THE
RELUCTANT SPIRITUALIST

THE
RELUCTANT
SPIRITUALIST

THE LIFE OF MAGGIE FOX

NANCY RUBIN STUART

HARCOURT, INC.

Orlando   Austin   New York   San Diego   Toronto   London

www.HarcourtBooks.com

With appreciation to the American Philosophical Society for permission to reprint fifty-nine
letters from the Elisha Kent Kane papers; to the Department of Rare Books and Special
Collections of the University of Rochester Library for reprint rights for ten letters from the
Isaac and Amy Post family papers; to the Friends Historical Library of Swarthmore College
for permission to reprint an unpublished letter from the Post family papers; and to the
Manuscripts and Archives Division of New York Public Library and the Astor, Lenox, and
Tilden Foundations for permission to reprint two letters from the Horace Greeley papers.

Library of Congress Cataloging-in-Publication Data
Stuart, Nancy Rubin.
The reluctant spiritualist: the life of Maggie Fox/Nancy Rubin Stuart.—1st ed.
p.   cm.
Includes bibliographical references and index.
ISBN 0-15-101013-7
1. Fox, Margaret, 1833–1893. 2. Spiritualists—United States—Biography.
3. Spiritualism—United States—History—19th century.   I. Title.
BF1283.F7S78   2005
133.9'1'092—dc22   2004015704

Text set in Adobe Garamond
Designed by Liz Demeter

Printed in the United States of America

First edition
K J I H G F E D C B A

To the memory of Aunt Lee
Who believed in laughter

CONTENTS

AT EIGHTEEN years of age Maggie Fox appeared as an "artless un-learned, unsophisticated young lady whose countenance [and] demeanor, all forbid the possibility of any deception," observed a *Cleveland Plain Dealer* reporter in 1851. Despite her appearance, though, she had already achieved national fame for her ability to raise spirits of the dead through rapped signals, or knocks.

My discovery of the movement Maggie and her sisters sparked evolved out of my research for a previous biography, *American Empress: The Life and Times of Marjorie Merriweather Post.* Born in 1887, Mrs. Post had been a lifelong advocate of Christian Science, a faith inspired by the teachings of Mary Baker Eddy in reaction to what she believed were the abuses of spiritualism.

As I learned more about those abuses and the movement itself, I became increasingly intrigued by Maggie Fox because of her apparent ambivalence about mediumship. My goal in exploring her life and writing her biography was to transcend the chronological tale of a generation of Americans embroiled in the spiritualist movement and depict the story of a woman who struggled for personal autonomy against that powerful enthusiasm.

While it is true that the life of any individual is always larger than the sum of its parts, it is to those parts that the biographer must look. Through an examination of Maggie's letters, memoirs, newspaper interviews, and accounts of her contemporaries, I gradually came to understand that the famous medium's emotional fragility and sensitivity—the very qualities that aided her clairvoyance and telepathy—were as intimately tied to her downfall as they were to her meteoric rise as a celebrity.

As her biographer I had hoped for a secret cache of letters that would reveal Maggie's voice as a teenager and young adult, but written documents were few and far between. A notoriously poor record-keeper—and, as Maggie's academic mentor Susanna Turner repeatedly observed, incorrigibly careless about dating her letters— the medium's voice was nevertheless partially preserved in several letter collections, in later newspaper accounts, and in two ghost-written memoirs.

The most important of those books was Maggie's 1865 record of her romantic relationship with Arctic explorer Elisha Kent Kane, *The Love-Life of Dr. Kane*. Replete with his letters but containing only a frustrating few from Maggie, the collection had been edited by two of the medium's friends, author Elizabeth Ellet and *Brooklyn Eagle* reporter Joseph La Fumee. In 1865, after a long, agonizing lawsuit, Maggie finally agreed to have *The Love-Life of Dr. Kane* published to prove that she had not only been romantically involved with that Arctic explorer but had secretly become his wife.

Fortunately, many of the letters in *The Love-Life of Dr. Kane* have been preserved at the American Philosophical Society in Philadelphia. After reading them, I was assured that the tone and intent of the correspondence reproduced in *The Love-Life of Dr. Kane* was largely accurate, if slightly amended in form. One pleasant surprise was my discovery of a collection of letters preserved at the American Philosophical Society by Robert Kane, Elisha's brother, that Maggie had written subsequent to her lover's death. Through them I was able to gain some insights into her thoughts, wishes, and moods in the decade following the explorer's demise.

In 1888, twenty-three years after publication of *The Love-Life of Dr. Kane,* Maggie contracted with journalist Reuben Briggs Davenport of the *New York Herald* to write her life story. Entitled *The Death-Blow to Spiritualism,* that book, like Maggie's previous volume, was written to justify still another part of her life—this time, the practice of spiritualism itself. Within its hastily compiled pages Maggie denounced spiritualism as a fraud, claiming that since childhood she and her sister Katy had been forced to work as mediums under their older sister Leah's relentless grip.

While paraphrased comments, direct quotations, and descriptions of Maggie's earlier life were included in *The Death-Blow to Spiritualism,* this book contained several misstatements. To me, the most disturbing were Davenport's descriptions of Maggie as an "eight year old" in 1848 when she started rapping, a "child" and a "juvenile mischief-maker"—misrepresentations probably written to convince readers of her initial innocence. In actuality, by March 1848, Maggie was almost fifteen-and-a-half years old—old enough to know right from wrong. The title itself echoes a sensational *Herald* headline published that same autumn. Meant to shock readers outside of New York, dissuade them from spiritualism, and vilify her eldest sister Leah, the book provided still more insights about Maggie's rationale for her behavior.

Two archival letter collections—the first in the Elisha Kent Kane Collection at Philadelphia's American Philosophical Society and the second in the Post Collection at the University of Rochester's Rare Book Library—provided additional proof and color to the outlines of Maggie's life as described in *The Love-Life of Dr. Kane* and *The Death-Blow to Spiritualism.*

Still other collections, including those at the New York Public Library, the General Society Library of New York, the Friends Historical Library at Swarthmore College, and the public libraries of Rochester, Buffalo, Troy, Albany, and Cleveland, provided additional information about Maggie's séances as well as spiritualism's envelopment into the popular culture of late nineteenth-century America.

Added to those sources were two books written by members of the Fox family. The first, published in 1885 by Maggie's eldest sister Leah, under her third husband's surname, "Underhill," and entitled *The Missing Link in Modern Spiritualism,* was meant to promote spiritualism at a time when the movement was losing popularity because of the abuses perpetrated by some of its mediums. Leah's book is one of the few accounts of the Fox sisters' transformation from small-town curiosities to international celebrities. Beyond the obviously self-serving and self-flattering tone of *The Missing Link in Modern Spiritualism,* the book contains so many obviously embroidered spiritualist miracles that I found its main value was its chronology of the Fox sisters' rise to national prominence.

In the twentieth century, a third-generation Fox in-law, Mariam Buckner Pond, published a novelistic nonfiction account, *Time Is Kind: The Story of the Unfortunate Fox Family.* "There is no one left to be hurt," Pond wrote in her introduction in that 1947 memoir. Drawing upon family lore and biased in Leah's favor, *Time Is Kind* nonetheless provided new intimate details about Maggie's life and that of her family.

Less personal, but more historically informative, was *Modern American Spiritualism,* a sweeping account of spiritualism during its first two decades written in 1870 by medium-historian Emma Hardinge, wife of the spiritualist publisher Reverend Samuel B. Brittan. While crafted to aggrandize the spiritualist movement, Hardinge's book included useful excerpts from newspaper articles—though they were often missing dates.

From these and other sources included in the bibliography at the back of this book, Maggie's story gradually emerged. Still, mysteries about the heroine of *The Reluctant Spiritualist* continue to abound.

Did Maggie and Katy fabricate the raps and then inadvertently conjure up the spirit of the Hydesville ghost—only to discover that they could eventually raise an entire world of spirits? Or was American spiritualism a hoax, as Maggie publicly announced in the fall of 1888 only to recant her denunciation a year later? The raps remain another contentious aspect of her tale. If, as some of Maggie's cynical peers insisted, they were produced by a trick and not supernaturally inspired, how did she and her sisters demonstrate them so consistently, forcefully, and often extemporaneously, as some of the era's newspapers and periodicals reported? Those who have tried to replicate the trick, at least as Maggie described it in *The Death-*

Blow to Spiritualism, have been frustrated in their efforts, thus leaving the origin of the raps a lingering mystery.

Beyond the strange story of Maggie's personal struggle as a spiritualist in search of her own identity stretches a swath of religious beliefs, scientific debates, medical facts, and hopes for the postmortem existence of the human spirit. At this writing, no one has yet settled that debate. Like Maggie and the controversies that surrounded her, the answers remain tantalizingly just beyond our grasp.

THE
RELUCTANT SPIRITUALIST

H U M B L E   B E G I N N I N G S

There is no death! What seems so is transition;
This life of mortal breath
Is but a suburb to the life elysian.
—HENRY WADSWORTH LONGFELLOW

AMERICAN SPIRITUALISM—a movement that at its peak claimed more than a million followers—was born of out of the basic human longing for contact with a loved one lost to death. But to literalists, spiritualism's true spark came in 1848 from something no more or less powerful than a bored teenage girl.

Her discontent, Maggie Fox would explain in interviews with the New York press some forty years later, had been stirred by the relocation of her parents, John and Margaret Fox, from Rochester, a cosmopolitan city of thirty thousand, to a rented farmhouse in the rural hamlet of Hydesville in Wayne County, New York—a day's boat ride away.

For months the elder Foxes had toyed with the idea of moving. Maggie's older sister Maria and her husband already resided in Wayne County, while her brother, David, had married and purchased a farm nearby in the township of Arcadia. There was, after all, as David and his young wife, Elizabeth, reminded their elders, plenty of space down the hill from their home for a second farmhouse. Peppermint, then a lucrative cash crop, already grew on David's land and there was room for John to plant his own fields. When John and Margaret Fox learned that the Hyde family, the area's major landowners, needed a new blacksmith, they seized the opportunity. On December 11, 1847, the elder Foxes, accompanied by the last of their brood, the petulant Maggie and her little sister, Katy, loaded their possessions into a wagon, hitched it to a strong horse, made the long, chill drive east into Wayne County, and finally arrived at the farmhouse at the corner of Parker and Hydesville Road.

From earlier visits to her relatives in Wayne County, the pretty, dark-eyed teenager considered the woodlands, high rolling pastures, and wide fields of Wayne County dull. Within a few weeks of moving into the Hydesville farmhouse, Maggie's initial impression was reconfirmed when she and Katy were forced to remain inside their parents' new saltbox home out of the desolate countryside's icy winds and drifting snows.

That is not to say that Maggie and her family were completely isolated from others. Nearby lived several friendly farm families, among them the Redfields and Dueslers and, most important of all, Dr. Henry Hyde and his son, Artemus. The Hydes, for whom the hamlet was named, seemed to own nearly everything in sight: large tracts of farmland, their nearby mansion, the farmhouse where the Foxes lived, and the forge where John was employed as a blacksmith. As democratic as they were prosperous, the Hydes also became good friends of Maggie's parents and they took "a great fancy," in Maggie's words, to her and eleven-year-old Katy, who was still in braids and pinafores.

The benevolence of the Hydes, combined with the proximity of other Fox relatives, undoubtedly had much to do with the family's decision to move to Hydesville. At sixty-one, the wiry, taciturn John Fox—or Voss, as his family name was known in his ancestral Germany—was already planning for his old age and that of his good-hearted wife, Margaret Rutan Fox, the mother of his six surviving children, the last being Maggie and Katy.

~❧~

The saltbox farmhouse was meant to be a temporary residence, but it suited the Foxes well, because it was conveniently adjacent to the forge and large enough to accommodate their small family. The front door opened directly into a front room behind which, on the right, was a bedroom where the elder Foxes slept. To the left was a kitchen and beyond it a pantry. A staircase separated the two back rooms and led to a cellar and an attic.

A hundred feet or so behind the farmhouse a small waterfall flowed from the Ganargua River, or Mud Creek as the locals called it, flanked by two mills, one for flour, the second for lumber. The property's western corner bordered Parker Road, two miles away from David's farm. Close by was the red clapboard schoolhouse where Maggie and Katy learned their lessons. Nearer still was the Methodist Episcopal Church, where the devout Foxes attended services every Sunday.

To the lively and imaginative Maggie, nearly fifteen at the time, such surroundings seemed monotonous, an appalling contrast to the stimulation she enjoyed in Rochester, whose streets were filled with shops, markets, well-dressed pedestrians, and the cacophony of its daily life. Several months earlier, during the summer of 1847 while visiting David's farm in nearby Arcadia, Maggie had wistfully written her middle-aged friend Amy Post that she deeply missed Rochester. "Oh Amy it is a very gloomy day [here]," she scrawled on August 24, 1847. "I love the noise and confusion of the city… [and]…am like the woman who becomes so accustomed to her husband's snoring that I could not get to sleep without it."

∼✻∼

While there were new chores to perform—fetching water from Ganargua stream, totting wood to the fireplace, and sweeping snow from the front steps—there was little in the way of amusements to cheer the bored teenager. With Katy, she would tease their "simple, gentle and true-hearted" mother, as Maggie described Mrs. Fox years later, or indulge in tickling matches with their niece, Lizzie Fish, the teenage daughter of their eldest sister, Leah, who visited from Rochester that first winter in Hydesville.

The nights were the worst of all, the time, as Maggie had written Amy Post, when she felt the most lonesome. What were the families like, she, Katy, and Lizzie idly wondered, who had lived in the farmhouse before them? Strangers must have lived in their home, and died there too. And perhaps their ghosts still haunted the place? Maggie's trusting and superstitious mother had helped lead the girls to this speculation: Not only did Margaret Fox believe in the existence of ghosts, but she often mentioned that her own grandmother and other Rutan relatives were known to have a sixth sense, or the ability to communicate with spirits.

"Until first suggested to us by our mother...the thought of 'spirits' had never entered our heads," Maggie later told her biographer. That was all the help the girls needed to hatch a mischievous plan. Why not frighten Mrs. Fox and, still more challenging, the skeptical John Fox? The inventive threesome started waking at night, tying apples to strings, and then dropping and retracting them on the floor to mimic the sounds of footsteps.

Night after night Maggie's mother awakened to the sound of those ghostly footsteps. She would jump out of bed, light a candle, and rush anxiously into the room where her young charges slept. Hearing her footsteps, the giggling trio would hide the apples, crawl into bed, and greet the concerned matron with feigned expressions of fright.

The apple trick inevitably excited other schemes. Once, after Katy learned to snap her fingers, she and her companions decided to create similar sounds with their toes. Lizzie was the first to perfect the trick. Planting one foot on the headboard of the bed, she applied pressure to her big toe, and then thrust her second toe against it in the opposite direction. The result was a resounding popping or knocking sound as she snapped her toe joints. Determined to keep up with their older relative, Maggie and Katy practiced that same technique and soon became so adept that they could "knock," as they dubbed their stunt, while standing on the floor in shoes or barefoot or even while sitting in a chair. After weeks of practice,

Maggie explained, the girls' flexible joints grew so accustomed to the knocks that "we could do it with hardly an effort."

By late winter Lizzie had returned to Rochester. Nevertheless Maggie and Katy persisted in their game, vying with each other to see who could make the loudest sounds. Sometimes, the girls did so with their fingers. To avoid being seen, one of them would sit "with one hand hidden by an elbow resting upon the table, or the woodwork of a chair," unwittingly goaded on by Mrs. Fox, who "in her earnest belief, pour soul, excited us to do a great deal more than otherwise, we would have done."

Before long, Maggie and Katy had incorporated their tricks into their daily lives as a kind of sport, much as contemporary teenagers blast music from their rooms to annoy their parents today. Executed silently and persistently upon the furniture, the repeated raps sometimes caused a table or chair to vibrate and even move from its original position, inevitably frightening the already agitated Mrs. Fox.

In contrast was her husband John's diffidence. More skeptical by nature, the aging blacksmith did not believe in ghosts and continued to insist that there was a practical reason for the sounds. Yet the nocturnal noises persisted, upsetting his wife so much that he agreed to move Maggie and Katy into their bedroom to sleep on a trundle bed.

Even at such close range to their parents, the girls brazenly persisted in their antics. "It was not very loud…yet it [the spirit] produced a jar of the bedsteads and chairs that could be felt by placing our hands on the chairs, or while we were in bed," Mrs. Fox later complained. Afterward, rejecting her exasperated husband's pleas to ignore the sounds, the unnerved woman would rise and search the farmhouse by candlelight.

꩜

But even that would not satisfy Maggie and Katy. Having convinced their mother that their new home was haunted, the girls now decided to impress her with their ability to talk to the ghost. Deliberately the girls chose the night of March 31—just before

April Fool's Day—for their performance. That particular evening, as their father sat in the main room by the fireplace, Maggie, Katy, and their mother went to bed. Soon after Mrs. Fox fell asleep, eerie sounds ricocheted through the house, this time so forcefully that she bolted upright in bed.

So, too, did Maggie and Katy. Then, boldly, Katy peered into the darkness and addressed the ghost. "Mr. Split-foot, do as I do," she said, snapping her fingers in the cadence of the earlier noises.

In response came a corresponding series of knocks. Brightly, Maggie then clapped her hands four times and commanded the ghost to rap back. Four knocks followed. As if on cue, Katy then made soundless finger-snapping gestures that, in turn, were answered with raps.

Suddenly Katy decided to drop all pretense, or at least offer her mother some sort of excuse for the sounds. "O, mother, I know what it is. Tomorrow is April-fool day and it's somebody trying to fool us," she began.

To Katy and Maggie's surprise, Mrs. Fox refused to entertain the notion. In the long weeks of nocturnal disturbances, the woman had become unshakably convinced that the ghost was real. She was, it seemed, no more able to surrender her belief in the spirit than she could harbor thoughts of duplicity from her beloved Maggie and Katy. Mrs. Fox decided to test the spirit herself. Initially, she asked it to count to ten. Once that was successfully accomplished, she asked how many children she had borne. Seven raps came back. But how many were living? Six raps. What about the ages of those children? Again, the spirit responded correctly, hesitating to knock out an age for the seventh. Then, Margaret sadly recalled, "Three more emphatic raps were given, corresponding to the age of the little one that died...my youngest child."

"Is it a spirit? If it is, make two raps," she asked. "If it was an injured spirit make two raps." Promptly two knocks were returned, allegedly causing the house—or perhaps Mrs. Fox—to tremble. Finally, she asked the spirit who it had been in life.

Maggie and Katy must have thought fast. The spirit, they rapped, was a thirty-one-year-old married man, dead for two years, and the father of five. "Will you continue to rap if I call in my neighbors that they may hear it too?" Margaret asked. A pause followed and then, she recalled, "raps were loud in the affirmative." As a chagrined Maggie later explained in her biography, she and Katy could not answer any other way. Confessing now would have incurred their parents' wrath—perhaps even the wrath of their preacher.

Soon afterward John left to fetch their nearest neighbor, Mary Redfield, reputed for her outspoken manner. The farm woman arrived ready to reprimand the Fox's city-bred daughters for their foolish fears about ghosts. Yet the moment she gazed upon the frightened expressions on Maggie and Katy's faces, she realized she had miscalculated the situation. The two girls, according to Mrs. Fox, were "clinging to each other and trembling with terror," leading Mary to understand that "there was something more serious than she had supposed." When the spirit revealed uncanny details about Mary Redfield's life and age, she grew so agitated that she scurried across the road to tell her friend, Mrs. William Duesler.

Few could have imagined then, least of all the two mischievous girls in that humble farmhouse, that they had just witnessed the birth of spiritualism in America.

❧

Life had not been easy for Margaret and John Fox—"good honest people," as Maggie later described them. At sixteen, Margaret Rutan Smith, born of French, English, and Dutch extraction and living in rural Rockland County, New York, had wed John Fox, a native of New York City, in 1812. Initially the newlyweds lived in Rockland County, where John worked as a blacksmith. A year or so later their first child, the spirited Ann Leah, was born, followed by Maria, Elizabeth, and their only son, David. Yet, whatever pride the young couple took in their sturdy young brood was soon marred by John's fondness for drink. His alcoholism meant dissension, poverty, and possible starvation for Margaret's family. By the mid-1820s the anguished and resolute matron packed up her four children and moved to Bath, Canada, her hometown, to join her maternal family.

Heartbroken and missing Margaret and his children terribly, John ultimately conquered his addiction in the early 1830s. The penitent blacksmith journeyed to Canada and persuaded his estranged wife to reconcile.

Soon afterward, on October 7, 1833, little Maggie, or Margaretta as she was named, was born in Consecon, near Bath. Three and a half years later, on March 27, 1837, Catherine, or Katy, arrived, followed by a final daughter who died in early childhood. Subsequently the elder Foxes and their two sets of youngsters moved back to Rockland County.

According to Maggie's description in her 1888 confessional account, *The Death-Blow to Spiritualism,* "The two broods of children had distinctive characteristics," from the beginning. The older group was practical, staid, and reflective, while Maggie and Katy tended to be imaginative, intuitive, and ethereal. Within a year, Maggie's parents moved again, to Rochester, New York. What motivated that relocation is not clear but may have been related to concerns about their eldest daughter, Ann Leah, familiarly known as Leah.

In 1828, at the tender age of fourteen, that handsome young woman had been courted by a man named Bowman Fish. While marriages were rarely encouraged in girls before the age of sixteen, Leah nevertheless wed and settled in Rochester. Within the next few years—exactly when is not known—Leah bore a daughter, Lizzie. Unfortunately, the marriage became increasingly unhappy. "Mr. Fish discovered when too late that he had married a child, and soon became indifferent to this home and family," Leah later explained in her own memoir, *The Missing Link to Modern Spiritualism.* Leaving Rochester under the "pretense of going on business to the West," the man never returned. Only later did Leah learn that he had married a rich widow in Illinois.

Endowed with a strong survival instinct, Leah eventually parlayed her piano-playing skills into work as a music teacher—then one of the few professions open to women. Within a short time, the young, single mother was supporting herself and Lizzie by giving lessons to the children of affluent Rochesterians.

꙰✾꙰

By the late 1840s Rochester was becoming the "first inland boom town," in the words of twentieth-century historian Paul E. Johnson. Even before the 1825 completion of the Erie Canal, the city's unique position on the Genesee River, surrounded by large tracts of fertile farmland, had been an ideal location for mills to grind grain, thus giving Rochester its sobriquet, Flour City. Once the Erie Canal linked Rochester to other upstate cities, such as Syracuse and Buffalo, Rochester's waterways filled with boats shuttling passengers across New York State. Daily, too, dozens of freight boats, loaded with flour, fruit, and other goods, were towed east by mules or horses to Albany, before being floated south on the Hudson River to New York City.

Visiting author Nathaniel Hawthorne, who came to Rochester in 1835, marveled at the city's vitality. Rochester's streets, he noted, bustled with "activity and eager life," and its "sidewalks and center...crowded with pedestrians, horsemen, stage-coaches, gigs, light wagons, and heavy ox-teams, all hurrying, trotting, rattling, and rumbling, in a throng that passed continually but never passed away."

Rochester's prosperity inevitably attracted swindlers, wastrels, and atheists, an influx that alarmed the groups of reformists dedicated to eradicating godlessness, poverty, the commercialization of the Sabbath, and the abuse of alcohol. Swept along by the religious revivalism known as America's Second Great Awakening, scores of charismatic preachers had descended upon the communities surrounding the Erie Canal to win the souls of its citizens and convert them to a variety of evangelical and radical sects.

Among the most famous were the Shakers—so-called for their spasmodic movements while in the throes of an ecstatic spiritual possession. A splinter group from an English Quaker community founded by "Mother" Ann Lee, the pacifist group had survived only with difficulty during the revolutionary period in eighteenth-century New England. By the nineteenth century, the Shakers, under the leadership of Joseph Meacham, had reappeared in up-state New York. They made New Lebanon their headquarters and embraced the ideas of simplicity, community, celibacy, and com-munication with the dead, particularly the spirits of Native Americans.

Upstate New York also was the cradle for the Mormon Church, or Church of Jesus Christ of Latter-Day Saints, which began on Sep-tember 21, 1823, when Joseph Smith of Manchester reported being visited by an angel messenger named Moroni, who described hidden gold plates containing the complete gospel of Christ. The resultant "book of Mormon," which Smith claimed to receive in September 1827, was said to contain an abridged account of God's revelations. Embracing both the Bible and the Book of Mormon, Smith's new Mormon Church was officially organized on April 6, 1830. Among its beliefs was the concept that souls waited to be born and, con-versely, the dead could be saved through retroactive baptism. Most controversial, though, was the Mormon practice of polygamy—a practice that, combined with the faith's new biblical interpretation, provoked such outrage that Smith's followers relocated to Ohio and later trekked more than one thousand miles to Utah.

Still another denomination from upstate New York that at-tracted public attention was the Millerites, founded by Reverend William Miller, who urged his followers to eschew all ambitions and worldly goods in preparation for a Second Coming, predicted between 1843 and 1844. Even after the first projected Day of Judg-ment of March 22, 1843, failed to materialize as promised, many of Miller's devoted followers—virtually all of whom had abandoned or given away their earthly possessions—patiently waited for the second projected date of October 22, 1844. After that failed to materialize, Miller's remaining flock—still an estimated fifty thousand—embraced the new denominations of the Seventh-Day Adventists and the Advent Christian Church.

In the wake of these and other religious enthusiasms, a spiritual cynicism settled over the area. Charles Grandison Finney, the era's most famous evangelist preacher, dubbed the terrain between the New York's Adirondacks and Great Lakes the "burnt-over" region. He compared the souls of potential converts ruined by an overabundance of religious passions to wide swaths of northern woods laid bare by forest fires.

∽✤∾

Spiritualism—the idea that the human spirit can exist beyond death and can communicate with the living through a medium—was hardly a new idea in the nineteenth century. Efforts to talk with the dead had been practiced by cultures as diverse as those of Ancient Greece, the biblical Middle East, the Voguls of northwestern Siberia, and, more recently, in America by the Oglala Sioux.

As schoolgirls neither Maggie nor Katy was acquainted with that history. The advent of their mediumship and its effect upon that region's religious turmoil was all the more startling for their innocence.

By the time neighbor William Duesler had arrived at the Foxes' home that infamous evening of March 31, it was around 9 P.M. and other curious neighbors, having heard the rumors, already had arrived. Perhaps because Duesler had once lived in that same farmhouse, he was among the first to enter the bedroom where the spirit had supposedly rapped for Margaret. There the farmer found John Fox. Mystified, the blacksmith later admitted his own confusion, saying, "I do not know of any way to account for these noises, as being caused by any natural means."

For all his initial skepticism, Duesler was so startled by the shaken appearance of the usually calm and stolid John Fox that he entertained the possibility that something unnatural had occurred. Fearing that his family had done something harmful to "raise" the spirit during their own tenure at the farmhouse, Duesler began questioning the ghost about its history. The ghost explained through a series of knocks that he had been a peddler and was murdered in the Foxes' farmhouse for his money.

Mrs. Fox later said that since the hour was late, she, Maggie, and Katy left the farmhouse and slept at the home of one of their neighbors. To the subsequent frustration of historians of spiritualism, Duesler's account failed to mention whether Maggie, Katy, and Mrs. Fox left before—or after—he questioned the spirit.

By early Saturday morning, April 1, rumors about the haunted farmhouse had already spread. Before long the farmhouse overflowed with neighbors—some three hundred by Mrs. Fox's account—all searching for clues.

At dusk, the spirit—who had been silent all day while the neighbors monitored the house—began to rap again. Yet the ongoing clumsiness of its response through raps was hardly satisfactory. William Duesler consequently devised a solution, writing out the letters of the alphabet and assigning a number to each. Now the ghost could spell out words and even whole sentences.

The resultant story, rapped out by the increasingly panicked, if highly imaginative, Maggie and Katy, explained that the spirit was a peddler named Charles B. Rosna who had been murdered for his money by a former farmhouse tenant. His body, the spirit insisted, was still buried in the house, along with his pack, or peddler's trunk.

Maggie and Katy found themselves trapped. "Soon it went so far and so many persons had heard the 'rappings' that we could not confess the wrong without exciting very great anger on the part of those we had deceived. So we went right on," Maggie would explain forty years later.

For the teenager, as for her younger sister, deception seemed the path of least resistance. Even in their "burnt-over district," thousands of residents continued to believe in the supernatural. It was, after all, only a few years since the failed Millerite Day of Judgment, just two decades since Joseph Smith met the angel Moroni, and still an era when preachers frightened followers with warnings about the devil's ability to inhabit a human body. Exorcisms were still common practice among some members of the clergy. Through that superstition-clouded lens, many Americans perceived new technologies like the steam engine and the telegraph as manifestations of the supernatural. In such a context, the appearance of a ghost who talked with the living thus seemed entirely within the realm of possibility.

Suddenly, too, Maggie and Katy were treated with importance and respect. No longer did their neighbors look upon them as giddy city-slickers. Literally overnight, the sisters had achieved a mystique that baffled even the most suspicious adults. To Maggie and Katy the price of confession must have been too steep to pay when compared to the rewards of local celebrityhood.

⁓✢⁓

By Sunday, April 2, William Duesler and his neighbors decided to investigate the spirit's claim that his body was buried in the farmhouse basement. Upon entering the cellar they heard what Duesler described as "a sound like the falling of a stick about a foot long and half an inch through, on the floor in the bedroom over our heads." An examination of the bedroom proved fruitless. "I can in no way account for this singular noise, which I and others have heard," Duesler admitted. Like John Fox, Duesler ultimately agreed that, "It is a mystery to me, which I am wholly unable to solve."

Several suspicious locals pointed out that the spirit rapped only when Maggie or Katy was present—proof, they insisted, that the girls must have produced the sounds. Another, equally adamant set of neighbors, trusting in Maggie and Katy's innocence, retorted that the ghost rapped for the girls because they were the first ones to befriend it.

Inevitably, the April thaw that loosened the snow-covered hills of upstate New York sent a muddy stream of rumors into neighboring counties about the haunted farmhouse. Within a few days one of those streams flowed into the Finger Lakes town of Canandaigua, where it reached attorney E. E. Lewis.

Perhaps Lewis had a streak of investigative reporter in him. By April 11, he was in Hydesville interviewing virtually every adult who had been involved—including Margaret, John, and David Fox, and William Duesler. Paradoxically, the only ones missing from his account were those who knew the story best—Maggie and Katy. Exactly why they were not included is not clear. Possibly they were considered too young to be reliable interviews, or perhaps Mrs. Fox, who was vigilant about protecting her daughters from any taint of scandal, refused to allow their names in print.

During the investigation, Lewis interviewed Lucretia Pulver, a young woman who was convinced there had been a murder in the farmhouse several years earlier. According to her tale, she boarded for three months in 1843 with the farmhouse's tenants, Mr. and Mrs. John Bell. As was often the rural custom, Lucretia worked as the Bells' household servant in exchange for room and board.

One afternoon a foot-peddler arrived at the Bells and was invited to stay overnight; Lucretia was told to go home to her parents. Intrigued with the peddler's colorful wares, which included perfumes and sewing equipment, the girl asked him to stop by her parents' home the next morning.

To her surprise, the peddler did not appear, and by the time she arrived at the Bells, he had disappeared. That same morning the Bells suddenly announced that they were going away for several days. Three days later when the girl returned, she went into the farmhouse cellar and found herself sinking knee deep in loose dirt. "After I got up stairs, Mrs. Bell asked me what I screamed for, and I told her," Lucretia recalled. "She laughed at me for being frightened, and said that it was only where the rats had been at work in the ground."

Adding to Lucretia's curiosity was the sight of John Bell lugging heavy bins of dirt into the basement at night. He was doing so, Mrs. Bell insisted to the increasingly suspicious schoolgirl, to cover the rat holes.

At that point, Lucretia might have forgotten the incident except that her mistress began displaying new thimbles and even presented her with one worth fifty cents. The costly item, Mrs. Bell explained, was from that same foot-peddler who, she said, had appeared several times since.

The odd thing, Lucretia told Lewis, was that she had never seen the peddler again, neither visiting the Bells nor anywhere else in Hydesville. Now, though, the farmhouse was filled with strange noises at night. And since the peddler's visit, the Bells' dog would "sit under the bedroom window and howl all night long." Concluding her peculiar tale, the young woman admitted, "I did not know what to think of the noises I have heard." Neither, perhaps, did E. E. Lewis, who being well aware of the dangers of libel, made a point of omitting the Bells' name in his published pamphlet.

Had Maggie and Katy already heard that story? And if so, did they decide to use it on March 31 when their mother asked them to rap out the spirit's story? Other locals may have suspected as much. To settle the controversy, Maggie's brother David assembled his neighbors and began excavating the farmhouse cellar.

Yet, even that effort was frustrated. Due to the unusually wet spring of 1848, the basement filled with water as the men shoveled, making all attempts at discovery impossible. As David explained to Lewis, "We could not lower the water much, and had to give it up." As to the existence of ghosts, Maggie's brother claimed he was dubious: "I have heard of such things, but never saw or heard any thing but what I could account for on reasonable grounds." Nevertheless, he was forced to admit that "I cannot account for this noise as being produced by any human agency."

Ultimately, rumors about Lucretia's accusations reached the Bells, who, since 1846, had been living miles away in Lyon, New York. "Poor Bell was shunned and looked upon by the whole community as a murderer," Maggie later recalled.

In an effort to clear his name, the embattled man produced a certificate of good character signed by forty-four people testifying that they had "'never known anything against him' and 'believed him to be a man of upright and honest life' and 'incapable of committing the crime of which he was suspected.'"

Casting additional doubt on Lucretia's story was the fact that no one in Wayne County ever recalled a peddler named Charles B. Rosna. Nor could anyone find the peddler's wife or children in upstate New York.

Refusing to be ruffled by the controversy, Lewis persisted in his investigation, interviewing former tenants of the Hydesville farmhouse. He found Michael and Hannah Weekman, a young couple who had rented the saltbox home a year before the Foxes. Like Lucretia, their female servant, Jane C. Lape, claimed that she had witnessed something strange in the farmhouse.

One day, while working in the kitchen, she was startled to see a man standing in the adjoining bedroom; curiously, though, the only way he could have entered the room was to walk directly past her. "I had been in the kitchen some time at work, and knew that nobody could have gone into that room," she recalled.

Rapping noises were another peculiarity of the house that often disturbed the Weekmans' sleep at night. For a while the couple tried to pass it off as the rattling of loose boards on the old house, but one night they were awakened by frightened cries of their young child from the attic bedroom. Running upstairs with her husband and servant, Hannah found their eight-year-old-daughter sitting up in bed, sobbing hysterically. When questioned the little girl insisted that "something had been moving around and over her head and face; that it was cold, and that she felt it all over her." The child was so traumatized that she refused to sleep in her own bed for weeks.

Soon afterward the Weekmans abandoned the farmhouse. "I do not believe in *spooks,* or any thing of that kind; but I hardly know what to say about it now;—so many have heard the noise that it seems as if something must be the matter." A year later when the Foxes moved in, no one mentioned the Weekmans' abrupt departure. Until Lewis's interview, the neighbors did not know about the reasons for their move.

~✿~

On November 23, 1904, fifty-eight years after Lewis collected his interviews, the *Boston Journal* reported that part of an old cellar wall of the famous Hydesville farmhouse—the "spook house" as it was popularly known—had begun to decay, revealing "an almost entire human skeleton between the earth and crumbling cellar walls, undoubtedly that of the wandering peddler, who is claimed to have been murdered in the east room of the house and whose body was hidden in the cellar. The findings of the bones practically corroborates the sworn statement made by Margaret Fox, April 11, 1848. The Fox sisters claimed to have been disturbed by the rappings and finally by a system of signals got into communication with the spirit." The bones later disappeared—no one seemed to know how or where—but a tin pack that had been found nearby, typical of those carried by mid-nineteenth-century peddlers, was preserved.

In April 1916, a Pennsylvania spiritualist had the cottage dismantled and moved to the Lily Dale Spiritual Association of Lily Dale, New York. There, in 1955, the farmhouse burned down. The tin peddler's pack was saved from the fire and remains on display at the Lily Dale Museum along with the Fox family Bible. The National Association of Spiritualist Churches is currently building a meditation garden on the site of the original Hydesville cottage.

Today, as in the spring of 1848, the curious regard Maggie and Katy's claims about a buried peddler with as much wonder as suspicion. Were they the innocent victims of a supernatural power whose identity and story had been only imperfectly revealed? Or were Maggie and Katy clever imposters who had deliberately duped an entire community?

THE SPIRIT OF A DREAM

As to the actual fact of these manifestations, we think there
cannot be a shadow of a doubt...That the rappings are
produced by an invisible and (to us) intangible agency.
—WILLIAM FISHBOUGH, *Univercoelum*, February 3, 1849

INEVITABLY, rumors about the alleged haunting of the Hydesville
farmhouse shattered the tranquil life of the Foxes. From dawn to
dusk, scores of the curious arrived in rented carriages or appeared
overland with their own horses and buggies, waiting outside the
Fox home for a chance to hear the raps for themselves.

"Hundreds have visited the house, so that it is impossible for us
to attend to our daily occupations," the usually reticent John Fox
complained to E. E. Lewis on April 11. "I hope that, whether caused
by natural or supernatural means, it will be ascertained soon."

Hoping that others could "ascertain" the cause, the overwrought
Mrs. Fox had encouraged those visitors by inviting them to hear
the spirit for themselves. At night, rows of chairs were placed in the
front room before Maggie, Katy, and Mrs. Fox's visitations with the
spirits began.

"She [her mother] used to say when we were sitting in a dark
circle... 'is this a disembodied spirit that has taken possession of
my dear children?'" Maggie recalled in her memoir, *The Death-
Blow to Spiritualism*. But whatever initial satisfaction Mrs. Fox
gained from sharing the raps with others was fleeting, overshadowed by fears about why her family had been cursed with the
haunting. Maggie guiltily recalled her mother became "pale and

worn-looking and thought that great misfortunes were to happen and prayed often and fervently."

"I can well remember," she explained to a reporter forty years later, "how my heart used to smite me at times when I looked upon her and knew that Katie and I were the cause of all her trouble."

Their father, though, remained stubbornly suspicious of the spirit, in spite of the fact that he had attempted to talk with it that first night, according to neighbor William Duesler. Consequently, Maggie and Katy surrounded John with raps while he was at his morning prayers. "When he would be kneeling upon his chair, it would sometimes amuse the children [Katy and her] to see him open wide his eyes as knocks would sound and vibrate," Maggie admitted.

Even so, John refused to acknowledge the sounds. "When I am done praying that jigging stops," he would later grumble to his wife.

Being devout Christians, the elder Foxes continued to bring Maggie and Katy to the nearby Methodist Episcopal Church on Sundays. But within a few weeks, the young minister, Reverend George York, had expelled the family, accusing them of blasphemy and devil worship. Their neighbors suspected the same; some of them feared the Foxes were in league with the devil, and must have encouraged their daughters to join them by engaging in some kind of "witchcraft."

⁓❧⁓

By early May 1848, E. E. Lewis had arrived in Rochester, bringing a draft of his pamphlet, *A Report of the Mysterious Noises Heard in the House of John D. Fox, in Hydesville, Arcadia, Wayne County.* Already rumors about the haunting had begun to circulate in the city. The entrepreneurial Lewis believed that a printed report containing first-person testimony was likely to sell hundreds, perhaps even thousands, of copies.

Explaining in the introduction that "We have spent several days in that place, for the purpose of investigating this strange affair, and if possible to solve the mystery...," Lewis admitted that "It may be the result of trickery, or fear, or superstition, or all combined." Conversely, he added, "...if any one has been able thus to deceive a large, intelligent and candid community for such a length of time as this has been carried on, it certainly surpasses any thing that has ever occurred in this country, or any other."

Paradoxically, one of the Rochesterians who still had not heard about the events at Hydesville was the Foxes' eldest daughter, the thirty-five-year-old Leah Fox Fish. Her mother had been too upset to write for the past month, Leah later explained in her memoir, *The Missing Link in Modern Spiritualism*.

One morning as Leah instructed the daughters of Jane and William Little at the piano, their mother burst into the parlor and called her aside. Knowing that Leah's maiden name was Fox and that her parents had recently moved to Wayne County, Jane Little introduced Leah to E. E. Lewis.

"Is your mother's name Margaret? Have you a brother David?" the attorney inquired.

"For mercy's sake, what has happened?" Leah asked.

Without a word, Lewis handed her the proof-sheets of his pamphlet. A few hours later Leah, her daughter Lizzie, and two of the matron's friends, Belle Grover and Adelaide Grainger, booked tickets on a night packet boat to Newark.

⁓❧⁓

By the spring of 1848, the religious climate was still unsettled and ripe for progressive new ideas. America's cities were expanding, its populations swelling with immigrants from Ireland and Europe, its factories and ports booming, all of which contributed to a rising mortality rate. Nearly a third of all city-born infants died before their first birthday and young mothers—bearing an average of five children each—were frequently struck with puerperal fever and other birth-related complications. The urban overcrowding and poor sanitation of that era also spawned epidemics of cholera, whooping cough, influenza, and diphtheria, threatening the lives of even the most sturdy adults. In Massachusetts, one of the few states then collecting mortality figures by gender, the average life span for men was 38.3 years; the average woman lived to be 40.5 years old.

In reaction, citizens sought ways to improve their health, embracing diet reforms such as vegetarianism, water cures, exercise, and mineral baths—and even, thanks to domestic reformer Catherine Beecher, the rejection of the then-fashionably tight female corset.

Simultaneous with America's urbanization and booming economy new material goods flooded into the marketplace, among them factory-spun textiles, clothes, dishes, and furniture, prompting a new materialism among the rising middle class. In tandem with the new cult of conspicuous consumption, citizens increasingly dismissed the Calvinistic concept of original sin in favor of the more liberal tendencies stirring within other Protestant denominations.

One of the earliest champions of that liberalization was Dr. William Ellery Channing, the Rhode Island–bred founder of Unitarianism. As early as 1819, he had rejected traditional Christian dogma in favor of a religion based on man's natural divinity. Believing that "reason and conscience are divine witness to truth and light," Channing asserted that neither religious ritual nor attempts to make reparation for man's original sin constituted true worship of the divine. Instead, he suggested that a better approach would be to show brotherly concern for one's fellow man and a dedication to helping the less fortunate.

Ultimately, Channing's theories influenced other Protestant clergymen who, already imbued with the European Romantic idea of man's intrinsic divinity, encouraged their flocks to embrace those reforms.

By the 1830s and 1840s America's new breed of humanitarians had founded dozens of charities and embraced social causes as diverse as prison reform, co-education, temperance, and abolition of slavery. Simultaneously, new spiritual philosophers such as Amos Bronson Alcott and Ralph Waldo Emerson appeared on the lecture circuit and in print. Founders of the social and literary movement known as transcendentalism, they asserted that man's inner spirit inevitably led him to social good.

"What is popularly called 'Transcendentalism,' among us, is Idealism.... Mankind have ever divided into two sects, Materialists, and Idealists," Emerson explained in a lecture entitled "The Transcendentalist" delivered at Boston's Masonic Temple in January 1842 and later published under that same name. "The materialist insists on facts, on history, on the force of circumstances, and the animal wants of man; the idealist on the power of Thought and of Will, on inspiration, on miracle, on individual culture... the idealist, in speaking of events, sees them as spirits... takes his departure from his consciousness, and reckons the world an appearance."

Still another contributor to America's dawning liberalism was its westward expansion, prompted by the recent acquisition of territories from the Mexican War. From New England to the western frontier, new communities and factory centers appeared, seemingly overnight. So, too, did the nation's growing network of canals, new fleets of steam-powered boats, and expanding railway system, making once-isolated towns and communities a mere train ride away.

To many Americans the most dramatic wonder of the age was the telegraph, which, thanks to the entrepreneurial genius of inventor Samuel F. B. Morse, transmitted sounds that could immediately be translated into words over wires strung for hundreds of miles through desolate stretches of land.

By the late 1840s, anticipation of a better life and the concept of "progress" had become an American touchstone, a national expectation. "It is an extraordinary era in which we live. It is altogether new. The world has seen nothing like it before... The progress of the age has almost outstripped human belief," orator and statesman Daniel Webster proclaimed on November 17, 1847, on the opening of a new link of the Northern Railroad that had reached Lebanon, New Hampshire.

Another sign of that optimism was the establishment of forty utopian communities in America. Inspired by the socialistic philosophy of influential French philosopher Charles Fourier, who had embraced socialism and eschewed the advent of industrialism, America's utopian leaders had similarly rejected capitalism and much that went with it—including traditional sex roles and conventional dress. The transcendentalist-oriented Brook Farm of Massachusetts of 1841–47 was one of the best known of those communities. Still more controversial was John Humphrey Noyes's Oneida Community of Madison County, New York, which advocated a modified version of free love known as "complex marriage."

To popular journalist-author Sarah Jane Clarke Lippencott, or Grace Greenwood as she was known to readers, America seemed alive with progressive ideas and avid groups of social reformers. "We found the cars crowded...filled to overflowing with Barnburners, on fire with free-soil democracy, and turbulent with patriotic enthusiasm," she wrote in her sketchbook *Greenwood Leaves* after boarding a night train from Utica to Rochester in 1848.

Earlier, French social commentator Alexis de Tocqueville had visited the United States and admired the bounding energies of its citizens, the booming trade, rising factory systems, and resultant prosperity. He predicted that a quest for new outlets for spiritual satisfaction was inevitable. "I should be surprised if among a people uniquely preoccupied with prosperity mysticism did not soon make progress," wrote de Tocqueville after touring the United States in 1835. And while the "desire of acquiring the good things of this world is the prevailing passion of the American people, certain momentary outbreaks occur, when their souls seem suddenly to burst the bonds of matter by which they are restrained, and to soar impetuously toward Heaven."

A dozen years later de Tocqueville's prediction would be fulfilled when Andrew Jackson Davis, a visionary youth known as the "Poughkeepsie Seer," published his bestselling book *The Principles of Nature, Her Divine Revelations, and a Voice to Mankind.* According to the eight-hundred-page book, the material world was only a shadow of a spiritual one. The dead were in daily contact with the living, even if the latter did not recognize that. While Davis had already promoted that message in the *Univercoelum,* a New York City weekly edited by Universalist minister Reverend Samuel B. Brittan, his book would reach a far wider audience.

"It is a truth that spirits commune with one another while one is in the body and the other in the higher spheres—and this, too, when the person in the body is unconscious of the influx and hence cannot be convinced of the fact...," Davis opined. Now, he added, "...this truth will ere long present itself in the form of a living demonstration. And the world will hail with delight the ushering in of that era when the interiors of men will be opened, and the spiritual communion will be established."

The nature of contact between the living and the dead, Davis hastened to explain, would be benevolent, rather than the malevolent hauntings long associated with ghosts and the Satan-fearing advocates of Calvinism. "I perceive that all spirits are engaged in loving their neighbors and advancing their welfare; and here is good will without distinction."

In such a benevolent aura, people should no longer fear death. When "spirit leaves the human form and is introduced into this Sphere [they] retain the same bodily form in the spiritual Sphere," Davis assured his readers. Once having discarded false notions about the afterlife, human spirits "become enlightened by the light and love of heaven" and ascend to higher levels of spiritual society.

Even after achieving the third level, Wisdom, the soul could continue to evolve, passing through a series of concentric circles, or spheres, until it reached the seventh or highest—what Davis described as "the infinite Vortex of Love and Wisdom, and the great Spiritual Sun of the Divine." Above that was the "Univercoelum" or "Universe."

Davis's prophecy of imminent spirit appearances had been revealed in a trance, during which he walked forty miles into the wilderness of the Catskill Mountains. There the young man claimed he met two distinguished figures from history. The first was the second-century A.D. Greek philosopher Galen. The second was the eighteenth-century Swedish scientist, theologian, and mystic Emanuel Swedenborg.

According to Swedenborg, all human experience was only a reflection of a larger spiritual one. The human soul was what gave meaning and expression to the concrete world. "As there is a spirit in every man, and...in respect to his life a man is a spirit...the body [is] merely to enable a man to live on the earth. In fact...the body does not live or think at all," Swedenborg proposed.

Profoundly influenced by that mystic's views—whose scientific writings were translated into English in 1845—the Poughkeepsie Seer developed a benevolent mystical philosophy of his own. By 1848, Davis's *The Principles of Nature* was widely available in bookstores across the East and Midwest, including one owned by D. M. Dewey in the Rochester Arcade.

Now, something eerily similar to Davis's predictions about the approach of the spirit world seemed to have occurred in the Fox home.

~❧~

Leah devoted several pages of her memoir to her rushed trip to Hydesville. Arriving at her parents' farmhouse she was dismayed to find it deserted, its front door locked and windows shuttered. Not knowing what else to do, Leah ordered the driver to David's white, welcoming farmhouse two miles away, where they found the other Foxes. Nearby stood the still-unfinished frame of the home her father John was building for his family.

David and his young wife Elizabeth graciously welcomed the Rochester party into the house. The once-cheerful Mrs. Fox sat unhappily clutching her Bible in one of the front rooms. Leah observed that her mother seemed "completely broken down by the recent events...never smiled...her sighs and tears were heart-rending. We begged her to hope for the best, and try to think differently; but she could not. She wished we could all die."

The family's move had been at his insistence, David quickly explained. He wanted to both shield his parents, Maggie, and Katy from the constant press of the crowds at the Hydesville farmhouse and to end the spirit's contact with the family.

So far that had not been possible. The troublesome knocks seemed to have followed Maggie and Katy from the Hydesville farmhouse. When the girls were together, Mrs. Fox tearfully observed, the strange sounds seemed louder. Conversely, when they were separated, the noises grew weaker. At this point, accounts begin to diverge. According to Leah's memoir, she volunteered to bring Katy home with her to Rochester so that finally "we could put a stop to the disturbance."

Maggie's interpretation was different. As *The Death-Blow to Spiritualism* explained, Leah had invited both her and Katy to accompany her and Lizzie to Rochester. But Maggie, for all that she missed Rochester, mistrusted Leah and stayed behind. Her eldest sister, Maggie insisted, had a "cold and calculating brain," so hardened and rooted in reality that she would never believe in the existence of spirits. In her adult diatribe against Leah, Maggie contended that by the time her sister arrived in Wayne County she had already hatched a plan to make money from the hauntings.

As Reuben Briggs Davenport, the journalist who wrote *The Death-Blow to Spiritualism* for Maggie, phrased it, "Some idea of the profit which could be derived from awakened public interest in the matter, seems to have come to her very promptly." Yet in the spring of 1848, it is unlikely that the relatively unschooled and unsophisticated Maggie mistrusted Leah as much as she later claimed. Only gradually, over a series of years, would the young woman's attitude sour toward her eldest sister. Judging from Maggie's behavior and cooperation with Leah in 1848, she, as well as Katy, must have regarded Leah with affection and respect.

Inadvertently, Maggie revealed that in her memoir. Soon after her arrival, Leah took Maggie and Katy aside, looked them straight in the eye, and forced them to confess. Withering under their older sister's relentless stare, the girls agreed to "undress and show her the manner of producing the mysterious noises." Leah assured them that she would keep their secret—but only if they would teach her their trick.

Dutifully the girls showed her what they did. To their surprise, Leah could not seem to catch on to the trick very easily or manipulate her toes well enough to make the same sounds. "She found great difficulty in producing the same effect...as the joints of her feet were no longer as pliable as in childhood," Maggie explained.

Having been found out, she and Katy could hardly protest when Leah insisted on taking at least one of them home with her. Of course, Leah's daughter, Lizzie, was an offender too, and once the trio returned to Leah's home at Rochester's Mechanics Place, Lizzie and Katy resumed their antics.

At twilight a sound rocked Leah's house so forcibly that it seemed "as if a pail of bonnyclabber [thick sour milk] had been poured from the ceiling and fallen upon the floor." Later that night she was awakened by screams from Katy and Lizzie. According to Leah's account, her daughter claimed that a cold hand passed over her face and down her back.

Leah also insisted that she had become the victim of other chilling events—among them, the spectacle of an invisible hand shaking a box of matches in her face and the mysterious rising of a Bible from under her pillow. The next night the "spirits" disturbed her sleep again with a noisy clog dance, culminating in applause from a ghostly audience that rushed downstairs, slamming the door behind.

Convinced that her home was haunted, Leah said she now felt compelled to move. Before long, she found another apartment in a two-family house on the quiet, tree-lined Prospect Street in Rochester's fashionable Third Ward. In a peculiar coincidence, it was adjacent to a cemetery, the "Buffalo Burying Ground," the oldest in the city.

The move also coincided with the arrival of Maggie and Mrs. Fox. That same night, Leah grimly reported in her memoir, the "spirits"—who sounded suspiciously like immature teenage girls—once again returned. "We could hear them shuffling, giggling and whispering, as if they were enjoying themselves at some surprise," she wrote. They became so exuberant that they shook Leah's bed (which she was sharing with Margaret), lifted the mattress, and "let us down with a bang."

These, Maggie later admitted, were simply an extension of their earlier capers in Hydesville. Now, though, Maggie and Katy had a new purpose—to taunt Leah with their rapping prowess. They seemed to have even less sympathy for their incurably superstitious mother, who, as usual, was terrified by the return of the spirits and the "curse" they represented.

With her husband in Hydesville, Mrs. Fox insisted that they needed a new protector. She summoned her foster son, the soft-spoken Calvin Brown, who lived nearby in Rochester. At twenty-four years of age, the strapping, handsome young man, who had lived as a teenager with the Foxes after his mother's death and now served part-time in the New York Militia Regiment, seemed a fitting choice.

Calvin's arrival provided the girls with a new challenge. For Leah as well, the arrival of their gentle foster brother seemed fortuitous, representing a new audience upon whom she, in consort with Maggie and Katy, could perfect her raps.

Solemnly, Maggie and Katy gave Leah their word to behave according to her instructions. That first night, after a loud noise awakened the household from their sleep, Leah directly addressed the spirit.

"Flat foot, can you dance the Highland fling?" she asked. Before long the room was dutifully filled with thumping sounds. Then the spirit went wild. Panic-stricken, Mrs. Fox called Calvin to the bedroom. Observing that his foster mother and Leah had moved their mattress to the floor, he scolded them. To do so was only encouraging more mischief. *His* mattress, he announced rather proudly, would remain on its bed frame in his room.

That was all Maggie and Katy needed to hear. No sooner had Calvin retired than they awakened him with a "shower of slippers." Then, after being hit with his own walking stick in the darkness, Calvin reached out for the flitting, elusive spirits, receiving a "palpable bang for every thrust he made" and ultimately grazing his lips on a brass candlestick.

Years later in *The Death-Blow to Spiritualism*, Maggie admitted that she and Katy had engineered the entire attack on their beloved Calvin. "Of course we slily [slyly] did it, as we did many other hoydenish tricks," she confessed. Virtually all the events reported in Leah's account also were described in Maggie's memoir—the whispering, giggling, scuffling, groaning, and "tragic mimicry were natural to childish daredevils like themselves."

The next night, the spirits visited again, according to Leah, and this time quite aggressively. Katy claimed she saw the apparition of a dying man wrapped in a white sheet whose death rattle was so intense it sent vibrations through the bed. Then, the girl fell into a death-like trance. Alarmed, Calvin held a mirror to Katy's mouth to see if she was alive.

As soon as she revived, Katy retold the "official" story of the spirits in Hydesville, burst into tears, and repeated twenty or thirty verses of poetry ending with the lines "To be with Christ is better far." Maggie also became alarmed, but she remained quiet. It was, after all, too late to retract their prank. While their cousin Lizzie soon refused to continue, Maggie and Katy were too invested to stop.

Admittedly, the girls were growing up in an age of trickery. By the mid-nineteenth century, the "arts of deception," as contemporary historian James W. Cook recently observed in a book of that title, were widely admired. Humbuggery, in fact, was nearly a national pastime. Its most famous representative was P. T. Barnum. His cleverly staged exhibition of Joyce Heath—who claimed to be the one-hundred-sixty-one-year-old black nurse of George Washington—had kicked off his legendary career in 1835. "The public," as Barnum famously observed, "appears disposed to be amused even when they are conscious of being deceived."

Professors of chemistry invited members of their audience to inhale nitrous oxide, or laughing gas. Still other experts on the new "science" of phrenology—a reading of personality from bumps on the head first described by eighteenth-century European Dr. Joseph Francis Gall—made a living by fingering the skulls of their audiences. Illusionists of every stripe crisscrossed the country entertaining an incredulous public. Shadow-boxers, mesmerists, and hucksters sold powders and elixirs purported to cure everything from acne to cancer.

At the elegant Lower Broadway theater known as Niblo's Gardens, spectators gaped at displays of panoramic *trompe l'oeil* paintings that seemed three-dimensional. Still others were stunned by the sleight-of-hand skills of early touring magicians like Monsieur Adrien. Americans also marveled at the seemingly supernatural abilities of a clock-like figure, Maelzel's automaton chess-player, which, as it turned out, was secretly manipulated by a human being. And the term "confidence man" was coined in 1849 when genteel-huckster William Thompson swindled a watch from a trusting stranger.

But if the spirit of the age set a mood for Maggie and Katy's pranks, their lives under Leah's insistent rule enhanced them, inuring them to the differences between fact and fiction so often that they could no longer distinguish between the two.

∼❧∼

Katy's breakdown seemed to encourage the girls in their tormenting of Calvin. At dinnertime his end of the table would inexplicably rise.

Nimbly, the teenagers pulled his chair out from under him. Once they did so as the unsuspecting young man rose to pour a pitcher, causing him to land on the floor with a crash, covered with water.

Other times, according to Leah's memoir, Calvin was awakened by woodworking sounds—sawing, cutting, and banging—followed by the appearance of a coffin that moved mysteriously through Calvin's bedroom, powered by unseen hands.

While Maggie and Katy spent their days dreaming up still other pranks, Leah decided it was time to share the spirits with an audience beyond her immediate household.

～※～

Leah turned to her old friends Amy and Isaac Post, a radical Quaker couple. Dedicated social reformers, the plainly dressed Amy and her druggist husband were guided by an "inner light" inspired by their Hicksite Quaker heritage. The Hicksites, a radical group named after charismatic Quaker preacher Elias Hicks, had insisted in 1827 that believers must separate themselves from the secular world and all non-Quakers. After the Posts moved to Rochester in 1836, the couple became so passionately involved in the city's social reform movements that they broke those rules. Before long their Hicksite leaders protested and the Posts, disgusted with their intolerance, broke with the sect.

They organized a group of like-minded individuals called the "Progressive" or "Congregational Friends," who pledged to support abolition and other social reforms. As leaders of the Western New York Anti-Slavery Society, Amy and Isaac Post often housed runaway slaves seeking sanctuary in Rochester's active Underground Railroad. They also invited anti-slavery speakers such as William Lloyd Garrison, publisher of the abolitionist *Liberator* and emancipated slave Sojourner Truth, to Rochester.

Leah's decision to share her new ideas and the "spirit manifestations" with the Posts was carefully calculated; the soft-spoken, middle-aged Amy and Isaac were not only neighbors, but had served as surrogate parents. Initially, when Leah told them about the hauntings, the Posts had laughed. Yet, after taking measure of their younger friend's serious tone, they listened more intently. Worried, they gently inquired if she, Maggie, Katy, and Mrs. Fox were "suffering under some psychological delusion."

Soon afterward, at least according to Leah's *The Missing Link in Modern Spiritualism,* the spirits proved their existence to the Posts. One night, while the Foxes were at home, a bass note on Leah's piano began tolling independently, as if played by an invisible hand. Coincidentally, Amy and Isaac stopped by for a visit. Wondering at the sound, the Posts called in their friends Henry and Abigail Bush to observe the event.

Like the Posts, the Bushes were stunned. They could not ignore the note's similarity to a death knell. Henry Bush fell to his knees. He offered a prayer asking the Almighty to "sustain this family" and wondered, "If, in his great wisdom, he had chosen them as instruments through whom mankind should be benefited." The piano continued to toll and finally at 1 A.M., the mystified Bushes and Posts left Leah's house.

Soon afterward, a wagon pulled up at Leah's front door. Stephan Smith, Mrs. Fox's son-in-law, husband of her daughter Maria, climbed out. "Oh Stephan, who is dead?" gasped Mrs. Fox. "We have had a terrible warning of death all night."

Stephan explained that Mrs. Fox's granddaughter, little Ella, David's child, was critically ill. Immediately Mrs. Fox and Maggie packed and rushed off with Stephan for Arcadia. Minutes later, according to Leah's memoir, the tolling piano stopped. A day or two later a messenger appeared bearing sad news: Soon after Mrs. Fox and Maggie had arrived at David's farm, little Ella passed away.

༅

That same June of 1848, Amy and Isaac Post embraced spiritualism. In a November 23, 1848, letter to his brother and sister-in-law, Joseph and Mary Post, Isaac described how it happened. One afternoon when the Bushes arrived for dinner with the Posts, one of the Fox sisters invited Amy and the Bushes into the bedroom. "I looked in the door with my own countenance so doubting and saw Abigail & Henry looking as tho they stood before the Judgment seat...Abigail in her most gentle manner asked some questions. I heard very distinct thumps under the floor and several apparent answers."

Since then, Isaac explained, he had many conversations with the spirit, as had Amy, his children, and even his Dutch servant girl. "But you must understand we do not get answers without one of the Sisters...present and not always then....I know it is impossible for me to convey the reality. It has been investigated by many and I believe every candid person admits that the girls do not make it. We have seen it in so many different positions that we see no possibility for man to do it."

Isaac and Amy certainly were vulnerable. Although the couple had three living sons, two other children had been lost to illness— three-year-old Henry in 1837 and their only daughter, four-year-old Matilda, in 1844. Heartened by the idea of communicating with their little ones in spirit, the Posts became the first friends to proclaim their belief in the Fox sisters' "spiritual manifestations" in Rochester and the new faith of spiritualism.

The timing and location for that proclamation had been ideal. By virtue of Rochester's boomtown prosperity and the diversity of its population, the city accommodated free thinkers, religious radicals, and liberals. Moreover, the notion of a collective "spirit"— a benevolent force that endowed each human being with the capability of righting the world's wrongs—was moving through America's religions, and the Posts and their friends already had embraced it. Intrigued with Leah's concept of spiritualism, the Posts and their circle perceived it as the first stirrings of a universalism or communalism—a brotherhood of the human spirit that mirrored their own resolve to find an alternative faith devoid of intolerance.

The purported spirit of Isaac Post's mother reinforced that connection through a message, delivered during one of the Foxes' early
séances, urging him and Amy to use spiritualism to further their
own social reforms. "Isaac, my son, thy feeling is not exactly right
towards low spirits, as thee calls them," Mrs. Post's spirit chided her
son. "A reformation is going on in the spirit world, and these spirits seek the company of honest men like you. It will do them great
good and thee no harm."

⁂

By mid-June 1848 the seeds of spiritualism had scattered across the
tidy lawns fronting the handsome Greek Revival homes and clapboard cottages of Rochester. The Fox sisters regularly held séances
for the Posts and their friends. From the few extant accounts of that
period, Maggie and her sisters seem to have raised spirits as a trio
and alternately as a twosome, but always with Leah in charge and
as interpreter of the raps.

One of the best-preserved accounts of their performance came
from a skeptic, Lyman Grainger, who became a convert to spiritualism after attending a séance. His story, retold in a November 1,
1848, letter by his friend, Reverend Lemuel Clark of nearby Otsego
Hills, was later printed in a historic journal.

At the insistence of Lyman's wife, he had hosted one of the Fox
sisters' séances. Once the guests arrived, they were directed to sit in
a circle in the Graingers' parlor and recite the Lord's prayer in uni-
son. The oil lamps were then darkened while guests held hands,
anxiously awaiting the spirit's first "manifestations." Before long the
eerie raps began, growing louder in intensity as Leah interpreted
the messages from the Hydesville spirit.

The ghost, Lyman recounted, was accompanied by a second
spirit that night—Harriet, the Graingers' daughter—who had mysteriously died after following her physician husband to Michigan.
To learn more, the now-curious Lyman was thus compelled to attend another session.

At that second séance, Harriet's raps became increasingly urgent as she explained that her husband had poisoned her. Even with that horrifying information, Lyman continued to scoff, "condemning the whole affair as a fraud." Nevertheless, he was intrigued enough to attend a third séance—one in which Harriet's spirit revealed so many intimate details about her life that Lyman admitted he was "overcome by the evidence of truth."

Unmentioned in Lyman's letter was the close friendship between his wife, Adelaide, and Leah. The former had accompanied Leah on her trip to Hydesville in May and might have shared details about her life and Harriet's.

Skeptical as he was, Lyman disregarded that. But he needed one more proof. In a final test, Lyman invited his friend Reverend Lemuel Clark to a séance during which Lyman decided to test the ghost himself. "Will the Spirit please move the table to Brother Clark," he said. Simultaneously, to avoid deception, he instructed the other guests—including Katy and Leah, who were conducting that séance—to raise their hands above their heads.

"Not a muscle moved visibly, no intensity of will was marked upon any countenance, as we would naturally expect, where a person was making a sly but powerful effort with any limb, but every countenance was mild and placid," Reverend Clark recalled. "Yet [each] bore the impress of the deepest awe, while the table moved steadily, and firmly towards me, as if impelled by the strength of a man."

Soon other Rochesterians and residents of nearby towns reported hearing strange sounds in their homes. Often such reports came from those who had attended a Fox sister séance. By late October 1848, George Willetts, another former Hicksite Quaker, wrote anxiously from the nearby village of Waterloo to his cousin Isaac Post. "As to the rappings heard at Rochester and which I heard when then away from the girls [the Fox sisters] I hear it very frequently, and much more now than then but I have not got to that condition where I can talk with it or have it answer questions. I hear it very frequently on my coat cellar and…a great deal on the pillow and around the bed…sometimes on the floor and the table." "I hope," he added anxiously, "I shall be able to talk with it."

He was not the only Waterloo resident to report the strange sounds. "The Thomas McClintock folks all say that they have heard the same. Also Elizabeth Stanton," added Willets in his letter. "Gerritt Smith's daughter was on a visit to E. Stanton and heard about it. She went home and told her mother who had full faith in it and the daughter wrote to E. Stanton a day or two since that her mother has heard it several times, so if it is humbug it seems to spread fast."

The previous July, several Quaker abolitionists had gathered first at the home of Jane and Richard Hunt and then at the McClintock's fine brick house in Waterloo. The organizers, who included Mary Ann McClintock, Lucretia Mott, Elizabeth Cady Stanton, and Matilda Wright, formalized their ideas for women's suffrage around the mahogany parlor table where the raps would later reportedly be heard.

Spiritualism, born out of the same discontent with social restrictions and punitive theologies as the suffrage movement, ended up even sharing the same table. The subsequent meeting at the Seneca Falls Universalist Wesleyan Church on July 19–20 would ignite the women's suffrage movement, setting the stage for a seventy-two-year battle that resulted in the 1920 passage of the Twenty-First Amendment. Among the hundred men and women who ultimately supported its resolutions, some were already sympathetic to spiritualism—Amy Post, Sarah Post Hallowell, Elizabeth Cady Stanton, Mary Ann and Thomas McClintock, and Sarah Burtis.

For the next quarter of a century, spiritualism, with its benevolent view of the soul and advocacy of social reform, was a serious concern for many suffragists. As one of its leaders, Susan B. Anthony, observed in her diary of 1854 while visiting with Lucretia

Mott in Philadelphia, "Spiritualism as usual being the principle topic...[we had] an intuitive feeling that we were not to cease to exist when the body dies."

~✤~

In thrall to their eldest sister and trapped in a regime of séances, Maggie and Katy had fewer opportunities for independence than other young women of their era. Their discontent may explain why the spirits grew increasingly boisterous during the summer of 1848, as Leah reported in her memoir. It was then that "a change came over the spirit of our dream. Things in spiritual matters, grew from bad to worse."

The immediate source of the trouble was the death of Leah's elderly neighbor, Mrs. Vick, who was soon replaced by a new tenant—a "diminutive sickly-looking man" whose wife complained about loud noises emanating from the Fox side of the house.

One night, after his dinner was disturbed, the neighbor appeared at Leah's door, threatening to have them arrested if the sounds persisted. In a pique of temper, Maggie and Katy retaliated with noises that Leah described as "heavy artillery." Another night the girls sneaked into the neighbor's rooms, jerked a pillow from beneath his head, and terrorized his family with eerie noises. Exasperated, the man reported the disturbance to the landlord. The following morning Leah was served with a summons, demanding her immediate removal from the house.

To save face over the embarrassing incident, the matron assured readers of *The Missing Link in Modern Spiritualism* that her friends rallied and by September 1, 1848, had helped her and her family move into a "pleasant little cottage" on Troup Street.

While not stated in Leah's memoir, she must have reprimanded Maggie and Katy or at least made them painfully aware that their rambunctious behavior had caused the move. Henceforth, they must practice a cooler, more muted form of spiritualism, Leah urged her sisters, encompassing visions of peace, tranquility, and a gentler visitation. The spirits, after all, were part of a loving divinity that was all-forgiving. In their communion with spirits, Leah later wrote, she, Maggie, and Katy began to visualize an image of their youngest sister, who had died in late infancy.

During that transitional period Isaac Post reminded Leah that a better way to communicate with the spirits was through the use of an alphabet board—similar to the one her brother David had used in Hydesville or as William Duesler described in his account. While the Foxes' precise method was never fully explained in either Leah or Maggie's memoir, it seems to have utilized a similar list of alphabetic letters. As Leah pointed to each individual letter, the spirit rapped on the appropriate one that would help spell out a word and then a sentence.

"Dear Friends, you must proclaim these truths to the world. This is the dawning of a new era; and you must not try to conceal it any longer. When you do your duty, God will protect you; and good Spirits will watch over you," read the first message the spirits allegedly rapped out from Leah's alphabet board.

In subsequent séances, she and her sisters agreed that five raps meant the spirits needed the alphabet board when communicating a complex message. While Samuel Morse's telegraph had been operating publicly since 1844, it was the new "spiritual telegraph," as Isaac Post now referred to spirit communication, that sent messages to the living from the other world. It was then, Leah added in her memoir, that a message arrived from her maternal grandfather, Jacob Smith, insisting that she allow her "good friends to hold communion with their friends in heaven." Immediately after copying the message on paper, Leah shared it with others in her circle. They brought the message to Isaac's apothecary shop.

Through that announcement, spirit communication became available to the public and, although Leah would deny it, was on its way to becoming a business.

To many Rochesterians who heard about Leah's invitation, spirit communication seemed titillating news. In an effort to satisfy curiosity-seekers, organize requests for séances, and protect the Fox sisters from unsavory visitors, the ever-loyal Isaac enlisted help from four friends—R. D. Jones, Edward Jones, John Kedzie, and Andrew Clackner.

Through Isaac and those men, the news spread of Leah's offer to hold séances with spirits who resided in a heaven-like "Summerland." Among the earliest recorded out-of-town adherents was Isaac's niece Matilda Rushmore, of Westbury, Long Island. Writing about her aunt Willett's funeral on January 28, 1849, Matilda explained that in spite of her grief, "I was enabled to rejoice that in our spiritual home, love shall be our bond of union...I believe the more our spiritual senses are unfolded, the closer shall we perceive...the relations, between this, and the other life—and even our tears for the departed, will be dried in the assurance, that... death has only gifted them with more powers."

❧

In Rochester, meanwhile, Leah seemed to have begun believing in spirit powers herself and even attempted to prove their existence to Maggie and Katy. Day after day, Maggie ruefully recalled in her memoir, Leah "tried hard to convince her younger sisters and her own child that there were really such things as spiritual communication."

Katy and Maggie's protests—if there were any—were so weak that ultimately only Leah's daughter Lizzie confronted her mother. "Ma," she would exclaim when Leah attempted to impress her with a belief in some of the frauds she perpetrated, "How can you even pretend that that is done by the spirits? I am ashamed to know even that you do such things—it's dreadfully wicked."

In contrast, the now-fifteen-year-old Maggie, for all her earlier high spirits, seems to have been intimidated. Trapped into a lie of her own making and forced to maintain a regular schedule of spirit evocations, Maggie gradually withdrew into an acquiescent, if nervous, and emotionally dependent state.

By the winter of 1848–49 Leah reigned supreme as translator of the raps and spokesperson for a new and profitable business, while, as Maggie later recounted to a reporter from the *New York World,* "Katie and I were led around like lambs."

"A MERE FRAUD COULD NOT LIVE SO LONG"

Let those who ridicule the excitement that has been created, and
laugh at those who, after a thorough investigation, have been
driven to the conclusion that this is a supernatural appearance—
let them step forward and solve this mystery, if they can.

—E. E. LEWIS, *Mysterious Noises,* 1849

"IMMORTALITY: I notice that as soon as writers broach this question they begin to quote. I hate quotation. Tell me what you
know," the American philosopher Ralph Waldo Emerson wrote in
his journal in May 1849.

Emerson's piercing observation cut deep into the nineteenth-
century debate over theological concepts of the divine. How, his
statement implied, could anyone—theologian, philosopher, or ordinary man—know with certainty what happened after death?

As dean of transcendentalism, Emerson had little patience with
opinion unless it was based upon experience. Like his younger contemporary, Andrew Jackson Davis, Emerson and fellow transcendentalists (including Henry David Thoreau) were influenced by
Swedenborg, who believed that a spiritual realm paralleled the
natural world on Earth. By experiencing life in all its colors and
respecting nature, human and otherwise, man could experience divine wisdom.

"There is a soul at the center of nature and over the will of every
man, so that none of us can wrong the universe," Emerson asserted
in his essay *Spiritual Law.* "It has infused its strong enchantment

into nature that we prosper when we accept its advice... The whole course of things goes to teach us faith."

While Emerson would not learn about the Fox sisters for many months, he too espoused the view that the world of spirits was benevolent. But there he and many of his fellow transcendentalists drew the line. In 1845 Emerson critiqued one of Swedenborg's central concepts, the idea that one could speak with spirits. That thought, he maintained, was simply too literal an interpretation— an "excessive determination to form" as he put it—that trivialized the seriousness of a religious experience.

Of course, the ability to communicate with individual spirits was the very essence of spiritualism. While it was unlikely that Leah, who had only a seventh- or eighth-grade education, understood the nuances of Emersonian thought, she was well acquainted with the Quaker concept that every individual had an "inner light" reflecting the divine. Combining that concept with Andrew Jackson Davis's prediction of the spirits' earthly arrival, Leah fashioned a new faith devoid of traditional religious trappings.

In the place of hell, she explained, there was a benevolent afterlife, a Summerland for all souls, regardless of race, religion, or the sins of a lifetime. Repentance and the enlightenment souls acquired in that afterlife also offered them a chance for redemption. In contrast were those souls dedicated to high moral purpose, which ascended more rapidly through spiritual spheres, until they reached the highest, or seventh, sphere.

As spiritualism developed, the faith would continue to be only loosely defined as a set of beliefs, an intuitive construct rather than a carefully articulated school of thought like transcendentalism. John Humphrey Noyes, founder of upstate New York's utopian Oneida Community, would describe spiritualism as "Swedenborgianism Americanized." Spiritualism would have a more popular appeal for most Americans than transcendentalism largely because it promised direct contact with individual spirits and a joyous afterlife.

Leah modeled her new séances upon the familiar pattern of a traditional religious service. Once guests arrived, they gathered around a table and recited an opening prayer. Then they sang a hymn, such as "The Spirit's Song" or "Hymn of the New Jerusalem," which was named after the church that had memorialized Swedenborg and his teachings. Its words, set to piano music by Leah, were taken from an obscure nineteenth-century poem entitled "The Haunted Spring." What followed was a joining of hands and a few moments of silence that bore a striking resemblance to the start of a traditional Quaker meeting. Simultaneously, Maggie or Katy or both closed their eyes and fell into a half-conscious dream state, or trance. Before long, their audiences heard the faint sound of ghostly raps.

While trances had long been associated with biblical figures and medieval saints, American audiences of this era had become familiar with a new type of dream state, the mesmeric or hypnotic trance first noted by the eighteenth-century Austrian doctor Friedrich Anton Mesmer.

Mesmer had theorized that the balance of a critical fluid called "animal magnetism" was essential to physical and mental health. Illness, he conversely believed, was the result of imbalances in that fluid which could be cured if the patient was properly "magnetized" by holding magnets over his head. After Mesmer's death, one of his disciples, Marquis de Puysegur, made the discovery that while magnetizing his patients some of them fell into a sleepy, trance-like state—mesmerized, as Puysegur dubbed the condition. While in that state, he observed, many of them seemed more intelligent, more aware of their lives, and more perceptive about other people and events than when wide awake. A notable few even achieved a unique state of "extreme lucity" during which they became telepathic, clairvoyant, or prophetic.

By the early nineteenth century, mesmerism had become popular in England, first as a curiosity, then as a field of serious medical study, championed by eminent physician Dr. John Elliotson, professor of clinical medicine at the University of London and founder of the London Phrenological Society. Thanks to Elliotson's advocacy, mesmeric healing was soon enthusiastically practiced by a number of influential literary figures such as Charles Dickens and Harriet Martineau. So startling were the results of mesmeric healing—largely through the powers of suggestion, psychologists later realized—that even Queen Victoria's husband, Prince Albert, became converted and admonished the medical community for disdaining to investigate it more thoroughly.

Mesmerism, and its corollary "magnetic healing," galvanized the United States in 1837, when Charles Poyen, a self-proclaimed Professor of Animal Magnetism from France, made a widely publicized tour of New England. Almost overnight, Poyen became a regional sensation. After volunteers from his audiences stepped forward to offer themselves as hypnotic subjects, they followed Poyen's orders to sing, dance, and march about. No less theatrical but far more serious were Poyen's demonstrations upon other hypnotic subjects who later claimed that they had been cured of backaches, rheumatism, liver ailments, and other complaints by his healing techniques.

Even more astonishing to Americans were those who, while entranced, could suddenly and unaccountably locate lost objects, describe events occurring miles away, and read the minds of others in the audience. Such clairvoyant feats, repeated from Connecticut to Maine, led many of Poyens's advocates to see mesmerism as a gateway to a higher spiritual existence.

That same year, an English version of the French mesmerist Joseph Deleuze's *Practical Instructions in Animal Magnetism* was published, followed by pamphlets illustrating the art of the hypnotic trance. After the 1839 appearance in America's major cities by English phrenologist and mesmerist Robert Collyer, the concept of animal magnetism became part of the American vernacular.

George Bush, a renowned professor of Hebrew at New York University, was among the most prominent of those supporting a link between mesmerism and spiritual communion. As he insisted in his 1847 book *Mesmer and Swedenborg*, "The most important facts disclosed in the Mesmeric state are of a spiritual nature, and can only [be] viewed in connection with the state of disembodied spirits and the laws of their intercourse with each other."

Mesmerism's demonstration of the plasticity of the human mind and its use to attain higher levels of awareness fed quite naturally into Leah's new concept. To her, the trance was a critical first step through which the medium's identity was temporarily erased in preparation for its possession by spirits from a higher plane.

Yet while "Electricity and Magnetism…play some part in the machinery of this intercommunication," as Leah obliquely observed in her memoir, the trance was hard work.

"Frequently our friends would become so deeply interested in their manifestations that they would forget we…needed time to recuperate our mortal strength," Leah recalled. "They did not know that every echo, as it came through our medium forces, consumed a portion of our vitality."

To Maggie, the séance was emotionally exhausting for reasons that went beyond the trance. While Leah may have hypnotized the teenager, it is never mentioned in the latter's memoir. Instead, Maggie was expected to remain alert and acutely sensitive to Leah's every expression and action before audiences. "In all of our séances, while we were under her charge…we knew just when to rap 'yes' and when to rap 'no' by signals she gave us," she said. A subsequent account published by a jealous relative suggested that Leah sat close enough to Maggie and Katy during those séances to signal them by quietly poking them.

Complicating the need to remain alert were the complex questions from some séance guests, or sitters as they were called. Among the most difficult, Leah recalled, were financial and romantic ones. "Many of our visitors were anxious to learn…how to make a fortune. Some wished to know the secrets of others; some dissatisfied with their domestic relations, sought the aid of the Spirits.…Some wanted to know what numbers they should buy in a lottery, to be successful; others…to be advised in their stock speculations."

Fearful of responding incorrectly, Leah often paused, stalling for time in order to think up a satisfying answer. Simultaneously the presumably entranced Maggie sat waiting for Leah's signal to knock. In the ensuing silence the guests began to rustle, then whisper, and finally openly express their discontent. How valid could such spirits be, they demanded, if Leah and her sisters could not answer such questions?

After several such awkward encounters, Leah found a solution. "The Spirits, knowing this [the difficulty of providing an appropriate answer] would give the signal 'done.'"

In spite of her tenuous new following, many Rochesterians remained dubious of Leah's séances, some even calling them "of evil origin, unnatural, perplexing, and tormenting." As in Hydesville, members of the Rochester clergy were foremost in that outcry, condemning the sisters as witches or heretics. Some citizens characterized them as heartless vultures who preyed upon grieving citizens, offering false comfort in exchange for funds. Others, having heard rumors about the Fox sisters' conversations with spirits, considered them mad. The most skeptical merely snickered, contending that the sisterly trio had to be either magicians or outright frauds, albeit very clever ones.

"These young women will have to be pretty smart, if they deceive everybody," sneered the *Rochester Daily Democrat*.

"How then," the *Rochester Courier and Enquirer* asked its readers, "can any rational man suppose such a Being [the Almighty] would undertake to convey intelligence on his creatures by unintelligible thumping on a table."

Under a communal cloud of suspicion, Leah watched her piano students drift away, taking with them her small income. "What shall we do? We cannot endure this much longer," Leah lamented in her memoir of that bleak period. "We scorned the idea of receiving

money from visitors...felt it would be degrading...for the exhibition of spiritualism," she explained.

To send her sisters back to Hydesville—where the community
already regarded them with suspicion—seemed an uncomfortable
alternative. Leah and her sisters were better off remaining in
Rochester, even though that meant they needed to find a way to
support themselves. Ultimately, though it went unmentioned in her
memoir, Leah decided to charge a fee for her séances—about $1 a
head. By the early 1850s, she was collecting $100 to $150 a day—
sums that, according to Maggie, her eldest sister greedily "pocketed"
for herself. Left unsaid was the fact that Leah used some of that
money to house, feed, and clothe Maggie and Katy.

❧

Rochester's dissatisfaction with spiritualism paralleled Maggie's
own. Week after week, the teenager dutifully followed Leah's bidding, appearing for the séances, falling into a trance, and rapping
out messages upon command. Maggie was becoming increasingly
restive, though, brooding over what a friend would later describe as
"this life of dreary sameness and suspected deceit."

"When I look back on that life I almost say in defense that I
never took any pleasure in it," Maggie later confessed to the *New
York World*. Adding to the awkwardness of her situation, by 1849 the
sixteen-year-old was becoming a beauty. Her fresh-faced appearance
not only charmed the mourning men who attended the séances, but
also beguiled their romantically inclined wives, sisters, and mothers.
Many of the visitors perceived her as an angelic creature, an emblem
of untouched purity through whom spirits could willingly pass.

"Our whole family was, at that time, under bondage, as it were,
to Ann Leah...she ruled over us as with a rod of iron," Maggie
later recalled in her own memoir. "I have feared that woman all my
life. Remember, she is twenty-three-years older than I am...[and
exudes a] mixture of terrorism and cajolery."

Relief for Katy came from Eliab Capron, a friend of the Posts and a member of the Progressive Friends, who offered to have her live with him and his wife in nearby Auburn. Skeptical of the spirits, Capron explained to Mrs. Fox that he believed Katy's separation from Maggie and Leah would put an end to the sounds—but soon he became an ardent convert himself.

Meanwhile, Maggie's relief was also at hand: John Fox had finally finished the family's new home in Arcadia and Mrs. Fox planned to return there with Maggie. At this, though, the spirits— or Leah—became enraged. "No, you cannot go; you must remain here and do your duty," they insisted, according to Leah's memoir. But the refusal seems to have sparked Maggie's rebellion because suddenly she stopped rapping.

Finally, Maggie had her way. No longer would she knock on command, no longer would she make any sounds in her older sister's séances whatsoever. Leah was horrified. Without Maggie, spiritualism had little chance of flourishing. To make matters worse, Leah remained incapable of producing raps as efficiently or convincingly as her teenage sister—a fact that she nearly admitted in her memoir. When the spirits stopped rapping, Leah wrote, she tried to convince them to resume. Yet it was impossible to "get the sounds" on her own.

Whatever grim pleasure Maggie gained from Leah's frustration was matched by Mrs. Fox's jubilation at the ensuing silence. Believing that the spirits had fled at last, the relieved matron now felt free to join her husband in Arcadia.

For reasons that have never been explained, Maggie agreed to remain in Rochester with Leah. The hush that now settled over Leah's shrunken household may have been disquieting, bringing with it an unexpected sense of loss—a disappearance of people clamoring for séances, a string of dull, forgettable nights, an absence of gifts from admiring believers, and, most threatening of all, the inevitable dwindling of household funds.

How would they live? Leah fretted. Moreover, what was to be done about the scores of bereaved Rochesterians who still hoped for a chance to talk with their beloved dead? What was to be said to dear friends like Amy and Isaac Post, who believed in the testimony of the spirits? By refusing to rap, by putting spiritualism to the lie, Maggie would inevitably bring shame upon them all. And perhaps that would cast doubts upon their other reformist causes as well.

⁂

Maggie's revolt lasted just twelve days until Eliab Capron and Isaac Post's cousin George Willetts visited the house, offering to help contact the recalcitrant spirits. One look at the trusting twosome who had befriended Maggie and her family was all that the teen-ager needed. Suddenly the raps returned. "They came in with the well-known joyous sounds, all over the hall, as if they were glad to meet us all again...," Leah recounted. "It was to us, like the return of long absent friends."

Leah seized the moment to promote the spiritualist cause more vigorously. She argued that the only way to end widespread resis-tance to the spirits—the condemnations, the bad press, and the persecutions that she and her sisters had endured—was to intro-duce the spirits to a large audience. Without further delay a meet-ing was called at the home of Amy and Isaac Post. There, the spirits issued an order: "Hire Corinthian Hall." The designated night was Wednesday, November 14; the time 7 P.M.; the price of a ticket 25 cents. Eliab Capron agreed to deliver the opening lecture. Amy and Isaac, and his spiritualist committee, promised to accompany Leah and Maggie to the stage.

"The citizens of Rochester will have an opportunity of hearing a full explanation of the nature and history of the 'MYSTERIOUS NOISES,' supposed to be *super natural,* which have caused so much excitement in this city and other places for the last two years. Let the citizens of Rochester embrace this opportunity of investi-gating the whole matter, and see if those engaged in laying it before the public are deceived, or are deceiving others, and if neither, account for these truly wonderful manifestations," announced the *Rochester Daily Advertiser* on the morning of November 14, 1849.

⁊✻⁊

As promised, the doors to the auditorium at Corinthian Hall opened promptly at 7:00 on Wednesday evening. By 7:30 P.M. that moonlit night, four hundred citizens, members of the local press, and a reporter from Horace Greeley's Manhattan-based *New York Tribune* had rushed to their seats to view what they anticipated to be a sensational exposé of spiritualism.

Looking pale and drawn, Leah and Maggie sat before the crowd on a platform backed by four Corinthian columns and a red damask curtain. Just beyond the two sisters stood a nervous Eliab Capron, dressed in a dark evening suit and posed at the lecture podium. The audience, according to the *Rochester Daily Democrat,* was in "the best possible humor," ready to be entertained by what they generally considered the Fox sisters' absurd claims.

To quiet the tittering audience, Capron began his talk by reminding the audience that many of the world's greatest discoveries—including those of Galileo, Newton, and Fulton—had been subjected to ridicule. A vivid rendition of the history of the Hydesville ghost and its transfer to Rochester followed, capped by Capron's vivid description of spirit noises heard in his own home in Auburn. Dramatically, Capron then invited the audience to listen for the ghost themselves. Faint but distinct raps soon echoed through the packed auditorium—noises that Capron enthusiastically touted as proof of the spirit's existence. So too did the *Rochester Daily Democrat,* which reported, "We venture to agree with the lecturer at Corinthian Hall on Wednesday evening, that those who were present…could not but admit the evidence of their senses, that THE GHOST was there." Echoing that conviction was the *New York Tribune* story, which noted, "During [Capron's] relation of these facts, the sounds were distinctly heard…"

Yet the audience was less than impressed. In contrast to "the irrepressible awe which usually accompanies such a manifestation of
supernatural presence," noted the *Daily Democrat*, "...the more the
ghost rapped with that muffled tone, the higher rose the spirit of
mirth."

Nevertheless, Capron and the manager of Corinthian Hall
seemed to have anticipated all eventualities, including the likelihood of audience disbelief. At the conclusion of the lecture-
demonstration, the spirit—or more likely Capron, as the *Daily
Democrat* fuzzily explained—asked that "a committee of five were
to be appointed, who should investigate...the chances for deception in this matter, and to report not what it is, but what it is *not.*"

As to the rappings themselves, the newspaper sharply observed,
"it may be important to state that it appears only when some of the
frailer sex are present, who have been, indeed the chosen companions of the goblin."

❧

The next day a five-man committee chosen from among Rochester's
most respected citizens met with Maggie and Leah. Who chose
them remains unclear, but it was expected that Rochester's best and
brightest would carefully weigh the questions and tasks used to test
the pretty teenager and her older sister. Even the location for their
first examination—at Rochester's Sons of Temperance Hall—had
been kept secret until the last minute to prevent any trickery on
Maggie and Leah's part.

Yet, to the committee's frustration, nothing could be proven or
found suggesting any deception. Maggie and her sister Leah appeared cheerful and cooperative as committee members introduced
themselves and began a series of examinations. They requested new
demonstrations of raps, and answers to questions—and finally removed the sisters to separate rooms. By mid-afternoon, two members of the committee even stretched the bonds of Victorian
propriety by holding the sisters' feet with one hand while placing

the other on the floor. But "though the feet were not moved, there was a distinct jar on the floor," reported the *New York Tribune*. "On the *pavement* and the *ground* the same sounds were heard... they all agreed that the sounds were heard, but *they entirely failed to discover any means by which it could be done.*"

That night, Maggie and Leah appeared again before an audience at Corinthian Hall. Timorously the committee reported that its investigation had been inconclusive. The report, noted the *New York Tribune*, "seemed to fall like a thunder bolt on many of those assembled, who had obviously come with the expectation of receiving one of a very different and far less favorable, character."

Grumbling members of the audience rose to their feet, demanding that a second committee be formed of men known to be skeptics of spiritualism, in hopes that the rapping "humbug" could be exposed.

The following day Maggie and Leah submitted patiently to yet another inquiry. This time they were escorted to the law offices of Frederick Whittlesey, vice chancellor of the State of New York. Equally formidable were the other committee members, among them physician H. H. Langworthy, Judge A. P. Hascall, and New York State Circuit Justice John Worth Edmonds.

What Edmonds saw that day, as he later recalled in a memoir espousing spiritualism, changed his life. "I was at that time a disbeliever; I had all my wits about me, and was on the sharp look out for deception," he insisted.

The fifty-year-old judge assiduously refrained from commenting on the beauty of the medium he met that day and merely issued a dry report of the events. "As I entered the room, she [Margaretta Fox] was seated at one side of the table; the rappings came with a hurried, cheerful sound on the floor where I sat... It was ventriloquism, I said to myself," he recalled. "I put my hands on the table directly over the sounds, and distinctly felt the vibration as if a hammer had struck it. It was machinery, I imagined."

But what kind of machinery, Edmonds, Whittlesey, and the

other committee members debated among themselves. Had it been some sort of mechanical device? How had the teenager and her older sister managed to use it? Where could it be stored—especially since the location of each examination had been kept secret until the last minute?

Whittlesey's committee faced still another audience at Corinthian Hall. They explained to the disgruntled crowd that, among the committee's efforts, Dr. Langworthy had placed a stethoscope on Maggie and Leah's lungs in hopes of discerning an internal reaction to the raps. No such association was made. Moreover "there was no probability or possibility of their being made by ventriloquilism, as some had supposed—and they could not have been made by machinery."

The following morning the managers of Corinthian Hall, cognizant of the mounting excitement that surrounded the Fox sisters and their claims, decided to open the auditorium's doors a fourth time at the reduced rate of twelve-and-a-half cents per head so anyone could afford to attend. Knowing the crowd would be clamoring for results, a third committee redoubled its efforts to find the source of the raps. To rule out the possibility of any "mesmeric" currents passing between Maggie and Leah and their suspected machinery, the men asked them to stand upon a table beneath which was glass, a known non-conductor of electricity. The same reasoning later led them to ask Maggie and Leah to stand upon feather pillows and rap with their long skirts tied around their ankles.

The mysterious knocks continued to envelop the sisters. In frustration the committee appointed one of their wives and two other women to examine Maggie and Leah's gowns, petticoats, and underwear. For the two sisters the necessity of a strip search—even by women—in an era when feminine modesty extended to those of the same sex was humiliating, and they began to cry.

When she heard them, the Fox sisters' faithful friend Amy Post begged to enter the room. Finally, in one last test, the three-woman committee asked Maggie and Leah to get dressed while leaving their feet bare. The results were equally frustrating.

"When they were standing on pillows, with a handkerchief tied around the bottom of their dresses, right to ankles, we all heard the rapping on the wall and the floor distinctly," the three women recalled in a certified statement given to the men's committee and later reprinted in the *New York Tribune*.

Committee members had to concede that they could not debunk the women's claims. The sisters' appearance that night should have been triumphant. But an ominous note had been delivered to the five-man committee, which shared it with Maggie and Leah. "Do not go to the Hall this evening; for if you report favorably to the girls, you will be mobbed."

By the time Maggie and Amy returned with Leah to her cottage on Troup Street, Maggie announced that she could not—and indeed, would not—appear at Corinthian Hall that Saturday night.

Well aware of the twelve days of silence that had settled over Leah's house, Amy Post met her young charge's objections blandly.

"We will go by ourselves, and sit down quietly and see how we shall feel about it," Amy said in a gentle but firm way.

Leah agreed. "If you will go I will go with you, if I go to the stake!" she vowed.

That reaction inevitably augmented Maggie's guilt. Just before they were to leave, she softened. "I cannot have you go without me. I must go, though I expect to be killed," Maggie tearfully conceded.

An hour or so later, Maggie sat stiffly in a chair on the auditorium platform at Corinthian Hall. Next to her was Leah and nearby her trusted friends, Amy and Isaac, George Willets, Eliab Capron, and the Reverend Asahel Jervis. The group had already discovered a warmed barrel of tar hidden in one of the auditorium stairwells. And beyond the narrow platform where Maggie sat, the new audience seemed rougher than previous ones, hurling openly hostile comments at Maggie, leering brazenly at her, and making ribald jokes.

Even when members of the third committee rose and appeared at the podium to present their conclusion, the crowd refused to quiet down. Somehow, finally, one man managed to spit out his committee's woeful conclusion: Try as they might, the five men could not find any explanation for the "knocks" that followed the Fox sisters.

"But stamping, shrieking, and all kinds of hideous noises... obliged him to desist," according to Isaac Post. Suddenly in a blinding cascade of light, firecrackers exploded toward the back of the auditorium. In the resultant smoke and din, men howled that the "females" had lead balls in their dresses that must have accounted for the sounds. The only way to solve the mystery, they bellowed as they pushed their way to the stage, was to inspect the Fox sisters for themselves.

The Posts, Reverend Jervis, George Willetts, and the Corinthian Hall manager, William A. Reynolds, immediately surrounded Maggie and Leah. As the crowd advanced toward the sisters, even the soft-spoken Willets grew violent, threatening that if the "mob of ruffians who desired to lynch 'the girls'" succeeded, it would be "over his dead body."

The group was rescued when Rochester's police-justice S. W. D. Moore and his men appeared from their hidden posts and hastily escorted Maggie, Leah, and their friends out of the smoke-filled auditorium.

⁓✦⁓

The press offered a decidedly mixed reaction to the Corinthian Hall demonstration. The *Rochester Daily Advertiser* haughtily observed that "the wary and eagle-eyed are kept out and excluded from opportunity of investigation," while the *New York Tribune* observed that "It is difficult to understand why spirits, who act with as little reason as children or idiots" would spend time "thumping the wall."

No publicity is bad publicity, though. Knowing that, just a day before the Fox sisters' final appearance Eliab Capron had published a pamphlet, *Singular Revelations: Explanation and History of the Mysterious Communion with Spirits Comprehending the Rise and Progress of the Mysterious Noises in Western New York, Generally Received as Spiritual Communications,* which would sell six thousand copies in less than two months' time.

Predictably, Leah and her sisters were swamped with requests for séances. "The people came from every direction. We knew not what to do," Leah recalled in her memoir. Katy and her mother (who must have resigned herself to the spirits at last) moved back to Rochester and joined Maggie and Leah.

Now, however, in contrast to the liberals who arrived for the first séances, a more conservative group of Rochesterians appeared. Among the curious was none other than Judge Hascall, who had served on Corinthian Hall's second committee, followed by other prominent doubters such as the local judges Summerfield, Chamberlain, and Hedden. Joining them was the Reverend Dr. Charles C. Hammond, still another member of the Corinthian Hall committee. By the winter of 1850 that minister, having observed three séances, was convinced of Maggie and Leah's telepathic abilities. "On the 20th of February, the two youngest sisters made my family a visit. Here the sounds were heard; questions involving subjects wholly unknown to them, were answered; a large, heavy dining-table was moved several times; and on expressing thanks at the table to the Giver of all Good, some six or eight sounds responded to every sentence I uttered...," he recalled.

Energized by spiritualism's promise of an afterlife, Hammond eventually became a medium himself and in 1852 penned an influential book, *Light from the Spirit World.*

Indeed, so many seekers felt a personal connection with the spirits that Leah was forced to divide their requests for séances with her sisters. Without Leah's authoritative presence, though, guests often disrupted Maggie and Katy's sittings. "The séances of the Misses Fox were constantly broken up by inharmony, rudeness and determined opposition, on the part of some of the visitors," wrote early spiritualist historian Emma Hardinge in her *Modern American Spiritualism.*

Convinced of their own spiritualist powers, some visitors began jabbering in unknown tongues, much like the Shakers who lived in nearby upstate communities. Other guests, in imitation of the spiritualist practices of Native Americans, bellowed in Indian-style war-whoops. Still others insisted on spelling out "apostolic letters in miserable grammar and worse spelling."

The chaos not only ruined the girls' séances, but threatened Leah's long-term plans to promote her séances and those of her sisters as the ultimate expression of the spirits. She, of course, was their ultimate earthly authority, the self-appointed leader of the new spiritualist faith. And to prove it, the spirits came to Leah's rescue by demanding an orderly system of telegraphy that paralleled the spreading telegram wires of Samuel F. B. Morse.

Mindful of the purported association between electricity, mesmerism, and clairvoyance, and determined to give spiritualism a revered aura, Leah credited patriot Benjamin Franklin, the famous Father of Electricity, with a call for a well-organized spiritual telegraphy. On February 16 the great patriot's spirit was said to have appeared at the Rochester home of Nathaniel Draper and his medium wife, Rachel. In attendance were Maggie, Katy, and Leah, accompanied by Reverend Asahel Jervis of the Methodist Church and his wife, Mary.

That evening, according to an article in Rochester's *Daily Magnet* that was later reproduced in Hardinge's *History of Modern American Spiritualism,* Maggie and Katy were directed by the "magnetized," or hypnotized, Mrs. Draper to divide the guests into two groups. No sooner were the two groups seated in rooms at opposite ends of the house than they heard loud noises resembling the rat-tat-tat of the telegraph office—signs, it was explained, of the imminent approach of the Father of Electricity.

Five days later, on February 20, the groups reassembled. Again Maggie was cloistered in a room with the Drapers and Mary Jervis, while Katy and Leah sat in a distant room with Reverend Jervis. Once again, they heard the sounds of a telegraph.

"Now I am ready, my friends. There will be great changes in the nineteenth century. Things that now look dark and mysterious to you will be laid plain before your sight. Mysteries are going to be revealed. The world will be enlightened. I sign my name, Benjamin Franklin," was the message that Maggie transcribed.

A few minutes later, Reverend Jervis appeared at Maggie's parlor door with an identical message that Katy had rapped out from Franklin.

The demonstration, published in the February 24 edition of the *Daily Magnet,* captured the public imagination. By the end of the winter of 1850, recalled native Rochesterian Dr. Alvah Strong in a talk to the Rochester Historical Society some sixty-five years later, "All Western New York was excited by the reports and the doctrines of Spiritualism."

The *Daily Magnet* report also attracted attention from certain big-city observers, including *New York Tribune* editor Horace Greeley, who had visited Rochester a month earlier. Greeley disparaged the alleged spiritual appearance of Franklin reported in the *Daily Magnet* and characterized the ghost's message as a "humbug and a counterfeit no matter which world he belongs to." But he admitted, "The whole subject is interesting and worthy of thorough investigation. We think Clairvoyance is at the bottom of it."

✠⚙ 4 ⚙✠

"So Continuously in the Public Eye"

These circles should not make their sessions more frequent than
twice a week; because those things which become too familiar are
thereby deprived of their sanctity, and hence, also of their power to
benefit the assembled individuals.

—Andrew Jackson Davis, *The Philosophy of Spiritual Intercourse*

In the wake of Maggie and Leah's public appearances in
Corinthian Hall some Rochester residents had become so fascinated with spiritualism that they immediately attributed any
strange sounds in their homes or shops to "spirit manifestations."

One of the most famous converts was a Mrs. Sarah Tamlin, who
was awakened one morning before dawn by a persistent rapping
sound. As she opened her eyes she realized that a smoldering wick
from a candle stand had floated to the floor and was about to ignite
the curtains. Soon after that "timely warning saved the house and
very probably Mrs. Tamlin from being consumed by the flames,"
she became a medium.

Other locals, alarmed by knocking sounds heard in buildings
near the falls of the Genesee River, became convinced that the
waterways of the famous Flour City were haunted. After consulting
with Professor Loomis, a *Scientific American* commentator on the vibratory effects of dams upon buildings, a Manhattan newspaper, the
New York Express, noted that "Prof. Loomis has pointed to a very
simple and easy method of checking this vibratory action of the
dam, and the people of Rochester, who have been troubled by an invisible spirit, will find it easily exorcised by mechanical means."

The *Rochester Daily Advertiser* reiterated the *Express's* conclusion, but conceded it would likely be ignored: "We question whether such an explanation will satisfy such as are determined to see 'the ghost.'"

By early spring 1850, some residents of Maine, Vermont, New Hampshire, Massachusetts, and Connecticut, intrigued by personal reports of those who had witnessed séances and become new mediums themselves, were embracing spiritualism. Adding to the movement's popularity was the release of a second edition of Capron's booklet, *Explanation and History of the Mysterious Communion with Spirits.*

The first edition had been hugely popular and the second appeared likely to follow in its path, especially after receiving a front-page review in Horace Greeley's *New York Tribune.* "When that remarkable book *Nature's Divine Revelations* by Andrew Jackson Davis was published, we saw fit to give our readers a full...summary of its contents," observed that liberal newspaper on January 18, 1850. The periodical had already provided a "succinct history of the origin and character of these [the Fox sisters'] noises as developed in several public exhibitions at Rochester...through our [previous] columns." Now the *Tribune* excerpted key sections of Capron's account of those same events.

Capron's story soon traveled even farther than New York City. Two weeks later, on February 1, 1850, several men and women from Philadelphia "formed into an experimental circle...and after a very few sittings, succeeded in obtaining through raps, clairvoyance and other methods, satisfactory communion with the spirit world." This, according to medium Emma Hardinge in *Modern American Spiritualism,* was one of the earliest spirit circles organized outside New York State. Others quickly followed in St. Louis, Missouri; Cincinnati and Salem, Ohio; Battle Creek, Michigan; and San Francisco, California.

A month later, bookseller D. M. Dewey of Rochester's Arcade Hall published a pamphlet about the Fox sisters that added to their fame. Shrewdly, as Dewey noted in the introduction to his awkwardly entitled pamphlet *History of the Strange Sounds, or Rappings, Heard in Rochester and Western New York, and Usually Called the Mysterious Noises Which Are Supposed By Many To Be Communications from the Spirit World, Together with All the Explanation That Can As Yet Be Given of the Matter,* "the undersigned...is in no way responsible for the peculiar doctrinal conclusion any of the writers have adopted." After the pamphlet sold thirty thousand copies within a few months, Dewey acknowledged that he, too, was a spiritualist.

Still more useful to Eliab Capron, however, would be the legitimization of spiritualism by some of America's leading scientists and thinkers. Simultaneous with the second edition of his own pamphlet, Capron seems to have either approached or been approached by several prominent men who wanted to bring the Fox sisters to New York City for lecture-demonstrations. By early February 1850 he had presented the idea to Mrs. Fox.

After the events at Corinthian Hall the once-despondent matron no longer feared the spirits or prayed for her family's release. At least according to Leah's memoir, Mrs. Fox had changed her mind. Inexplicably she now seemed to consider spiritualism a fortuitous visitation, an honor conferred upon her daughters by a divine intelligence that accorded them respect and fame.

Nevertheless, she remained intensely protective of Maggie and Katy. A product of the Victorian ideal of true womanhood—the social demand that women occupy their "proper sphere" and act with purity, piety, submissiveness, and a devotion to home and hearth—Mrs. Fox expected the same for her daughters. She refused to allow Maggie and Katy to travel to the rough-and-tumble city. Admittedly, her daughters had already deviated from that ideal by appearing in public to conduct séances and witnessing the hostile behavior at Corinthian Hall, but there was no reason to expose them to still more. No, she could not allow her daughters to visit New York City.

But Capron did not relent. "I regret this very much," he replied to Mrs. Fox on February 10, "as the persons who have sent for her...stand among the first in the nation for science and influence. It would be of great advantage to your family to have such men satisfied in regard to the family and...would forever clear all who are now being ridiculed and lied about, from all charges of fraud."

The trip would take little more than a week, he assured Mrs. Fox, during which time he and Mrs. Capron would watch over Maggie and Katy. Nor would they be the teenagers' only chaperones: the Poughkeepsie Seer himself, Andrew Jackson Davies, volunteered to look after the girls. The renowned phrenologist Edward Fowler also extended an offer for Maggie and Katy to live in his home in New York City.

Even if Katy could not be spared from the busy schedule of Rochester séances, why not let seventeen-year-old Maggie make the trip? The invitation, Capron reminded Mrs. Fox, came from a man "who wishes his name kept a secret for the present" but one who could potentially boost the spiritualist cause. "You and all the defenders of the 'spirits' could have...one of the best public defenders in the United States," he pleaded.

Again Mrs. Fox refused. For the moment, there would be no trip to New York City. Yet before long, other invitations would appear, including one from showman Phineas T. Barnum, who passed through Rochester every summer with his "Traveling Exhibition" featuring Tom Thumb, the Feejee Mermaid, and other curiosities from his popular American Museum in Manhattan. The possibility of visiting New York must have thrilled Maggie. If her beloved Rochester was lively compared to Hydesville, what then would it be like to live in New York City—even if she had to rap under Leah's relentless control?

~❧~

At the end of March two influential visitors from Springfield, Massachusetts arrived in Rochester, the free-thinking Universalist minister Reverend R. P. Ambler and his friend D. F. Coman. The purpose of their visit, they explained to Leah, was to investigate spiritualism.

Already several New Englanders had issued reports about visitations from spirits. One of the most disturbing came from Reverend Eliakim Phelps and his son Austin of Stratford, Connecticut, who said they were tormented by a boisterous nocturnal ghost. They insisted that a series of strange domestic antics disrupted their household: dishes that jumped, candlesticks that walked, cold turnips inscribed with hieroglyphic writings that dropped from the ceiling, and forks that appeared inexplicably bent. In one instance, eerie voices called for helpings of squash pie.

No less mysterious were reports emanating from a Massachusetts Methodist minister, LeRoy Sunderland, and his physician friend Dr. Larkin, who received messages from the dead "by raps and movements of a cradle" belonging to Sunderland's infant grandchild, according to Hardinge's *Modern American Spiritualism.* After inviting the public to witness séances then occurring at the home of the baby's mother, Mrs. Margaretta Cooper—who would become a famous medium in her own right—Sunderland began publishing his journal, *Spiritual Philosopher.*

To the ever-opportunistic Leah, the appearance of the two gentlemen from Springfield could not have been better timed. They arrived at just the right moment to witness a special séance planned for April 1, 1850, commemorating the second anniversary of the Hydesville knockings.

Leah's memoir did not record the details of that séance but insisted that Ambler and Coman were "greatly astonished by the evidence they received." The two men proposed that Leah and her sisters demonstrate their talents to residents of Albany, a city of about 50,000 people and the capital of New York State.

Leah had not forgotten the "howling mob" at Corinthian Hall, she told Ambler and Coman. Nor had her more emotionally fragile sister Maggie. And while the climate toward spiritualism seemed far more receptive now than in November 1849, Leah would need assurances before agreeing to go out of town. A local trial run was needed. Ironically, the designated location—perhaps because it was the largest auditorium in the city—was Corinthian Hall.

Maggie, Leah, and Katy appeared at Corinthian Hall on April 25, 1850, and the evening went smoothly, according to Leah. "The hall was crowded. The lecturer [Reverend Ambler] was eloquent and the audience pleased. The rappings were profuse. Public opinion had changed since the first lectures on the subject. Friends rushed the platform to congratulate us on our triumphant success."

⁕

Maggie, Katy, and Leah arrived in Albany on April 30, 1850, accompanied by their watchful mother and the ever-protective Calvin Brown. As promised, Ambler and Coman promoted Maggie, Katy, and Leah's first appearance at the newly opened Van Vechten Hall on State Street. Following the Corinthian Hall format, the reverend would introduce the sisterly trio with a lecture about the history of spiritualism while Coman served as their businessman, arranging for publicity and distributing tickets to curious residents.

On the appointed night, the *"elite* of Albany" turned out in droves and were not disappointed. They clamored to host parties in honor of the mysterious sisters and signed up for private séances with them. While the Fox sisters converted many residents into believers, they also inflamed doubters among Albany's leaders. One of these was Jacob C. Cuyler, editor of the *Morning Express,* who sent Leah a message on May 13 informing her that the judges of Albany "would be pleased" to call upon her, Maggie, and Katy at 4:00 that same afternoon. The implication of the request was obvious: The sisters had to accept the invitation or face the risk of being run out of town. At the appointed hour, a full corps of Albany's magistrates—seventeen of them—arrived at Delavan House, for a séance that Leah claimed was an unequivocal success.

Even so, accusations of blasphemy and witchcraft were already running rampant through Albany. Some viewed the Fox sisters as servants of the devil. To others, they were madwomen at best and, at worst, imposters and frauds intent on bilking gullible residents.

"A strong army was raised up for our protection," was all Leah wrote about the civic hostility she and her sisters evoked. "And this result," she hastily added, "...was invariably the case through all our subsequent public career."

On May 24, 1850, the Fox family left Albany, heading north to the nearby Hudson River city of Troy. Leah and her sisters made the trip, she explained, out of the goodness of their hearts, to honor the requests they had received from many residents of Troy.

"We really hope all who think that the 'noises' are shallow and transparent humbug will visit the young women and expose them," wrote the *Troy Daily Whig* the day of their arrival. After four days of séances the newspaper softened. "Those who have heard the 'noises' agree in classing them among the things which challenge explanation. The most thorough tests have been applied, and still the 'mystery' is as great as ever."

Nevertheless, the attacks continued and the Foxes left Troy just as they had Albany, in a flurry of praise and denunciation. But the detractors in Troy seemed to be more specifically female. "A murmur arose among the 'women' whose conduct toward us...was cruel and unchristianlike," Leah sourly recalled. Several women even "insinuated that if the mediums were men, their husband would not become so deeply enlisted in this unpopular, and seemingly weird subject." The most outspoken of the female critics, after all, had a husband who was "much younger than herself, handsome and prosperous."

It should have been no surprise that the sisters evoked jealousy because their popularity was based, at least in part, on their sex. At a time when it was considered poor manners for gentlemen to stare at attractive young women at parties, dinners, and at other social occasions, Leah displayed herself and her pretty younger sisters for hours on end to men who could gaze upon them without reproach.

At that very moment, one hundred and fifty miles north of Troy in Waterloo, some of Leah's "progressive" Quaker and reformist friends were attempting to frame a more equitable understanding of the relations between the sexes.

Presented on June 3–5, 1850, as "An Address to the Women of New York" during the Yearly Meeting of Congregational Friends and signed by the pro-suffrage Thomas McClintock and Rhoda De Garmo, the resultant document read, "We maintain *equality of rights* irrespective or sex. What *man* has a right to do, *woman* has a right to do and *she herself* is to be the judge of the propriety and expediency of any given course of action...In no other way can she be true to the world, herself or her God."

Controversial as such words were, they reflected the same impulse for harmony and tolerance as the joyous, brotherly spirits of Leah's Summerland. Critics would tar feminism and spiritualism with the same brush, branding both movements as absurd flights of fancy and, worse, contributors to the erosion of home and hearth.

Many spiritualists, like feminists, would eventually come to regard the institution of marriage warily, historian Ann Braude observed in her 1989 book *Radical Spirits: Spiritualism and Women's Rights in Nineteenth Century America*. All too often, they contended in that sexually restrictive age, men married women out of lust rather than genuine love. Parents also tended to pressure young women into marriage as an economic necessity because so few occupations were open to women. Those who refused to wed, moreover, were consigned to an impoverished spinsterhood; often they remained home with aging parents or became dependents in the home of a married sibling.

In 1853, New York women's rights activist Mary Fenn Love shocked her family and community by traveling to Indiana and divorcing Samuel Love, her husband of nine years and father of her children, on the unusual grounds of spiritual and emotional incompatibility. Adultery was the usual—and often sole—acceptable reason for divorce.

By the end of the Civil War many spiritualists considered marriage valid only when based upon mutual compatibility. "Mediums decried the 'body and soul destroying marriage institution in favor of one that was a soul union, not a curse,'" observed the *Religio-Philosophical Journal* of January 1864. Without benefit of a happy union spiritualists believed that the soul could not reach its highest potential during its earthly existence.

~✤~

On Monday, June 4, the Fox family steamed down the Hudson, finally landing at one of the fifty piers that lined Manhattan's Battery. Who invited them, and why Mrs. Fox finally allowed the visit, have never been explained.

At the dock the scene was dizzying. Swarms of roughly clad men hauled Southern cotton, West Indian sugar cane, and crates of Continental goods freshly unloaded from the fleets of clipper ships that bobbed at anchor offshore in the harbor.

Nearby rushed boisterous fishmongers, newsboys, hot-corn girls, apple vendors, stevedores, fashionably dressed men and women, and men in green neckties directing clusters of newly arrived immigrants to boarding houses. Perched atop their hansom cabs, hacks sat ready to take travelers to elegant uptown hotels such as Irving House near Gramercy Park or the older Astor House on Broadway.

In such an atmosphere, the novelty and excitement of seeing Manhattan for the first time overshadowed Maggie's resentment toward Leah. The adventure of the big city and its inchoate promise of a better life "half intoxicated" Maggie, lulling her into overlooking her reservations.

~✤~

Maggie and her family took rooms in a hotel at Maiden Lane and Broadway. In Leah's memoir she said they stayed at Barnum's

Hotel—although it was, she immediately added, "not [to] be confounded with the great showman by that name." The reference, in a coincidence that has caused innumerable misinterpretations, related to a hotel briefly owned by A. S. Barnum. Just two blocks south on Broadway was the impresario Barnum's American Museum, a spacious white building.

There, in exchange for 25 cents, visitors could spend a fascinating day in an enormous series of exhibits and halls that boasted a wholesome "family atmosphere." It had become a favorite destination for sightseers, much like our contemporary Disneyland.

Barnum's brand of "humorous hokum" at the American Museum included "an encyclopedic synopsis of everything worth seeing in this curious world"—exotic animals, midgets, fortune-tellers, phrenologists, clairvoyants, and freaks like the Rubber Men, Siamese Twins, and the Swiss Bearded Lady who inevitably drew large, gaping crowds. Proud of his reputation as a trickster whose winking displays challenged even the most discerning minds, Barnum once opined that "Everyone is open to deception. People like to be led in the region of mystery."

For tourists with more serious educational leanings, Barnum's American Museum also featured panoramas, travel exhibits, and wax figures depicting historical events. For conservative ladies who considered the theater improper, there was even a formal "lecture room" for Shakespearean dramas.

Two blocks north, in a parlor adjacent to their hotel rooms, the Fox sisters conducted séances and received guests. Among the first to call was Horace Greeley, the liberal, bespectacled editor of the *New York Tribune,* whose offices were nearby and who was a friend of P. T. Barnum. But convenience had less to do with Greeley's visit than curiosity.

By 1850, the outspoken, crusading editor from New Hampshire was one of America's most controversial and respected journalists, imbued with a deep passion for the rights of the common man and a feverish commitment to abolition, prison reform, temperance, and homesteading. After years of supporting utopian causes, diet reforms, and cleaner streets, Greeley had clawed his way up from running nearly bankrupt penny-publications to establish the *New York Tribune* as one of the city's most powerful newspapers. Impassioned, ideological, and stubborn, Greeley comes down to us today as the editor whose advice to men without influential families or fortunes was popularized into the famous slogan "Go West young man." "He thought the world might be reformed in a day—in his day," his friend Feman Brockway recalled.

For months Greeley had wondered about the Fox sisters. Was spiritualism mere puffery, produced by skilled mountebanks and tricksters, albeit in the fetching form of the Fox sisters? How could anyone believe in an earthly return of spirits at a time when scientific investigators such as naturalist Louis Agassiz, ornithologist John James Audubon, and biologist Asa Gray were explaining natural phenomena in terms of rational laws?

For weeks those questions were debated, becoming part of a bitter rivalry ensuing between Greeley and James Gordon Bennett, the stubby, scrappy Scotsman who was editor-in-chief of the sensationalized *New York Herald*. On February 3, Bennett had jeered at Greeley in print, characterizing him as a poseur who pandered "to the worst appetites of the morbid...there is not a more dangerous demagogue in our midst...nothing in the way of novelty, either pertaining to earth or to heaven is too absurd to be advocated and solemnly defended from the pestiferous poison of Fanny Wright and Fourier, down to the Rochester knockings from the spiritual world."

On March 6, Greeley penned a cautious *Tribune* editorial defending his curiosity. "There is something in the mode of producing the noises that we do not find satisfactorily explained and very likely some exercise of Clairvoyance or some kindred psychologic phenomenon."

By June 4 or 5, the first to greet Greeley at Barnum's Hotel was a smiling Leah, whose dark eyes and rounded figure were handsomely set off by a green-striped muslin dress. Near her stood the more retiring brown-eyed Maggie, dressed in a rose-colored gown complimented by a white under vest and sleeves. Close by, too, was the lighter-skinned, gray-eyed Katy, still in long brown braids, and wearing an embroidered muslin over a long blue dress. As Greeley gazed at the three young women, fresh from the hinterlands of New York, he became inspired to take them under his wing in what would prove a lifelong commitment.

After an initial exchange of pleasantries, Greeley questioned Leah about her plans for séances. Horrified at the idea of charging a mere dollar a head, the editor suggested that she raise the price to five dollars. To collect less than that was unwise, as anything could happen in the rough-and-tumble city—an urban maze of nearly 540,000 people, more than half of whom were immigrants from Ireland, Germany, and England. A hefty price tag for admission, Greeley explained, was a necessity, to "keep the rabble away."

Subsequent to that introduction, the editor attended his first séance. Years later, in his autobiography, Greeley insisted that his initial encounter with the spirits had been deeply disappointing. "I called upon them and heard the so-called 'raps' but was neither edified nor enlightened thereby." Yet, he remained intensely inter-ested in spiritualism. While attributing his fascination to his con-cerns for his chronically ill and depressed wife, Mary, with whom he mourned the recent death of their four-year-old son, Pickie, the editor also felt some kinship with Maggie, Katy, and Leah, initially supporting spiritualism in his paper and serving as their advisor and friend for the next twenty-two years.

Other prominent New Yorkers were soon attending readings. Just two days after the Foxes arrived, in fact, they held a séance at the home of a journalist and former Baptist minister, Reverend Dr. Rufus Griswold, the erstwhile rival of the late Edgar Allan Poe.

Griswold had invited a formidable coterie, among them the eru-dite colonial historian George Bancroft, former secretary of the U.S. Navy; William Cullen Bryant, poet and editor of the progressive *Evening Post;* Nathaniel Parker Willis, editor of the society-minded

Home Journal; and James Fenimore Cooper, author of the famous *Leatherstocking Tales.* Among the brightest literary men of their generation, virtually all of them were skeptical of anything alleged to be supernatural.

Still, whatever apprehension Maggie and her sisters felt about that meeting was carefully concealed. The sisters cheerfully appeared with Mrs. Fox promptly at 8 P.M. at the Griswold townhouse on lower Broadway. Willis later observed to the well-to-do readers of the *Home Journal* that he found Mrs. Fox a "stout lady of the ordinary small-town type of maternity [followed] by three young ladies considerably prettier than the average."

Most puzzling to Willis was the relaxed and personable manner of the young women—especially when compelled to produce such a critical exhibition before those eminent historians, social commentators, and authors. Maggie, Leah, and Katy Fox "have nerves so plumply clad in health and tranquility, that it is difficult to reconcile their appearance with the fact that they have been worked upon for two years by the phenomena of unexplained visitations," Willis observed.

Regardless of such speculation, Willis, his host Griswold, and their literary companions, having vowed to withhold all judgments until the evening's end, respectfully took their places for the séance. For the first half hour, noted reporter George Ripley of Greeley's *New York Tribune,* there was only silence, causing the observers to shift in their seats with "obvious symptoms of impatience."

Leah then asked the men to draw closer to the table in a tight circle. "Soon after faint sounds began to be heard from under the floor, around the table, and in different parts of the room...[they] gradually increased in loudness and frequency...so that no one could deny their presence," Ripley recalled. After a good deal of "coquetting"—or chatter with the spirits—a Dr. Marcy asked one of the ghosts who claimed to be his relative to identify himself and his age. To his astonishment, the spirit responded that he was a child and accurately described himself and the circumstances of his death.

Equally inexplicable were other responses given to poet and essayist Henry Tuckerman. After he asked the spirits questions silently or telepathically, he heard Leah translate raps into correct answers. Following still other demonstrations of Maggie, Leah, and Katy's uncanny abilities, Ripley added, "Mr. J. Fenimore Cooper was then requested to enter into the supra-mundane [otherworldly] sphere, and proceeded to interrogate the spirits with the most imperturbable self-possession and deliberation."

In a long series of questions Cooper grilled one of the spirits about the details of its death. To the author's amazement, the ghost identified itself as Cooper's young sister who had died decades earlier from a riding accident. "Mr. Cooper did not pursue his inquiries any further, and stated to the company that the answers were correct, the person alluded to by him being a sister who, just fifty years ago, the present month, was killed by being thrown from a horse," reported the *Tribune*.

Afterward, at the suggestion of the perplexed guests, Maggie, Leah, and Katy moved from a sofa to a series of standing positions in various parts of the room. Still later, the *Tribune* continued, the men "went into a parlor...and the sounds were then produced with great distinctness, causing sensible vibrations in the sofa, and apparently coming from a thick hearth rug before the fire-place, as well as from other quarters of the room."

As the evening progressed, Nathaniel Parker Willis and his companions "were struck with the [sisters']...combined good-humor and simplicity...the ease and unpretentiousness with which they left their visitors [from both worlds] have their own way...[and] evidently won the respect and liking of all present."

As to the origins of these strange sounds, Ripley opined at the end of his *Tribune* account, "We are as much in the dark as any of our readers. The manners and bearing of the ladies are such as to create a prepossession in their favor. They have no theories to offer in explanation of the acts...and apparently have no control of their incomings or outgoings."

Concurrently, other New York newspapers, among them the *Journal of Commerce* and the *Express,* retracted their earlier accusations of devil-baiting and fraud. A perplexed James Gordon Bennett concluded in a June 8 *Herald* editorial that his reporter's "impression seemed to be unanimous in the company that the ladies were in every sense incapable of any intentional deception."

Nevertheless, he added, "It is believed by many sagacious persons learned in curious psychology, humbug and metaphysics, that the 'knockings' are in no manner or degree spiritual, but only a development of a new phase of intellectual and mesmeric sensibility peculiar to the present age."

Nine days later, as still more New York newspapers continued to praise the Fox sisters' appearance at Griswold's home, Bennett seethed in a June 17 editorial, "It is lamentable to read the nonsensical accounts which are daily paraded in the newspapers, in reference to the females who get up 'these knockings,' and who have caused some degree of excitement among the ignoramuses and old women of the town. What excuse can be offered for the conduct of a dozen of leading names…great historians and extraordinary romance writers [who] now actually believe their own imaginary statements?"

After all, he reminded readers, "For two shillings our citizens can go and see an open and professed ventriloquist, who will make more unearthly noises, imitate knocking, bell ringing, cork drawing, pigs squealing, and do a hundred other things more wonderful than the ventriloquists of the Rochester knockings, who have so successfully and ludicrously humbugged these twelve great philosophers."

~❖~

Bennett's ranting editorials aside, the ongoing publicity appearing in the New York press had surpassed Maggie and her sisters' wildest dreams. Enhancing their prominence were notices placed in the *Tribune*—probably at the suggestion of Horace Greeley—notifying readers of the time, place, and "rules of order" for the séances.

Tickets were issued at Barnum's Hotel for three sessions a day—
from 10 A.M. to noon, 3 to 5 P.M., and 8 to 10 P.M.

At the appointed hours, thirty New Yorkers—among them
ministers of various denominations and members of the legal, medical, literary, and business professions—filed into a large room opposite the hotel lobby where attendants had set up a long table and
chairs, Leah recalled. Rarely did their guests treat them discourte-
ously or with any lack of respect. The one discordant note was the
appearance of suspicious committees of ladies, who requested that
the sisters undress in a private room in an effort to detect fraud.

Between the public sittings, the sisters saw wealthy individuals
willing to pay higher fees for private séances. One of them was
a dashing socialite attorney, George Templeton Strong, who famously kept a journal. He noted on June 16 that nothing of any
consequence had transpired that week in New York City, the only
exception being "the Rochester knockings which enlightened performances I've attended twice and about which I'm mystified. The
production of the sounds is hard to explain and still stranger is the
accuracy with which the ghosts guess of whom one is thinking—
his age, his residence, vocation and the like."

Inevitably, other citizens reacted less favorably, certain that
trickery accounted for much of the information revealed in séances.
Holden's Dollar Magazine published one of the most scathing cri-
tiques in September 1850.

For some reason, the reporter had attended a small session, one
that accommodated no more than eight or ten guests. On one side
of the room Leah, Maggie, and Katy sat on a sofa before a long table
covered with a cloth. Upon first hearing the ghostly raps, sniped the
Holden's reporter, they sounded "like a knocking on wood covered
with cloth, and we have produced a very similar sound by drum-
ming on a table covered with a cloth with the ends of our fingers."

He was even less impressed when the sisters raised the spirit
of the late South Carolina senator John C. Calhoun, former vice
president under John Quincy Adams and Andrew Jackson. When

asked if Calhoun's spirit favored the "immediate abolition of slavery," his spirit replied with "loud knocks in the affirmative." Somewhat later in the session another member of the audience inquired if Calhoun "was in favor of the abolition of slavery according to *a gradually progressive serial law of labor.*" Once again, the raps signaled agreement. "Now to our mind here was plainly a contraction of the spirit against itself," the magazine said. "Both the individuals supposed they had J. C. Calhoun's spiritual opinions on the subject, and yet they did not agree at all."

During that same séance, *Holden's* insinuated, the sisterly trio had rehearsed one audience member to attest to the truth of the spirit messages. "One young gentleman was at the end of the table sitting next to one of the young ladies, and appeared quite intimate with her, whispering and laughing with her through most of the performance," observed the *Holden's* reporter, "and exchanging written remarks on slips of paper for their own amusement."

Later though, the young man, claiming that he was a stranger to the Fox sisters until that séance, insisted to the audience that the spirits had answered every question correctly he had asked telepathically. Yet, *Holden's* haughtily observed, "It struck us that he had a peculiar aptitude for making himself intimate with young ladies at first sight."

In a final salvo, *Holden's,* echoing Nathaniel Parker Willis, wondered about the Fox sisters' casual attitude toward spirit communication. During the two-hour session, for example, Mrs. Fox returned from a walk with a handkerchief of peanuts, which "she distributed among them, and which they ate with a relish which showed they did not undervalue the good things of this world, even when attending to the revealings of spirits from another."

Holden's wryly concluded, "While there are thousands who really believe them to be revelations from the spiritual world...We had no faith in them before we went, and less, if possible, when we came away."

To these and other criticisms, Leah had a ready explanation.

Any inconsistencies in answers received during séances arose from dishonest or deceptive spirits who sometimes mischievously appeared as uninvited séance guests. "When manifestations and communications were consistent, we believed them to come from good Spirits: but when they were to the contrary, we condemned all as evil." The séance, after all, evoked all sorts of ghosts. Therefore mediums had to be wary of answers received from "promiscuous parties [uninvited spirits] who were constantly in attendance."

Subsequent guidebooks on mediumship stressed a similar message. One of the earliest was the 1852 *Light from the Spirit World* written by Reverend Dr. Charles Hammond, who had become a spiritualist after witnessing an impressive demonstration of Maggie and Katy's telepathic skills in Rochester during the winter of 1850. Above all, he later warned his readers, those who wanted to become mediums must avoid "anxiety, care, vexation, disgust, desire and wish, [for they] unfit the mind for control by spirits." Moreover, "when mediums wish to realize the truth, they must be passive… [for] the spirit can not force a correct expression of its thoughts upon the mind of a person who is positive against it."

Hammond's publication reflected the unique traits attributed to the Fox sisters and popularly thought to characterize all mediums. Such personalities tended toward fragility, nervousness, and a ready vulnerability. Like the daguerreotypist who used silver-coated copper plates to reflect images of the living, gifted mediums recorded impressions of the dead.

To New Yorkers who drew such parallels, the Fox sisters and spiritualism seemed yet another of the era's inexplicable technological feats. Despite the *Holden's* criticism, the Fox sisters remained a sensation. Inexpensive souvenirs emblazoned with "Rochester knockings" appeared in stores, prompted by a Broadway song, "The Rochester Knockings at Barnum's Hotel," crooned by the popular Mary Taylor that summer. Even George Ripley of the *New York Tribune* informed the sisters quite merrily one day that "You are the lions of New York."

Outside their hotel, crowds lined up for tickets day and night, while more private clients begged for sittings. Finally it became so overwhelming that the sisters planned to go home and rest. In the meantime, though, Horace and Mary Greeley invited them to be guests at their farmhouse in the still semi-rural section of New York near the East River known as Turtle Bay.

It was then, Horace Greeley observed in his autobiography, that he attended a second séance. "There, along with much that seemed trivial, unsatisfactory and unlike what might naturally be expected from the land of souls, I received some response to my questions of a very remarkable character, evincing knowledge of occurrences of which no one, not an intimate of our family in former years, could well have been cognizant," he admitted.

He added his voice to the chorus of the converted in a glowing *Tribune* testimonial. "We are convinced beyond a doubt of their [the Foxes'] perfect integrity and good faith in the premises. Whatever may be the cause or the origin of the 'rappings'...we believe that these singular sounds and seeming manifestations are not produced by Mrs. Fox and her daughters nor by any human being connected with them."

A week later Greeley reiterated his new faith to his friend Colonel Thomas Kane of the U.S. Army. "I am sure it cannot be accounted for by merely human agency. It is a puzzle which you will some day be interested to investigate," he wrote. "A mere fraud could not live so long and spread so widely."

In that same letter, Greeley thanked the colonel for forwarding a letter from his older brother, the thirty-year-old Arctic explorer Dr. Elisha Kent Kane. "Nothing I have read from the Arctic regions for years pictured them so freshly...[or was]...so interesting," the editor wrote, promising to publish Kane's letter in the *Tribune* later that same week. Within a year, the mysterious channels of chance and luck would bring Dr. Kane and spiritualism together in real life.

"JUSTICE IS SURE, THOUGH SOMETIMES VERY SLOW"

Our city streets are thronged with an unseen people who flit
about us, jostling us in thick crowds, and in our silent chambers,
our secret closets and our busiest haunts; their piercing eyes,
invisible to us, are scanning all our ways.
—EMMA HARDINGE, *Modern American Spiritualism*

ON MONDAY, September 30, after a two-week sojourn at the
Greeley home in Manhattan, Maggie, her sisters, and Mrs. Fox left
New York City. Along with their heavy packing trunks, the four
women brought expensive gifts—silk dresses, hats, and "casawrecks" or velvet wraps—for their upstate relatives. After a brief
stop in Rochester, Maggie, Katy, Leah, and Mrs. Fox headed out to
David's farm—already considered the family homestead—for a
badly needed rest.

David and his family warmly welcomed them home, according
to a 1945 family memoir, *Time Is Kind*, written by Mariam Buckner
Pond, a daughter-in-law to one of David Fox's grandsons. Especially anxious to see the travelers was Maggie's father, John.

Lulled by the fading sun and an autumnal chorus of cicadas,
Maggie found the return to Arcadia welcome respite. She played
with young cousins and strolled the hilly countryside dotted with
peppermint fields, goldenrod, and Queen Anne's lace, relishing an
escape from what she would later characterize as a "tiresome life...
tiresome because I have to meet with all kinds of people." Ironically, what the teenager now perceived as rural tranquility was the

same landscape she had complained about to Amy Post three years earlier as being dull and boring.

Yet the incandescent glow of fame that surrounded the Fox sisters in New York City was not easily dimmed. A reminder of that glow came in a September 30 *New York Tribune* editorial that arrived in the mail.

"Mrs. Fox and her three daughters left our city yesterday on their return to Rochester after a stay here of some weeks," began Greeley's laudatory editorial, "during which they have freely subjected the mysterious influences by which they seem to be accompanied, to every reasonable test, and to the keen...scrutiny of the hundreds who have chosen to visit them...."

Greeley explained that he had personally investigated the mystery of the raps while the Fox sisters were guests in his home. "We devoted what time we could spare from our duties...and it would be the basest cowardice not to say that we are convinced beyond a doubt of *their perfect integrity and good faith.*"

The mail also brought invitations from Manhattan and other cities requesting séances—so many that the energetic and ambitious Leah insisted Maggie and Katy leave the sleepy township of Arcadia and return to Rochester to address them.

No sooner had they arrived at the Troup Street cottage and unpacked their clothes than the trio was surprised by a visit from an old acquaintance—the newly appointed Supreme Court Justice John Edmonds, who had witnessed the Corinthian Hall examinations of 1849. Edmonds was on the brink of becoming a spiritualist himself but he had not arrived for a reading. Instead he carried a message from Horace Greeley, who invited Maggie and Katy back to New York. Earlier when the Foxes were staying with the Greeleys, Horace had tried to get Maggie and Katy into school, even volunteering to pay the tuition. Yet his well-meaning plea had fallen on deaf ears. While Mrs. Fox listened politely, she explained that she could not accept his offer. Leah could not spare Maggie and Katy from the séances; in fact, the family depended upon the appearances of the two young women at the séance table to generate more income.

Greeley, however, felt the neglected schooling of the two sisters was not only shortsighted, but tragic. If Mrs. Fox would not allow Maggie to return to school, perhaps Katy, at least, could be spared? At thirteen the girl was much too young to stop her education, Greeley argued. Moreover, with her brains and a proper education, Katy might even make contributions to the world as important as those of his late friend and *Tribune* reporter, the radical essayist-philosopher Margaret Fuller.

Horace's wife, Mary, supported his argument, though for more selfish reasons. Obsessed with the death of her little son, Pickie, the sickly and eccentric woman was, as her husband observed, becoming "more and more confirmed in the commotions with the spiritual world by 'rappings.'" If Katy could live with them, she could summon the spirit of little Pickie whenever Mary desired.

Mrs. Fox finally agreed to the visit. But while Katy enjoyed school, she became discontent. Not only was the shabby farmhouse near the East River far from the city center, but Mrs. Greeley's housekeeping and cooking, like her unhappy temperament, were hard to negotiate.

On October 26, Katy wrote her maternal great uncle, John Smith, to lament, "John, it is impossible to live with Mrs. Greeley. I have cried myself almost sick. Why did I leave my mother?"

～✹～

Within a week or two of Katy's departure for New York, a second invitation arrived for Maggie from the Robert Boutons, a friendly family that she and her sisters had met in Troy the previous spring. Would Maggie be willing to travel to their home, the Boutons asked, and give séances to interested friends and relatives? To Leah this seemed an attractive idea. Maggie would be chaperoned by friends and gain valuable experience by conducting séances on her own, and also could inspire the spiritualists of Troy.

Maggie liked the idea, too. It meant temporary freedom from Leah and a chance to visit with Robert Bouton's young sister-in-law, who had become a friend. She arrived in Troy in early November, where the Boutons treated her as their honored guest.

But unsuspected currents of hatred toward spiritualism still flowed in Troy. A group of religious zealots who equated spiritualism with devil-worship learned of Maggie's reappearance in Troy and made a surprise attack on her life.

"We are endeavoring for Maggie to go to another place. If she has mentioned [its]...name...keep it a secret as you value her life," Bouton wrote Leah on the night of November 13. "A deep plot is laid to destroy her."

Bouton's first intimation of trouble had come earlier that same evening when he, his family, and Maggie, returning from some event in East Troy, rode in a carriage to the shores of the Hudson River.

To their surprise, the boat that usually carried them across the Hudson was missing. In its place stood several sinister-looking men who suggested that Bouton's driver transport the party across the long Troy bridge. Sensing that the lonely structure was a "glorious place for murder," Bouton directed the driver to another route, only to be stalked all the way home by that same party of men. A timorous Maggie, surrounded by the Boutons and being chased by the men, ran into the house and bolted the door.

"After we had retired," Bouton breathlessly continued, "[they] attempted to break into the room occupied by Margaretta and my sister-in-law. They were furious on being defeated, and threw stones against the house and fired through all the windows."

Somehow, Bouton secured a temporary "means of defense." But the next morning the vigilantes once again tried to break into the house. Panic-stricken, Bouton telegraphed Leah several times over the weekend, begging her or Mrs. Fox to appear in Troy. "You must be here by Monday night. It is of *vital* importance," read the man's last message.

When Leah arrived at the Troy railroad station at 8 P.M., the seriousness of Maggie's situation became apparent. A gentleman waited for her at the curb. "It is alright, it is Leah; I know you by your resemblance to Maggie," the man reassured her, motioning her quickly into a carriage. Inside was another gentleman, his hand poised on a loaded revolver, which he used to defend Leah after they arrived at the Bouton home, which was still stalked by hostile men.

"I found Maggie sick and nearly paralyzed with fear," Leah recalled. "We had not been in the house ten minutes when several shots were fired and stones thrown, breaking everything in their way. We crouched beneath the furniture and lay on the floor to escape the bullets, expecting at every moment some stray shot or stone would strike us."

Finally the vigilantes retired for the night. While physically unharmed, Maggie remained profoundly unnerved. The nights were the worst. "She would start in her sleep and cry out fearfully, believing she was still besieged by the mob," Leah recalled.

While Leah never explained how she and Maggie escaped, she somehow brought her sister to nearby Albany to rest at the Delavan House hotel. Even then, the vigilantes of Troy remained on their trail. A day or two later, she learned from friends that the same group of hate-mongers had arrived in Rochester and were seen prowling around the Troup Street cottage. Yet, like "every other attempt at violence against us," Leah concluded, "they met with nothing but discomfiture."

The episode left Maggie shaken. After the incident at Troy, Maggie's high-spirited adolescence effectively ended. Whenever the young woman was faced with a frightening personal situation in future years, she became helpless, physically ill, and took to her bed. She would do so for the rest of her life.

⁕

Within weeks of the Troy incident, Leah pushed ahead with her campaign to promote spiritualism. On December 16 Maggie and

Leah, bundled in heavy winter cloaks, arrived in snow-bank-filled streets of Buffalo and took rooms at the fashionable Phelps House hotel. They were so warmly received, their days filled with "crowded séances," that Leah decided to extend their visit into mid-winter.

Among their most memorable callers were two University of Buffalo doctors, the "gentlemanly" Dr. John Wilson Coventry and the highly respected Dr. Charles Alfred Lee. They claimed to be interested in spiritualism, but their true motives were just the opposite. They would spend the next year trying to destroy the sisters' reputations.

For months Lee and Coventry had been alarmed at the spiritualist fever that had spread over New York with such rapidity, especially among its professional class. Several of their medical colleagues, who ascribed to the healing claims of Andrew Jackson Davis, had become spiritualist converts, believing it would make them better physicians. Others, it was whispered, consulted spirits before making a diagnosis or writing a prescription. Spiritualist beliefs had also penetrated the legal profession: Certain lawyers and judges were said to consult regularly with the spirits before rendering legal decisions or trying cases in court.

Like Lee and Coventry, Dr. Austin Flint, editor of the *Buffalo Medical Journal,* was equally eager to expose spiritualism and rid the country of what seemed like a "retrogression to the dark ages." By the winter of 1851, Flint, Lee, and Coventry had focused on Maggie and Leah, whose séances at the Phelps House hotel were drawing large crowds of believers and new converts.

The storm broke early Tuesday morning, February 18, 1851, when Leah and Maggie received a surprise visit from Dr. T. M. Foote, editor of the *Buffalo Commercial Advertiser.* He urged her and Maggie to pack their bags and board the next train out of Buffalo because they had been exposed.

A "Letter to the Editor" from Flint, Lee, and Coventry had appeared that morning in the *Commercial Advertiser,* accusing Maggie and Leah of producing raps by dislocating and relocating their knee joints: "...On carefully observing the countenances of the two females, it was evident that the sounds were due to the agency of the younger sister, and that they involved an effort of will. She evidently attempted to conceal any implications of voluntary effort, but in this she did not succeed: a voluntary effort was manifest and it was plain that it could not be continued, very long without fatigue."

Almost immediately, Leah called for an official investigation designed to explode the physicians' "new and comical knee-joint theory." Nor would she be cowed by the press. The day of Dr. Foote's visit, Leah threatened him with a lawsuit, demanding that he grant her equal time in the *Commercial Advertiser*.

On February 26, the formal examination began. As visitors walked into the private parlor of the Phelps House hotel, they saw Maggie and Leah sitting upon chairs or sofas before the grim-faced Flint, Lee, and Coventry. Day after day the doctors listened to the raps, twisting and turning the sisters this way and that and ordering them into various positions on sofas and chairs. Once when Maggie was asked to stretch her legs out on the sofa and Leah placed hers on the floor, the raps ceased. When asked why, Leah had a clever answer: The spirits refused to rap because of the doctors' obviously hostile attitude.

After two grueling weeks of examinations, the Buffalo physicians left the hotel to finalize their report, which appeared in the *Commercial Advertiser* and the *Buffalo Courier and Inquirer* the next day.

Unsurprisingly, they reconfirmed their kneecap theory. When only Leah's feet were placed on the floor, "The Spirits 'did not choose to signify their presence,'" they observed. Thus they concluded that the "younger sister"—Maggie—was solely responsible for the sounds. Flint, Lee, and Coventry had attempted to discern the movement of Maggie's kneecaps during raps by grasping her knee and lower leg for a half an hour or more at a time. The sight of bearded, distinguished physicians grasping Maggie's leg for lengthy periods must have been ludicrous, as well as discomforting to the teenager.

While "there were plenty of raps when the knees were not held, and none when the hands [of the doctors] were applied... the conclusion seemed clear that the *Rochester Knockings* emanate from the knee-joint," Flint, Lee, and Coventry reported in the *Commercial Advertiser*.

As always Leah insisted upon having the last word. The resolute ringmaster of spiritualism had already taken preparatory steps for a public defense. As soon as Flint, Lee, and Coventry left the Phelps House, Leah invited three prominent men who had carefully observed the physicians' examinations—Captain J. C. Rounds, Judge John Burroughs, and Dr. P. A. Gray—to conduct their own investigation. Maggie was thus compelled to submit to still another round of examinations.

But this time, or so Leah and her committee claimed, the results were dramatically different. Like the doctors before them, the second group of examiners held Maggie and Leah's legs and knees, but insisted that raps were distinctly heard through the Phelps House parlor at the same time. Nor, they claimed, were any movements felt in their limbs.

Their findings, reported by Leah in the same *Commercial Advertiser* that ran Flint, Lee, and Coventry's conclusions, indicated that the second committee had conducted "a far more satisfactory test, as they could distinctly hear the sounds under their feet," feeling the floor "jar... [even when] our feet were held, nearly... a foot from the floor."

Anyone who doubted those facts could verify them with onlookers, Leah reminded readers of the *Commercial Advertiser*, and those onlookers, in turn, "can refer you to dozens of other respectable persons, who have witnessed the same."

Most ludicrous of all, she added, was the accusation that the raps emanated from Maggie's knee joints. That, after all, was a physical impossibility. To prove it she suggested that Flint, Lee, and

Coventry "tell your readers what condition our poor joints would be in by this time, after three years' constant service in this almost ceaseless operation."

❧

No sooner did Maggie return with Leah to Rochester in the trying spring of March 1851, as the latter characterized that season in her memoir, than another accusation of fraud was leveled against the Fox sisters. What made this one particularly embarrassing was its source, Ruth Culver of Arcadia, who, according to Pond's family memoir, was the jealous sister-in-law of David's wife, Elizabeth.

For reasons that have never been clearly understood, Mrs. Culver took it upon herself to swear before several witnesses that she knew the secret of the raps. She had learned them from Katy—or Catherine as she was still sometimes called—who had secretly revealed how she rapped with her toes. For two years, Mrs. Culver added, she had believed in spiritualism until Katy shared the secret.

Mrs. Culver added that toe-rapping was "very hard work to do." To help the process along Katy had suggested that she either "warm my feet, or put them in warm water, and then it would be easier work to rap." Nor was that unusual. Even Katy had admitted that often she soaked "her feet three or four times during the course of an evening" of séances.

Subsequently Mrs. Culver had placed her toes in warm water before attempting to rap. "After nearly a week's practice with Catherine showing me how, I could produce them perfectly myself," she said, adding, "I have sometimes produced a hundred and fifty raps in succession."

During the same practice sessions, Katy supposedly instructed her in other tricks of mediumship. Among them was the importance of sitting close to the one that spelled out the raps so that certain signals could be conveyed through touch and then knocked out with the appropriate letters. Another trick involved asking séance clients to write several questions on paper. While doing so, the rapper had a "chance to watch the countenance and motions of the person and in that way...could nearly always guess right," Katy explained.

Whatever reply Katy or Leah made to those charges has not been preserved. Leah, at least, seemed to have ignored them. A few months later she told friends in Cleveland, "If you ladies had passed through one half the abuse I have, for the past two years or more, you would not wonder that I am personally indifferent to what all my enemies may say against me."

Nevertheless, on April 17, 1851, Ruth Culver's story appeared in many newspapers, casting serious doubts on the validity of modern spiritualism, as Emma Hardinge observed in her *Modern American Spiritualism*. And Horace Greeley was so deeply embarrassed by Mrs. Culver's story that he never publicly supported spiritualism in print again. Privately though, the controversial editor remained faithful to the sisterly trio, continuing to impress upon Maggie and Katy the importance of education.

☙❧

The fast-talking "Reverend" C. Chauncy Burr was yet another accuser to appear that spring and claim that he knew the source of the raps. Boasting that he could replicate them with his toes, Burr was feverishly touring the East with his brother and giving demonstrations.

He even ventured onto the Fox sisters' home turf and gave a free demonstration at Corinthian Hall on May 1. An "immense" audience had turned out to watch as "Mr. Burr pretty effectually used up the Knocking theory in his argument," observed the *Rochester Daily Democrat*. When his brother Raymond appeared and produced the knocks, "We were quite astonished at the perfect imitations of the 'genuine' which he gave. We were not prepared for so clever an exhibition of his power to make the same identical raps... without the least physical exertion. His manifestations, if equally successful in the table and other tricks, will, it seems to us, complete annihilate the rappers."

The report had enraged, if not surprised, Leah. Days earlier friends had warned that Reverend Burr also had pre-empted her appearance in Cleveland's largest auditorium, Melodian Hall, by booking himself there just before her arrival with Maggie and Katy.

Burr was a wily opponent and soon had notices of his arrival plastered all over Cleveland. By Monday, May 5, residents of the city were primed for the challenge.

"There are to be Rapping times in Cleveland this week," announced the *Plain Dealer*. "Mrs. Fish, the celebrated Rochester lady…will be here…The Messrs. Burr will also be here and…will attempt to prove the whole spiritual theory a humbug, and the mediums imposters. So we are to have both sides of this interesting question…Afraid of no truth, we shall patronize both sides, and report progress to the people."

True to its word, the newspaper published a synopsis of Burr's lecture at Melodian Hall the following day. He sneered at other advocates of spiritualism—among them Horace Greeley, who, Burr gleefully noted, "at the outset was quite disposed to believe, though now—I am warranted in saying—he is fully convinced of his error." As for the Poughkeepsie Seer, Andrew Jackson Davis, Burr added, "we do not deem…wholly dishonest but…by no means free from the imputation of humbug."

By May 7, on the eve of Burr's third appearance at Melodian Hall, the *Plain Dealer* ran another story headlined "Are the Rappers Knocked, or the Knockers Rapped." Noting that "the spiritualists have, as yet, had nothing to say, and the Burrs have it all their own way," the *Plain Dealer* lamented the fact that after spiritualist attorney Joel Tiffany had challenged the Burrs to a public debate, the reverend and his brother had declined.

Leah, meanwhile, took matters into her own hands. Since Maggie and Katy had not yet returned from New York, Leah traveled to

Cleveland without them. Soon after arriving by boat on Lake Erie's western shore, she was introduced to John Gray, editor of the *Plain Dealer*, and immediately befriended him and his wife. On May 8, coincidentally, the *Plain Dealer* reprinted a news brief from the *Buffalo Republic* in support of Maggie and Leah: "Mrs. Fish and the pretty Margaretta are to be in Cleveland this week with their host of rapping spirits to astonish the good people of the Forest City."

Burr's third demonstration was less than impressive, according to Leah, who secretly attended one of his presentations. As before, Burr began by delivering an inflammatory lecture on spiritualism, and then his brother, Raymond, demonstrated how he could reproduce the eerie sounds of the spirits. First he struck his big toe upon the sole of his wide boot, then dislocated the joint and pushed it back into place with a popping sound. By the end of the week, Leah gleefully wrote in her memoir, the repetitive demonstration had so badly inflamed Raymond's toes that they were bloodied and swollen—a secret she had wheedled out of the head waiter at the Burrs' hotel.

Within a month of the Burrs' appearances, the *Cleveland Plain Dealer* had entirely dismissed their claims. "Notwithstanding the burlesques of the Burrs, the exposé of the Buffalo Faculty...and other learned dunces...besides the scoffs of the prejudiced and ignorant against the 'rappings,' the cause...is gaining ground on every side. One month ago, there were not fifty believers in the city; now there are hundreds, including some of its best minds."

By then, Burr was frantically crisscrossing Ohio, appearing in auditoriums and lecture halls and continuing to slander the Fox sisters in his lecture-demonstrations. Resolved to silence the man, Leah engaged attorney Joel Tiffany to bring him to court.

But Leah had little time for relief. After she had waited for weeks, Maggie and Katy finally arrived in Cleveland, chaperoned by a Rochester spiritualist, Mrs. John Kedzie. The teenagers, fresh from New York by way of Rochester, had arrived in a rebellious mood, ready to mutiny. They had stopped in Cleveland only temporarily, they explained, and intended to travel on to Cincinnati with Mrs. Kedzie to conduct séances under her management.

At this betrayal Leah flew into a rage. Then, discovering that Maggie and Katy had also left Rochester against the wishes of Mrs. Fox, Leah telegraphed her mother and demanded her immediate appearance in Cleveland. "Mrs. Kedzie's coming out here has caused us much trouble for she goes to every person she meets and tells them that Leah is not the proper person and a bad manager," Leah peevishly wrote Amy Post on July 2. The worst of it, she added, was the girls' mischievousness. "Much of the trouble is caused by the girls who are always planning out something and then if they fail in their calculations, they throw the whole thing upon my Shoulders."

No sooner did Mrs. Fox arrive than Maggie regretted her decision to travel on to Cincinnati. Mindful of her experience in Troy, fearful of an equally tenuous reception in Cincinnati, she suddenly balked. As Leah put it, "Maggie could not be persuaded to go further." As a compromise, the high-strung teenager would remain with Leah and Calvin—who seems to have arrived with Mrs. Fox—in the friendly city of Cleveland while Katy and Mrs. Kedzie traveled to Cincinnati themselves.

Maggie's old conflict was beginning to claw at her again. She was torn by a desire for independence from Leah and her dutiful obligation to uphold the family's honor. Still, she had been threatened with death twice. Only Leah, it seemed, could insure her safety on the road. Maggie ultimately clung to her eldest sister—hostile, ambivalent, but compliant.

Tiffany the attorney soon informed Leah that he had collected enough evidence to haul Burr into court. In July, after an original complaint was filed at the Lake County Courthouse in Painesville, the Foxes met in Ohio's capital, Columbus, for a formal hearing. Upon Burr's appearance at the state courthouse, Leah recalled in *The Missing Link in Spiritualism,* local residents pelted him—and the government building—with bricks, broken eggs, and sticks. In contrast, when she, Maggie, and Katy arrived the next day, a friendly crowd greeted them, shouting, "Welcome to the Fox family."

Although the case would drag on for months, the court upheld Leah's accusations and fined Burr $10,000 in damages. Subsequently, Leah gleefully noted in her memoir, Burr was "almost hooted and pelted out of the State."

～❦～

Soon after the Columbus hearing, the Foxes arrived in Cincinnati on the Ohio River, only to learn that the city was in the midst of a cholera epidemic, a bacterial infection transmitted through unclean water. Despite the public health emergency, the thirst for séances was intense and people flocked to the sittings.

Cholera was not the only health issue that loomed over the séances that summer. Calvin, traveling as the family's protector, suddenly fell seriously ill. Initially, he had contracted what seemed a bad cold until he began to cough up blood from his lungs—a sign of consumption, or tuberculosis.

Leah wrote Amy Post on July 22, "Calvin is feeble, been very sick, raised a great quantity of blood. We fear for his life." To Maggie, who in spite of her earlier pranks was inordinately fond of her gentle foster brother, his illness was especially upsetting. In the doctor's opinion Calvin's case was hopeless.

One morning, according to Leah's memoir, the dying young man took her hands and those of Mrs. Fox in his. "Dear Mother and Leah, the only regret I feel is…leaving you…to the persecutions of your enemies," he said.

Then, gazing at Leah and addressing her as "dear sister," Calvin observed that his best legacy was to give her his name. "If we were married now, your widowhood would be a great protection," he said, referring to the Victorian expectation that women be shielded by a male authority figure, whether dead or alive. Should Leah become a widow, she would command more respect than as a divorced mother.

Weeping, Mrs. Fox left Leah and Calvin alone to make a deci-sion. "We were married September 10, 1851, on what was supposed to be the death-bed of our beloved Calvin, and then I became Mrs. Brown," Leah wrote coolly in her memoir.

Whether the marriage was at Leah or Calvin's instigation—and whether in name only—the union had a seemingly miraculous effect upon the ailing man. Gradually, Calvin's health improved enough for him to linger in what Leah described as "tolerable com-fort" for several years as a semi-invalid.

~❧~

Despite the battle against Burr and Calvin's serious illness, the Fox sisters' trip was deemed a success. Exuberantly, Katy wrote Amy Post from Cincinnati on October 30, "We have many friends here, & they are all very kind."

During their travels Maggie and her sisters seemed to have added several showy aspects to the "spiritual manifestations" that enhanced their mystique. "The Spirits do such wonderful things," Katy explained to Amy. "They ring bells, move the tables and when our feet are held, we have convinced many skeptical people of the truthfulness of spiritual communication."

After touring several more cities, including Pittsburgh, Pennsyl-vania, the Foxes returned to Rochester in late 1851, feeling entitled to rest and repose. Fame and fortune were once more impossible temptations to resist, though, especially as invitations continued to arrive at Leah's home. "Invitations and appeals of the most urgent character rained upon me from important individuals, and from collective bodies of prominent men in the respective cities and towns," she wrote, all of which added to the opinion of her friends "that we should establish ourselves in one of the great centers of population and movement [so that] people could conveniently come and hear for themselves."

While spiritualist committees—or groups of followers—from Cleveland and Cincinnati urged the Fox sisters to settle there, they decided to return to New York City. Privately, Maggie was thrilled with that decision. Months earlier, on August 23, 1851, while she was still in Cincinnati, she had written Mary Greeley, hoping for a second invitation to New York. While politely inquiring about the ailing woman's health, and reminding her to "kiss the little ones" for her, the real purpose of Maggie's letter was to find out when Horace would return from Europe. "Do you remember, Mr. G. promised to let us go [to New York City] as soon as he returns," she reminded the editor's wife.

By the winter of 1852, whatever answer Mrs. Greeley returned— if she replied at all—had become irrelevant. The spirits and the fervent admiration they had incited among thousands of people had carried Maggie back to the luminescent City of New York, where sound and light seemed as eternal as the rappings themselves and where all dreams seemed possible.

"REMEMBER THEN,
AS A SORT OF DREAM"

Alas, my countrymen, methinks we have fallen on an evil age!
If these phenomena have not humbug at the bottom, so much
the worse for us. What can they indicate in a spiritual way,
except that the soul of man is descending to a lower point
than it has ever before reached while incarnate?

—NATHANIEL HAWTHORNE, *The Blithedale Romance*, 1852

WHILE THE FOX sisters triumphantly toured Pennsylvania and Ohio, the spark of excitement they had ignited in New York City steadily fanned into a flame. In Manhattan industrialist Charles Partridge, Universalist minister Samuel B. Brittan, society physician John F. Gray, New York University professor George Bush, and other influential citizens had organized an enthusiastic group of believers know as the New York Circle. The famed phrenologist and medical student Edward P. Fowler acted as their leader and medium.

One of the New York Circle's earliest efforts to spread the word was a spiritualist conference hosted by Charles Partridge in his Manhattan mansion at 20 West 15th Street. The ebullient Partridge, the millionaire owner of a match company, had originally scoffed at spiritualism, but became converted after attending one of Maggie and Katy's séances in Manhattan during the summer of 1850. To Partridge, Maggie and Katy's spirit messages had virtually "rolled back the stone from the door of the sepulcher."

In his usual business-like style, Partridge issued a memo-style invitation to spiritualists and their friends outlining the goals of the meeting:

1. That the Divine Author of the Universe is a conscious Spiritual Being.
2. That he has revealed somewhat of the spiritual world in ages long since passed, and especially that the Jewish people were a medium of such revelation.
3. That in our own day and through our own American people, manifestations are being made from the spiritual and into the natural world, whereby immortality and unbroken continuity of the personal existence of all men is being daily demonstrated.
4. That an honest, frank and tolerant interchange of views and conclusions will tend to promote a beneficial use and extension of such spiritual manifestations.

My purpose in inviting this meeting is furthermore...to ascertain whether anything...can be done...in reference to the advancement of harmonious and profitable intercourse with the world of spirits.

Scheduled for Friday, November 14, 1850, the conference drew large groups of the curious and the converted to Partridge's spacious drawing rooms. It was so successful that members of the New York Circle decided to meet weekly in rented halls and auditoriums to accommodate their growing membership.

◈

Simultaneous with that growing enthusiasm was the appearance of new spiritualist periodicals. Among the earliest were the 1850 *Spirit World* and LeRoy Sunderland's *Spiritual Philosopher* of Boston, followed in 1851 by Reverend R. P. Ambler's *The Spiritual Messenger* of Springfield, Massachusetts. In 1852, the *New Era,* another Boston-based spiritual journal, was published.

Enhancing the movement's extraordinary growth was its seeming infectiousness—spiritualism spread from one person or household to another, from mediums to their séance audiences, to those who had only heard about séances. Theoretically mediumship was open to everybody—a reflection of Leah's "brotherhood of souls" concept, which, in turn, was based upon Andrew Jackson Davis's writings. But in contrast to Davis's "harmonial" philosophy—which insisted that man practice rationalism, scientific thought, and intuition to help him accept his distant, abstract relationship to the spiritual universe—Leah's concept was much more concrete. She offered access to individual spirits through dramatic raps and séances. That contact probably propelled the movement's growth and its popularity far more than Davis's theoretical ideology, historians Ann Braude, author of *Radical Spirits: Spiritualism and Women's Rights in Nineteenth Century America,* and Rob Cox, author of *Body and Soul: A Sympathetic History of American Spiritualism,* observed.

Typically, sensitive young women were the first to embrace spiritualism and were always represented in greater numbers than men. Empowered as spiritual experts, women mediums could speak aloud in public for the first time—albeit in a trance—in voices and with mannerisms and opinions that were forbidden to them in real life by the mores of Victorian propriety.

The powers of suggestion had a lot to do with the spread of the movement as well. In Boston, soon after LeRoy Sunderland's conversion to spiritualism, Helen Leeds suddenly announced her new spiritualist powers. Before long, seven other Boston women discovered that they, too, were mediums. Among the best known was Mrs. Sisson, "a fine clairvoyant physician," in the words of historian Emma Hardinge, and Mrs. W. R. Hayden, wife of the Boston editor of *The Star Spangled Banner,* who traveled to London in 1852, where she introduced the spiritualist movement.

No less prominent was Sarah Helen Whitman, former fiancée of Edgar Allan Poe, who wrote trance-inspired poetry. She explained in an 1851 letter to the *New York Daily Tribune* that her work resulted from the dramatic rappings she heard in her Providence, Rhode Island home. Another convert was the Reverend Dr. Charles C. Hammond, the Rochester Universalist minister-turned-spiritualist, whose 1852 book *Light From the Spirit World* instructed readers in the art of mediumship. Lucina Tuttle's book *The Clair-voyant's Family Physician* was published that same year and enhanced the alliance between mediumship and the healing arts. So rapidly was the movement spreading that even the skeptical author Nathaniel Hawthorne wove rappings and spiritualism into the plots of *The House of Seven Gables* and *The Blithedale Romance.*

By early spring 1852 spiritualism was said to have forty thousand followers in New York City alone. Daily, letters arrived at the homes of members of the New York Circle, describing the advent of spiritualism in other regions. Out-of-town spiritualists arrived in New York City, eager to attend meetings of the New York Circle. One of them was a Dr. Greaves of Wisconsin, who claimed that in 1850, even before a young girl in his state had heard about the "Rochester knockings," she was receiving messages from deceased friends of her parents.

Still another tantalizing story told to the New York Circle came from a Mr. Nimthorne of Bridgeport, Connecticut, who claimed a medium raised the spirit of a man killed in a railway accident. As the spirit appeared, its aura replicated the whistle, the chugging sounds of an approaching locomotive, and hisses of steam escaping from its chimney.

Equally dramatic was an anecdote Charles Partridge shared with the New York Circle. At a spiritualist lecture in Templeton, Massachusetts, he heard Edward Hooper recount the eerie experience of sitting at his desk in his Fitchburg home, when his hand started moving across a piece of paper without any guidance from him. The message it left was even more startling: "Your father is dead."

Unnerving as the message was, Hopper was stymied because his father, then in England, was in good health. Five days later, however, Hooper received a letter from Britain announcing his father's sudden demise.

Inspired by such stories and the attendant groundswell of spiritualist enthusiasm, the New York Circle planned a public forum on February 26 at the Hope Chapel on Broadway. Thirty-seven-year-old Reverend Samuel Bryon Brittan, a former Universalist minister and co-publisher of Andrew Jackson Davis's short-lived *Univercoleum*, led the meeting. Brittan would later wed medium–historian Emma Hardinge. Individually and together they would become leading spokesmen for the spiritualist movement.

"From this time… Spiritualism, its claims, facts, theories and all its general features… have been ably represented on New York platforms on an average once in every week, regular Sunday services, morning and evening, and an afternoon conference, has placed it prominently before the New York public as a great religious [and] no less than a reformatory and scientific movement," Hardinge would later boast in her 1870 history.

~✿~

It was little wonder that the arrival of the Fox sisters in New York City in January 1852 was met with such enthusiasm. Through the contacts of a friend and some family connections, Leah was able to lease a brownstone at 78 West Twenty-sixth Street, in a neighborhood of "first-rate excellence."

Their "fine three-story house" was just a few steps away from the new seven-acre Madison Square Park. The area was being promoted as "the most fashionable part of our rapidly increasing city," according to Edwin Burroughs and Mike Wallace, authors of *Gotham*. Nearby, on Fifth Avenue, legendary millionaires such as William Astor and August Belmont were busily building mansions. Soon department store magnate A. T. Stewart would erect a magnificent marble-walled home "uptown" on Thirty-fourth Street.

The Fox sisters' home was considerably more modest. Like other three-floor row houses of the era, it was fronted by a high stoop, or row of stairs, and a handsome front door opening to a vestibule, beyond which was a hallway. From the hallway—behind which was a hand-carved wooden stairway—visitors entered spacious front and back parlors. The home conveyed such an atmosphere of comfort and prosperity that the thrifty Mrs. Fox worried over its extravagance. Leah assured her mother that spiritualism would provide them a substantial source of income. And she was quickly proved right.

Even before Maggie, Katy, and Leah were unpacked in their new home, they were besieged with requests for séances—"sit-for-raps," as New Yorkers colloquially dubbed them.

"Our rooms were frequented by much of the best society in New York; and it was common to see the street encumbered with long files of carriages," Leah reminisced in *The Missing Link in Spiritualism*. "Particularly the intellectual and literary classes were familiar visitors, both at our circles and in our private lives." And many, she proudly added, "became our most intimate friends."

Their enterprises had become more professional, aided by the worldly advice of those friends and lessons learned on the road. Now, in contrast to the hectic schedule of séances that Leah and her young sisters pursued during the stay at Barnum's Hotel in 1850, the trio only allowed sittings twice a day—from 3 to 5 P.M. and 8 to 10 in the evenings. There were, however, two exceptions—Saturday afternoons and nights and Wednesday evenings, which were reserved for private parties and, inevitably, higher profits.

Guests at West Twenty-sixth Street who met with Leah—usually the most prestigious and best-paying visitors—were escorted to the brownstone's back parlor, where, by then, she apparently demonstrated convincing raps of her own. Maggie and Katy, in contrast, greeted their clients in the front room of the basement, watched over by the ever-vigilant Mrs. Fox or the ailing Calvin whenever his health allowed.

"An invasion of armies can be resisted, but not an idea whose time had come," French novelist Victor Hugo had observed in *The History of a Crime*. And unquestionably that time had arrived for spiritualism, leaving Maggie and Katy little opportunity for anything but séances—not even extended lessons with the tutor who was probably hired by Horace Greeley to help them with their studies.

Insistently, clients like the debonair attorney George Templeton Strong, who had previously attended séances in 1850, returned to the Fox sisters for more sessions. On Saturday, May 15, after escorting his friends and wife, Ellie, to a sitting with Leah, the attorney noted in his diary, "The developments of this spiritual school have become very extraordinary and extensive…Tables loaded with heavy weights are made to dance vigorously."

Despite his skepticism, Strong admitted his ongoing fascination, saying, "It is a strange chapter in the history of human credulity at all events, and as such worth investigating."

Not all those who wanted to investigate spiritualism at West Twenty-sixth Street, however, were allowed to do so. Mindful of threats, Leah and Mrs. Fox routinely scrutinized all guests at the door. Those deemed troublemakers or rowdies were abruptly turned away. Séance guests, who despite Greeley's advice were still expected to pay only a dollar per ticket, received a list of instructions outlining séance etiquette at the door.

"The communications are mainly conversational, in answer to questions such as can be reasoned to by the Spirits in the monosyllables Yes and No," the sheet explained. One rap signified "no," three raps meant "yes," and two raps "suggested something in between such as "not now, not yet, not quite [or] don't know." Five raps meant that the spirits wanted the alphabet board to spell out words. Continuous loud raps, however, were a danger sign. They indicated a "want of Harmony in the Circle, and may generally be taken as a reproof in consequence of some violation of the Rules of Order."

Since guests were expected to be polite, no one was to speak in a loud voice or "otherwise interfere with the person in communication…as its violation results in great loss of time and disturbs the Harmony, which is essential to reliable communication." Sitters were also expected to be cooperative. Any failure to do so "usually results in [the spirits']…partial or complete cessation."

The fourth and most self-protective rule of all was strikingly modern in its declaration of non-accountability. "The ladies, in

whose presence the manifestations are made, will use their best ex-
ertions to satisfy all inquiries, but since the manifestations, alike in
their commencement, character and duration, are *above their personal control,* they cannot promise that all persons, or all inquiries,
will obtain answers."

✦

So on October 9, 1852, two days after Maggie's twentieth birthday,
she and Mrs. Fox arrived in Philadelphia by train. Before long, they
were established in the elegant bridal suite of Webb's Union Hotel
on Arch Street. As Leah anticipated, the arrival of the pretty young
medium and her mother created a stir among the city's spiritualists.
Within a few days, their rooms were flooded with calling cards and
requests for séances. In Philadelphia, as in New York, "prominent
and fashionable people of the city came to hear the mysterious
knockings and to have their questions answered. Clergymen and
doctors, scientific and literary persons, the lovely and the learned,
the sentimental and the stern, were daily in attendance," as Maggie
recalled in her memoir.

Even in that exalted company the ever-protective Mrs. Fox remained a stern gatekeeper. Mindful of the terror at Troy and its effect upon Maggie, she restricted her daughter's first séances to
guests who were already confirmed spiritualists.

"Public" séances were to be held only in the afternoons and
evenings. Mornings were a time for Maggie to relax, read, and con-
centrate upon her studies—especially French, which she had just
begun with her tutor before leaving New York.

Yet within a few weeks of the arrival in Philadelphia, the careful
schedule that Mrs. Fox had drawn up for Maggie would be inadvertently and permanently disrupted by the short, handsome
gentleman who appeared one morning at Webb's Union Hotel. Directed to the bridal suite by the hotel manager, the man knocked at
its door, which was promptly answered by Mrs. Fox. Behind her,

sitting by the window in an aureole of sunlight, sat a pretty dark-haired girl who was engrossed in a book.

~✤~

"I beg your pardon. I have made some mistake," the trim young man stammered upon first meeting Mrs. Fox and Maggie, according to her memoir. "Can you direct me to the room where the 'spirit manifestations' are shown?"

Smiling, the matron assured the gentleman that these were the same "spiritual parlors" and that she was Mrs. Fox. Introducing himself as Dr. Elisha Kent Kane, a native of Philadelphia, the man explained he had come to arrange for a private séance. Taking measure of his obviously refined and well-dressed form, Mrs. Fox agreed and invited him to have a seat at the séance table.

Our knowledge of this first meeting comes from Maggie's memoir, *The Love-Life of Dr. Kane.* Ghostwritten by journalists who were Maggie's friends and bent upon defending her reputation, that memoir is the only existing account of her relationship with Kane. Within it are some of Maggie's letters; still more telling is Kane's correspondence to her, which dominates the book. Some letters have perhaps been slightly amended, but judging from many of the originals still preserved at the American Philosophical Library, most of them are accurately reproduced.

Maggie, according to *The Love-Life of Dr. Kane,* barely looked at the gentleman visitor. Instead, while seated at the table, she coolly continued to pore over her French lesson while the stranger chatted amiably with her mother, stealing furtive looks at Maggie as she bent over her volume.

"One of the very first things that drew me towards you, was your ladylike manner and deportment. A little affectation about it, but still very gentle and quiet, and modest, and retiring, as a lady's should be," he wrote Maggie rather moralistically some months later.

Of his warmer emotions, however, Kane gave no immediate indication. During the séance, the gentleman merely seemed curious as he questioned Maggie about the spirit of his recently deceased younger brother, Willie. At the end of the séance, he politely thanked her and Mrs. Fox before closing the door behind him.

Maggie's first meeting with Kane did not seem extraordinary. To her, he was simply another curious client, although she was "pleased with his manners and conversation." What was surprising was Dr. Kane's return visit to the bridal suite again the next morning. But now, even though he requested a second séance, he seemed barely attentive. Instead it seemed to Maggie that the diminutive, if sturdy, young man regarded her with a disquieting intensity.

"This is no life for you, my child," the thirty-two-year-old physician observed after the séance. From his perspective, it was inappropriate and even dangerous, given Maggie's tender age, for her to be living as a public figure. Instead, he suggested that she should be in school.

Nevertheless, Elisha now began appearing daily at the "spiritual parlors" of Webb's Union Hotel—sometimes several times a day. Often he came with friends and relatives to whom he explained that he attended Maggie's séances in hopes that the spirits could help him locate the remains of Sir John Franklin, a British Arctic explorer.

Despite Elisha's obsession with Sir John Franklin—whose rescue he had unsuccessfully attempted in 1850–51—Maggie soon gleaned that the sessions were nothing more than an excuse to gaze upon her again. Initially, Maggie was attracted to Elisha's candor, sincerity, and what she perceived as "his brotherly tenderness for her interests," she wrote in *The Love-Life of Dr. Kane*. If his intensity radiated more than pure altruism, if the emotional complexities of his personality were obvious to the perceptive Maggie, she did not yet acknowledge such impressions. And by the widely acknowledged rules of Victorian etiquette outlined in such manuals as William Alcott's *A Young Woman's Guide to Excellence* and the anonymously written *True Politeness*, it would have been improper for her to have done so.

As Maggie would insist in her memoir, all she saw was kindness, coupled with what Elisha's first biographer, William Elder, later described as a charming but understated personal style. Characteristically becoming quiet when the conversation became glib, Elisha "had a way of looking attentive, docile, and interested as a child's fresh wonder but no one would mistake the expression for the admiration of inexperience or incapacity," Elder noted, "while underneath [he was] as tense and elastic as a steel-spring under pressure."

Elisha's restrained manner, combined with a reformist urge to help others, was part of the Kane legacy. His father, Judge John Kintzing Kane, of the U.S. District Court for Eastern Pennsylvania, was an officer of several cultural and philanthropic organizations, among them Girard College and the American Philosophical Society. On Elisha's maternal side was a great-grandmother who had nursed wounded American soldiers in Philadelphia's Walnut Street prison during the British occupation at the time of the American Revolution. Elisha's mother, the charming beauty Jane Leiper Kane—so lovely that in 1824 she was chosen to accompany the Marquis de Lafayette to a Philadelphia dress ball—bravely stood guard while the Kane home was threatened during a political furor over the election of a Pennsylvania governor. "I thank God, I have a husband and a brother whose patriotism does not startle at words," she said.

In 1850 Elisha's idealistic brother Thomas Leiper Kane—later a colonel in the U.S. Army famous for his defense of the Mormons of Salt Lake City—resigned from his appointment as a U.S. commissioner after the 1850 passage of the Fugitive Slave Act. A dedicated abolitionist, Thomas felt that as a commissioner he could not bring himself to capture runaway slaves.

In that same altruistic tradition, Elisha apparently regarded Maggie as needy, a bright, beautiful young woman who had been led down a crooked path that was bound to destroy her life.

Privately, Elisha also was deeply smitten, fascinated by the seemingly sophisticated yet child-like Maggie's ability to charm strangers who attended her séances. In that sense she was a distinct departure from the young women he knew in his social class. Gentle and non-controversial, these women of leisure apparently bored Elisha. He once cynically observed to his aunt Eliza Leiper that they accomplished little in life and typically "sat simpering behind an embroidered screen or a teapot."

The more time he spent with Maggie, the stronger his fascination became. Once, Elisha slipped Maggie a note during a séance. "Were you ever in love?" it read.

Embarrassed, not knowing how to respond, Maggie playfully answered, "Ask the spirits." There was something about Elisha that resonated within her as well, that brought out her old playfulness and the fun of flirtation, a *joie de vivre* that had been stifled during her years as a medium.

No less winning was Elisha's solicitous attitude toward Maggie's mother, Mrs. Fox. Graciously, repeatedly, Elisha offered to escort both women around Philadelphia in his carriage to see the sights. By early winter, the trio's outings had become customary and Mrs. Fox eagerly anticipated them almost as much as Maggie did. Typical of the friendly formality of those excursions was a December 7, 1852, note that Maggie carefully preserved in the reprinted papers of her memoir. "Dr. Kane will call at three o'clock for the purpose of accompanying Mrs. and Miss Fox upon an afternoon drive."

But for all his intense interest in Maggie and presentation as a gentleman-doctor of leisure, Elisha was a driven man, deeply engrossed in serious scientific exploration. While temperamentally energetic and adventurous as a child, he had been stricken in adolescence with heart-damaging rheumatic fever. Acknowledging that his son's life was likely to be brief, his father consequently urged the young man to pursue his dreams, to follow a life of action. "Elisha, if you must die, die in harness," John Kane told his son after his recovery.

The judge's words became Elisha's credo. In 1842, after graduating from the University of Pennsylvania Medical School, twenty-two-year-old Elisha enrolled in the U.S. Navy as an assistant surgeon. Cavalierly dismissing his earlier illness, the young doctor gave vent to his wanderlust. He sailed the continents of Europe, Asia, and Africa in the capacity of a naval surgeon and scientific explorer, risking his life for the sake of adventure at every opportunity.

His deeds—climbing the jagged Organ Mountains of Brazil, descending into the crater of the still-active Taal volcano in the Philippines, engaging in hand-to-hand combat against the Mexicans of Nopaluca and, while wounded, stitching up the severed artery of his enemy, Major Gaona—had already made Elisha well known by 1850.

Foremost among his concerns was the loss of Sir John Franklin. The British explorer and his 129-member crew had disappeared in 1845 on an Arctic expedition in search of the Northwest Passage, a legendary northern sea route from Europe to India that had eluded sailors and geographers since the days of Columbus.

The search for the Northwest Passage was nearly forgotten for two centuries after the daring 1618 voyage of William Bylot and William Baffin, who sailed into the channel between Greenland and northern Canada only to be blocked by its treacherous ice-bound waters. The channel was later named for Baffin. In 1818, British explorer Sir John Ross rediscovered those waters, though he was blocked at the entrance to Lancaster Sound. Two years later Ross's second in command from the 1818 voyage, William Edward Parry, penetrated Lancaster Sound, sailing as far west as Melville Island. There, his hopes rising, Parry observed two other straits that offered the possibility of further navigable passageways—Wellington Channel and Prince Regent Sound. Yet conditions were such that he could travel no farther.

In 1845 Sir Franklin vowed to continue on Parry's route. A seasoned naval officer and veteran explorer of the northern coast of America, the fifty-nine-year-old Franklin set off with two ships, the

Erebus and *Terror,* for a new exploration. "No service is dearer to my heart, than the completion of the survey of the northern coast of America and the accomplishment of the Northwest Passage," the doughty Franklin announced shortly before his departure. So sure of the expedition's success were some of the officers aboard the *Erebus* and *Terror,* it was said, that they boasted they would accomplish their mission in just one season.

Franklin, by order of the British Admiralty, was instructed to enter Lancaster Sound, then continue west through Barrow Strait until reaching the approximate longitude of Cape Walker, and from there proceed as far into the Bering Strait as conditions allowed. If the path was blocked, Franklin was permitted to attempt the unexplored Wellington Channel. Beyond that, the explorer and his crew were on their own. Two summers passed without word from Franklin. By 1848 the British Navy and the explorer's grief-stricken wife, Lady Jane Franklin, were debating how best to rescue him.

In March of 1850, marking time in what he considered a boring tour of duty with the U.S. Coastal Survey, Elisha read about President Zachary Taylor's proposed American Arctic expedition to assist in the search for Sir John Franklin. Elisha promptly volunteered his services. With the matter languishing in Congress, a wealthy businessman named Henry Grinnell stepped forward with a generous offer to purchase and outfit, at his own expense, the two ships necessary for the expedition if the U.S. Government would furnish the necessary officers, crew, and provisions. On May 12, around the same time Maggie and her sisters were conducting their first séances in Albany, Elisha received a telegram ordering him to New York City for the new Arctic expedition.

As thrilled as Elisha was, his parents were horrified. "I cannot rejoice that he is going on this expedition; his motive is praiseworthy, but I think the project a wild one," Judge Kane confided in his daughter Bessie when he heard the news. That same sentiment was echoed by his wife, Jane, who lamented, "I feel as if I had not waked from a hideous dream...but still a heavy weight oppresses me and I feel as if Elisha had parted with us for an interminable period, perhaps forever."

To their relief, Elisha returned safely in late 1851. That rugged voyage under the command of Captain Edwin De Haven on two brigs, the *Advance* and the *Rescue,* failed to produce either Franklin or the promised "Passage to the Pacific" (as the Northwest Passage was sometimes called), but the experience inspired the gifted Elisha to write a memoir about his Arctic adventures. Entitled *The U.S. Grinnell Expedition in Search of Sir John Franklin,* Elisha's book was the only published account of that voyage.

The glorious sunrises, looming glaciers, and icy canyons of the Far North, coupled with the ongoing mystery of Franklin's whereabouts and the Northwest Passage, continued to tantalize Elisha. Finally, he resolved to make a second Arctic voyage. By 1853 nothing had become more important, he said, echoing his favorite poet, Alfred Lord Tennyson—who happened to be Franklin's nephew—than having his name appear on an Arctic map.

Across the Atlantic, Lady Jane Franklin held out similar hopes for Elisha's success. Ever since her husband's disappearance in the Arctic, she had focused her energies entirely upon the rescue efforts. Failing that, the handsome, outspoken widow hoped for a discovery of Franklin's remains or at least some understanding of his fate in the frozen lands of the Far North.

To continue to search would require enormous energy, still more money from the government, and perhaps funds from groups of scientifically minded donors and geographers. Elisha had to do a great deal of fund-raising if he hoped to lead a second expedition to the Arctic in the spring of 1853. He scrambled from one East Coast city to another, presenting lectures to government agencies, scientific societies, and private individuals.

Yet even in the midst of his duties, Elisha's thoughts constantly fixed on Maggie. On a sunny Sunday, December 12, while preparing a lecture for the American Geographical and Statistical Society, the smitten doctor-explorer dashed off a note to Maggie at her hotel. "Might he ask Miss Fox at what hour she would be disengaged before his departure?"

Maggie had apparently refused one invitation, but Elisha was not a man to give up. "The day is so beautiful that I feel tempted to repent my indoor imprisonment," he wrote. "If you will do me the kindness to change your own mind, and take a quiet drive, I will call for you at your own hour." Maggie's response has not been preserved, but even if the ride never occurred, the fact that she saved his letter spoke to her obvious interest in her suitor.

Diplomatically, knowing that Maggie's budding affection was related to her mother's approval, Elisha continued to court Mrs. Fox. On December 18, just before he left Philadelphia for Manhattan, he learned that the other Fox sisters were living on West Twenty-sixth Street and invited several of his New York friends there for a séance. "If you have any messages to send to your daughter, I should be happy to convey them," he suggested to Mrs. Fox.

He also explained in that same letter that he could "not resist the temptation of sending the accompanying little trifle of ermine, for Miss Margaretta's throat." Acknowledging that the matron was "fastidious as to forms"—socially appropriate behavior—Elisha urged Mrs. Fox to "permit me to place it [the fur] in your hands" so that she could present it to Maggie. "Pardon the pocket-worn condition of the enclosed note," he added in a final decorous apology.

Nor did Elisha stop at that. In addition to ingratiating himself to Mrs. Fox, the naval doctor stopped at West Twenty-sixth Street where he was received by Leah and Katy.

Soon afterward Mrs. Fox received a letter from Katy that "A very pleasant gentleman, Dr. Kane, has called on Leah and me, and has attended several of our meetings." On January 10, 1853, after learning that Katy was about to visit Philadelphia, Elisha again wrote Mrs. Fox offering to escort her daughter from the railway station at Camden, New Jersey to the steamboat that would carry her to Philadelphia. As "this would not be very pleasant to a young lady unaccompanied by a friend," offered Elisha, "I will be happy to meet Miss Kate on the boat."

During the trip the sixteen-year-old Katy found Elisha such a good companion that she soon came to regard him as a brotherly figure, chatting with him about spiritualism and other subjects. Katy's feelings were returned in kind. As Elisha later wrote Maggie, "Kiss Katy for me, and tell her I am *your* friend, and therefore her own."

To underscore his honorable intentions, Elisha also brought his favorite cousin, Mrs. Helen Patterson, to one of Maggie's séances. That first meeting was so successful that a day or so later Elisha wrote Mrs. Fox that he planned to "call with Mrs. Patterson, at half-past two, in hopes of persuading Miss Margaret to take the vacant place in her carriage. Tell Miss Maggie to dress warmly."

~⚜~

Yet, the chill temperatures of the winter of 1852 were less biting than Elisha's ongoing contempt for spiritualism. He had told Maggie very early in their relationship that he didn't believe in it and thought she should remove herself from such a compromising life. Several weeks later the literary-minded physician wrote Maggie a poem entitled "A Prophecy." Within it, he characterized his sweetheart's existence as a medium as "Weary! Weary is the life/By cold deceit oppressed." Should Maggie continue to pursue spiritualism, Elisha ominously predicted, "Thou shalt live and die forlorn."

Doubtless, such pronouncements rattled Maggie, especially when she recalled her unhappy experiences in Troy and Buffalo. Along with Elisha's criticism came the gifts he constantly showered upon her—flowers, books, and music of the rarest and finest quality. Maggie's confusion about him intensified.

By January, Elisha's relationship with Mrs. Fox had progressed so far that he felt he could be as frank with her about spiritualism as he was about his feelings for Maggie. "Although I am still skeptical as to our friends in the other country [Summerland] I am a firm believer in my friends in this." To prove it, he had "taken the liberty of presenting to Miss Margaret a little memento of our short acquaintance" and an "accompanying trifle" for Mrs. Fox.

Soon afterward, Elisha drew Maggie aside to a corner of the hotel parlor away from her mother. In a low voice, according to her recollection in *The Love-Life of Dr. Kane,* "he again spoke of the melancholy way in which she was living—pursuing a calling which the world thought ambiguous at least, and deplored the fact that deceit was generally attributed to those who engaged in such matters." He reminded her that she was fitted by nature for better things, for "the highest destiny of woman"—in other words, as a wife and mother.

Then, with great solemnity Elisha asked if Maggie was willing to quit spiritualism and "devote herself to acquiring an education, with such habits as would efface the memory of the past, and fit her for an entirely different sphere." Mutely, Maggie stared at him, struggling to understand her suitor's intent.

"…When you are thus changed, Maggie," Elisha added quietly, "I shall be proud to make you my wife. Can you resolve to leave all that surrounds you…to forget the past, and think only how you may become worthy of one whose existence shall be devoted to you?"

Believing his sweetheart's affection could not be as secure as his own because of her youth, Elisha suggested that Maggie carefully consider his marriage proposal before making a decision. "You must not engage yourself to be my wife unless you can give me all your love—your whole heart: unless you can sacrifice for all other anticipations and prospects," he warned.

Elisha explained that his father expected him to marry into a wealthy and prominent Philadelphia family much like his own. It was even anticipated that he would wed a particular woman in his circle, but as he told Maggie, "he had no attractions to fetter his love." Now realizing that he was in love for the first time, Elisha intended to inform his father that the planned union "was an utter impossibility."

⁂

Later that afternoon a thrilled Maggie shared her news with Mrs. Fox. Her mother, a veteran of her own marital trials with her husband John, was less than pleased. For all Elisha's charm, affability, and lineage, she reminded the suddenly downcast Maggie that he was in the midst of planning a dangerous journey to the Arctic. To her, Elisha's proposal seemed ill-timed and hardly in Maggie's best interests.

Soon afterward, in what must have been an awkward meeting with Maggie and Elisha, Mrs. Fox politely repeated her sanguine message: While she sincerely hoped that he would return safely from the Arctic, it was entirely possible that Elisha might not survive. Such a scenario would, of course, leave the betrothed Maggie in a precarious situation; having given up spiritualism for school and then waiting several years for Elisha's return, Maggie would essentially become a widow—albeit one without any means of support or plans for the future.

Whatever concessions Elisha made to Mrs. Fox's objections—if there were any—have not been recorded. In response he seems to have redoubled his declarations of love. Maggie, he insisted to his understandably conflicted sweetheart, was like a camellia he once gave her: "Like you, it must not be breathed upon." And again, he explained to her and her mother, she must have a proper education so that she would be "fitted to occupy a high position in society."

To give Maggie a graphic illustration of what that "high position" meant, Elisha drove her, his cousin Mrs. Patterson, and her husband a few miles outside Philadelphia to see the Kanes' country estate, Rensselaer. Once the carriage rolled to a stop outside the front door, Elisha stepped out to help the ladies descend. As he did so, Mrs. Patterson leaned over and whispered to Maggie, "Miss Fox, Elisha loves you. I can see that!"

Later when they returned to the carriage, the young physician took his cousin's hand, pulled down her glove, and showed Maggie a beautiful diamond ring set in black enamel. To her surprise, he arrived at the "spiritual parlors" the next day with three engagement rings for Maggie's selection. Thrilled and surprised, Maggie chose a diamond surrounded by black enamel similar to Mrs. Patterson's ring.

Elisha was just as excited—an exuberance that even spilled over before strangers. Once, after enjoying a quiet carriage ride into the country followed by lunch at an inn, Elisha introduced Maggie to the proprietor—who must have noticed the tenderness between the couple as they dined—as "the future Mrs. Kane."

Another winter day Elisha and Maggie drove to Philadelphia's Laurel Hill Cemetery, where the Kanes had recently arranged for the construction of a large family vault. "Here, Margaret, will be your last resting place," he whispered as they stood looking at the still-unfinished tomb. Then, after talking about his fifteen-year-old brother, Willie, who had died the previous August, Elisha took Maggie in his arms, calling her his "godsend," who had filled his empty heart. To Maggie, it seemed that Elisha had done the same for her—and much more.

After years of being dominated by Leah, of being forced to maintain a lie for the sake of her parents, of watching Katy grow into a committed medium and gradually coming to believe in the spirits herself, Maggie now understood that hers had been a tortured life—one she would leave behind once she became Elisha's wife. Thrilled by the promise of that bright future, Maggie demurely encouraged her suitor to "love on." For him, she tenderly confessed in a subsequent letter, "I would do anything."

Only one disagreement remained between them—the existence of the spirits. Maggie remained adamantly opposed to repudiating their existence and confessing herself a fraud. "I feel that I have convinced this skeptical unfeeling world that I am innocent of making these sounds," she insisted to Elisha.

He did not believe her. Instead, Elisha lectured Maggie so often about the "sinfulness" of her profession that she playfully, but pointedly, dubbed him "preacher"—a nickname that fit so well that even he laughed, affectionately adopting it in his most light-hearted moments when writing to Maggie

Some of Elisha's "preachings" found their way into his poems. One was entitled "A Story," but brashly subtitled "Thoughts which ought to be those of Maggie Fox." In keeping with Elisha's ongoing harangue, the four-stanza poem evoked a wistful image of Maggie as a "laughing girl" who was happy before she practiced a "deceit-ful art."

To save herself, the poet advised her to pray to her father—who had never accepted spiritualism—for "one trusting hope" as well as "one trusting love... to snatch me from a life forlorn." Significantly the poem was signed "Preacher."

❧

Cavalierly dismissed both in Elisha's poem and his courtship were the expectations his prominent parents had for the kind of woman he would wed. Knowing they would never approve of a lowly "rapper" as his bride, Elisha insisted upon keeping his engagement a secret.

"What pretty girl was that driving—or walking—with you?'" Elisha's friends often asked him. But rarely would he give them a candid answer. Nor did he confide in his younger siblings, Colonel Thomas Kane of the U.S. Army; Robert, a young patent attorney; Bessie, his musical sister; or even John, his third and favorite brother, who, like Elisha, was a physician.

Instead, Elisha offered evasive answers, maintaining the pretense that he visited Maggie only because of correspondence with Lady Jane Franklin. Lady Jane had not only appealed to the British Par-liament, the American president Zachary Taylor, and the U.S. Congress to finance a rescue mission, but also had called upon the spirits to discover the whereabouts of her husband.

"Wrap my letters up carefully and give them to this young

gentleman," Elisha urged Maggie in one of his notes perpetuating the ruse. Since the gentleman in question was one of his brothers, he warned, "Do not let him suppose that you have anything more than mere spirit business with me." Assuring Maggie of his ongoing affection, Elisha added, "I sent down my favorite brother to you, in all this snow and rain. Nothing but my real love for you keeps me from coming."

To Maggie, such secrecy came as a keen disappointment, even though a silence about love affairs was all too common among courting couples—especially when they were of unequal social status.

Soon afterward, on the eve of another trip to New York, Elisha begged Maggie to "write to me letters of love." Since he was leaving the next morning, he planned to visit her hotel to bid her goodbye—or at the very least wave to her from her window. Realizing that Maggie was committed to giving a séance, Elisha promised to wait beneath her window until she was through. Then, she could signal him by raising both curtains. Even if they did not meet, he hoped that she would write him that night in care of Delmonico's in New York, "telling me your movements."

Maggie's response has been lost, but judging from Elisha's subsequent letter Maggie must have accused him of treating her unfairly. Perhaps she was entirely too taken with him, especially since he was soon leaving for the Arctic. Perhaps she thought too much of him.

"Do not be afraid of 'thinking too much' of me," Elisha passionately wrote back. "For even if the drear old Polar winter should make me a perpetual exile, the memory of a dead affection would be better than a recollected coolness. If you think me afraid of letters, here is my contradiction." Beneath that line, Elisha gave her his postal address at his naval station in Philadelphia.

Mollified, Maggie wrote back. "I am delighted, my dear friend, to know that I will have the pleasure of your company this evening. But I fear you will be too much fatigued to ride,—will you not?" she sweetly asked before coquettishly adding, "Now Doctor—be candid—am I not correct when I say you are enigma past finding out? You know I am. Many thanks for the music."

Beyond the couple's playfulness, however, loomed the troublesome—and, in Elisha's view, embarrassing—issue of spiritualism. In early January he found another reason to lash out when a man who dabbled in spiritualism committed suicide. The death, described in a January 8 story in James Gordon Bennett's *New York Herald,* was said to have occurred after the man had attended one of Leah's séances.

"Your sister's name is mentioned in the inquest of the coroner. Oh, how much I wish that you would quit this life of dreary sameness and suspected deceit," Elisha railed at Maggie from his desk in a Manhattan hotel.

Insulted and upset by the implications of Elisha's outburst, Maggie demanded a meeting. But that, he immediately responded, was impossible because he was committed to nearly round-the-clock meetings with scientists, geographers, and private individuals—potential sponsors for his Arctic expedition. "I cannot get away from New York, nor see you on Saturday...I wrote you by mail to tell you of this unlooked for detention," Elisha added. Yet he would do his best. He would try to catch a train to New Brunswick, rent a carriage, and "perhaps be able to reach Philadelphia in time for a Sunday afternoon's ride." Given that effort, "Do you think many friends would take all this trouble for you? Never doubt me any more."

Elisha also said he would never question Maggie's intelligence or her abilities again. "Your letter surprised me. I had no idea you wrote or thought so well and ably," he wrote haughtily. "Indeed, you were born for higher things...."

Nevertheless, he continued, "You say 'that you do not understand me'—'I am a riddle'—'an enigma' and all that nonsense. Dear Maggie you understand me very well. You know that I am a poor, weak, easily deceived man, and you think that you are an astute, hardly seen-through woman managing me as you please. Now tell me the truth—don't you?"

The truth, Elisha admitted, was that he was conflicted about his attraction to Maggie. "But with all this I am a weak man and a fool; weak, that I should be caught in the midst of my grave purposes by the gilded dust of a butterfly's wing."

Admittedly, Maggie had "many traits" that lifted her above her profession, such as her refinement and "lovable" nature. The pity of it was that "with a different education, [you] would have been innocent and artless; you are not worthy of a permanent regard from me. You could never lift yourself up to my thoughts and my objects; *I* could never bring myself down to yours."

Beneath Elisha's stinging words was a frustrated and hopelessly enamored man. "This is speaking very plainly to my dear confiding little friend Maggie Fox, who sometimes thinks she loves me more than a friend. But Maggie, darling, don't care for me any more. I love you too well to wish it, and you know now that I really am sold to different destinies: for just as you have your wearisome round of daily money-making, I have my own sad vanities to pursue. I am as devoted to my calling as you, poor child, can be to yours. Remember then, as a sort of dream, that Doctor Kane of the Arctic Seas loved Maggie Fox of the Spirit Rappings."

Maggie made no reply. In the ensuing silence, her suitor regretted his words. Chagrined, he likely telegraphed Maggie an apology. A day or so later he wrote, "I will see you, if time or money can achieve it, by Sunday at one or two o'clock; you will ride with me. Answer to Girard street, as I will go there first if I get back, dear Maggie, and we will talk the thing over...If you say so, I will bring Mrs. _____ to prevent any doubts with your excellent mother. I always want to treat you both with respect."

The details of that meeting and the couple's subsequent reconciliation are unknown. The argument may have been simply a lovers' quarrel. Nevertheless, it was becoming clear to Maggie, dazzled as she was by Elisha, that he could be as difficult as he was passionate, as secretive and denying as he was insistent about declarations of love.

"But for the Polar Ices"

Believing where we cannot prove.
—Alfred Lord Tennyson, *In Memoriam*, 1850

WHEN MAGGIE returned to New York City in mid-January with Katy and Mrs. Fox, a dizzying series of séances, dinners, and other social engagements swept her up almost immediately. Her tight schedule had been cleverly arranged by Leah, who disapproved of Maggie's engagement.

Never one to mince words, Leah "flared in a torrent of protest" when she heard of Maggie's intentions, according to Pond's memoir *Time Is Kind*. The idea, she told her mother and sister, was foolhardy. First, there was an obvious discrepancy in wealth and social position—a situation that might lead the Philadelphia doctor, for all his vaunted charm, to manipulate Maggie into a compromising position that would ruin her life. Sexual seduction, of course, would spell disaster for Maggie, as it would for any woman of that era. Once relegated to the status of a mistress or wanton woman, few, if any, proper gentlemen would consider her for a wife.

Equally worrisome to Leah was Elisha's disapproval of spiritualism and insistence that Maggie return to school. Both ideas would cut into the family's séance business.

Another consideration was Maggie's position in the public eye, which could well be diminished while she dallied with Elisha. Other young mediums were competing for attention—not only LeRoy Sunderland's daughter, Margaretta Cooper, but also others who were still girls, such as the pretty, golden-haired Cora Scott of Buffalo, who already dazzled audiences with her trance séances.

The sisters needed to capitalize on their position as the famed orig-inals for the sake of their income. Leah implored Maggie to aban-don all thoughts of marrying Elisha. She also angrily turned to Mrs. Fox, whom she accused of foolishly permitting the romance in the first place.

"He is a vain, pompous little man!" Leah groused. "…Why, what will people say? Just when…we're being repaid for all we have gone through, you can't let Maggie turn from us all!"

Only Calvin defended Maggie, pointing out that Dr. Kane had been pleasant and attentive when visiting him, Leah, and Katy in December. Nor did he think Elisha was vain and pompous. From his perspective the doctor-explorer was a man of admirable courage and fortitude, a national hero whose polished and self-assured manners reflected his station in life.

In response Maggie withdrew from everyone—including her suitor. "Why do you not write to me?" Elisha wrote on January 23. "Have you forgotten your friend? Or does your new life drive from you the recollection of old times?"

In two days, Elisha explained, he would be on the road again—to talk at Baltimore's Maryland Institute and then journey to Wash-ington "to meet the great men"—a reference to presentations before the Senate Committee on Naval Affairs and the Navy De-partment. Later that month he would give a public lecture at the Smithsonian Institution.

Yet the importance of those meetings dimmed compared to the misery Elisha suffered from a week of silence from Maggie. He wrote, "Oh dear Maggie, when I think of you in your humble call-ing, and of myself with my toiling vanities and cares, I only feel that I am about to leave you; and feeling this, how very, very much I love you. I am a fool for this, yet I know that you have some good reason for not writing."

As a token of her love, could Maggie send him a lock of her hair? "Unless it comes," Elisha wrote with sudden petulance, "I will not come to see you." Then, regretting his words, he assured Maggie of his undying affection. If "trouble presses his cold hand come to your one friend, for he alone has no coldness."

Elisha also sent Maggie a copy of *Undine*. Friedrich De La Motte's popular story concerned a water nymph and the peripatetic knight who loved her. After they wed, the water nymph was granted an immortal soul.

To that gift Maggie responded with only tepid politeness. "All the warmth and affection seem to be on my side," Elisha complained in a hurried letter written between lectures. "You write to me entirely as to a friend—a kind non-committal letter."

Even so he ached to see her. "I miss you when I look over my crowded table with its books and papers...I miss you when I mount my horse for one of my wild rides....I miss you when listening to the empty nonsense of my fashionable friends, who think themselves so much better than yourself."

What was there about Maggie, Elisha pondered, that drew him so powerfully to her in comparison to other women? "I'll tell you. It is not beauty, for they are as beautiful as you. It is not kind words or demonstrations for they go further than you. But it is in that strange mixture of child and woman, of simplicity and cunning, of passionate impulse and extreme self-control, that has made you a curious study. Maggie, you are very pretty, very childlike, very deceitful, but to me as *readable* as my Grandmother's Bible."

Toward the letter's conclusion Elisha proposed that they meet one afternoon between 4:00 and 4:30 P.M. at Satler's Cosmoramas, a fashionable art gallery at Twelfth Street and Broadway. "Walk out every day alone, or with Kate, and then if I should come to New York, we can easily see each other without exciting the suspicions of [presumably Leah] you know who." When they met, Elisha added, he planned to bring along a gift of pocket handkerchiefs—an item that Maggie habitually misplaced.

Maggie tentatively agreed, but at the last minute, mindful of Leah's earlier reproach, changed her mind. Young ladies, after all, were not supposed to meet men on the sly but only with the knowledge—and consent—of their families. "You will forgive me, my dear friend, for not meeting you. Strange that I should have made such a promise—so imprudent!" Maggie began. "How must it look in your eyes [and surely I care as much for you as any one]! The idea seems to me so unbecoming."

Still, if Elisha was willing to call for her at West Twenty-sixth Street, she would be "most happy to do so, as I have no other engagement during the day." First, though, the doctor must write a proper invitation and she would share it with Leah.

In addition to Leah, Maggie had a second, equally formidable protector: Dr. John Gray. He was a prominent New York physician, friend of Judge Edmonds and one of the founders of the New York Circle—a "thorough-going, but reasonable spiritualist," according to one of his contemporaries. So impressed was Dr. Gray with the Fox sisters' gifts when he first met them in the summer of 1850—and so distressed at their lack of a prominent and authoritative male figure to steer them through New York's intricate social networks—that he had volunteered to become their counselor.

The sisters and Mrs. Fox looked to Dr. Gray for advice on the nuances of local etiquette. That the conservative physician may have erred on the side of excessive primness mattered little to Leah. But to Maggie and her younger sister Katy, his insistence upon the highest standards of propriety was dismaying, inevitably curtailing the high-spirited adventures that the two teenagers craved.

Any act that could be even vaguely construed as improper, Dr. Gray warned, had the potential to ruin Maggie and Katy's reputation as well-brought-up young ladies and cast them—and by association, spiritualism—into a decidedly dubious light. Proper women were supposed to be sweet, soft-spoken, passive, and passionless beings, as expressed in the recently published ladies' book of 1850 *Greenwood Leaves* by Grace Greenwood. "True feminine genius," she instructed readers, "is ever timid, doubtful, and clingingly dependent: a perpetual childhood." And Maggie was expected to comply with that model, rather than embrace the bold clamor for equal sexual rights led by upstate suffragists such as Elizabeth Cady Stanton, Lucretia Mott, Susan B. Anthony, and Amy Post.

⁂

By February 1853, Maggie felt so sure of Elisha and so confident that his intentions were honorable that she willingly risked convention to see him. Elisha—in spite of his insistence that she be a lady—was not averse to such risks. In one of his numerous attempts to meet with Maggie away from the disapproving eyes of West Twenty-sixth Street, Elisha arranged to visit her at the townhouse of his Arctic patron, the wealthy shipping magnate Henry Grinnell.

At the designated hour, a carriage arrived promptly at West Twenty-sixth Street. But just as Maggie and Katy were about to depart, Dr. Gray happened to arrive for a visit. Inquiring about their destination and learning the truth from Mrs. Fox, he forbade them to make the trip.

"You thought strange of our not calling on Thursday afternoon when you sent the carriage," Katy wrote Elisha apologetically the next day, but "Mother told him she thought we were going to Mrs. Grinnell's." Dr. Gray "begged us not to go" and then threatened that "if we went against his wishes he would never advise us again."

The physician warned Maggie and Katy that if they went to the Grinnells, they would be guilty of a serious *faux pas,* Katy explained. In fact, Dr. Gray insisted that he would "not *allow* his own daughter to call on a gentleman *no matter* how well she knew him. And he says he has the same cane over Maggie and me."

Whether through stubbornness or passion, Elisha would not be discouraged. "Do say when I can see you. I leave for Boston tomorrow at three P.M. to be gone for a week," he wrote Maggie urgently on February 12.

Immediately she replied that she would wait at home the next day to see him. Yet it was not to be: When Elisha arrived the next morning, Mrs. Fox and Katy met him at the front steps and insisted that Maggie had already left for the day.

Devastated, Elisha dashed off a frantic letter to his sweetheart. "Dear, dear Maggie: Have you ceased to care for me?—me, whose devotion you now can see, and of whose true, steadfast, love every fibre of your heart assures you?"

Elisha feared he would not see Maggie for weeks because she was leaving soon for Washington, D.C., with Katy and Mrs. Fox. If his failed rendezvous with Maggie was a matter of miscommunication, he promised that he would immediately return to New York. Was it possible for her and Katy to leave West Twentieth-sixth Street at 10:00 the following morning? If so they should "turn to the right until you come to the first cross street, when upon turning again to the right you will see me. Do, dear Maggie, do!" Elisha pleaded.

Maggie, who had spent a miserable morning waiting for Elisha, was horrified when she received his letter. First weeping, then yelling at Mrs. Fox and Katy, she stomped off to her room and wrote Elisha. Then, to ensure that the message would be immediately received, she followed it with a telegram notifying him of her forthcoming letter.

Meanwhile in Boston, Elisha penned a second, peevish letter, accusing Maggie of perceiving him as a "cute, cunning dissembler, a sort of smart gentleman hypocrite, never really sincere, and merely amusing himself with a pretty face."

After receiving Maggie's letter he felt comforted and responded in a different tone. Elisha's letter included a newspaper article about his lecture at Boston's New Music Hall, characterizing him as "full of energy, intelligence...enthusiasm...with an organization which makes one think of Damascus steel."

The review, Elisha observed, had hardly impressed him. Instead, having been humbled by Maggie's silence and the critique it implied, Elisha had somberly examined his own behavior and begun to question the vanity of his ambitions. "How disgusting is this life, to be discussed by the papers! I need not be so proud, Maggie, for I am no better than the 'rappers.'"

Increasingly, he admitted in another letter, he was questioning his presumably high-minded stance against Maggie's dedication to spiritualism. "When I think of you, dear darling, wasting your time and youth and conscience for a few paltry dollars, and think of the crowds who come nightly to hear of the wild stories of the frozen north, I sometimes feel that we are not so far removed after all. My brain and your body [her youth and beauty] are each the sources of attraction [for audiences], and I confess that there is not so much difference."

Perhaps for the first time in his life, love—and the threat of its demise—had softened the doctor-explorer, causing him to rethink his dreams and recognize his and Maggie's common humanity.

❧

In anticipation of Katy and Maggie's imminent journey to Washington, D.C., Elisha sent her an expensive traveling bonnet. Upon its arrival at West Twenty-sixth Street, Leah had discreetly "asked no questions," according to *Time Is Kind,* but quite likely surmised the identity of the sender. She must have been glad to be sending Maggie out of town. General Waddy Thompson, a fellow spiritualist who was a former South Carolina senator and ambassador to Mexico, had arranged the trip. At the very least Maggie's sojourn would provide powerful Washingtonians with first-hand acquaintance with the Fox sisters and simultaneously separate Maggie from her persistent suitor.

Elisha regarded Maggie's trip with trepidation, fearing his sweetheart would be regaled with attention from other men. As an additional reminder of his devotion, Elisha sent her two sets of fine lace blouses. "One," he explained, "an under-handkerchief of *Honiton,* with sleeves to match; the other of French work, for morning wear. Do be careful and dress well about your neck and arms, for I want my Maggie to appear as a lady wherever she is."

Soon after Maggie's arrival, Elisha anxiously inquired, "How does Washington come on? Many beaux? Many believers? Many friends? Answer these questions, you wicked little Maggie."

"Do you want some advice?" Maggie's "preacher" began again. "Never venture out in Washington except in the very best company. If you can get a *real* gentleman, grab him; but have nothing to do with the vulgar members of Congress."

If she could not find an appropriate means of "seeing the sights," Elisha suggested that she postpone such excursions and "wait till your friend comes."

But Elisha's trip to Washington had to be postponed. Harried, overworked, and prone to disease, Elisha fell ill, so seriously that he was forced to remain in Boston—"this miserable rainy town," as he described it—for at least a week before returning to Philadelphia.

"Maggie, I am sick—sick at the hotel—sick with hard work, and with nobody to nurse or care for me. You saw how wretchedly I looked when in New York; I am far worse now and without any chance of resting," Elisha penned. "Is it any wonder, then, that I long to be with you, to have again, the lazy days and sit by your side talking nonsense...Is it any wonder that I long to look—only to look—at that dear little deceitful mouth of yours; to feel your hair tumbling over my cheeks, as I write the spirit messages from another world—our world, Maggie—the world of love!"

How much the strain of his professional obligations added to Elisha's querulous attitude toward Maggie can only be conjectured. Just a few days earlier, he had learned that the British Navy had adopted its own plan for sailing north through Smith Sound. Captain Edward Inglefield would lead a rival rescue and exploratory mission with a steam-powered vessel. "Nothing is left me, therefore, but a competition with the odds against me; and for this, even, I must hasten the preparation for my departure," he lamented on March 8 to his friend John Pendleton Kennedy, former Secretary of the U.S. Navy.

Moreover, the illness that started in Boston had gradually evolved into a familiar syndrome of fever and swollen joints, suggesting that Elisha was suffering another bout of the rheumatic fever that periodically ravaged his body. In response to a telegram he sent Maggie describing his condition, she wrote, "I am grieved to hear that you are ill. You say that you will telegraph every day. Do not forget to do so, for I am uneasy about you."

By way of distraction, Maggie explained how frightened she became during a solo shopping trip—permitted, apparently, by Mrs. Fox—when she got lost in Washington. Finally, after arriving back at her small hotel, Mrs. Sullivan's Lodging House on F Street, she was so relieved that she burst into tears. Nearby, one of her new Washington acquaintances, General Charles C. Hamilton, a veteran of the Mexican War, asked why she was upset. Upon hearing her story, the general "laughed heartily and insisted...that no young lady could ever lose her way in Washington unless she had some *affaire du coeur.*"

"I did not deny the charge," Maggie admitted, adding, "Doctor there is a rumor—so the General tells me—that you and I are to be married before you go to the Arctic."

This, Maggie's one letter to the ailing Elisha in mid-February, struck him as so insensitive to his desperate emotions that he threatened to withdraw from the relationship. And then, to impress Maggie with the seriousness of his threat, he sent a letter announcing as much to Katy.

"Dear Miss Incomprehensible Kate," Elisha's querulous letter began, "your sister has doubtless told you that I have formally resigned every thing but her friendship; so that henceforward you are both of you alike in my eyes; and I do not see why you should not take half of my correspondence. As a friend, I think you will like me quite as well as in the other relation; and I am sorry to say that your sister will like me better."

Elisha could not help pressing his theme—insisting that Katy, like Maggie, should give up spiritualism before she became further entrapped. While in Boston, he explained, he had attended a séance during which a female medium's message from a spirit had so profoundly upset a guest that he fainted in grief.

"Now Katy, although you and Maggie never go so far as this, yet circumstances must occur where you have to lacerate the feelings of other[s]…There will come a time when you will be worse than ____ a hardened woman, gathering around you victims of a delusion.…Now cannot I help you and Maggie?"

To this, Katy earnestly retorted. "I am very anxious you should know that the sounds are not made by machinery. Neither do I know how the rappings are produced. Oh do not look upon Maggie and me as deceivers. Do not class us with that mean woman [the Boston medium] for we are not like her."

"What has so sadly changed you?" she implored. She confessed that while she tried to keep Elisha's letter secret, Maggie had "begged so hard that I *had* to let her *read* it. She was very much affected and looked melancholy all day and *not* said one *word*."

Just what was it that Elisha expected her and Maggie to do? "Shall we tell the spirits never to rap again. If so, we will. I am perfectly willing to follow your advice," Katy added. Even so, she could not help delivering a parting salvo. "Our rooms have been thronged daily, not many believers?"

Alarmed by Elisha's angry message to Katy, Maggie wrote at once. "Your letter was received this morning; strange, strange letter. Then I have lost, forever, lost the friend I loved so dearly? Often, while reading your letter to Kate, an involuntary tear started to my eyelid…Should we never meet again in this world, we will in another. Then you will know I have loved you, and love you still. Oh, how sorry I am to hear you are ill! I wish I could be with you. Farewell. As ever, your Maggie."

Maggie's letter did not mollify her demanding lover, who cruelly responded, "I saw that you loved me, but not enough. Dear child, it was not in your nature. You would give me everything when near me, but forget me when away. So I made up my mind, and in a moment you became *my friend*."

But just a few lines later he softened. "If it be that you really in your deepest center care for me, say so; if it be the feeling of a friend, only, say so; and in the one case I will see you again—in the other, never."

Maggie's reply, if there was one, has not been preserved. But within a few days, an apparently chagrined Elisha arrived in Washington with his younger brother John and took rooms at Maggie's simple F Street hotel.

The men's rooms, located in a fourth-floor suite directly above those of Maggie, Katy, and Mrs. Fox, were an unconventional choice for the prosperous Elisha and his brother. In her memoir, Maggie assured readers of her beau's high morals and attributed the hotel choice to Washington's shortage of rooms elsewhere.

Even with the lovers' proximity, however, their relationship continued to be stormy. While Elisha observed the requisite social niceties of formally requesting meetings, Maggie—perhaps for reasons of youth, immaturity, or carelessness—did not always honor them. Swept into Washington's social swirl, pressed to attend concerts and plays by spiritualist men such as former senator Waddy Thompson, former Wisconsin governor Nathaniel Tallmadge, General Edward Bullard, and others, Maggie occasionally forgot her appointments with Elisha. Elisha descried Maggie as a "humbug" after she failed to keep one of their meetings and scolded that she could have at least sent her mother to keep the date.

Elisha's pressing schedule compounded those tensions. By midwinter he had patched together enough funding and equipment from various sources—a small sum from the American Philosophical Society, instruments from the Smithsonian Institution, and ten crew members from the U.S. Navy—to support the Arctic voyage. Elisha was busy with a thousand and one details: "worrying the [Naval] Department," as *Time Is Kind* put it, "examining recruits, inventing cooking stoves, pricing rounds of beef, while his pen was running, his telegraph flying."

In between he managed to coax Maggie away from her spiritualist duties. Once, as Maggie dashed out of a séance, she dropped a note on the parlor floor. Katy retrieved the note, only to have Mrs. Fox snatch it out of her hands. It read: "Dearest Pet: Come out for a moment from those coarse people to your friend waiting for his little Maggie. Surely you can rest a minute! Come, dearest fluttering bird. Come!"

Somehow, the couple managed to have a few minutes of privacy here and there. One entry in *The Love-Life of Dr. Kane,* for instance, revealed that on several occasions he was present while Maggie brushed and rearranged her "tumbledown hair" in the parlor mirror. Another time as Maggie reached for a cup of cough medicine on the mantelpiece, she knocked it over and spilled the contents on herself. Just then her suitor walked into the room, "hurried to her assistance and carefully washed her hair, face and neck…delighted to…snatch the opportunity of kissing the disarranged locks and wet forehead."

As in the early days of their romance in Philadelphia, Maggie and Elisha took carriage rides together in Washington, apparently without a chaperone. They rolled past the still-unfinished Capitol building, the White House, the aqueduct of Rock Creek Park, and out to the surrounding countryside, where they stopped at various inns for lunches and dinners.

During such quiet times together, Maggie became convinced that Elisha's love was sincere—and now welcomed his wish that she abandon spiritualism for school.

She articulated her changed view in a letter to Elisha just before he left Washington. "I have been thinking over the very tiresome life I have been living, tiresome because I have to meet with all kind of people. These things oppress me—indeed dear Preacher, very nearly drive me crazy," she confessed. Echoing Elisha's own words, she wondered what "have I ever done that I should be denied the pleasures of a quiet home, the blessings of love—the rewards of virtue. I have given my whole time to this subject for six years. I think I have done my part. I am innocent of making these sounds."

Now, Maggie wondered, "my dear, dear friend, for you are the only human being who has ever urged me to better things, what shall I do when you leave for your distant pilgrimage of danger? Who then will extend to me a helping hand. For you I would do anything yet you will be with me no longer. Can I not educate myself and then live in a sphere of usefulness and refinement by my own effort. Do come and talk this over with me for I have one of my fits of low spirits."

~❉~

By early March, Elisha returned to Philadelphia carrying with him a joyous secret: Maggie had agreed to abandon spiritualism and attend school to become a "refined, educated, conscientious woman" so that one day she would become his wife.

The seriousness of that promise, which meant that Maggie was abandoning her family, had likely caused her anxiety, guilt, and sleepless nights. Soon after Elisha left Washington, his high-strung sweetheart contracted influenza. Fearing the worst, Elisha telegraphed her repeatedly, offering to return to Washington to comfort her.

"Very, very sorry, dear darling, that you are sick," Elisha wrote on March 10. "Sick in gloomy Washington, with nobody to sympathize with you, except fusty old Tallmadge, and foolish Waddy Numbskull." Surely she missed the "greeting smile, the warm kiss, and the resting breast of 'cousin Peter' [one of Maggie's several nicknames for Elisha]. Do, dear Maggie, hurry and leave this wretched life. Come, dear little one, and nestle in my arms. But for the Polar Ices, they should be your home."

Still the road to that home was bound to be rather grim. "Listen, Maggie; instead of a life of cherished excitement you must settle down into one of quiet, commonplace repose. Instead of the fun... delicious merriment of xxx (we won't trust this to paper) you will have the irksome regulations of a school, the strict formal precepts of a lady abbess, a *schoolmistress*," Elisha explained on March 17.

Ironically, Katy, in a faint echo of Elisha's sentiments, now complained to Leah about the stress that she and Maggie had suffered while conducting séances in Washington, D.C. In contrast to the orderly, businesslike séances in New York, those she and Maggie held in the nation's capital were often unpredictable and unpleasant.

"I am sick of this life," Katy began. "Last evening a party of twelve fine-looking gentlemen visited our rooms. All but two were as drunk as they could well be. They made mean, low remarks. Only imagine Maggie and me, and dear mother, before a crowd of drunken senators."

Finally, "Maggie left in disgust," Katy reported. "...Oh dear Leah, I long to be laid in a peaceful grave! I care not how soon. I would live on a crust of bread and drink cold water if I could live a different life...I told them that if my sister, Leah, were here with us, they would not dare insult us. They would be escorted from our rooms."

Upon receipt of that letter, Leah immediately summoned Maggie, Katy, and her mother home to New York. Maggie, saying little, retreated to her room while Leah, sensing her sister's changed attitude, immediately grilled Mrs. Fox about Elisha. Appalled by the man's audacity in renting rooms at Mrs. Sullivan's Lodging House, Leah once again accused Mrs. Fox of complicity with Maggie. To encourage Elisha was dangerous, not only because of his suspect intentions but because of his relentless pressure upon Maggie to abandon spiritualism.

Given Elisha's resolve, Mrs. Fox retorted, there was no use bucking the relationship. Nor, she added, was there any point in talking to Maggie again because she was in love with the doctor-explorer. Indeed, once Elisha appeared in Washington, the formerly obedient Maggie had thrown caution to the wind and had even abandoned séances on a moment's notice whenever he beckoned.

From his hotel room in New York, meanwhile, Elisha sent Maggie notes through Cornelius Grinnell, the twenty-eight-year-old son of his Arctic patron, Henry. Once, while delivering Elisha's messages, Cornelius observed that Maggie was a "very interesting girl" but so jealously guarded by her relatives that he had little opportunity to talk with her.

"Bear up, dear little one, against your sorrows: for God knows I feel more for you than myself...when the thing blows over we will meet again," Elisha reassured Maggie in one of his letters. If they were "rent asunder by these curious meddlers," they could at least "look back upon old times with comfort." Since Maggie thought he should not write any longer—cruelly destroying "this last pleasure"—he suggested that she write him instead. Above all, he mentioned in another letter, "Be careful not to mention me before the Tigress."

As Elisha's euphemism for Leah suggested, a struggle was underway at 78 West Twenty-sixth Street. At its conclusion an exhausted Maggie wrote Elisha soliciting his advice one more time. "Mother has been perfectly willing to let me go to school all the time...[and] give up the knockings," she curiously claimed. "Now you know best. Do you think I had better go or not. Mrs. Brown [Leah] says she has said all she is going to say about it."

Solicitously then, Maggie concluded, "do come this evening... I am dying to see you....You need not even see Leah."

Soon after that evening, Elisha received an extraordinary, if characteristically formal, letter from Mrs. Fox. "After mature deliberation I have concluded to give my consent to Margaretta's attending school as you proposed," she wrote. That consent, she pointed out, was based on an understanding of Elisha's "kind and disinterested proposition....I do not think it would be proper for any member of the family to have the money to dispose of...but should prefer to leave it to [you to] make the selection [of the school]."

Delighted as he was with Mrs. Fox's letter, Elisha worried that Maggie would ultimately retract her decision and revert to the rappings. "I have had but one thought how to make you happier, how to withdraw you from a deception from a course of sin & future punishment, the dark shadow of which hung over you like the wing of a vampire," he reminded his sweetheart. "Maggie, dearest Maggie, when you are tempted to forget my love & false friends misrepresent me and my motives—read this truthful letter & see if I have not proved myself a truly devoted self sacrificing friend & lover."

Ultimately, it was Leah who would challenge Elisha's sincerity. Realizing that she could no longer fight him, Leah decided that she would at least wring some profit out of Elisha. Less than a month after Mrs. Fox's letter, Maggie's opportunistic sister wrote to remind Elisha of his recent offer to provide some "relief of my dear husband or myself." In all confidence, Leah explained, Calvin's poor health had precipitated a financial crisis in her household. "The long continued illness and a consequent interruption of business with the large family to [support] by our little income has drawn upon my funds as to bring me in arrears for my quarter's rent." She owed $175.

Was it possible for Elisha to send Leah $100—"not as a donation but as a loan—for my circumstances are such that I only need a little time to repay any such favour....If you could in your abundance loan me $100 I have other friends who I can call upon for the remaining deficiency...you would relieve me from present embarrassments and lay me under lasting obligations to you."

Immediately Elisha forwarded money to Leah. Scrawled on the back of her letter—carefully saved in his papers and preserved at the American Philosophical Society—he tersely noted that he "sent her $75 without acknowledgement."

By doing so, the anonymous donation implicitly rebuffed Leah's offer of "lasting obligations" and hence any future chance for demanding more.

If there were to be any "obligations" from a member of the Fox family, they would come from Maggie, in whom, as Elisha wrote a day earlier, he felt certain that his "confidence will never be abused."

✦

To ensure that confidence, Elisha had left nothing to chance. "I have been inquiring after schools like a good fellow; seeking out *many*, that my little Maggie may have a choice," Elisha wrote her on March 17. To remind her of his Arctic journey, he was also searching for a "fine Newfoundland dog—a big, brave, steadfast friend—who will keep love of me alive *in you*."

Elisha consulted with the Grinnells; Dr. Francis Hawks, president of the Geographical Society of New York, and other influential friends to find a suitable school for Maggie, whom he presented as a young woman he wanted to help out of purely altruistic motives. A friend of Dr. Hawks's suggested a Misses Caroline and Mary Edward's school in New Haven, Connecticut. Elisha also consulted with his favorite aunt, Eliza Leiper of Lapeida, Pennsylvania— once again characterizing himself as Maggie's disinterested sponsor.

Delighted to help her nephew, Eliza replied with an intriguing idea. One of her friends was Susanna Turner, wife of the manager of a cotton mill in Lapeida, whose homely daughter was a capable tutor. The Turners lived in a comfortable, if relatively modest, home in the nearby hamlet of Crookville where Maggie could study, take music lessons, and generally benefit from the "opportunity of improvement" found in the family's lifestyle.

"My opinion is decidedly in favour of this situation," Eliza explained. "I know Mrs. Turner's family unexceptionable, Mother & daughters well informed, tastes cultivated, cheerful dispositions & religion."

Enthusiastically Elisha conveyed her opinion to Maggie. "Through her influence I can get you a quiet, yet cheerful home where you will be the only boarder, and where you may have a governess, and a room, and a piano all to yourself. It is true, dear Mag, that this home will be a plain country gentleman's...but you will be all the happier for that. You will be to them only as a lady. No one shall know, not even my relative, where the money comes from." After the summer, he added, she could enter another school on the list—a Madam Moulenard's at Albany, for instance—and return to Mrs. Turner's home during vacations.

Elisha's only request from his aunt was that she say nothing about his charge's "unfortunate conversations with 'spirits.'" "Miss F.," as Elisha referred to Maggie, "is very sensitive on the matter and a knowledge on her part that it was known would impair the moral influences of her retirement and probably cause her to withdraw."

That same day, Elisha wrote Maggie of his aunt's recommendation, informing her that he would explain the details to Mrs. Fox. If his sweetheart and her mother preferred they could see the school first, and then return to New York so that Maggie could pack. "There, dear Maggie," Elisha brightly concluded, "you will be a lady; your own mistress, and a person regarded with respect by the whole house."

"Your own mistress," Elisha had written. The idea of being released from Leah's tyrannical grasp and living like a normal young woman in charge of her own life seemed a dream come true. Maggie finally told Leah that she had made her decision: She was going to abandon spiritualism for the sake of an education.

❧

After a brief visit to Philadelphia, Elisha rushed to New York, scurrying back and forth from Manhattan to the Brooklyn Navy Yard supervising preparations on the *Advance,* the 144-ton brig that would carry him and his crew to the Arctic. Well acquainted with the craft from his previous Arctic voyage, Elisha was busily instructing carpenters to make it still more impermeable to the chill northern waters, when he was once again struck—this time more seriously than in Boston—by another spell of rheumatic heart disease. Its source, an infection caused by the streptococcal bacteria that lie dormant in heart valves for months or even years, typically rendered its victims feverish and crippled with painfully swollen joints or polyarthritis—if, in that pre-antibiotic era, they survived at all.

Alarmed, Elisha's friend Cornelius Grinnell had the ailing doctor-explorer brought from his hotel to the Grinnell home on Bond Street. There, aided by William Morton, a devoted member of the crew from that first Arctic journey, Cornelius shouldered responsibility for preparing the *Advance* while his father Henry handled Elisha's correspondence.

Typically, attacks of rheumatic fever lasted about three months, but the hard-driving explorer could not tolerate such a delay. Elisha consequently disparaged the seriousness of his disease, describing it as having caused him only "three weeks of helplessness on my beam ends." He knew full well—as he had written John Pendleton Kennedy that past March—that the only way the *Advance* could compete with Captain Inglefield's screw-steamer was to arrive in Greenland's Melville Bay that June. While his illness meant that the sailing date would be postponed until late May, Elisha was determined to overcome all difficulties.

"You have heard of my attack of inflammatory rheumatism and of the kind friends who have nursed me through it to returning strength and convalescence," Elisha wrote his aunt Eliza on May 1. Nevertheless, he added, with characteristic resolve, "My expedition will not suffer and I regard it as Providential that this outbreak found me surrounded by the blessings of home."

Still, the "blessings of home" at the Grinnells' was not enough. Soon afterward, longing to see his sweetheart, Elisha impulsively sent a carriage for Maggie. To his surprise, he received a curt note that read "cannot possibly come." On the eve of Maggie's expected departure for school, just as he was recovering, Elisha discovered that she was to conduct a séance for Jane Appleton Pierce, wife of the recently inaugurated American president, Franklin Pierce. Like thousands of other bereaved Victorian women, the dark-haired Mrs. Pierce was mourning for her dead children. Two had perished in infancy and early childhood and her remaining child, eleven-year-old Benny, had died before her eyes during a train derailment.

While Elisha, like the rest of the nation, empathized with the Pierces' tragic loss, he nevertheless urged Maggie to cancel her séance. "Don't rap for Mrs. Pierce," he begged, "Remember, you promised to me, a promise my heart has just told me has been twice broken within these forty-eight hours. How much oftener I don't know." Instead, Elisha suggested, she should "Begin again... and be careful—very careful, lest in an idle hour you lose my regard and your own respect. The carriage shall call for you tomorrow.... Receive this note kindly, and write me an answer for although my hands let me write, I am very-very sick."

Alarmed by the tone of her lover's note, Maggie arrived at the Grinnells' townhouse the next day. There, Henry's gracious fifty-year-old wife, Sarah Minturn Grinnell, greeted her hospitably and showed her into a parlor where Elisha lay listlessly on a couch in a crimson dressing gown.

One look at Maggie changed everything. Brightening, he immediately sat up and chatted and then, in an effort to amuse her, asked Sarah to show Maggie a gorgeously colored mechanical bird whose clock-like mechanism enabled it to spread its wings and trill a song. "If that belonged to me," Elisha whispered to Maggie when their hostess was out of earshot, "it should be yours." During that same happy afternoon, Maggie amused her hostess with stories about her adventures as a medium to the politicians and military men of Washington, D.C.

The following day, Elisha wrote Maggie that he was "not so well this morning, but very glad to have seen again the light of your eyes...Mrs. Grinnell was much pleased with you. Everybody who really knows you *is*, for my Maggie is a lady; and by the time that

THE RELUCTANT SPIRITUALIST 139

she has had a course of Mrs. Turner's music and French, nobody will know her as the spirit-rapping original phenomenon!"

⚜

Soon after Elisha began to recover from his rheumatic attack, Maggie's brother-in-law Calvin hemorrhaged so severely that it was clear he would not survive. On Wednesday, May 4, 1853, Calvin passed away. For Maggie, his death was a deep blow. She lost both a beloved foster brother and a sympathetic defender. Sensitive to his sweetheart's grief, the barely recuperated Elisha postponed a trip to Philadelphia and appeared at West Twenty-sixth Street for the funeral service on that Friday. Calvin's embalmed body lay in state in a back parlor. As he and Maggie stood side by side, Elisha suddenly grabbed Maggie's hand and in the presence of other spiritualists promised to marry her immediately after his return from the Arctic. "I will be true to you, till I am as the corpse before you," he vowed.

The family traveled to Rochester for another service the following week. But death shadowed them there as well. Though brother David's little son George seemed "perfectly well" when the visitors arrived that Sunday, May 8, the boy awoke the following Tuesday morning with a nasty cough and a spiking fever. By noon, surrounded by his weeping parents and relatives, the child died. "It nearly killed my brother," Maggie wrote Elisha, for her brother's son was "the most perfect little beauty you ever saw."

The grieving young woman added plaintively, "Dear Ly, do come as soon as you possibly can. I am so lonely. Yours Evermore, Maggie."

⚜

With a late May departure date looming, Elisha, in spite of his still-swollen joints, spent long hours at the Brooklyn Navy Yard overseeing the *Advance*'s final preparations. Designed to be a scientific exploratory mission as well as a rescue effort, the *Advance* was loaded with a variety of thermometers and navigational devices from the Naval Observatory, magnetic instruments from the U.S. Coast Guard, and traps to collect botanical specimens for the Philadelphia Academy of Natural Sciences.

In addition, tents, whale boats, sledges, goods to barter with the Eskimos, and a "large, well-chosen library" were placed aboard to keep Elisha and his crew amused during the long Arctic nights.

The provisioning of food was another challenge. Mindful of his earlier mission to the Arctic, Elisha stocked the *Advance* with what he thought would be several years' worth of foodstuffs that would protect against scurvy. These included two thousand pounds of canned pemmican—cakes made of dried meat and fruit—as well as meat biscuits, pickled cabbage, and malt extract for beer.

"No one knows as well as an Arctic voyager the value of foresight," Elisha had written in his first book. Yet, paradoxically, everything about his second expedition was conducted in a rush—from Elisha's unsuccessful efforts to win high-level support from the federal government, to the hastily assembled crew of seventeen officers and seamen, to his speedy application and acceptance into a Philadelphian Masonic order, which presumably strengthened the bonds between him and several of his officers.

There were, of course, sound reasons for Elisha's urgency. He was concerned about the brevity of the good weather in the Far North. In addition to Captain Inglefield's expedition, several rival rescue missions were underway, which, if successful, would quash his chance, as he once told Maggie, to "leave after me a name and a success." By spring 1853 at least seven expeditions had already attempted to locate the whereabouts of Franklin and his men.

To console himself during what he knew would be an arduous journey, Elisha wanted a visual reminder of Maggie. Consequently he arranged for prominent Italian artist, Joseph Fagnani, to paint Maggie's portrait. The sittings, held in Fagnani's Manhattan studio, commenced almost immediately upon Maggie's return from Arcadia and concluded on May 26, just a few hours before she was to depart for Crookville.

The resultant portrait revealed a slim, innocent girl-woman, and "the winning grace of her modest demeanor and the naive refinement in every look and movement," as she was described in *The Love-Life of Dr. Kane*. Somehow, too, Fagnani had caught her mood on the eve of her farewell from Elisha—wistful, faintly optimistic, but accepting of the challenge that lay ahead. There would be months, perhaps years, of separation from him, accompanied by long days of study in a new home far from New York City.

Painfully aware of that imminent separation, Elisha wrote on May 25, "If my to-morrow be clear and my poor body permit, I will call at half-past twelve to spend a parting hour with you. Do, dear darling, hasten your preparations, for I want to see you in your own home [that is, Mrs. Turner's] before I take my longer journey."

To that end he had already sent Maggie a fine packing trunk. "Will you do me a favor?" he asked. "As soon as Morton hands you this, write me a dear, sweet, loving little letter and send with it a lock of your hair. It will soothe me to sleep."

Despite such assurances of love, the couple's last hours together were painful. On Thursday afternoon, May 26, Mrs. Fox and Maggie met Elisha at the train station and together the threesome somberly traveled to Philadelphia. As they entered the Girard House hotel, some of the guests exchanged "excited murmurs and glances," for "Philadelphia knew that Maggie Fox, one of the Rochester Rappers, had adjured the cause of Spiritualism for the sake of their famous native son," according to *Time Is Kind*.

During an evening dinner with Mrs. Fox in a private room at the Girard House, the couple pondered the painful questions that Elisha had raised in a recent note. "Pet, lamb, in a few days we part: I on my arduous track—you to the quiet enjoyment of a happy home. Are we ever to meet again? Are we to walk arm in arm over sunny fields....Are we ever to be more to each other than we now are? Or is this—our soon-coming farewell—to be eternal?"

At the end of the dinner, Elisha gave Maggie a blue notebook, within which she promised to keep an account of her activities during his absence. "When you come back, dear Lish, you will find my heart in it," she promised.

Mrs. Fox left the couple alone for a few moments for a final farewell. Afterward, according to *Time Is Kind*, Maggie threw herself on the floor, "her body wracked with sobs," as Mrs. Fox knelt helplessly beside her. The next morning a pale, tear-stained Maggie and her mother boarded the carriage that Elisha had hired to carry them to Crookville, a manufacturing town on Ridley Creek.

The eighteen-mile, four-hour journey over country roads was tedious and probably fraught with emotion—memories of the arguments that had passed between them over Elisha's attentions, of the subsequent quarrels with Leah, of Maggie's decision to forsake spiritualism, of the recent deaths of Calvin and little George.

Still, Maggie's first glimpse of the Turner home was heartening. The house, she cheerfully noted in her new journal, was surrounded by a picket fence and "very tastefully" landscaped with rare flowers and "handsome trees." At its front was a "pretty piazza covered with honeysuckles and roses [that] forms a most inviting entrance." To the hopeful Maggie it spoke to the dream of bucolic domesticity that Elisha promised her once they wed.

After warm greetings from the Turners and assurances that Maggie was in good hands, Mrs. Fox explained she was immediately returning to Philadelphia. Weary, and still mourning the deaths of her son-in-law and grandson, the gray-haired matron seemed anxious to leave. "It was as if she could not face this particular problem one instant longer than need be," wrote Pond in *Time Is Kind*, adding that "there was no show of feeling as the two parted," causing the Turners to wonder at "the cold exterior" of the mother and daughter.

In contrast was the rush of warm feelings that came from New York. "When I think of our parting evening—its last hour, its last minutes—I am oppressed with the unreal vagueness of a dream. Oh, my Maggie, think of me—always think of me—with respect…lean on me, me, hope in me, bear with me—*trust me!*"

Elisha had immediately written upon his return from Philadelphia to Manhattan.

Urging his beloved to "live a life of purity and goodness" in his absence, he promised they would subsequently enjoy a "passion sanctified by love and marriage." Like his favorite poet, Tennyson—who often compared emotional states to nature—the literary-minded Elisha predicted that "golden fields shall spread before us, their summer harvest—silver lakes mirror your very breath." Above all, Elisha euphorically pleaded in that letter, "Let us live for each other."

❧

But he was worried about Maggie. To assure himself that she was all right, he called on Mrs. Fox at West Twenty-sixth Street the same Friday night. Hearing how upset Maggie was "and in how disconsolate a condition.... He could not bear this [and] short as his time was, resolved on another journey to Crookville to...have a last parting."

The next morning, Saturday, May 28, Elisha took a train back to Philadelphia, bringing with him several items that Maggie had left behind in her rooms. One of them was a canary, which in his haste to hire a carriage, he forgot in the Philadelphia terminal.

By early afternoon Maggie's harried suitor had arrived at the Turner residence. Once again, as at so many other critical junctures in her life, her reaction was not recorded, but from the description of Mrs. Turner's response in *The Love-life of Dr. Kane,* Maggie must have been openly delighted. Immediately upon watching the young couple, Susanna Turner understood, Maggie claimed, that their relationship went well beyond friendship and "how deep and sincere was the Doctor's love for her young charge."

To soften the poignancy of their final farewell, Elisha advertised a reward for the lost canary. Writing from New York on the eve of his departure for the Arctic, he triumphantly announced that he had succeeded in recovering "our little bird." Its return, Elisha added, was still more proof that "every thought, every wish is met by me. Never doubt my love."

He begged Maggie, "Guard and cherish the little wanderer thus returned to the fold. Make it an evidence of my thoughtful attention to your every wish. An emblem, too, dear darling, of my own return, when, after a dreary flight, I come back to nestle in your bosom."

HOPE DEFERRED

I wish, dear Ly, that you would hurry home.
—MAGGIE FOX TO ELISHA KENT KANE, 1853

AT NOON on a sparkling Tuesday, May 31, 1853, Elisha and a crew of seventeen men and officers sailed out of New York Harbor on the *Advance* bound for Newfoundland. Behind them, on the shores of the Battery, stood hundreds of well-wishers cheering and waving banners. As the *New York Herald* observed the next day, the expedition had become "an object of intense curiosity" to the public.

Two steamships filled with more friends, relatives, and officers, including Elisha's father, brothers, and Cornelius Grinnell, flanked the brig. "As the vessel passed along the North River [today the East River] she was saluted with cheers from the crowds...and by guns from the shipping," Cornelius wrote Maggie. Elisha, he added, was in "good spirits...[appearing] quite well, having entirely recovered from his rheumatic attack."

Cornelius had promised to be one of several guardians supervising Maggie's education. He would serve as the link between Elisha and Maggie, he explained. The *Advance* was expected to arrive at St. John's, Newfoundland, in two weeks. At that point, he wrote Maggie, either he or his father, Henry, "may expect to hear from them" and would forward any letters Elisha had written her.

Nevertheless Maggie continued to feel anxious. Fretting over Elisha's health and safety, worrying about the late arrival of her trunks, and missing the daily approval and stimulus of séance guests, she slowly settled into her studies—an adjustment, as her beloved suitor had warned her months earlier, that was bound to be challenging.

The newspapers of New York and Philadelphia buzzed with rumors about the famed medium's disappearance from New York City. But they did not penetrate the rural hamlet of Crookville, where Maggie wrote Elisha effusively and sent her letters, as instructed, through Cornelius Grinnell.

Maggie soon had one of Elisha's letters in her hands. "Just standing out to sea," Elisha wrote. "Maggie, my own sweet pet, be comforted...Your letter gave me pain, pain because it showed me that you were unhappy."

To avoid upsetting his sweetheart, Elisha made no mention of the rough weather the *Advance* had encountered on their eighteen-day journey to Newfoundland, the first leg on their voyage to northern Greenland. Nor did he dwell on his still-fragile health or the debilitating and chronic bouts of seasickness that were laying him low, as had happened on other voyages. By the time the *Advance* arrived at St. John's, Elisha's health was so tenuous that shipmate Henry Goodfellow observed that he had the "subdued look of a broken-down invalid...and was far from being either well or vigorous."

In a letter sent to Newfoundland, Maggie reported that since arriving in Crookville, several friends and relatives had already visited her—among them her mother, her sister Katy, and an older Manhattan friend who was to be her female guardian, the widowed Mrs. Ellen Cochrane Walter, an acquaintance of the Grinnells.

Over the past few weeks, Maggie breathlessly continued, Mrs. Turner had become a "very dear friend to me and so is Mrs. Leiper [Elisha's aunt Eliza]. You said they would all love me. Did you not tell them to say [that], Ly?" Then, promising that she would not "tease my Ly any more," Maggie assured him that their "sacred promise" was foremost in her mind.

The rest of Maggie's letter was undiplomatically filled with news about spiritualism. By then her Katy and Mrs. Fox had moved to an apartment of their own on Tenth Street. Leah had leased rooms nearby on Fifteenth Street. Maggie proudly observed that Katy, whose skills included healing, had "cured" Dr. Bayard of facial neuralgia.

At that moment, spiritual manifestations "are spreading all over the world." In fact, Maggie thoughtlessly chattered, "some of the greatest men in the world have become believers in the spirits." Recent converts included abolitionist William Lloyd Garrison, writer Nathaniel Park Willis, and the Foxes' old friend, New York State Supreme Court judge John Worth Edmonds. The judge had just published *Spiritualism*—a book that so outraged his colleagues that he would be forced to resign from the Supreme Court.

In spite of Maggie's continued enthusiasm for spiritualism, the devoted tone of her letters suggests that her clairvoyant or telepathic skills were constantly being directed toward Elisha. In that same letter, she admitted that she had "conversed with the spirits when Mrs. Walter was here...and [they] asked a number of questions about you."

In response, Elisha wrote quite poetically that during his long hours at sea he often visualized Maggie in that "quiet old country house—counting time by the village clock which rises above the willows...or under the shade of some drooping chestnut, startling the birds...with dreamy tokens from the spirit-world." If that were true, Maggie should "imagine him by her side" so that he could answer her questions.

If, at the end of four months at the Turners', she wished to "try another school-girl life" she was free to select one of the other schools they had previously considered, including those in Albany or North Carolina, whose tuitions either Cornelius Grinnell or Dr. Hawks were permitted to pay.

His one remaining fear was that she would be lured back into spiritualism. In conclusion, Elisha added in his last message, "The only thing...that your true friend can find it in his heart to utter" was to "see little of...[Leah] and *never sleep within her house.*"

≈✤≈

After that exuberant exchange, Maggie did not hear again from Elisha. But that, as Henry Grinnell explained, was to be expected because on June 17 the *Advance* had sailed from St. John's for Greenland.

Elisha's health revived during that journey. Suddenly, noted fellow sailor Henry Goodfellow, the sickly captain "seemed stronger" and began to assume his duties "with the alacrity of a well man."

Ironically, as Elisha grew more vigorous in the northern air, Maggie languished in Pennsylvania. Initially, as her letters to her lover implied, she had applied herself industriously to her studies and "never lost a minute." But soon she began to flag, citing a toothache and other "bodily infirmities," which her mentor, the vigilant Susanna Turner, grumbled, made it increasingly "difficult to accomplish much."

Never a country girl to begin with, Maggie now felt so cut off from others that in mid-summer she wrote Cornelius Grinnell, asking his opinion about switching to a traditional girls' school such as Mrs. Willard's in Troy, New York. There, Maggie reasoned, she could reconcile with old friends who lived nearby and be closer to her family in upstate New York.

"If my advice were asked," Cornelius replied a few days later from his yacht, *Albion,* in Newport Harbor, she should stay at Mrs. Turner's since she found it so "comfortable and pleasant in all respects." Instead of reminding her that Elisha had wished her to remain at Crookville for at least four months, he added that at Mrs. Willard's that "you might not enjoy yourself so much." From his perspective, nothing seemed better suited to Maggie's needs "than the course you are now pursuing at Mrs. Turner's."

But try as she might, the young woman continued to languish. By late September, she had become so listless and depressed that when Ellen Walter arrived from New York for a second visit she became alarmed. Maggie's unhappiness, the older woman quickly gleaned, went much deeper than the fashionable languor so often adopted by lovelorn men and women of the Victorian era.

Months earlier, when the Grinnells first introduced Ellen to Maggie and explained that she was to be her New York guardian, the widow had privately questioned the wisdom of the young woman's removal to a small country town. Now, given Maggie's depression, Ellen felt obliged to contact her mother as well as her family's physician, Dr. Edward Bayard, the handsome forty-nine-year-old brother-in-law of Elizabeth Cady Stanton. As it happened, that homeopathic doctor knew a great deal about romance and its disappointments, having once unsuccessfully proposed to young Elizabeth Cady while married to her sister. Edward suggested that a change of scenery might help, especially a visit to Manhattan, where she would again enjoy the companionship of friends and relatives.

"I am very lonely and should love very much to go and spend a few days with my friend Mrs. Walter," Maggie consequently wrote her primary guardian, Cornelius. "Will you please do me the kindness to write to Mrs. Turner and tell her to let me spend, say one week…" Maggie promised to "take my French books and study one hour every day."

Having obtained Cornelius's approval, Maggie left Crookville and arrived at Ellen Walter's home on Clinton Place (now Eighth Street)—close to Katy and Mrs. Fox's new apartment on Tenth Street but at a safe distance from Leah's home. Still, no sooner was Maggie settled in Ellen's welcoming home than she "suffered from a severe illness brought on by mental disquiet." Maggie, apparently, had become depressed and then, according to Dr. Bayard, had fallen victim to a "brain fever"—a non-specific medical term then used to describe an illness that was probably meningitis or encephalitis. Such an infection, he explained to Ellen Walter, was dangerous and could only be cured by "a long and carefully supervised rest."

A month later Susanna Turner wrote from Crookville, expressing dismay that Maggie had been "struck down with such a malady." While reminding her young charge to be patient with her recovery, Susanna sternly reminded Maggie that afterward she

would have to "work harder than ever, to make up for lost time."
Maggie did not reply.

Five weeks later Susanna wrote again. "Not having received any
communication from you since I wrote," she began sharply, she
was inquiring about Maggie's health. If she was still sick, the young
woman certainly should have had someone notify Susanna. If not,
and if "you are merely remaining to indulge in the gaieties of the
city, you should write to me yourself."

In her role as Maggie's educational mentor, Susanna explained,
she had certain obligations, having promised Elisha to behave "like
a mother to you... to cultivate your understanding" and to awaken
those "latent energies which lay dormant through neglect." How,
Susanna continued, was she ever to explain this recent "lapse from
duty" to her "high minded friend" Elisha?

Two days later, Ellen Walter defended Maggie in a letter. Explaining that the young woman was "very much distressed" by
Susanna's insinuations, she insisted that Maggie was still under the
medical care of Dr. Bayard and still "far from well." It was only in
the last few days that Maggie had recovered sufficiently to look "at
all like herself."

Because of the precarious state of her health, Maggie had not
"partaken of the amusements and gaieties of the city, not having inclination nor the strength" to do so.

From Crookville, a chastised Susanna meekly explained that she
had not meant to say "one word to wound [Maggie's] feeling" and
that she was unaware of the "protracted nature of her indisposi-
tion." Gingerly, she assured Ellen that her charge should take time
returning to Crookville "till she is fully able to travel. Please present
my kindest love to her, in which Mr. Turner heartily joins."

Taking Susanna at her word, Maggie did not return to
Crookville until after New Year's 1854. From there she once again
wrote Elisha effusive letters. These Maggie first shared with Ellen,
with whom she had grown close during her illness and who, in turn,
forwarded them to the Grinnells. "I thought yours to the Doctor

very sweet and touching from their sympathy and the pure affection breathing through them. What is more to be prized than a pure, devoted heart?" Ellen wrote Maggie approvingly that March.

By then, Ellen had visited Maggie in Crookville again and patched up her differences with Susanna Turner. While Maggie must now resign herself to the rigor and isolation of the Crookville home, Ellen urged her to have faith that there would be "better times ahead" when her studies were complete so that she would "shine all the brighter."

Maggie remained highly distractible. Anything, it seemed, even a carelessly written newspaper article speculating about Elisha's progress in the Arctic, set off new waves of anxiety. She had, of course, been counseled to behave otherwise. An important aspect of a lady's behavior was self-control.

To calm the jittery young woman, Cornelius suggested that she immediately write Elisha. At that moment Cornelius had a unique opportunity to send letters to the Far North, ironically via England, where Elisha's rival, Captain Inglefield, was again sailing on a second voyage to the Arctic in April. "You should therefore put your letter in the post-office [addressed to me] Thursday afternoon, if possible, or early Friday morning," Cornelius instructed Maggie.

Yet somehow her letter was lost; on March 30 Cornelius wrote that he still had not received it and missed the deadline for its dispatch to England. In frustration Maggie wrote Cornelius again, begging for news about Elisha. Her letter was not preserved, but Cornelius offered a terse reply: "We do not expect to hear from Dr. Kane until next September or October."

❧

It was at that very moment that her beloved Elisha and his men were pitched in a grim battle against the sub-zero climates of the Arctic. The previous August, after sailing north from Upernavik to Smith Sound, the doctor and his crew, fearing the treacherous ice floes known as the Arctic's "middle ice," had manually hauled the storm-battered *Advance* several miles along Greenland's northeastern coast into uncharted territory near the latitude of 78° 50'. Subsequently, geographers would name that wide body of ice-clogged water Kane Basin.

Ominously, the "new ice" of the advancing winter was spreading unusually fast over the open waters of Smith Sound. With little warning on or around midnight on August 26, the *Advance* became hopelessly locked in the frozen waters.

Dawn revealed a formidable vista, a "shelf of ice that clung to the base of the rocks overlooking the sea, but itself overhung by steep and lofty cliffs"—some as much as one thousand feet high, Elisha observed, like "long tongues of worn-down rock." The sea contained hundreds of icebergs etched like teeth against the pale sky, giant projectiles caught in floes or in watery currents that had been flash-frozen in midstream. The icebergs gave Elisha "some apprehensions," as he wrote with dramatic understatement, about the *Advance's* hoped-for "liberation."

❧

By September 10, Elisha realized he and his men would be compelled to spend the winter in the cove where they had been trapped. He named the cove Rensselaer Harbor after his family's Pennsylvania country house, Rensselaer. Then, attempting to wrest some advantage from their predicament, Elisha ordered his men to unload some of the scientific equipment and establish an observatory on a nearby islet. The next eight months passed slowly, each week bringing new challenges and difficulties. Elisha and his crew suffered a plethora of ills, including frostbite, snow-blindness, scurvy, near-starvation, rodent infestations, and a nervous disease that destroyed their sledge dogs.

Seven months later, on March 23, 1854, at the peak of Maggie's inexplicable anxiety in Crookville, Elisha and his crew were in dire straits. In minus 75-degree temperatures, three crew members returned to the *Advance* "swollen, haggard, and hardly able to speak."

They had dragged themselves back from an exploratory mission along the frozen Arctic coast. Another four men from their party, they rasped to their horrified captain, "were all lying frozen and disabled" somewhere in a field of icebergs to the north and east of the brig.

Hastily Elisha and several crew members collected supplies and set out to locate their missing peers. After trekking miles into the Arctic wasteland, the team miraculously discovered the four frost-bitten crewmates lying in a tent beneath a hummock marked by an American flag and a Masonic banner. "We could not halt long. Each of us took a turn of two hours' sleep; and we prepared for our homeward march," Elisha recalled. What ensued was a death-defying stumble over the icy terrain. They dragged the four ailing crew members, strapped to sledges, through fields of towering icebergs. After four hours, Elisha and his men reached the *Advance*.

Like the rest of his crew, Elisha returned from that grueling seventy-two-hour trek half-delirious from the cold and strain. "The week that followed the disaster left me nothing but anxieties and sorrow," he wrote. "Nearly all the men involved were tossing on their sick-bunks, some of them frozen, others undergoing amputations, several with dreadful premonitions of tetanus." And by April 8, two of the sailors had died.

~❧~

In Pennsylvania, Maggie's anxiety grew increasingly intense and in mid-April she wrote Cornelius requesting permission to return to New York. Even then, she remained restless and for the next several months shuttled between Crookville and New York trying to juggle her longing for comfort from Manhattan friends with her promise to Elisha to complete her education. She was in New York when Susanna Turner notified her that a letter from Elisha had arrived. Since the Crookville post office was so unreliable, Susanna explained, she hesitated sending it along to New York.

Within another day, Maggie had returned to Crookville to read it. The letter, whose date is unknown, had likely been carried from a whaling boat a year earlier when Elisha was still in Upernavik.

"Dear dear Maggie: In the midst of ice and desolation, I still think of you. Can you, while hope and sunshine linger round you, turn a thought to me?...For am not *I* in your heart? Yes, dear Mag, your very heart of hearts—now and always! Ly." And in a touching postscript, Elisha added that her portrait had become "a great comfort to me. I often gaze on its quiet loveliness."

Adding to Maggie's joy was news from Cornelius that Captain Inglefield, having just completed a second Arctic voyage, might be carrying more recent letters from Elisha. On August 17, Cornelius predicted that "we may look for the Doctor about the 10th of October. Trusting that his life and health have been spared, and that he may have been successful in finding some trace of the lost ones."

But now it was Elisha and his crew who were in jeopardy of being lost. Several weeks later Cornelius ruefully reported that Captain Inglefield's journey had yielded no news of Elisha. More discouraging yet was Cornelius's letter of October 17 explaining that "we have no tidings yet of the Doctor, nor do we look for him until the latter end of the month." If Elisha is not home by the end of November, he gently explained, Maggie must accept the fact that Elisha "intends to remain another winter in the Arctic regions."

Intends? Or had no choice? Either way the probability was nearly too much for Maggie to bear. In November she insisted upon returning to New York, hoping against hope that Elisha would appear.

But a second winter passed drearily without a word.

~✥~

Five thousand miles north of New York City in Rensselaer Harbor, Greenland, Elisha was equally despondent. Their best hope for escaping the ice had been during the summer—June and July. But there had been no thaw. On July 10, 1854, he wrote his second brother, Thomas, fully realizing that the letter might never reach him. "Never, dear brother, can poor Elish go through all this again—Fresh trials are ahead, for the ice is unbroken around me—and I am well aged and worn."

Only one possibility for rescue remained before the encroaching winter freeze—boarding a light whaleboat (aptly named the *Forlorn Hope*) whose slender size might enable Elisha to skirt the ice floes and sail six hundred miles south to Beechy Island. There, at Sir Edward Belcher's base camp, he could possibly borrow a launch to sail north and retrieve the rest of his crew. "I know it is a hazardous venture, but it is a necessary one…and an incumbent duty," he wrote before he and several crew members boarded the craft.

By July 31, that venture too seemed destined to fail: After several grueling weeks sailing south in Lancaster Bay, the *Forlorn Hope* ground to a sickening "dead halt." Elisha and one of his men then climbed to the top of a 120-foot iceberg to confirm their worst fear. "We saw that all within a radius of thirty miles was a motionless, unbroken and impenetrable sea," Elisha wrote.

That view, Elisha knew, coincided with the frozen waters of Baffin Bay, which had partially melted and divided in two sections during the summer of 1853, making it possible for the *Advance* to sail north through the eastern opening. Since then, however, unusually bad weather and storm currents had locked together both parts of the ice pack, trapping the *Advance* to the north and making any "further attempt to penetrate to the south…hopeless."

To Elisha, that realization was a death warrant. Barring some miraculous means of escape, he understood that he, his crew, and the *Advance* were frozen into the ice for another full Arctic winter. He returned to the *Advance* to share the news. Eleven members of Elisha's crew were so terrified with the prospect of spending another winter in Rensselaer Harbor that they elected to risk a hazardous journey south themselves. Elisha provided them with two boats and sledge; then he turned his efforts to making the *Advance* secure and igloo-like for himself and his remaining crew members for the coming winter.

As their food supplies dwindled, as fuel for light and heat grew scarce, Elisha and his sickly crew spent their days in nearly perpetual Arctic darkness. On December 7, in the midst of that grim struggle, a group of Eskimos, the Inuit, arrived at the iced-over *Advance*. With them were two of Elisha's deserters, who begged for help to save the rest of the crew. The other deserters were camped two hundred miles south, ill, starving and incapable of traveling.

While the scurvy-riddled condition of his remaining crew prevented Elisha from rescuing them himself, he bartered precious stocks of food with the Eskimos in exchange for their agreement to retrieve the men. As Elisha feared, the strangers simply disappeared with the food. Ultimately, though, a friendlier group of natives from Netlik transported the rest of the humiliated deserters back to the brig.

Somehow, they made it through the winter. By March 31, Elisha could even observe that "We have managed to get enough game to revive the worst of our scurvy patients and have kept in regular movement the domestic wheel of shipboard."

He and the crew spent April and May 1855 hunting for game and organizing supplies for an "early departure" from the *Advance*. By May 17 the ice had melted enough for him and his men to prepare for the long journey south. Carrying what they could, he and his crew donned clothes sewn from their heavy blankets, packed scientific equipment, mounted their whaleboats upon three sledges, and abandoned the *Advance*. Elisha had Maggie's portrait strapped to his back.

What followed was a grueling thirty-one-day trek. Members of the Second Grinnell Expedition, hobbled by four sick men, walked 316 miles, dragging the boats over eighty-one miles of ice floes. According to sailor Amos Bonsall, the exhausted crew was heroically guided by Elisha, who "not only cheered the dispirited and quieted the querulous and discontented," but also administered their scant provisions "as to give no one the slightest cause for complaint."

By June 16, Elisha and his men had reached Cape Alexander at the base of the frozen Smith Sound. "Our boats are at the open water. We see its deep indigo horizon, and hear its roar against the icy beach. Its scent is in our nostrils and our hearts," he scrawled exuberantly in his journal.

They launched themselves into the ocean in three open boats with little remaining food or water. Ahead lay a perilous five-hundred-mile journey through the icy and notoriously storm-tossed waters of Baffin Bay.

❦

The long months of silence from the North had rattled Elisha's family and friends in Philadelphia, New York, and Washington, D.C. Alarmed by whalers' reports of a bad winter, Judge Kane and Henry Grinnell had rallied their peers for a rescue mission in November 1854. They were soon joined in their exhortations to the government by former Secretary of the Navy John Pendleton Kennedy, and scientists Joseph Henry of the Smithsonian and Alexander Dallas Bache of the U.S. Coast Survey.

Even so, congressional approval came slowly. Finally lawmakers passed a joint House-Senate resolution for a rescue mission on February 3, 1855. Signed by President Pierce on February 5, the agreement allocated $150,000 for the mission.

To head the rescue, the U.S. Navy appointed Henry Hartstene, a twenty-seven-year veteran of naval service and seasoned Antarctic explorer. He would command a two-ship squadron, consisting of the *Release,* a 327-foot clipper bark, and the *Arctic,* a 558-ton propeller steamer, in what was called the Hartstene Rescue Mission. Among its officers was Elisha's devoted twenty-year-old brother, John, a recent graduate of the University of Pennsylvania Medical School, who had begged for a temporary naval assignment.

How or what the Grinnells explained to Maggie about their personal efforts or other details of the mission is not known. The father and son did send her a series of polite letters with probable estimates of Elisha's arrival.

As Henry explained in one addressed to Maggie on April 30, 1855, "If the Doctor returns this year, he will probably be here in October next; but if he is not home by that time, he cannot get here before October 1856." To soften the news, Henry added, "The Government Expedition in search of him and his party will leave here on the 1st of June, and...are expected to return in October following."

Susanna Turner, never being one to waste time, attempted to use those estimates of Elisha's probable return from the Arctic as a goad directing Maggie back to her studies.

"I trust in kind Providence that Dr. Kane will return in the course of this ensuing fall," Susanna began in a diplomatic letter of July 3, 1855, to Maggie. After the initial excitement of his arrival, she predicted that Elisha would inquire about her educational progress. "He will expect to find your mind stored with the elements of useful knowledge...a companion whose conversational powers have been cultivated."

Given those expectations, Maggie must ask herself if she had used her time well. If her conscience assured her that she had, the young woman had no reason to feel guilty. But even if that were true, Susanna added, "It is my earnest hope and prayer that you will improve in every hour."

She might as well have saved her breath. Once again Maggie was in Manhattan—and this time at the request of Ellen Walter, who unexpectedly arrived in Crookville one hot summer day and claimed that Maggie was needed in the city because one of her close friends was deathly ill. *The Love-Life of Dr. Kane* did not mention the name of that friend, but subsequent letters suggest it was probably Dr. Edward Bayard. Nearly two years earlier the homeopathic physician had carefully tended Maggie during her bout with "brain fever." And now, after fruitlessly seeking help from Katy, he had turned to Maggie to use her own rarely mentioned but apparently formidable "healing gifts" to cure acute facial neuralgia.

Two weeks after her arrival in New York, Maggie finally wrote Susanna Turner that she had no plans to return to Crookville until mid- or late September. "I really feel sorry that you should have been called away just at the time when every moment was doubly precious," Susanna replied with obvious annoyance.

Nor was she the only one put out. Within a few days, Cornelius also had reprimanded Maggie. He informed Susanna that the young woman would be back in Crookville by August 1 "to commence again [her studies] in right good earnest."

※

Elisha and his men had made it to Baffin Bay but faced a new set of challenges. Fast-moving ice floes alternating with jagged chunks of ice constantly threatened the three whaleboats as they threaded their way south. Adding to their trials was a shrinking supply of provisions; they had little more than tea and broth, hardly enough to sustain the already malnourished men.

On July 11 their tortured progress south abruptly ended. The ice floes had coalesced into an impassable wall. From the top of a steep iceberg, Elisha looked out upon the distant Cape York, the northernmost promontory of Melville Bay that was their destination.

"My eyes never looked on a spectacle more painful," he recalled. "We were ahead of the season: the floes had not broken up. There was no 'western water.' Here, in a cul-de-sac, between two barriers, both impassable to men in our condition, with stores miserably inadequate and strength broken down, we were to wait till the tardy summer should open to us a way."

Determined to keep up his crew's morale, Elisha kept his worries to himself, hoping that the summer sun would soon melt enough of the ice pack so that they could pass. Their imprisonment did yield an unexpected surprise. They spied seabirds—lummes, as Elisha called them—nesting in the ledges of the steep cliffs of rock and ice, some more than eleven hundred feet high, that encircled the captain and his crew. "All of them," Elisha recalled later in his journal, "in endless abundance; imagine such a combination of charms for scurvy-broken, hunger-stricken men."

To commemorate that propitious location, Elisha named it "Providence Halt," and on July 18, after a week's rest and revitalization, the ice had melted enough for him and his men to recommence the journey. Three days later, after braving what he recalled was "tortuous but romantic travel through a misty atmosphere" that signified rising temperatures, they arrived at the longed-for Cape York.

Even then, the expedition's trials were far from over: They would be on the water for another twelve days. On August 1, Elisha and his crew finally sighted Devil's Thumb, a famous landmark in Melville Bay. Before long he and his ragged crew encountered Danish sailors in a large open boat—the first Europeans they had seen in two years.

Excited greetings were exchanged on both sides followed by the Danes' explanation that they had sighted two American rescue boats heading north in Melville Bay. Then came disheartening news: In April 1854, British explorer Sir John Rae had discovered Franklin's expedition, or more accurately, records of it, one thousand miles south of Rensselaer Harbor.

Elisha glossed over whatever disappointment he felt in his memoir of this second voyage, entitled *Arctic Explorations: The Second Grinnell Expedition In Search of Sir John Franklin 1853, 54, 55*. Instead, he focused upon his crew's delight as they sailed into the misty outskirts of Upernavik. "It is six o'clock. We are nearing the end of our trials. Can it be a dream?" he wrote. Altogether he and his crew had sailed thirteen hundred miles in three light whaleboats from Cape Alexander to Upernavik. Their expedition charted more than eight hundred miles of undiscovered territory.

Of that other dream—Maggie, whose image he had carried to Upernavik—he had not written at all, believing it unsuitable for a ship's journal.

After a warm welcome and "all manner of kindness from the Danes of Upernavik," Elisha and his men rested from their ordeal. Finally, on September 6, they boarded the Danish barque *Mariane*.

Five days later, a lookout sighted a steamer bearing an American flag. Immediately, hoping it was one of the ships of the American rescue mission, Elisha and his crew lowered the battered whaleboat, *Faith*—the sole remaining vessel from their journey south—and paddled furiously toward it. At the whaleboat's approach, Elisha's younger brother, John, peered down from the high deck of the *Release* upon the passengers in the *Faith*. "The men in the boat were long-bearded and weather-beaten; they had strange, wild costumes; there was no possibility of recognition. Dr. Kane, standing upright in the stern of the first boat, with his spy-glass slung around his neck, was the first identified."

❧

Maggie was ecstatic at the news. After twenty-six months of languishing, she insisted to Ellen and her mother that she must look beautiful to welcome Elisha in exquisite clothes befitting one who would soon become his wife. While usually frugal, the soft-hearted Mrs. Fox relented: After her daughter's long and agonized vigil, she could deny her nothing. In between fittings with dressmakers, Maggie made a hasty trip to Crookville to pack up her belongings.

The date of Elisha's return had not been announced because the *Release* and the *Arctic* had steamed directly south from Godhavn to New York Harbor. Consequently, it was not until Thursday afternoon October 11, 1855—when Captain Hartstene's squadron arrived at Sandy Hook, New Jersey—that the news was telegraphed to ships in New York Harbor and then to Manhattan.

All the way into the harbor other boats and ships raised and dipped their flags in tribute to the *Release* and *Arctic,* in recognition of the returning heroes. Cascades of cannon fire, shot from forts surrounding New York Harbor, saluted the passing squadron, alerting still other citizens to the historic event. Cheering crowds and a cluster of newspaper reporters awaited the heroes at the Battery landing.

In Brooklyn and New York City, excited citizens thronged the streets. "Few events within the range of possibility could have produced a livelier feeling of public joy than did the announcement yesterday of the safe return of the gallant Arctic adventurer, Dr. Kane, and his exploring party," observed the *New York Tribune*.

The *New York Times*'s front-page story was far more muted, announcing that "Dr. Kane, the intrepid Arctic navigator, after having been given up as lost, has returned safe home with the loss of but three men on his whole expedition." In spite of the perilous journey, the *Times* noted that "The Doctor has improved in physical appearance...a bronzed face, a long and heavy black beard, a shock of hair just whitening a little...a stouter body and a hand with a hearty grip."

Later, Elisha would tell a friend that since his return to Upernavik his health had become "almost absurd. I have grown like a walrus." The one telltale symptom of his hardships was his balding forehead, revealed in self-mocking "before" and "after" self-portraits sketched in his journal and in a subsequent daguerreotype.

That evening, in a hastily assembled party at New York's posh Astor House, Elisha was swarmed by friends and admirers who begged to hear about his Arctic adventures. Finally, after pushing his way out the door of the smoky Rotunda Bar at the Astor House toward a waiting carriage, Elisha traveled to the Bond Street home of Henry Grinnell. Trailing him was a *New York Herald* journalist, who reported in his column the next day that the shipping magnate greeted Elisha with "such a welcome as comes only from the depths of his heart."

❧

At Clinton Place, meanwhile, Maggie waited impatiently. Hours earlier, hearing the cannon fire from New York Harbor, she had become so edgy and excited that Ellen Walter had to forbid her to leave the house, reminding her that as a refined young lady, she was obliged to wait for Elisha's call. She and Ellen sat anxiously through the dinner hour and well into the night waiting for the front doorbell to ring.

By midnight, when it was obvious that Elisha was not going to arrive, the disappointed women finally retired. Waking early—if she slept at all—Maggie resumed her vigil. By noon she had become hysterical, fearing that Elisha had somehow forgotten her or, if not, had changed his mind about his affections.

Perhaps, Ellen suggested in one of her repeated efforts to comfort Maggie, Elisha assumed she was still in Pennsylvania. Realizing suddenly that no one had actually informed the Grinnells of Maggie's return to Clinton Place, Ellen sent off a note to Henry. Still there was no response. By that evening Maggie was so distraught that she asked to be escorted to Mrs. Fox's home on nearby Tenth Street. At last, the doorbell rang. Instead of Elisha, there stood Dr. Edward Bayard, gently suggesting that Maggie accompany him back to Clinton Place, where Ellen Walter had just received a visitor.

Awkwardly, Ellen Walter greeted Maggie and Dr. Bayard at the door. "It was all a mistake, a gentleman on business, not Dr. Kane!" she stammered uncomfortably. Now, given the lateness of the hour, she gently urged the tearful Maggie to spend the night with her.

What Ellen did not tell Maggie was that hours earlier, while Maggie was with her mother, Cornelius Grinnell had arrived with a message from Elisha. His absence, he said, was due to poor health, but he assured Maggie that he would see her in a few days. Privately, however, Cornelius confided in Ellen that Elisha was embroiled in a disagreement with his family over rumors of his engagement to Maggie.

Adding to the shock of the explanation was Cornelius's request that Ellen hand over Elisha's love letters. Outraged at the man's audacity, but managing to keep her temper, the poised widow explained that she had no idea where her young charge kept them.

At some point during the next twelve hours—Maggie's memoir does not say exactly when—Ellen shared the painful news about Elisha and his family with Maggie. Bewildered, the weeping girl secluded herself in her room.

The next morning, Elisha arrived at Ellen Walter's front door. Dressed in his naval uniform the now well-groomed, tanned Elisha nervously asked to see Maggie. Warily, Ellen Walter replied that "she is above stairs—but the child is completely broken down."

Nevertheless, Elisha insisted upon seeing her, beseeching Ellen so piteously that she finally relented.

Haggard and tear-stained, Maggie descended the stairs and entered the parlor. As she did, Elisha uttered a joyful cry. Then, folding Maggie in his arms and kissing her head and brow, Elisha reaffirmed his love, reassuring her that his feelings were "the same as when we parted."

Elisha blamed his inability to see Maggie immediately after his arrival on the public clamor that had immediately surrounded him. Then, gingerly, he broached the subject of their engagement. Their marriage, he gently explained, had to be "indefinitely postponed on account of the violent opposition" of his family. For the time being, Elisha ruefully added, they must "be to each other only as sister and brother!"

To confirm the seriousness of his statement, Elisha showed her a letter he had composed to calm his mother, Jane Leiper Kane, who, he explained, had become heartsick over news of his engagement to a lowly rapper. That letter stated that Elisha's relationship with Maggie had always been "merely friendly and fraternal; that no matrimonial engagement had subsisted, etc. etc." Then Elisha asked her to copy it over and sign her name.

Stunned, Maggie hesitated. "Do it for me, Maggie!" Elisha urged. "You shall never suffer! It is for my mother!" Ultimately, at least according to Maggie's memoir, she agreed to write the letter in her own hand, if only to restore peace between Elisha and his family.

Once Maggie finished, Elisha called Ellen Walter into the room to show her the letter. "Maggie, is this so?" asked the dumbfounded widow.

Returned to her senses by Ellen's penetrating expression, Maggie cried, "No, no—it is not so! Doctor Kane knows it is not!" Then, turning to her lover, she reminded him of what he "said in the carriage" about the details of their future wedding. A bitter argument followed after which Elisha left the house. Several days later, however, he reappeared and sheepishly returned the letter to Maggie. Without a word, she ripped the pages to shreds.

Still nothing had been settled. Exacerbating Elisha's confusion was a note he had received from his aunt Eliza Leiper, who, having visited Maggie during her stay in Crookville, was enraged by rumors that Elisha had deceived her with a promise of marriage. Incensed with the implied slur against her own reputation, Eliza "bade him clear himself of the imputation of having deceived that young girl—whom he had placed under her charge—or *never enter her house again!*"

This was too much for Elisha. His parents were fuming. The threat of being cut of from their financial—and emotional—support had thoroughly unnerved him. Now too, other beloved relatives were threatening to disown him. "See, Maggie, here is my favorite aunt turning against me for your sake!" Elisha cried with despair.

Whatever relief the elder Kanes gained from Elisha's report of his broken engagement was short-lived. Within a week of his return from the Arctic, Elisha's romance with Maggie Fox was announced in the newspapers. "A gentleman of this city informs us that Dr.

Kane, of the Arctic Expedition, is soon to be married to Miss Margaretta Fox, the second sister of the 'Fox Girls,'" announced the *Troy Daily Whig* on October 19, adding "...his said-to-be-affianced has been attending a young ladies' school in Philadelphia."

The rumor, being too sensational to resist, was repeated in the *New York Herald* a week later. By October 31 the story had stirred such controversy that the *New York Evening Post,* quoting the *Herald* and seeking to boost its own circulation, insisted that the story was "without a shadow of foundation." The next day both the *New York Express* and the *New York Times* republished the *Post* story verbatim. Simultaneously, the *New York Times* defended the validity of the source, but on November 2 acknowledged it was a mistake for "this contradiction had been insisted on by some party furious in the Kane interest."

On Sunday morning, November 3, in the midst of the uproar, Elisha appeared at Mrs. Fox's home on Tenth Street just as Maggie was leaving to attend church. A reporter dogged him. The newsman had essentially forced himself upon the explorer, determined to learn the truth about his engagement. Within minutes, he was grilling an indignant Mrs. Fox about her daughter's romance while an equally indignant Maggie chastised Elisha for allowing the reporter to call in the first place.

By November 6 the controversy had reached such a pitch that Horace Greeley, who had remained a close friend of the Fox family, finally protested in a *Tribune* editorial, "We wish the several journals which have originated reports *pro* and *con,* respecting the persons above named...[to] consider whether they have...perverted their columns to the gratification of an impertinent curiosity. What right has the public to know anything about an 'engagement' or non-engagement between these two people?"

In the midst of the furor, Maggie and Elisha continued to see each other. "I cannot tell you how unhappy it makes me to think of my affairs being in the mouths of so many strange persons, and the subject of newspaper comment," Maggie wrote in a letter reproduced in her memoir. What distressed her most of all, she added, was the damage such rumors did to Elisha's reputation. "It would grieve me (you must know how much), even were we never to meet again, to hear you spoken of as a person who had no regard for his honor or his word. I am but a simple girl and people might soon forget any idle gossip about me. But you are more widely known and a stain on your honor would be hard to efface." Yet she had "implicit confidence" that Elisha would "think of some right and proper means to silence all this disturbance and meddling."

Ultimately the silencing came from an unwelcome quarter. Elisha's mortified family, seeking to remove any spot of scandal from their son's name, persuaded the *Pennsylvanian* to run a story meant to crush rumors of any engagement to Maggie. Prior to Dr. Kane's departure for the Arctic, the article explained, a donation had been collected from several "liberal-kind-hearted gentlemen for the purpose of educating one of the Fox sisters, a remarkably bright, intelligent girl and worthy of better employment than 'spirit-rapping.' Dr. Kane, feeling somewhat interested from pure motives of humanity subscribed with a sailor's liberality to help the girl. On his return, by invitation of the gentleman superintending her education, he called to witness the improvement of his protégé; and from this simple incident has arisen the engagement story."

Dr. Elisha Kane's largesse to the young lady, the *Pennsylvanian* concluded, was merely the latest example of the "noble liberality of the Kane family."

Dutifully, Elisha remained firm in his insistence that he and Maggie maintain their platonic relationship. Instead of addressing Elisha familiarly as "Lish" or "Ly" in her correspondence, Maggie accordingly began her letters now as "My Dear Brother."

"Promise me once more that you will always love and bless me with a brotherly love," she wrote Elisha in late 1855, "and should fate, as you say, compel us to part, will you not solemnly promise to love and think of me as your own sister."

Weeks earlier, in the aftermath of Elisha's first upsetting visit following his return from the Arctic, Maggie's guardian Ellen Walter had suggested that Maggie stop seeing her former fiancé altogether because of the emotional turmoil.

Mrs. Fox had expressed similar views. Maggie protested, though, that she could not contemplate such a break: To do so was unimaginable, unthinkable, and intolerable, and such thoughts sent her into fits of weeping and dark moods. Attempting to accommodate her daughter, Mrs. Fox even listened patiently to Elisha's explanations for the broken engagement. His own funds were gone, he explained, having been spent to help finance the Arctic expedition; since his return, he had become financially dependent upon his father. Happily, though, he was writing a new book about his Arctic adventures and once it was published he would have enough financial resources to "spurn the interference of friends who had already wrought so much mischief."

But Mrs. Fox had become increasingly uncomfortable. Why, after all, should Elisha dominate Maggie's time—and consume her emotions—when he could not marry her? When he had no right to have asked her in the first place? Politely but firmly she asked Elisha to stop seeing Maggie permanently. It served no purpose, after all, as the ghostwriters of *The Love-Life of Dr. Kane* explained, for him to visit "a young lady whom his family was not willing to receive as his wife, and who might be injured both in her feelings and her reputation by a continuance of his attentions." But passion spoke louder to Elisha than propriety, even in the face of the scandal. Insensitive to the damage his presence was inflicting upon Maggie, he continued to call.

By December 6, Mrs. Fox had lost all patience. Writing Elisha that day, she explained that she had just received the propriety-minded Dr. and Mrs. Gray. "Mrs. Gray has just left my house and you were the theme of our conversation," Mrs. Fox began. Mrs. Gray "begged with tears in her eyes, never to let my daughter see you, or exchange words with you." If he did, added Mrs. Fox, "we would do right to have our friends publish you [defame you] to the world. I from this moment forbid you ever again entering my house. I forbid my daughter from receiving you."

In a rare admission of guilt, she added, "I have done wrong to have allowed Margaretta to see you. It is injuring her hitherto unblemished name. I am her mother and I must protect her and she must obey me....My child is as pure as an angel, and if you are seen coming here the world will censure her."

But Elisha would not accept banishment, "unless, he heard it from Margaret's own lips," according to Maggie's account in *The Love-Life of Dr. Kane.*

When he finally persuaded Maggie to see him, Elisha ruefully admitted that society's harsh opinion about his behavior was justified. Yet in truth, he peevishly insisted it was he, rather than Maggie, who was the "discarded lover." Throwing himself upon his knees, the tormented man then implored, "Speak, Maggie, my destiny is in your hands!"

Once again she replied that in view of his family's opposition, she would never marry Elisha. The situation would make him so unhappy that she would "rather part from him for ever than make him wretched in such a way!" Self-serving as this account from *The Love-Life of Dr. Kane* may be, it was probably an accurate reflection of the advice Mrs. Fox, Ellen Walter, and the Grays gave Maggie.

Still, she could not give him up. As the days grew shorter and colder, Maggie's friends and relatives became increasingly strident in their demands for her to avoid him permanently. The young woman finally addressed another letter to Elisha. "I have seen you for the last time. I have been deceived." She must, she explained, "either give you up from this moment and for ever, or give up those who are very dear to me, and who hold my name and reputation as sacred."

Since their romance was over, Elisha was entitled to the return of his love letters. "One thing do remember," Maggie added plaintively, "you have my love. I believe in your honor and truth, and cannot be changed."

Stung by Maggie's offer to return his love letters—implying that they must have been insincere—Elisha countered, "As to your dear generous offer of returning my letters, I tremble—not at the letters—but at the fear that you have not understood me. I have never distrusted you or even asked for those notes. With or without them, you were always the same to me." He had asked for them only out of fear that they might fall into the wrong hands. "I only felt and feared that suspicious, designing friends or enemies might see and abuse these letters and give me pain and trouble. I fear for them and for you."

In time, Elisha's hunch would prove more correct than either he or Maggie could possibly imagine.

"A Sort of Sanctuary"

We both know, my dearest, dearest that time will,
of course, gradually weaken our love, until at last
all will be as a dream, past forever.
—Maggie Fox to Elisha Kent Kane, August 15, 1856

Between 1853 and 1855 the soaring popularity of spiritualism and widespread reports of its accompanying manifestations—table tippings, automatic writing, spirit music, and dancing lights—led to new demands for scientific investigation.

"Table moving has got into France and Germany, and it is to be hoped that men of science there will do what ours have been too dignified and conservative to attempt: investigate its alleged phenomena and either prove them humbug, or study out their connection with the other facts of the visible world," observed attorney George Templeton Strong in a May 28, 1853, diary notation. "It throws new light on man's faculty of self-deception in relation even to subject of sense. Rochester knocking needs inquiry in the same scientific spirit and for exactly the same reason."

"It is surely one of the most startling events that have occurred for centuries...A new Revelation, hostile to that of the Church and the Bible, finding acceptance on the authority of knocking ghosts and oscillating tables...throwing light on the intellectual caliber and moral tone of the age," he added in another entry two years later.

Henry Raymond of the *New York Times* was equally puzzled. Considering the scientific progress of the 1850s—which brought innovations such as the Bunsen burner, the gyroscope, and the sewing machine motor—Raymond was astonished at the tenacity of spiritualism's advocates.

"Its influence is wider, stronger and deeper than that of any philosophical or socialistic theory, since it appeals to the marvelous in man, and takes hold directly upon the strongest sentiments of his nature," Raymond observed in the *Times*. "In five years it has spread like wild-fire over this Continent so that there is scarcely a village without its mediums and its miracles…it takes the form of a Church organization and has its religious services—its prayers, hymns, its sermons and conference meetings. If it be a delusion, it has misled very many of the intelligent as well as the ignorant."

By 1854, the "many," according to the spiritualists' own estimates, ranged from one to two million Americans. Moreover, there were astonishing varieties in spiritualism's expression. On a six-week trip to the West, Rochester-based medium Reverend Dr. Charles C. Hammond observed in the spiritualist *New Era* that he discovered a wide range of "speaking, pointing and dancing" mediums.

In Athens, Ohio, Jonathan Koons, a self-educated farmer who became a medium, was suddenly directed by the spirits to build a log cabin "spirit room" accommodating seats for twenty people. After starting his séances by playing a fiddle, Koons was joined by a ghostly orchestra that "began to speak orally through…trumpets" and other "spiritual pyrotechnics." A few hundred miles away in Columbus, Ohio, mediums George Walocutt and George Rogers painted portraits of people they never knew—which, eerily, relatives later identified as accurate representations of deceased relatives.

In Boston and Springfield, hundreds who attended the séances of young mediums Daniel Douglas Home, Henry C. Gordon, George Redman, and Rollin Squire testified that they watched those men being lifted into the air by unseen hands and flown over spectators' heads. In Buffalo, a Miss Brooks, "a young and interesting girl of a highly-respectable family," raised spirits who played symphonies brilliantly upon the piano while her own hands avoided the keyboard. In Hartford, Connecticut, crowds of ailing individuals waited at the door of Mrs. Mettler, whose trances were reputed to effect miraculous cures.

Many of the mediums claimed they discovered their clairvoyant powers by chance. Typically, as in the case of erstwhile actress Emma Hardinge—later the author of *Modern American Spiritualism*—the transformation occurred after their first attendance at a séance. Soon after this experience Emma fell into a trance. After awakening and becoming aware of her extraordinary gifts, she felt obliged to become a "public" or professional medium.

Dozens, perhaps hundreds, of mediums now toured the nation, each boasting a unique method for summoning the spirits. Among the best known, according to Hardinge's history, were the blue-eyed, blonde-haired Cora Scott (later Hatch) of Buffalo; a Miss Middlebrook and Miss Sarah Irish, "admirable mediums for tests by seeing, writing, trance"; Harriet Porter, who demonstated a "most wonderful prophetic speaking and seeing"; a Miss Seabring, an excellent table "tipping medium"; and the twelve-year-old Mildred Coole.

So striking was the youth and beauty of these and other female mediums that some skeptical observers attended séances in spite of their doubts. Among them was the anonymous New York City author of the 1854 book *The Rappers,* who, while attending a "grand spiritual circle" in the rooms of a Mrs. C, praised the "spiritual Mediums" as "the fairest part of creation." So lovely were that bevy of young women, he admitted in his book, that "it was enough to make a confirmed Alderman turn spiritual."

The young women, who had already toured Boston, Hartford, and other cities before arriving in New York City, were "a brilliant collection...of large, dark, dreamy and flashing, light and laughing eyes: of glossy ringlets and Madona [sic] curls, black, brown, auburn and golden, clustering on the sides of cheeks rivaling the bloom of the rose, or parted simply over brows, pale, high and

polished as alabaster. And such a collection of white, tiny and ta-
pering hands as were spread out in a circle on that table!"

Spiritualism had an equally vehement chorus of critics, who jeered
at the quality of the spiritual messages as well as the manner of their
delivery. Transcendentalist Ralph Waldo Emerson was increasingly
disgusted with the movement's rapid spread, and denounced it as
a "rat-revelation, the gospel that comes by taps in the wall and
humps in the table-drawer."

Poet James Russell Lowell ridiculed the idea that spirits had the
ability to raise tables and move chairs or sofas. After all, he sardon-
ically observed, respect should be paid to all spiritualists, among
them a certain Judge Wells, a man who was "such a powerful
medium that he has to drive back the furniture from following him
when he goes out, as one might a pack of too affectionate dogs."

Emerson's colleague Henry David Thoreau also snickered at the
movement even though it was popular in his own village: "Con-
cord is just as idiotic as ever in relation to the spirits and their
knockings. Most people here believe in a spiritual world which no
respectable junk-bottle which had not met with a slip would con-
descend to for a moment." In his opinion, those who believed in
spiritualism were simply "idiots, inspired by the cracking of a restless board."

The scientific community was equally disparaging. Dr. Robert
Hare, Professor Emeritus of Chemistry at the University of Pennsylvania, announced in 1853 that he considered it an "act of duty to
his fellow creatures, to bring whatever influence he possessed to the
attempt to stem the tide of 'popular madness' which, in defiance of
reason and science, was fast setting in favor of the gross delusion
called Spiritualism."

To prove his theory, Hare sat through several séances and became so disquieted by the sight of tables moving without apparent
human aid that he launched his own investigation. Before long the

chemist had fashioned several experiments, the most famous of which involved his creation of a "spiritoscope"—an apparatus using zinc balls, metal plates, weights, and an alphabet wheel. To his astonishment, when the medium he selected for the experiment placed her hands upon the spiritoscope's zinc balls, several nearby tables spontaneously moved. After additional experiments Hare became a convert, insisting that the spiritoscope had enabled him to reach the spirits of his father and two sons.

By April 29, 1854, Hare was so thoroughly convinced of the existence of spiritual communion that he attempted to present his findings at a meeting of the American Scientific Association, but was laughed off the floor. The following year he shocked the scientific community again with the publication of his book *Experimental Investigation of the Spirit Manifestations*. In August 1855, during a meeting of the American Association for the Advancement of Science in Albany, the distinguished chemist lost the respect of his colleagues when he demonstrated his new machine.

"The professor spends some hours every day with his hands on a spiritoscope, asking questions of his departed friends...Significant smiles were around; some laughed and some sneered; the professor's old friends turned their heads away with a look of painful pity," wryly observed the *New York Tribune*.

Justice John Worth Edmonds, who in 1853 had become a judge in New York's Court of Appeals, asserted that he too had begun as a skeptic. "For the first four or five months of my investigations my chief inquiry was, 'Is this a reality, or an imposture or delusion?,'" Edmonds wrote in his 1853 book *Spiritualism*. After attending several other séances, he confessed that he was unable to find a logical explanation for spiritualist phenomena. "The sounds were not produced by the instrumentality of any person present," he proclaimed. Nor could Edmonds understand how questions he asked only by thinking about them were telepathically answered by a medium.

Other prominent citizens such as George Templeton Strong continued to question the veracity of spiritualism, but as he grudgingly admitted in his journal it "was a phenomenon about which there's much to say."

꙳

By spring 1854 the prevalence of reports about uncanny spiritualist phenomena appearing in America's cities and towns attracted the attention of the U.S. Congress. On April 17, General James Shields, a senator from Illinois, and Senator Charles Sumner of Massachusetts presented a petition signed by fifteen thousand Americans requesting the appointment of a scientific commission to study spiritualist phenomena.

"The petitioners represent that certain physical and mental phenomena of mysterious import, have become so prevalent in this country and Europe as to engross a large share of public attention," began Senator Shields in an executive session of the Senate. "A partial analysis of these phenomena, attest the existence, first, of an occult force, which is exhibited in sliding, raising...holding, suspending and otherwise disturbing ponderable bodies apparently in direct opposition to the acknowledged laws of matter, and transcending the...power of the human mind....The memorialists [spiritualists] while thus disagreeing as to the cause, concur in the opinion as to the occurrence of the alleged phenomena; and in view of their origin, nature and...the interests of mankind, demand... a patient, rigid, scientific investigation, and request the appointment of a scientific commission for that purpose."

Ultimately a "pleasant debate" followed during which the senators suggested that the petition be referred to one of several possible groups—an organization of three thousand clergymen, the Committee on Foreign Relations, the Committee on Military Affairs, or perhaps the Committee on Post Offices and Post Roads, if only "because there may be a possibility of establishing a spiritual telegraph between the material and spiritual worlds."

Lawmakers ultimately tabled the petition, even as a new debate raged among the nation's clergy. Many clergymen became alarmed

Rochester around 1850 from a painting by G. G. Lange Darnstadt.
Courtesy of the Rochester Historical Society

Margaret Smith Fox. *Courtesy of the Trustees of the Boston Public Library*

John Fox. *Courtesy of the Trustees of the Boston Public Library*

HOUSE WHERE SPIRITUALISM
ORIGINATED MARCH 31, 184[ ]

NEAR NEWARK, N.Y.

The "spook house" on Hydesville Road, Newark, New York, where American
spiritualism began on March 31, 1848. *Courtesy of Robert L. Hoeltzel*

Maggie (left) and Katy Fox in 1852 from a daguerreotype by Thomas H. Easterly.
Permission of the Missouri Historical Society

Fagnani's famous portrait of
Maggie in 1853 painted for
her beau, Elisha Kent Kane,
just before his second
Arctic expedition.
*Courtesy of the Rochester
Historical Society*

Engraving of Katy Fox as a young woman.
Courtesy of the Rochester New York Public Library, Local History Division

Portrait of the Fox sisters from the early 1850s.
(Left to right) Maggie, Katy, and Leah.
Courtesy of the Rochester Historical Society

Leah Fox Underhill, leading force behind the rise of American spiritualism, around 1863.

Courtesy of the Trustees of the Boston Public Library

An engraving from about 1854 of a medium levitating a table during a séance.

Permission of the General Research Division, the New York Public Library, Astor, Lenox, and Tilden Foundations

Horace Greeley, editor of the *New York Tribune*. Ultimately dismissive of spiritualism, he remained a loyal friend to Maggie and her family throughout his life. *Library of Congress, LC-USCZ4-3888*

Daniel Underhill, president of the New York Fire Insurance Company and doting third husband of Leah Fox. *Courtesy of the Trustees of the Boston Public Library*

Portrait of shipping magnate Henry Grinnell, sponsor of the Second Grinnell Expedition led by Elisha Kent Kane. He and his son Cornelius served as guardians for Maggie Fox during Kane's Arctic voyage of 1853–56. *Library of Congress, LC-USZ62-110168*

A posthumous likeness of Elisha Kent Kane, painted from a photograph that was taken when Elisha returned from his second Arctic expedition. *Permission of the American Philosophical Society*

Elisha Kent Kane
daguerreotype 1855–56
by Mathew B. Brady.
*Permission of the Elisha Kent
Kane Historical Society*

Spiritualists flock to meetings at the Lily Dale Assembly in upstate New York in 1904.
Permission of the Lily Dale Assembly

on June 10 when former Wisconsin governor Nathaniel P. Tall-madge became a charter member of the Society for the Diffusion of Spiritual Knowledge.

"Your pulpits—and we speak kindly when we speak of them, for they have a holy office...have launched forth invectives. The cry of delusion and chicanery has been heard all over the land...," stated the Society's charter. "Policy was adopted...not only from the pulpits, but by the religious press of this country, namely that evil spirits have visited the earth still further to delude deluded mortals. What pity!...It is very strange, if they believe this thing— that evil spirits can come to do evil on their earth—that good spir-its will not be permitted by the good God also to come upon this earth to effect good purposes. We profess to believe both these propositions. We leave you to examine the subject for yourselves."

The doctrine was signed by Tallmadge—Maggie's old friend— and other prominent citizens, including Chief Justice Joseph Williams of Iowa, General Edward Bullard of New York, industri-alist Horace H. Day, and the Honorable Warren Chase of Wiscon-sin. (Annoyed by its exclusivity, Eliab Capron, the Fox sisters' first promoter, suggested that the organization was more determined to flaunt its elite membership before the public than to incorporate "the earliest and most experienced in the investigation.")

Sixteen months later, the battle grew even more vituperative as a growing number of religious leaders embraced spiritualism— among them prominent Unitarian ministers Thomas Wentworth Higginson and Theodore Parker. "Clergymen, formerly preachers of evangelical denominations, are now lecturing on Spiritualism and its wildest heresies to large congregations," observed William Raymond, founding editor of the *New York Times,* on October 16, 1855. "The whole West, and to a greater extent the whole country, has been deeply infiltrated."

Equally disquieting was the association between spiritualism and free love. Dubbed the "Free-Spirit-Love doctrines" by the New York press, its advocates, explained Horace Greeley's *New York*

Tribune with alarm, "believed that each man or woman has a natural, justly indefeasible right to dissolve his or her existing sexual relation to a person of the other sex, if such he or she shall at any time have contracted and enter into a new relation under the guidance of his or her spiritual affinities." To consult those affinities, lamented the *Tribune,* six hundred men and women were said to meet twice a week in New York at their love club at 555 Broadway.

On October 18, incited by the *Tribune* story and by suspicious members of the local clergy, two New York police captains and a city councilman broke into a meeting at 555 Broadway, arresting its members and its outspoken leader, Stephen Pearl Andrews. By the following week the case had been thrown out of court after Andrews denied that sexuality was a goal of the spiritualist meetings. Seasoned civil libertarian that he was, Andrews also successfully argued that since free love "breaks no man's leg nor picks his pocket" it could not be considered a crime.

Outraged at the outcome, the *Tribune* carped, "We do not know that any of Mr. Andrews's supporters disclaim the 'Free Love' theory.... That same 'free love' is in our view a most pernicious, perilous, destructive sophism sure to work the ruin of thousands."

Thereafter the accusation that spiritualism fostered free love was often repeated. By the late 1850s several former mediums even stepped forward to make such claims themselves. One of the most outspoken was Dr. Benjamin Hatch, a middle-aged dentist who in 1856 had married sixteen-year-old Cora Scott of Buffalo who was already famous for her gifts as a trance speaker. Hatch soon dominated Cora, her profits, and the social freedoms she once enjoyed.

By 1859, Cora was so miserable in her marriage—and the dentist so distraught by her cooled attitude—that both of them filed divorce actions. For years the case dragged through the courts, providing juicy copy for the newspapers.

Spiritualism was "depravity" itself, the embittered husband railed in his highly publicized 1859 booklet *The Hatch Divorce Case.*

Among "nearly all mediums...there is...a perpetual tendency to form extra-marital relations."

~✤~

In contrast to the sorrow that spiritualism brought upon Maggie Fox, her sister Leah seemed to thrive upon her work. Surrounded by admiring members of the New York Circle and followers clamoring for séances, Leah enjoyed a flourishing spiritualist practice during the years that Maggie lived in Crookville. Just a few months before Calvin's death, the anonymous author of a critical book, *The Rappers,* described forty-one-year-old Leah as "a fine-looking woman, portly in person and bearing, with jet-black hair, and an intellectual expression of countenance. She was richly dressed, and bore in her hand a gold watch, to which was appended a massive gold chain."

The watch, the writer wryly observed, had less to do with the spirits than with schedules, noting that "each mortal in Rapping Circles is...apt to talk so long to the spirits, that he interferes with the rest of his brother seekers after spiritual knowledge."

Time, even in Leah's spirit world, was money—just as it had been during the life of her favorite spiritual telegrapher, Benjamin Franklin.

During those same years, Katy had grown into a woman, though the author of *The Rappers* thought the seventeen-year-old to be "very young." Even in consideration of Katy's tender age, her "claim to beauty cannot be disputed. Her hair, which is black as the wing of a raven, was parted in two simple curls, after the Madona [sic] style, giving striking effect to a fair forehead of an intellectual character...."

Despite Katy's busy spiritualist practice, Maggie did not volunteer to resume her old activities when she returned home to live with Mrs. Fox and Katy. Instead, she sidestepped anything to do with spiritualism, and spent her days on domestic tasks, her studies, music lessons, and visits with friends—activities that Katy gradually came to resent, especially since she was now the sole supporter of the household. For all of Katy's previous fondness for Elisha, she could no more approve of his recent treatment of Maggie any more than she could condone her sister's ongoing communication with him.

Elisha sternly advised his former fiancée that she must continue to ignore Katy's resentments because she had promised him to permanently renounce spiritualism. "Do avoid 'spirits.' I cannot bear to think of you as engaged in a course of wickedness and deception," he wrote. "Indeed, Maggie, it is very sad. Say so to Kate."

❧

No sooner was Elisha again ensconced in Philadelphia than his father, Judge Kane, urged him to dump his publisher Harper and Brother, which had brought out *The U.S. Grinnell Expedition,* in favor of the more aggressive Philadelphia firm of Childs and Peterson. There was only one hitch: The new publisher demanded that Elisha's book on his second Arctic journey be written quickly. Barely recovered from that trial, the doctor-explorer only reluctantly conceded to that demand from his ambitious editor, George William Childs. Still more reluctantly he also conceded to another Childs request—that he write a more popular book than the scientific account Elisha originally envisioned. Childs argued that his new celebrity status made his book a likely bestseller.

To capitalize upon that status, however, meant that Elisha had to spend his days at his desk, transforming the less savory details of his adventures and the details of Eskimo life into popular prose. At first it went well; by keeping long hours and working well into the night, Elisha was able to send Childs and Peterson three hundred edited pages from his journal by mid-December 1855.

Encouraged by the author's productivity, Childs was soon pitching *Arctic Explorations: The Second Grinnell Expedition In Search of Sir John Franklin 1853, 54, 55* to the U.S. Congress, hoping, rather cheekily, that senators and congressmen would purchase copies to distribute to local schools and colleges as a patriotic gesture. When the plan was scuttled, Childs's next maneuver was excerpting the manuscript in newspapers immediately after Elisha completed each section.

But even while focusing his energies almost entirely upon the book, Elisha found time to maintain contact with Maggie. At Christmas he sent her and Katy bonbons. Later that winter, he visited several times, once for a sleigh-ride with Maggie and Katy along the wide paths of New York's still rustic Bloomingdale Road (now Upper Broadway). How much Mrs. Fox knew—or chose to know—about these meetings and the letters that accompanied them is unclear, but by March 23 she again felt compelled to prohibit Elisha from contacting Maggie.

"A letter was addressed to my daughter, Margaret, which, under the circumstances, I deemed it proper to open and read. It is best for the happiness and interest of my child that you should discontinue your visits and also leave off writing to her. My motives, I hope you will understand, and respect my feelings," Mrs. Fox declared.

Chagrined, Elisha diplomatically wrote Maggie, explaining her mother's discovery of his letter and enclosing a copy of his own note to Mrs. Fox. If the matron had the "slightest objection" to their pre-arranged meeting, it read, he would cancel it. Moreover, even if she allowed them to see each other, he promised "I had better make this my last visit," if only for the sake of Maggie's "reputation."

Elisha sorrowfully confided to Maggie that he considered himself only "half a gentleman" because of the oversimplifications he was forced to write about his Arctic explorations. Unhappily, as he wrote Childs, he was trying to be "more popular and gaseous—this latter inflated quality in excess. Most certainly my efforts to make this book readable will destroy its permanency and injure me. It is a sacrifice."

Even after promising Mrs. Fox that he would no longer see Maggie, he did not want her to forget him. On April 21, 1856, Elisha sent Maggie his engraved portrait. "Although a mere trifle, it may serve as an evidence of my high respect for your character, and will, I hope, assure you of my continued and brotherly interest in your welfare," he wrote.

Brotherly interest? If Maggie sent any response, Elisha did not preserve it. Then, something incredible happened, although later Elisha's family would hotly disclaim it. Several days after his engraving arrived, according to Maggie's memoir, Elisha arrived unannounced at the Foxes' house following the funeral of a friend. No one was home but the maid, Mary. Uncertain about protocol, she showed the gentleman into the front parlor. Hearing Maggie enter the house, Elisha hid behind the parlor door and as she entered the room, surprised her, and clasped her in his arms. "My own Maggie,—you are again mine—the betrothed wife of Dr. Kane! What more could you ask?" he said tenderly, with tears in his eyes, repeatedly kissing the surprised young woman's head.

Then, Maggie's memoir continued, Elisha removed a ring from his hand, which he claimed he had found in the Arctic, and placed it on Maggie's finger to commemorate their renewed engagement. In still another token of commitment, he also presented his sweetheart with a locket engraved with his late brother Willie's initials and containing his hair. No longer, Elisha explained, "did he care about anything but his love for Maggie." In fact, "He cared no longer…for the world's opinion or its sneers: his beloved was all in all to him."

What precipitated Elisha's new proposal is unclear: Perhaps, as Maggie's memoir suggested, his friend's funeral pointed out the brevity of earthly happiness. The memoir also did not explain why Maggie immediately accepted his offer. Implied but left unstated was her ongoing passion for Elisha. "I will wear our locket next to my heart and love it for ever and ever," Maggie promised Elisha. "It shall be my rosary. I'll wear it to save me from evil."

❧

After four anguished months of separation, Maggie and Elisha finally came into a happier time. Somehow, in spite of the explorer's pressed schedule, he managed several trips to New York, during which they enjoyed drives, dinners, lectures, and theatrical performances together. "I know I ought to be in Philadelphia," Elisha wrote while still in New York, "but I really cannot bear to leave." Somehow, Mrs. Fox must have become reconciled to their engagement.

In another letter from Philadelphia, Elisha explained that the "Royal Family"—Maggie's snide nickname for his relatives—had compelled him to remain "in our quiet city to attend a ball." The coming Friday he was obliged to "talk science and stupidity to a society of learned philosophers...[but] truly I had rather be with you, resting after my hard work like a boy in his holiday time."

This was a new Maggie. Older and no longer willing to hold back her feelings, Maggie expressed herself freely. "Then you are doomed to pass another day in Philadelphia," she wrote with dismay. "It is now five days since you left, and it seems a whole year to me. Oh, my lover and friend, hasten! My hours grow irksome when you stay so long!"

Again, as in the first days of their romance, Elisha grew playful and became indifferent to the gossip. One night, while attending the opera, Maggie misplaced her handkerchief. Elisha responded impulsively. "Here—take mine—pet lamb," reaching into his pocket and presenting one of his own, oblivious to the curious stares around him.

Maggie's enjoyed Elisha's irreverent debunking of the stiff-necked society that had so vehemently attempted to crush their romance. One night Elisha entertained her and Katy with an imitation of a stuffy society Philadelphia matron, dressed in a lacy cap and glasses peering down at an enormous book.

That spring Maggie, Katy, and their mother moved to a larger home at 50 East Twenty-second Street. Often, when Katie or Mrs. Fox had other visitors, Maggie and her suitor would retreat to a prettily decorated parlor. To him that third-floor room seemed "as a sort of sanctuary: a retreat to which we are driven by mischief-making eyes and tongues. There like wounded deer, we escape from the hunters; and if we, both of us, are conscious of doing no wrong, whose business is it if we seek a shelter?"

True to her promise to avoid the spirits, Maggie spent her days on her lessons and her evenings visiting friends, several of whom disapproved of her renewed relationship with Elisha. Fearful that his once-skittish sweetheart might bolt, Elisha wrote from Philadelphia, "Maggie, Maggie, if you are ever tempted to forget old times and false friends misrepresent me, go and read this letter, and see if for many years I have not proved myself a true-self-sacrificing friend and lover."

While working hard on the book he was counting down the three weeks until he could see Maggie again. "Even while at my student's desk, pondering over matters too dull for your bright brain, thoughts, sweet thoughts, distress me," he confessed. Equally distressing were the waves of exhaustion that swept over the doctor-explorer from time to time, leaving him weak and depleted of vitality—symptoms suggesting that he still suffered from the effects of rheumatic fever. All too often when Elisha and Maggie met that spring and summer, as she recalled in her memoir, her fiancé asked her to place her hand upon his heart to feel its violent palpitations.

Elisha nevertheless attributed his declining health to the grueling task of writing. "Authordom has again overdone me," he complained to his publisher Childs on June 7. "I shall have to take a spell [a rest] soon."

By July, Elisha had handed in a completed draft of the *Arctic Explorations.* "With little spirit of congratulation and much weariness, I send you this preface which completes my task," he wrote his editor sourly. "Drained and unaccountably weary...Now that the holy day is at hand, I am ungrateful enough to complain that it finds me without capacity to enjoy it."

Even a rushed trip to New York later that month did little to improve Elisha's spirits or his health. He was apparently in such poor health that he and Cornelius Grinnell traveled to the beaches of Long Island in hopes that the chill waters and sun-filled air would revive him. Yet nothing seemed to help. "I get weaker every day," Elisha wrote Childs anxiously. "I tried Long Island bathing with my friend Grinnell, but could not stand it."

Maggie and Elisha were about to endure still another long separation. Maggie was taking a family trip to Canada with Mrs. Fox to visit another of her sisters, Elizabeth, who was in poor health.

Far more daunting was Elisha's plan to travel to Switzerland, known for its high altitudes and cool mountain air, which he hoped would restore his health just as the chill climate of Greenland had. After he regained his vitality, he planned to stop in England on his return trip to the United States. The latter would be purely a business trip, one that Elisha had grudgingly agreed to at Lady Franklin's insistence.

While her husband's death had been confirmed in 1854 by explorer Sir John Rae, Franklin's devoted widow remained determined to learn more about her husband's final days in the Far North. Coincidentally, Franklin's brig *Resolute*, which had been frozen in the Arctic ice for two years, had drifted south to Baffin Bay, where it was retrieved and ultimately returned to England. In her characteristically high-handed way, Lady Franklin proposed that Elisha return to the Arctic with that ship for still another investigative expedition.

Elisha had briefly considered the idea, but flagging health, deadline pressures of completing *Arctic Explorations,* and his new engagement to Maggie mitigated against it. As the date for his departure approached, Elisha decided to change his itinerary, postponing his Switzerland sojourn until after he visited Lady Franklin in London to support her campaign at the British Admiralty to fund another Arctic expedition.

By August 1856, realizing that he might depart for England before Maggie returned from Canada, Elisha clung to her promise of betrothal. "You must remember that you are mine...you must hold yourself sacred, as my wife should be; there must be no flirting; you must receive no attention from gentlemen," he said to her during their last meeting in New York, according to Maggie's memoir.

"Shall I then disclose our engagement?" Maggie asked, half-teasing.

To Elisha her question was no laughing matter. "Yes—if brought to it," he said.

On August 15, 1856, the eve of Maggie's departure for Canada, she wrote Elisha all that was in her heart. "With you, my dearest, went my life...I felt alone. Sad and melancholy, Who would not feel gloomy when all they loved had gone and perhaps forever?... I love—I worship you."

❧

Fretting over Elisha's health and deeply missing him, Maggie found solace writing letters from Canada. Now, stripped of the mask of pseudo-sophistication and flirtation she once wore as a spiritualist, this was Maggie at her core, a child-woman who was still as guileless and dependent upon her elders for advice and succor as any other dutiful Victorian young lady.

One incident in particular points up her unworldliness. On August 15, 1856, after she, Katy, their mother, and their servant, Emma, boarded a train in New York and arrived in Syracuse, Mrs. Fox disembarked to check on their baggage in another car. Suddenly, the train pulled out of the station, leaving Mrs. Fox behind.

"Three more distracted girls than Katie, Emma and I, were never known," Maggie wrote Elisha, "perfectly unacquainted with traveling, and then we were destitute of one penny to pay our passage." The conductor, taking pity upon the hysterical trio, suggested that they get off at Rochester to wait for Mrs. Fox, whom he assured them would arrive on the next train from Syracuse. Somehow Maggie and her companions managed to secure rooms at a nearby Rochester hotel before returning to the station to await Mrs. Fox.

"The cars arrived punctually at the hour mentioned; but our

mother was not there. We went back perfectly crazy," Maggie recalled. Again, at the next arrival time—the last train of the day—
the three young women returned to the station. But still, after the
train steamed to a halt, there was no Mrs. Fox. Despairing, the trio,
having no other option, retired to the hotel for the night.

Mrs. Fox did not arrive until the next morning. While Maggie
failed to explain the reasons for her mother's delay in that letter, the
prospect of abandonment had horrified her. After that, Maggie
explained, "we were very careful...not to let her get off the cars
again without us."

Elisha responded from New York, advising Maggie and her family to avoid the heat wave that was sickening hundreds of city residents by remaining out of town until early September. "I myself am
very sick, and go this afternoon to Brattleboro, Vermont," he admitted. Still Maggie was not to worry because he would return and
spend several days in New York City before he was to sail. "You will
see me again before I cross the water, for I cannot leave until the
tenth [of October]; and as soon as your letter reaches me, will hasten to New York."

In spite of her fiancé's promise, Maggie continued to brood,
longing so intensely for Elisha that she stayed up one night until
dawn to write him. "Without you all is darkness, and every place
seems a grave. You ask if I mix in company? No, no! I join no merry
scenes. 'Lish, I have not laughed since we parted. By the time we
meet again I fear I shall quite have forgotten to laugh..."

Knowing Elisha's desire for her to lead a discreet and quiet life,
Maggie could not help adding a teasing note: "You will clothe me
in the habiliments of a nun, and send me to a convent to count my
rosary." Then, quite lovingly, she closed by assuring her sweetheart
that "on the wings of angels, I send you ten thousand kisses."

A week later, when Maggie and her family left Canada to visit
her brother, David, in Arcadia, the lovesick young woman wrote
again, explaining that she and her family planned to stay in upstate
New York longer than originally intended.

"I wish to see you again," she wrote Elisha. But since her mother had other obligations at David's home, it fell to Maggie to spend much of her time with the recalcitrant John Fox, who, having shunned spiritualism from the start, had stoically remained behind in Arcadia.

By attending to her father, Maggie wrote Elisha, she was doing a good deed, demonstrating the unselfishness that he admired and would expect in his future wife. Consequently, she added, she was doing her best to "overrule my feelings . . . [and] subdue my loneliness for I shall know that I am doing right and living once more free from the sting of an unhappy conscience."

What clearer signal could she give Elisha than to fit herself to his goals and compensate for the sins of selfishness and greed wrought by spiritualism? "I trust that by my kindness and denial of many pleasures, I can atone for my misery and ere long look upon myself as a free happy girl," Maggie added, echoing the refrain from one of Elisha's earlier poems that lamented how spiritualism had ruined her youthful joy.

❧

In preparation for Maggie's return to New York on September 23 or 24, Elisha arrived at her house to insure that everything was in order. Fearful he might miss the exact moment of Maggie's arrival, he even placed a note in her room, instructing her to send a secret message when she arrived. Ultimately there was no need for worry; on a hunch he arrived within minutes of Maggie.

As a welcome-home present, Elisha gave Maggie a bound volume of the galleys of his soon-to-be published book, *Arctic Explorations*. Later when they were finally alone, he told her about a diamond bracelet he had ordered from Tiffany's. Knowing that the expense of such a gift would immediately elicit rumors, Elisha exclaimed to his beaming fiancée, "They will all know now, Maggie, that I want it for my betrothed."

Now, too, finally feeling assured of Elisha's love, the once-restrained Maggie prepared a surprise of her own. One evening when her fiancé arrived for a visit, Elisha was told that she was not at home. "Is it possible…when she knew I was coming—and only a day or two before I must leave her, too!" Elisha exclaimed, sinking unhappily into a chair.

Suddenly Maggie darted out of a nearby closet, giggling and approaching him in a seductive and exotic costume. Enchanted, Elisha decided that he must preserve the moment: He would have Maggie photographed in that outfit. She was woman eternal, Eve, the enchanting nymphs of Greek myths—and more. To preserve that image, Elisha carefully instructed the photographer to have the picture taken on a "large plate—figure erect-complete Profile—Eyelids drooping, Countenance pensive and looking down."

By the next morning Maggie was having second thoughts. Was her costume too bold—too revealing for a proper lady? Hearing his fiancée's ambivalence, Elisha dashed off a note. "Dearest Pet," it read. "Do dress at once, and have the ambrotype taken. I will come up in less than an hour and see to your costume. Don't be afraid of your neck and shoulders. I want you to look like a Circe, for you have already changed me into a wild boar."

Elisha now addressed Maggie as if they were married, heightening subsequent confusion about their true marital situation. A few nights before his voyage, according to *The Love-Life of Dr. Kane*, Elisha arrived at Maggie's house and shared his anxieties with her. He worried that he might die young—perhaps while still overseas. "If I send for you, Maggie, will you come to me?" Elisha asked. "Certainly I will," Maggie responded solicitously.

"I fear you would hesitate," he admitted, "and yet you know you are my own—my wife! You remember what I have told you!" After a short pause, Elisha asked Maggie if she would like him to repeat his vow of marriage before her mother. Taking that pledge before a group of witnesses, he solemnly explained, would legally make them man and wife.

"Such a declaration, in the presence of witnesses, is sufficient to constitute a legal and binding marriage," Elisha said, according to *The Love-Life of Dr. Kane.* It was, he added, "a marriage as firm as if the ceremony took place before a magistrate." (To further persuade readers, the book's footnotes include citations from eight legal briefs.)

"Would you be willing *now* to enter into such a bond?" Elisha asked Maggie, looking deep into her eyes. She nodded.

Within moments, the couple had summoned Katie, Mrs. Fox, a servant, and an unidentified friend into the parlor. Standing next to Maggie, Elisha placed his right hand in hers, while his left hand encircled her tiny waist and declared, "Maggie is my wife, and I am her husband. Wherever we are, she is mine, and I am hers. Do you understand and consent to this, Maggie?"

With that mutual exchange of vows, Elisha and Maggie were wed. The marriage was as legitimate as one that had been performed in a church, Elisha explained to Mrs. Fox, promising her and Maggie that it would be publicly announced when he returned from Europe the following May.

⁂

Was Maggie and Elisha's impulsive and unorthodox marriage ceremony consummated in name alone? *The Love-Life of Dr. Kane* offers only vague hints rather than definitive answers. The second of the book's eight footnotes on the legitimacy of a marriage witnessed without benefit of a magistrate suggests that the couple may have remained celibate: "It is very clear that the marriage contract is valid and binding if made by words *de presenti,* though it be not followed by cohabitation."

Even so, the couple might have shared some intimate time together before Elisha's departure. The first hint is a note written the day after the ceremony by Dr. Kane to the new "Mrs. Kane." While obliged to attend a farewell dinner with some naval officers, Elisha intended to see Maggie afterward. "Will seven o'clock find you at home?" he wrote.

A second note written the next night—perhaps the last before Elisha's departure—was addressed to his "Dear Wife" and requested a meeting at 10:30 P.M. "I have a capital excuse for your mother," he wrote quixotically. "Do not say no, but send word the earliest hour, and I'll be with you."

On or around the time of the wedding, Elisha presented Maggie with the Tiffany's diamond bracelet. To insure their uninterrupted correspondence during his trip, he also gave her special envelopes—lined with muslin to hide her handwriting from unfriendly eyes—addressed to his London hotel. One of them, to be sent in an emergency signaling that Maggie needed his immediate return, had stars on its corners and was addressed to Henry Grinnell's English company in Liverpool.

Amid preparations for their future lives together, Elisha repeatedly dwelled upon death. "Maggie, what if I should die away from you!" he lamented. "Oh, my own Maggie, could I but die in your arms, I would ask for no more!" It was not death *per se* that he feared. "I can part from all the rest,—even from my mother—with calmness; it is parting with you, Maggie, that kills me!"

Elisha's obsession with death must have alarmed her. Later that night when his friend Morton arrived at the door to bring Elisha back to his hotel, Maggie greeted him mournfully. "Remember, Morton—take good care of the Doctor," she begged Elisha's faithful friend.

With little time left, Elisha took measures to insure Maggie's financial security if he did not return. In the event of his death, he had already informed Mrs. Fox, he had provided for Maggie in his will—a message he repeated to Maggie on Saturday morning, October 11, the day of his departure for England. The legacy, Elisha carefully explained, had been placed in a special trust added to his will that was signed and witnessed before Henry and Sarah Grinnell at their Bond Street home a day earlier.

Clinging to Maggie until the last minute, Elisha finally tore away from his bride and boarded the waiting carriage. Yet he still had Maggie's image before him—on the seat of the cab was Fagnani's portrait, which he planned to bring to England.

An hour or so later, Elisha appeared for a second time before Maggie. In a final poignant parting, he asked her to stand in the doorway so that he could see her until the last moment as his carriage pulled away. Then, suddenly, a few feet up the street, Elisha ordered the driver to stop and wait for him while he walked back to Maggie's house. He had, he explained when he reached his surprised sweetheart, forgotten to take her ambrotype, which he planned to have copied in oil by an English artist.

Gazing upon Maggie's tear-filled face, Elisha broke down and questioned the wisdom of the trip. "It is for you to decide, Maggie!" he cried. "My passage is taken, but that is nothing. Tell me, shall I go, or stay?"

This was not the first time Elisha had asked such a question, at least according to *The Love-Life of Dr. Kane*. But once again Maggie agreed that he was obliged to go.

❧

The *Baltic* steamed into Liverpool on Wednesday, October 22, 1856. After resting for two days at the Adelphi Hotel, a favorite of American tourists, Elisha wrote Maggie, "I have just time to catch the steamer, dear Tutie [one of his pet nicknames for her], to tell you of my safe arrival and to beg you write should you need anything. Pardon the haste of this letter and believe me always as of old."

Elisha's brevity had been deliberate. In an effort to avoid upsetting Maggie, he did not mention that he had remained for two days at the hotel to recover from a severe cold and bronchial cough. Feeling somewhat better, Elisha insisted upon leaving for London but, to his friend Morton's growing alarm, he was spiking a high fever by the time they arrived.

At the last minute, Edward Sabine—later Sir Edward Sabine, a prominent astronomer, geophysicist, and veteran of several Arctic expeditions himself—persuaded Elisha to scuttle plans to remain at a London hotel and hosted him in his own home. But for all of Sabine's hospitality, Elisha soon realized that he had made a mistake traveling to England before recovering in Switzerland. London's dank and coal-dust-polluted air, described so vividly in Dickens's novels, was a difficult enough environment for the healthy, but had dire implications for someone as ill as Elisha. Almost immediately Elisha contemplated boarding the next boat for a warmer climate—perhaps nearby Madeira, Algiers, or even back across the Atlantic to the West Indies.

Within a day of his arrival, however, Lady Franklin swept back into town. No sooner did the charming and still-handsome fifty-eight-year-old brunette present herself to Elisha at Sabine's home than she began pressing for his public support for a third Arctic expedition. Lady Franklin was so bent on her purpose that Elisha's ailing condition seemed to make little impression upon her. The widow insisted upon visiting him repeatedly at his bedside, badgering the Arctic hero with her plans for the new voyage. "She comes here daily and kisses 'my pale forehead,'" Elisha wrote Judge Kane. "Dear Father, the woman would use me if she could, even now."

Such a voyage, he repeatedly explained to Lady Franklin, was an impossibility because he intended to depart for Madeira as soon as possible to recover his health. The only reason Franklin's widow finally agreed to his plan, Elisha bitterly added in that same letter, was to facilitate his return to England. She did not seem to grasp the fact that Elisha had no interest in leading a third Arctic expedition.

Within a few days Elisha had regained enough strength to attend a Lords of the Admiralty reception given in his honor, where he was feted for his courage and contributions to knowledge about the Arctic. Five days later he suffered another setback. This time Elisha's health deteriorated so rapidly that another English friend, William Cross, brought Elisha to his country home, Champion Hill, for fresh air and insisted that he see Royal Physician Sir Henry

Holland. The doctor diagnosed his illness as another attack of rheumatic fever; a few days later Sir Holland saw him again, this time in consultation with Dr. Thomas Watson, and together they urged the explorer to leave London as quickly as possible for the sunny climate of Cuba.

By then, even Lady Franklin was so shaken by Elisha's health that she urgently wrote Cornelius Grinnell—then in France on business for his father Henry—begging him to come to England. The widow was demoralized, having lost her plea for Madeira and Elisha's support for a third expedition. As her faithful niece and secretary, Sophia Cracroft, wrote Henry Grinnell, "I cannot tell you how unhappy and absorbed my aunt has been by Dr. Kane's illness."

Meanwhile, in New York, Maggie wrote daily to Elisha. In early November she finally received Elisha's rushed note from Liverpool, but that was all. Unknown to Maggie, none of her letters sent to her lover's hotel in London had been forwarded to him.

By November 10, Elisha had grown so weak that he was unable to attend a long-anticipated meeting of the Royal Geographical Society in his honor. The next day when Cornelius arrived and gazed upon Elisha's white face and wasted body, he immediately booked passage for him and Morton on the *Orinoco,* scheduled to sail to Cuba on November 17.

Despite his own medical training and first-hand experience with rheumatic fever, Elisha seemed unaware that he was suffering from a new attack, perhaps because, in an effort to calm him, Drs. Holland and Watson had insisted he was suffering from nothing more than a severe chest cold. Somehow, if only through the power of denial, Elisha believed them—or at least pretended that he did. "My inability to throw it off is explained by my extensive want of power and this wretched land of fogs," he wrote to a friend.

Behind the scenes, however, urgent letters and telegrams about Elisha's illness were crisscrossing the Atlantic between Cornelius, his father Henry, Lady Franklin, and Judge Kane. On November 16 or 17, Cornelius escorted his invalided friend and Morton to Southampton to board the *Orinoco*. In New York, Henry Grinnell, having witnessed Elisha's last bout of rheumatic fever, feared for his survival. "My heart is bad, bad, bad, so is that of Mrs. G and all my family. I am preparing my mind for the worst. May God in his infinite mercy avert so great an affliction as depriving us of your noble son," he wrote Judge Kane on November 18.

From shipboard, with badly swollen fingers, Elisha wrote Maggie the only other letter she would receive from her new husband. "Dear Tutie: I am quite sick and have gone to Havana; only one week from New York. I have received no letters from you; but write at once to E. K. Kane, care of American Consul, Havana."

When she received his note a week later, the words ran through Maggie like an electric shock. Why had her beloved Elisha not received any of her letters? She had been waiting to hear from him since she received his hasty note from Liverpool. And she had written him every day. Had someone—perhaps a suspicious relative—intercepted her letters and then forbidden Elisha to write? Or had Elisha's health declined so rapidly that he simply could not write at all?

Exacerbating her alarm were bulletins that suddenly appeared almost daily in the press about Elisha's illness. "Newsboys shouted in the streets of New York the news of his critical condition. Oh, my God! It was anguish to my ears!" Maggie recalled in a *New York Herald* story years later. She penned a letter to Elisha in Cuba immediately.

"Your welcome little note was received this morning," she wrote guardedly. "You can only imagine my feelings when I heard that your physicians had ordered you to go to St. Thomas [a port of call before reaching Havana, Cuba]. I only hope that you may soon recover. I would give worlds to see you, but can hardly expect to have that pleasure till May, as our climate is so awful for invalids...I am not happy when you are away."

Then, unable to resist hinting at her emotions, she plaintively added, "Could I only see you, I would say much that I cannot write. In love yours faithfully Margaret."

~❊~

It was unlikely that Elisha read that letter because on Saturday, December 20, while aboard the *Orinoco,* he suffered a stroke. The blow, which paralyzed Elisha's right arm and leg, left him unable to speak. Within a few hours, as often happens with stroke victims, Elisha recovered partial use of his right limbs, but seemed confused and his speech remained thick and garbled, according to Morton, his attendant.

In Philadelphia, members of his family made hasty preparations to join him in Havana. Elisha's second brother, Thomas, the abolitionist, departed first. He arrived in Havana in time to meet Elisha and Morton and had his brother transported to a nearby hotel. Courtroom duties prevented Judge Kane from traveling to Cuba, but on January 7, 1857, his wife, Jane, and their other physician son, John, set sail.

In New York, Maggie waited helplessly, still having heard nothing. Again and again, she dashed off letters to her beloved. One of the most anguished, preserved in *The Love-Life of Dr. Kane,* read, "Why have you not written? Or if you were too ill to write, why have you not given Morton orders to do so?...only think how very cruel it is in you to leave me to all manner of awful imaginings!"

Maggie finally reached out to Henry Grinnell for news. He gingerly explained that since several members of Elisha's family were in Havana, they likely screened his correspondence. Her letters had probably been discarded before Elisha could see them.

Maggie decided to take matters into her own hands. She must, she told her mother, sail to Havana to see Elisha for herself. Mrs. Fox booked passage for Maggie and herself on a steamer for February.

Two thousand miles south, Elisha languished in a hotel bed, by then so feeble that his brothers, mother, and Morton took turns nursing him around the clock. At his request, his distraught mother Jane read to him from the Bible, much as she had done when he was a child. He seemed to take a turn for the better in late January, and the local doctors agreed he was stable enough to return to the United States.

But the bad winter weather of 1857—it was one of the worst years of the decade—delayed their travel plans. Consequently Elisha and his family were still in Havana on Saturday, February 10, when he suffered a second stroke—one that left him a paraplegic. Five days later, as Jane Leiper Kane was reading from the Bible, Elisha quietly slipped away.

On February 17, the *New York Tribune* announced a telegram received by Henry Grinnell: "Dr. Kane is dying. He cannot live but a few moments. Mind right, departing very hard." Almost immediately the paper replaced it with a new report of the Arctic explorer's death. When Maggie read the news, she blanched, turned to leave the room, and fainted.

"THAT YOU MAY KNOW
THE SACRED LOVE"

"Women possess no rights," said Zenobia with a half-melancholy
smile, "or, at all events, only little girls and grandmothers would
have the force to exercise them."
—NATHANIEL HAWTHORNE, *The Blithedale Romance*, 1852

AFTER ELISHA'S DEATH Maggie became physically ill with grief.
She was so hysterical and overwrought that she spiked a high fever.
Even after her recovery, Maggie remained listless and depressed,
shunning the daylight as if she wished to join Elisha in his grave.
No one—not Mrs. Fox, Katy, nor any of her friends—could comfort her, not even her father, John Fox, who had rushed from Arcadia to New York City upon learning of Elisha's death.

Elisha's death sent shock waves through the country. In the
months before his death, *Arctic Explorations* had appeared and become a bestseller. With the news of glamorous Dr. Kane's untimely
demise, America mourned as a nation. In cities and towns large and
small, mayors, statesmen, and dignitaries felt obliged to commemorate the hero's death with funeral ceremonies unprecedented in
the brief history of the United States, the likes of which were not
seen again until President Lincoln was assassinated.

The first ceremonies began in Havana the day after Elisha's
death. Family members, joined by Cuba's governor and highest of-
ficials, accompanied his coffin in a stately procession to the wharf,
where the American steamboat the *Cahawba* carried the body to
New Orleans. After the steamer reached that busy Mississippi port

city, the mayor of New Orleans and his Continental Guards carried Elisha's coffin to City Hall. His body lay in state for several days.

Similar solemnities were repeated as the steamboat progressed up the Mississippi River to the Ohio River. In Cincinnati, the governor of Ohio led the funeral procession from the river past the city's black-draped buildings to the railroad terminal. The faithful William Morton walked behind the hearse, followed by Elisha's three brothers in a carriage. At the depot the coffin was placed on a special funeral train that stopped at Xenia, Columbus, Baltimore, and other cities for still more observances.

Elaborate expressions of sorrow continued to pour forth—from newspapers and journals, from pulpits, from the legislatures of Pennsylvania, New York, Massachusetts, Ohio, and New Jersey. One of the sponsors for Elisha's second Arctic journey, the American Philosophical Society, commissioned a memoir of his life as well as a posthumous portrait.

By February 22, the *Philadelphia Public Ledger,* anticipating the arrival of Elisha's funeral procession, urged a still more visible display of civic grief: "The remains of the chivalrous Kane are on their way to their final resting place in this, the city of his birth, the city of his pride and affection." It was only fitting that there be "some open manifestation of the feeling and the sympathy which the news of his death has awakened...we suggest, therefore...that his remains shall be received in this city with suitable public honors in Independence Hall."

But Elisha's remains did not reach Philadelphia until March 11. In a misty rain, accompanied by muffled drums, seven crew members from the *Advance* covered the coffin with the brig's tattered flag and carried their captain to Independence Hall. There the hero's body lay in state for three days, decorated by Elisha's ceremonial sword and a magnificent wreath with the mysterious inscription "To the Memory of Dr. Kane, from Two Ladies." While many theories have been advanced about the identity of the senders—ranging from Maggie and Katy to women from Elisha's social circle—they remain unknown.

On March 14, 1857, the day of Elisha's burial, flags were flown at half-mast across the nation as Dr. Francis Hawks, president of the Geographical Society of New York, delivered a funeral eulogy. The funeral ended at Philadelphia's Laurel Hill Cemetery, where the body of Elisha Kent Kane was placed in the Kane vault.

❧

What Maggie knew—or cared to know—about those public ceremonies has not been described. For weeks after the initial shock of Elisha's death Maggie remained depressed, suffering from intermittent illness, fevers, and delirium. Anxious friends and family, among them Ellen Walter, Horace Greeley, the Bayards, and the Grays, hovered over her.

As the weeks passed they worried about more than her health. Being neither single nor widowed—and possibly no longer a virgin—Maggie's marriage to another man, at least for the foreseeable future, seemed out of the question. Nor, had it been proposed, would Maggie consider it. Instead, she clung to the one hope that she believed would insure her future—the legacy Elisha once promised in his will.

By early spring, Mrs. Fox wrote to Robert Kane, one of Elisha's younger brothers, an attorney and the co-executor of his will. "A few days after the Dr.'s death, Mrs. Grinnell called and told Margaret that she had been 'remembered to the last' and he had made a request which was left with you to deliver to Margaret," Mrs. Fox wrote. "Her trials have been great (as you must already know) greater than she could bear and we fear that unless changes soon take place she cannot survive them much longer. I wish you would come at once. We shall remain here in 22nd Street until the first of May when we will move to 35 East 19th Street."

While Mrs. Fox did not disclose the name of the owner of their new home, it belonged to Horace Greeley. The Greeley family rarely occupied the three-story row house, and the place was so carelessly kept that the lights often went out—an embarrassment causing the peripatetic editor to ask his neighbors to monitor his gas meter. Recently, the editor's unhappy wife, Mary—as discontented with Horace as she was with urban living—had moved north to the Greeleys' new seventy-five-acre country home in Westchester County, and Greeley offered his spacious New York home to the Foxes for their permanent use.

Maggie treated the prospect of the move indifferently, focusing her attention instead almost exclusively upon Elisha, becoming convinced that he had left her a deathbed message. Determined to learn the truth, she wrote Robert Kane on June 1, 1857: "I know the Doctor must have left some message for me, and know that you will not refuse to deliver it even though it gives you much pain in recalling the name of him whose memory is and ever will be sacred."

Assuring the attorney that she had religious faith in the sincerity of Elisha's love, Maggie implied their relationship went beyond a friendship: "I can never realize that he is gone—gone for ever. Only seven months ago I bad him farewell, here...in this very room, only an hour before his departure for England and little thought that it would be the last, long farewell."

The letter so worried the thirty-year-old attorney that he made a special trip to New York. While Robert assured Maggie that the dying Elisha had not left her any message, he appeared to be so kind and sympathetic that Maggie immediately warmed to him.

"My dear Mr. Kane: I am better. Dr. Gray comes now nearly every day. But your smile and kind words have done more than all," she wrote.

But sympathy was only one of Robert's motives for the visit. Unknown to Maggie and her friends, he was arranging the imminent publication of a book about Elisha—whose name he was determined to protect from unsavory rumors. Surprised by the national outpouring of grief over Elisha's death, Childs and Peterson realized his biography could mean another bestseller. By May the publisher had received permission from the Kanes for author William Elder to write a laudatory biography about Elisha's life.

When *The Biography of Elisha Kent Kane* appeared just a few months later, it was promoted as an authoritative book based upon recollections from the Arctic hero's own family. His goal, Elder explained in the introduction, was to "write a memoir of the man, which might serve to make his readers personally acquainted with him." It was a task, Elder proudly added, that had been greatly enhanced by access to Elisha's personal correspondence: "Bless the memory of the man for the happiness I have...in declaring that I have not been obliged to suppress a letter or a line for the sake of his fame!"

That, of course, was not exactly the truth. Elisha's relationship with Maggie had been omitted. In an oblique reference to those rumors, the *New York Times* faulted Elder for "not giving more copious extracts from the correspondence of Dr. Kane for it is in the private and unstudied letters of such men that we can best discover their real characters." Years later Greeley's *New York Tribune* went even further. Elder's biography, that newspaper observed, presented a gilded portrait of the explorer, but omitted "a deep undercurrent in the navigator's life, which the distinguished biographer knew nothing of, and which the family did not place at his disposal... [namely] the love-life of Dr. Kane...(involving) a private correspondence with a young lady in New York."

The biography might have been "more strictly true" if Elder had written honestly about Elisha's engagement—a commitment which "when he returned covered with the tinsel and show of glory" he so shamelessly repudiated "because his friends thought it beneath him." In the event that "the letters are ever published (an event not likely to occur, we learn) another important leaf can be added to the biography."

Initially Maggie had no thoughts about publishing the letters for revenge. To the still grieving and unworldly young woman, Elisha's letters were sacred symbols of his love, which she now wished to keep for herself to read over in the privacy of her room.

Still, there loomed the nettlesome issue of her support. For all her initial enthusiasm for studying at Mrs. Turner's and mastering the rudiments of a proper education, Maggie's frequent absence left her less than well-schooled and thus ill-equipped to teach school or serve as a governess—two of the few jobs then available to middle-class women. Equally serious was Maggie's awkward and indefinable marital status.

Yet during the second of Robert's solicitous visits in the summer of 1857, the gentleman diplomatically sidestepped all discussion about a legacy. Privately, the devoted Ellen Walter later reminded Maggie that the letters were potentially a powerful weapon, which could be used as leverage to force the Kanes into paying her Elisha's legacy.

Maggie felt conflicted. She was torn between the seemingly kindly Robert's expressions of concern for her well-being, her desire to keep Elisha's letters in her private possession, and the need for financial support. So she turned for advice to one of her famous acquaintances—Elizabeth Fries Lummis Ellet, a short, plump forty-year-old member of New York's literati whose three-volume *Women of the American Revolution* had won her national acclaim.

In spite of such accolades, Mrs. Ellet had a dubious personal reputation because of her meddlesome involvement thirteen years earlier in a love triangle with Edgar Allan Poe. In an uproar later known as the "bluestocking scandal," Poe had become enraged by her complicity with his dying wife, Virginia, over a love letter written by poet Frances "Fanny" Sargent Osgood. Poe had publicly suggested that Elizabeth, too, had written him indiscreet letters. To protect Elizabeth's honor, her brother, T. D. English, challenged Poe to a duel, which culminated in a fistfight during which the

author's face was badly cut with a seal ring. While Poe never produced any letters from Elizabeth, she was publicly tainted as a
scandalmonger.

Whether Robert Kane knew about the rumors or not, he reacted to Maggie's meeting with Elizabeth by accusing the author of
meddling in the younger woman's business. Enraged by his insinuations, Elizabeth Ellet wrote back, explaining that her only reaction
had been one of empathy and pity. "Her distress and feeble health
strongly moved my sympathy," Elizabeth recalled, "and in reply...
I advised her to put her affairs in the hands of some good lawyer."

Maggie, however, backed off, perhaps because of her depression,
lack of funds, habitual passivity, or simply out of respect for Elisha's
memory and his desire to please his parents. Retreating again to her
sickbed, she busied herself creating a special room as a shrine to
Elisha and spent hours gazing at his letters, gifts, photograph, and
a map of his wanderings. She vowed to model her life upon Elisha's
expectations, Maggie recalled in her memoir, virtually fitting "her
opinions of persons and views of things...entirely by her recollection of his."

Maggie also withdrew from friends Elisha had disliked. She
rethought her daily activities: Every chore, every deed ranging from
her choice of clothes to the books she read was measured by the
yardstick of her former lover's opinion. "Would dear Elisha like me
to do this?" became the guiding question of her life.

While Elisha had been reared a Presbyterian, he often told
Maggie he wanted her to convert to Catholicism. His reasons were
complex—as indeed was nearly everything about Elisha—but related to preventing Maggie from returning to spiritualism. Catholicism, then America's second most popular religion, strictly forbid
its followers from raising spirits of the dead. Hoping to persuade
Maggie to that faith, Elisha had accompanied her to mass at St.
Anne's Church on nearby Eighth Street on several occasions.

Now, remembering those visits, Maggie resolved to embrace
that religion. On August 15, 1858, after months of study with her

spiritual advisor, Father Quinn, a white-frocked Maggie was baptized at St. Peter's Church on Barclay Street before a crowd of curious spectators who still remembered her once-famous name.

"She is a very interesting and lovely young lady... [with] large dark Madonna eyes, a sweet expressive mouth, a petite and delicately moulded form and a regal carriage of the head, with an aristocratic air quite uncommon," commented a reporter from the *New York Herald Tribune*. Miss Fox, the reporter added, had been placed at a school by the late Dr. Elisha Kent Kane, who "loved her as a sister, and whose brotherly interest in the fair girl was deeply cherished even in his last moments."

In spite of that blissful description, Maggie's life was far from tranquil. She had been betrayed by Elisha's friends, who insisted that his relationship with Maggie had been purely platonic and altruistic. She suffered ongoing financial difficulties as well. Despite persistent appeals to Robert Kane to release funds from Elisha's bequest, nothing was paid. To resolve the matter, Ellen Walter finally paid a visit to Cornelius Grinnell, only to be curtly informed that he believed Elisha had discharged all obligations to Maggie before his death. The Arctic hero, Cornelius maintained, had educated Maggie with the intent of preparing her to become a governess— not his wife.

"This is the first time I have ever heard of it and indeed, were I given to laughing now a days, the joke would not pass unrelished," Maggie retorted in a letter to Cornelius. Equally ridiculous, she added, was a comment that his mother, Sarah Grinnell, made during the meeting with Ellen Walter that Maggie had refused to marry Elisha when he proposed: "This is a sad mistake and you should come to her and own if a falsehood, or misunderstanding on the part of you or your mother."

Elisha's love letters were the ultimate proof. Maggie's possession of them continued to gnaw at Robert Kane, who diplomatically continued his visits in such a kindly manner that she still perceived him as her friend. Naively, instead of pressing Robert for money in those meetings, the grief-obsessed Maggie asked him for descriptions of Elisha's last moments. "Come and tell *all* the Dr. said," she wrote Robert on May 18, 1858. "Do not feel afraid of me, a poor friendless girl…he [Elisha] must have left messages for me, and surely you must hold his requests too sacred, to refuse to follow his last wishes. Do come and tell me all, and I will trouble you no more…If there are any letters bring them."

In reply Robert broached the idea that she should cede Elisha's love letters so that they could be safely preserved. By doing so, he added in an appeal to the young woman's new religious leanings, she would accomplish a good deed by insuring their protection from misuse. Moreover, since his father, Judge Kane, had died the previous February—just a year and five days after Elisha—the receipt of the letters would spare his widowed mother, Jane, any additional anxieties.

Maggie was outraged. Barely containing her anger, she assured Robert that while she appreciated his concern for the letters, he should understand that she considered Elisha's memory sacred: "You know the Doctor's memory can not be more holy—even to his own mother than it is to me. Therefore you ought not to have mentioned the harsh word 'misuse' in connection with his name."

She added, "The letters are mine to guard and cherish as long as I live and when I may no longer be able to guard them I will place them with you, but do not think me so lost as to ever allow them to be published."

Thus began Maggie's own contra-dance of deception. Determined to be recognized as Elisha's fiancée, to defend the letters as her rightful property, and, perhaps, to get even with Robert, Maggie again contacted Elizabeth Ellet, this time suggesting that the author write a book that included the explorer's letters. Theoretically, her friend opined, such an exposé could vindicate Maggie's reputation. Yet, being unaware of Maggie's secret marriage, the author explained that Elisha's letters legally belonged to his heirs, the Kanes, and thus could not be published without permission.

Surely, Maggie retorted, it was possible for Elizabeth—who wrote so sensitively about women and their trials—to draft a book about her life. Warily, the older woman agreed, but with three caveats—that she would be well paid, that she would write it anonymously, and that her young client would accept the dire legal consequences attendant upon an unauthorized publication.

Meanwhile, Maggie's letter to Robert Kane elicited a response. That same spring, Robert visited her again, this time promising to honor Maggie's claim for a sum of $5,000. As a sign of good faith, Robert then forwarded $150 and subsequently sent along another $50.

But that was all. Once again, the legacy seemed permanently stalled. Losing patience, Maggie contacted Elizabeth Ellet again, this time admitting to the author that she had wed Elisha. Astonished, Elizabeth now counseled her to take a different approach. If indeed Maggie was Elisha's widow, there was no reason for her to publish his letters: To save her reputation, she only needed to make her marriage public.

Even so, Maggie now believed that the quickest way to avoid scandal was to have her romance and marriage to Dr. Kane published in a book. Before long the idea seems to have become an obsession. By early August 1858, shortly after her baptism, Maggie began to appear at Elizabeth's house, sometimes as often as several times a day, repeatedly soliciting the author's advice. Maggie groused that she been treated most unfairly. She believed that the $5,000 left in trust for her under Robert's aegis was to be paid out of the proceeds of Elisha's writings. Yet, while *Arctic Explorations* had become a bestselling book, she had received only $200 to date.

Finally, after ignoring Elizabeth's advice for more than a year, Maggie consulted with New York attorney C. Henry Hawkins. Robert then tried to intimidate Maggie, according to an account by Elizabeth some months later. "When instead of responding to the letter of her counsel, you went to her house, and as she said loaded her with violent reproaches for two hours—then went to Mr.

Greeley, who had nothing to do with her affairs—and to her advisor [Father Quinn] to induce him to use his influence to induce her to give up the letters...The matter," Elizabeth wrote, "certainly wore an aspect of intentional wrongdoing on your part."

As Elizabeth also observed, Horace Greeley, for all his professed concern about Maggie's plight, took Robert's side and agreed that the publication of Elisha's letters would be an injustice.

In Horace's view love between a man and woman was a private matter. Good or bad as that relationship may become, the details were not to be shared. Moreover, for all Greeley's support of suffrage, he considered women emotionally weak, overly excitable, and tending to illogic and hysteria—a bias that must have exacerbated his difficulties with his wife Mary.

The editor visited Maggie on August 31, 1858. Playing upon her sympathy, their long relationship, the altruistic tendencies of the Kanes, and Maggie's own desire to behave as a lady, Horace persuaded her to stop her intended legal action.

Later that same day, Maggie even wrote Robert about her "long sweet interview" with the editor. "All he said was gentle kind and sincere...I shall heal all wrong patiently and never flinch the kind and good I shall appreciate, the wicked...I shall forgive."

That same afternoon Horace also wrote to Robert, characterizing Maggie as a well-intended but emotionally volatile young woman. "She has suffered from the events of the last few days and appears to be truly sorry for the step into which she was dropped," he opined. Moreover, "she appears to be now in her right mind in all respects, says she will never see Mrs. E [Ellet], etc. etc. Of course, she means this, but may not always mean it. I trust, however, that with Mr. Q [Quinn] as her spiritual advisor and we in the house here, she can never again go so far astray as she did [with] Mrs. E."

Robert then wrote Maggie, "I have read your letter of yesterday and am sorry that you are so troubled in mind....Do not, then, I beg you, make yourself wretched over that which cannot now be helped. Believe how sincerely I am interested in your well being and how much happiness it will give me to co-operate with Mr. Greeley and Father Quinn."

In spite of those words, both men were traditionalists, interpreting Maggie's desperate behavior as a breach of traditional feminine passivity—and, as such, a symptom of emotional instability rather than a pragmatic response to being cheated by the family. While Mrs. Fox and Katy were sympathetic to Maggie, only two women seem to have understood her plight well enough to protest—Elizabeth Ellet and Ellen Walter.

Exasperated with the manipulations of the men and all too familiar with how Elisha had placed Maggie in that dilemma, Ellen Walter paid a visit to the Grinnells. The purpose of her visit, Ellen explained to Henry's wife Sarah and her son Cornelius, was to discover what provision Elisha made for Maggie on the eve of his departure to England.

Sarah and Cornelius remained noncommittal. No sooner did their butler show Ellen Walter to their door than Sarah sat down and wrote Robert Kane about the visit, saying, "I am inclined to think she was sent by a lawyer....I fear trouble from these bad people."

In response, Robert observed that while Mrs. Walter's visit may have been unpleasant, he did not believe that Maggie was behind it. Elisha's will was, after all, open to public inspection in Philadelphia. Still, to prevent any future difficulties, Robert decided to make two certified copies and send them to Father Quinn and Horace Greeley, "two gentlemen of our city who have taken a warm interest in Miss Fox and with whom I am addressing with a vision to making some provision to her."

Father Quinn shared a copy of the document with Maggie. In a codicil, witnessed by Sarah and Henry Grinnell, Elisha had requested $5,000 be paid in trust to Robert Kane to an unnamed recipient. In the case of Robert's death, the trust was to be administered by his younger brother, John. Obliquely, it read: "These trusts [were] expressed by me in a paper writing to be found among my private papers at the time of my decease and in which the trusts imposed on said death and bequest was declared."

Maggie felt certain that she was named in Elisha's private papers as the intended recipient. She promised an encouraging Father Quinn that she would treat Robert patiently while he made arrangements for the settlement.

From Father Quinn's perspective at least, a peaceful solution had been achieved. A few days later, on October 18, the priest wrote Robert still more encouraging news. Maggie was planning a trip to the country and in her absence wanted to entrust the priest with Elisha's letters. Since he saw Maggie nearly every week, Father Quinn also felt obliged to remind the attorney of his parishioner's core character: "I still find her the same constant, humble, modest and excellent soul. She needs money, but she is too timid to say this."

∽❋৵

In contrast to Maggie's timidity about her need for money, Leah boldly stretched out her hand. By 1857 spiritualism was reaching the peak of its popularity, carrying her along in its crest. Even Boston, for all of its Puritan and Calvinistic influences, had evolved into a hotbed of spiritualism, mediums, and séances. A major publishing center, Boston had long churned out periodicals related to spiritualism.

That spring George Lunt, a fifty-four-year-old poet, writer, and editor of the *Boston Courier,* had become disgusted with the revelation of a spiritual hoax by a Harvard College Divinity student. He set up the Cambridge Committee with Swiss-born naturalist Louis Agassiz and several other Harvard professors, vowing to drive spiritualism from Massachusetts, much as the Buffalo doctors had attempted seven years earlier.

Lunt's *Boston Courier* offered an award of $500 to any spiritualist who could prove his powers during a formal investigation before the distinguished committee. "We will pay $500 to...anybody who will communicate a single word, imparted to the 'spirits' by us, in an adjoining room; who will read a single word, in English, written inside a book, or sheet of paper, folded in such a manner as we may choose, who will answer, with the aid of all the higher intelligences he or she can invoke from the other world, three questions—which the superior intelligences must be able to answer," read the *Courier* challenge.

Leah accepted the challenge and traveled to Boston with Katy. By mid-June 1857, a handful of leading spiritualists, including George Redman, known for his telepathic gifts, and the teenage Davenport brothers, John and William, famous for their ability to float musical instruments in the air while song filled the séance room, had arrived at the second floor of Boston's Albion Building. The ensuing scene was as dramatic as it was colorful. The mediums appeared in a variety of dress and manner to display their gifts before a group of grim-faced professors and an eager corps of reporters looking for a sensational story.

After six days of examination, during which the *Boston Traveller* accused the Cambridge Committee of failing to cooperate with the mediums, the results were deemed inconclusive. "It was the unanimous opinion...with the exception of the representative of *The Courier,* that the whole affair was in no sense of the word an investigation," reported the *Traveller,* "and that nothing was proved or disproved by it."

Far more interesting than the ghostly spirits, opined a reporter from the *New York Tribune,* were the mediums themselves. To him, savvy Leah Fox and her somber sister Katy, the quixotic Davenport brothers, and the intimidating George Redman were "mostly persons of original and flexible character, cultivated by a droll, queer mode of life, and by much experience of mankind."

The mediums were, by now, used to battling skeptics and refuting claims that spiritualism caused insanity. Prominent spiritualists who went astray inevitably attracted the attention of the nation's doubters. One of the most tragic cases involved John B. Fairbanks, a patent attorney and former assistant editor of the illustrious *Scientific American Magazine,* who had been devastated by the death of his beloved sister. "Hearing such wonderful stories of the miracles performed by the Spiritualists, he became possessed with a most ardent desire to communicate with his departed relative," noted the *New York Tribune* on December 1, 1856.

After becoming a frequent guest at one of New York's spiritualist circles he converted. The obsessed Fairbanks then spent much of his time attempting to convert others, believing that "at all times he was attended by good and evil spirits."

On Saturday morning, November 29, 1856, a young woman in the next apartment heard Fairbanks raise a window and groan. Convinced that his late sister had appeared outside his fifth-floor apartment on New York City's Sixth Avenue, the attorney stepped out to join her, plunging to the sidewalk below. "...It would seem that the deceased was so infatuated with spiritualism as to entertain the belief that he could at will leap across the gulf that divides time from eternity and join his sister in the spirit world," read the coroner's report.

On March 14, 1857, when diarist George Templeton Strong—who remained intrigued enough with the "delusion" of spiritualism to attend several séances—arrived for one at Leah's house, he became impressed. After nearly a decade of practice, according to *Time Is Kind,* Leah's "raps had grown tremendously strong...often frightening in their force."

Strong then attempted to put one of Leah's spirits to a telepathic test. "I questioned it about an imaginary transaction fixing my thoughts on an answer—and that answer was given with great precision," he reluctantly admitted.

~✤~

Within six months of Strong's séance visit to Leah, America's fascination with utopian concepts was fading, the result of a depression following the Panic of 1857. The sudden economic downturn had left Americans, and especially New Yorkers, skeptical of nearly everything they could not see and touch.

The spark that ignited that antebellum fiscal crisis—one of the worst the nation had yet experienced—had flared in August 1857 when an embezzlement bankrupted the New York branch of the Ohio Life Insurance and Trust Company. In reaction, the nation's frightened bankers tightened rules for other types of financial transactions, which, in turn, prompted a frenzied selling off of stocks. Many stocks, *Harper's Weekly* somberly observed, "fell eight or ten percent in a day, and fortunes were made and lost between ten o'clock in the morning and four of the afternoon." In the ensuing scramble, bank failures and suspensions were posted daily outside newspaper offices while newsboys ran through the streets hawking penny posters that listed the latest misfortunes.

Still more bad economic news arrived on September 12, 1857, when the wood-hulled steamship the *SS Central American,* carrying $1.6 million in precious metal from the San Francisco mint, was caught in a hurricane and sank two hundred miles off the coast of South Carolina. News of the disaster, telegraphed to cities across the United States, created fresh waves of hysteria, causing thousands of frightened citizens to rush to banks to withdraw their funds in gold.

By October 3, even the New York banks that had held steady in the first stages of the fiscal crisis began to wobble and several crashed after thousands of angry investors stormed their doors to redeem their notes for gold. "We seem foundering," noted George Templeton Strong in his diary on October 10. "People's faces in Wall Street look fearfully gaunt and desperate."

By October 13, all but one of New York's fifty-eight banks closed their doors. They would remain shut until mid-December. The next day the national banking system collapsed. For the next eighteen months, the United States was mired in a depression.

In the midst of that national panic, spiritualism and Leah stumbled as well. In the latter's case, however, her troubles had less to do with finances than issues of trust. In November 1857, Leah had been invited to give a séance at the Jersey City home of the Simeon Posts. Honored to have the famed medium travel from Manhattan to their country home, the Posts had invited other guests for the designated night.

This, according to Leah's recollection in *The Missing Link in Modern Spiritualism,* was a special séance, one that reflected the increasingly elaborate expressions of spirit communication. As soon as the raps sounded in the Posts' parlor, the room filled with flickering lights that grew so bright that several people shrieked. To the entranced Leah, the outburst was an inexcusable lapse in courtesy. After chastising her guests, she led only a select few into an adjacent room to continue the sitting.

Once again the lights appeared, this time so brilliantly that they nearly blinded the onlookers. Simultaneously, Leah recalled, she felt faint, walked to a washbasin in the corner of the room, and thrust her hands into the cold water. Even that offered so little relief that Mrs. Post helped Leah to the back door for fresh air. Leah bent over and placed her hands in the damp soil.

The next morning the Posts returned to that same spot and to their surprise found particles of phosphorus in the ground. Politely but firmly they demanded an explanation through Leah's old spiritualist friend George Willets.

The implication, Leah later admitted in her memoir, was that she must have rubbed phosphorus on her fingers the night before, manipulating it to create sparks reflected on the walls. While other mediums were routinely subjected to accusations of fraud, it had been years since anyone had implied that Leah was dishonest. "I never used anything to conceal, or afford the Spirits a hiding-place for anything," Maggie's eldest sister insisted. "I...knew I was innocent, but did not know that I could prove myself."

It was then that Daniel Underhill, a middle-aged spiritualist widower, defended her reputation. Underhill, who met Leah for the first time while escorting her to New Jersey as a favor to his friend Simeon Post, was immediately taken with her spiritual abilities. "Mr. Underhill felt sure of my innocence. In his own purity of heart could not doubt me," as Leah put it. The accusations of late 1857 had nevertheless shaken Leah to her core. She would not forget them or the man who had helped her recover her good name. "Mr. Underhill came to my rescue in that dark hour of my life when old and trusted friends wavered in opinion," Leah bitterly recalled in her memoir nearly thirty years later.

As it happened, her hero, who was smitten with Leah, was the wealthy president of the Wall Street–based New York Fire Insurance Company. Leah married Daniel Underhill on November 2, 1858, in a ceremony held at Horace Greeley's home. The marriage was said to be one of convenience. Leah and Daniel had the same interests and both were widowed; Daniel also had a young daughter of whom Leah became inordinately fond. "There had been no romance in it—their pleasant companionship had simply culminated that way," relatives later told Pond when she wrote *Time Is Kind.*

Following a honeymoon in Cleveland, Leah settled into a comfortable existence in a fashionable brownstone on West Thirty-seventh Street. There, as the new Mrs. Daniel Underhill, Leah indulged her tastes with abandon, furnishing her new home in the heavy mid-Victorian style. Gilt wallpaper lined the home's formal rooms, which were furnished with rosewood chairs, sofas, mahogany tables, glass chandeliers, Oriental carpets, statuary, a piano, and an organ.

Daniel, a handsome, thick-bodied man with a taste for gourmet food, was a generous and patient mate, who pampered Leah at every opportunity. One example was the aviary he had built off their home's dining room. He filled it with rare songbirds in honor of his wife's love of music.

Daniel refused to allow his new wife to be subjected to humiliations over spiritualism. "He thought I had done my duty faithfully and that it was time for me to retire from public séances," Leah explained in her memoir. Henceforth, her séances were conducted solely in private sessions for clients who admired her gifts and, in turn, praised her to their wealthy and prominent friends.

Maggie makes only a brief mention of Leah's marriage in her own memoir, *The Death-Blow to Spiritualism*. It is possible that she may not even have attended Leah's wedding. While agreeing that her new brother-in-law was a pleasant and warm-hearted man, Maggie continued to avoid Leah, perceiving her as an ominous figure from her earlier life.

"Now that you are rich, why don't you save your soul?" Maggie asked Leah soon after her wedding. At that, Leah flew into a rage, angered by her younger sister's audacity.

Such outbursts, as Maggie, Katy, and Mrs. Fox knew all too well, were hardly unusual. Hoping to prevent them, the trio often sidestepped delicate issues with Leah—among which was the secret marriage between Maggie and Elisha.

Leah had long been suspicious, however. Why did Maggie continue to mourn so excessively over a man who had failed to marry and support her? Did it not make sense now for Maggie to re-embrace spiritualism? According to *The Death-Blow to Modern Spiritualism,* Maggie retorted that she had renounced séances out of respect for Elisha and had vowed to lead an honest life.

But honesty was not necessarily rewarded.

Robert Kane wrote to Father Quinn in January 1859, saying that Maggie had no legal grounds for a claim because Elisha had been destitute when he died. The sums Robert had already dispersed to Maggie, he explained, had come out of his personal resources.

"I have, I believe, already told you that I have never received from the Estate of the late Doctor Kane one cent of the five thousand dollars which by the terms of his will are a legacy to myself without words of trust," Robert wrote. "If I should press my own claims independent of this legacy I could exhibit an indebtedness to myself (as executor) on other accounts exceeding the above sum. I believe too that I have shown you that there is no estate of the late Doctor Kane."

Perhaps the financial depression was responsible. Maggie, how-ever, seems to have discounted Robert's assertion as a lie and blamed his delay for a settlement upon the nettlesome intervention of others. The chief meddler, an increasingly disgruntled Maggie contended, was Horace Greeley, in whose home her parents now resided. "It is very sad that your brother's wishes could not have been permanently followed by yourself without having Mr. Greeley to govern all," she rebuked Robert on January 7, 1859. "You are wholly governed by Mr. Greeley. I am convinced—and Mr. Gree-ley know nothing of my affairs—how useless."

Ten days later, Maggie, who, judging from subsequent letters, seems to have moved to an apartment at 15 Barclay Street, visited her parents at the Greeley townhouse. Discovering one of Robert's letters open on Horace's desk, Maggie scrawled a second angry note to the attorney. "One passage of that letter was very strange to me, where you tell him to direct you, that you will now as ever be wholly governed by him—what right has he to 'govern' in regard to me?" she asked. "Now Mr. Kane unless he is left out of the ques-tion entirely, I shall consider it a wrong."

No sooner did Maggie vent her anger than she regretted it. She wrote Robert on January 22, begging him to ignore her last letter. "At that hour I wrote you, forbidding you to use Mr. Greeley's name in connection with mine, I was in a very irritable state of mind," she admitted. "Mr. Greeley has ever been very kind and gentle to me and I still love and respect him."

The outburst did little to advance Maggie's cause. Instead, it convinced Robert of her emotional instability—and vividly illus-trated her inclination to defer to male authority figures. After see-ing Maggie on several occasions, he had been filled with pity for her. Pale, thin, and haggard from recurrent illnesses, uninterested in the pretty clothes and jewelry she once wore with such delight, Maggie now bore little resemblance to the lively, bright-eyed young woman who had so thoroughly charmed Elisha.

No less shocked at Maggie's gaunt appearance was Cornelius

Grinnell, who, in spite of Maggie's angry reprimand to him a year earlier, paid her a courteous visit during that same winter of 1859. The purpose of his admittedly belated call was to give her certain items Elisha's old friend Morton had carefully hidden during the doctor's last days in Havana—Maggie's unread letters sent to Elisha at the American Consulate, a packet of her earlier correspondence, and Fagnani's portrait.

To Maggie nothing could have been more moving, or spoken more forcefully to her of Elisha's love, than the receipt of those gifts. Seeing them again, knowing that Morton had kept them from Elisha's family, was to relive his love for her. To Maggie, they were a last message from her beloved. Just before leaving, Cornelius presented Maggie with one final gift—a copy of Elder's *Biography of Elisha Kent Kane*.

After his departure Maggie sat down to read it. While a reasonably accurate—if somewhat overblown—account of her lover's exploits, death, and funeral, there was neither a mention of Maggie nor the rumors of her controversial relationship with the Arctic explorer. For all intents and purposes, she had never existed in the official account of the life of Elisha Kent Kane.

"A Cloud of Reproach"

There is no passion in nature so demoniacally impatient, as that
of him who, friendly arm to check us, or if we fail in a sudden effort
to prostrate ourselves shuddering upon the edge of a precipice,
thus meditates a plunge...if there be no from the abyss, we plunge
and are destroyed. Examine these similar actions as we will, we
shall find them resulting solely from the spirit of the *Perverse*.
We perpetrate them because we feel we should not.

—Edgar Allan Poe, *The Imp of the Perverse*

The year 1860 started hopefully for Maggie. Subsequent to
Robert's insistence that Elisha had died penniless, Father Quinn
arranged a meeting between him and Maggie during which the attorney agreed to arrange a settlement. But the erratic payouts left
her frustrated, dependent, and always anxious that she would be
destitute. Robert, on his side, became irritated by her persistent demands and refusal—no matter what he did—to return Elisha's
letters.

Maggie's April 6 letter to Father Quinn reflected those tensions.
Maggie explained that she wanted to visit her brother, David, and
his family in Arcadia, but to do so meant that she needed an additional $5 per week for travel and related expenses. "Please inform
Mr. Kane of my intention to go and please tell him to send me a
distinct reply that I may know what to depend upon," she begged
her spiritual advisor.

In a second letter that month Maggie wrote Robert directly, asking him to return a small gold locket that Elisha gave her when he
renewed their engagement in the spring of 1856. She had, she

explained, given the locket to Elisha to attach to his watch fob as a reminder of their love just before his departure for England. "It has Willie's name engraved upon it and also a lock of Willie's hair. If you will bring a lock of the Doctor's hair with the locket and leave them with Mr. Quinn, I will remember the kindness eternally," she wrote.

Repeatedly, purposefully, she kept hammering upon the importance of Elisha's love. Her messages had an obsessively repetitive tone suggesting her inability to accept Elisha's death and move on to a new life. In a letter of September 15, she announced that Elizabeth Ellet planned to find her a new lawyer. Moreover, Maggie added ominously, Elizabeth was arranging an interview with Henry Grinnell to learn more about Elisha's relationship with Maggie.

She also requested additional funds for a trip to the country. The sojourn, she scrawled obliquely, was of utmost importance to her because she had to leave New York before Mrs. Fox and Katy—who were again visiting relatives in Canada—returned home. The letter showed Maggie was in a state of high anxiety and distraction:

> Mr. Kane, I am afraid that I shall be insane. I have no longer slept, neither day or night. I am fearfully frightened there is no longer the slightest use of concealing it. Today I was better but it will not last...If you will help me off [to the country] I will go where I will kill time and I will give you all the things belonging to the Dr. every letter—but attend to it before the day passes before you.... No matter where I go & I will give you every scrap of the doctors' letters & scared swear will never trouble you for...a cent of money—but my sacrifice be as great as yours, but if you are willing. I will do as I have stated. Do not wait.

Robert's reaction to the letter was not preserved, but it must have confirmed Greeley's earlier observation of Maggie as an inherently unstable young woman.

By November, after still more threats, placations, and promises made and broken, Maggie consulted Father Quinn. Why not forget about the settlement entirely, the priest suggested, and look instead to her mother and Katy for financial support? But Maggie refused to consider it. "As for accepting one penny from either my mother or Katie, that is impossible," Maggie retorted.

Nor, she wearily explained again, could she consider a return to her former profession as a medium. "I cannot turn Spiritualist and make money in that way as it was the Doctor's sacred request that from the first hour we met I should wholly and forever abandon the Spirits and the followers of Spiritualism," she reminded Father Quinn. Besides, as her spiritual advisor must have known only too well, "Now my faith and religion forbids it."

If anything, Maggie explained, her adverse circumstances had merely strengthened her resolve. "I am quick-tempered and nervous and say things every hour in the day that in quiet hours I am sorry for," she admitted, "but I shall die knowing that on my deathbed that I have lived otherwise, as he [Elisha] would have me live...in fact, I live but to guard myself that I may meet him with no stain...."

৵৯঵৶

Finally Maggie had had enough. Several of her friends most likely contributed funds so that she could hire attorney Dexter A. Hawkins (a relative and associate of her former consultant C. Henry Hawkins) to negotiate with the Kanes. On November 20, 1860, Hawkins wrote Robert Kane politely, informing him that Maggie was dissatisfied with the current method of payments: "She would like to have you state to her in writing, how much money she is entitled to per year. She would like to have the income divided into four equal yearly installments and either sent her directly from you, or else have the installments deposited by you in the hands of some responsible business man, who will pay the money over to her when she calls for it." If the amount was indeed $5,000, Mr. Hawkins added, she should have at least $350 a quarter from it—an amount upon which Maggie felt she could survive.

Hastily, in that same letter, Hawkins assured Robert Kane that his client had no intention of becoming litigious. "Miss F. does not contemplate or desire to force any legal measures in order to enforce her claims…but…simply requests in your hands, trusting that you will act justly and wisely."

On December 1, Robert coldly replied, "I do not see that I am interested either personally or professionally in the matter which Miss Fox has placed in your hands." Nevertheless, he added, "Taking your communication however, in connection with that which you addressed me some time since I believe it to be my duty to submit its contents to others."

Maggie coolly informed Father Quinn that she planned to seek a settlement through legal means. It was a personal rebuff to the priest, who had continued to preach patience. In recognition of that, Robert wrote Father Quinn sympathetically, expressing his regret that Maggie "seems to have withdrawn from you at least for a time that confidence…certainly due one who had intervened so kindly on her behalf."

Most worrisome, Robert admitted, was Maggie's implication that Elisha's letters had the potential to embarrass the Kane family. "I have perhaps an imperfect notion of the contents of the letters… and the publication of which has more than once been threatened as something so much to be feared by my family," he admitted. Despite his efforts to prevent Maggie from publishing the letters, Robert did not believe that the contents, whatever they were, could tarnish the glorious reputation of his heroic brother. Even so, just the mere publication of them would be an embarrassment.

"My patience has been tried by her eccentricity of behavior to call it by no less her term and the flagrant breach of faith with yourself," Robert continued, adding that he was tempted to wash his hands of the entire affair. "My only motive in trespassing so much upon the unwearying goodness of yourself has been the desire to aid a young woman in whose welfare my brother had taken a lively interest and whom I very foolishly believed to be frustrated with grief at his decease."

Robert apparently had come to believe that Maggie's grief was a ruse for blackmail. Consequently he must proceed with caution in all his dealings with her: "I cannot forget that I have a mother and sister and the suffering to which they would be subjected by seeing a work containing my brother's private letters placarded on the boards of every vendor of cheap literature and I am willing to do anything I can...to prevent such a misfortune."

By December 20, having heard nothing from Robert or his counsel since the letter of December 1, Maggie's attorney lost patience. "If I do not hear from you in response to my friendly interposition in the matter of Margaret F. Kane I shall infer that you decline to adjust the matter in a friendly way but prefer the court," Hawkins threatened, "and as for the reasons stated, it is not a case that admits of delay, I must advise Mrs. K. [Mrs. Kane, as Hawkins now referred to her] to call at once for the assistance of your courts."

Father Quinn, meanwhile, perpetually attempting to resolve the situation peacefully, had arranged for Elisha's letters to be entrusted to Maggie's old spiritualist friend and doctor Edward Bayard. To that, Maggie had happily agreed. And so, too, did Robert Kane, who, while unfamiliar with Bayard personally, knew and liked other members of his family in Philadelphia.

☙

One of Maggie's secrets was the episodic recurrence of eccentric behavior that seem related to the strange mental state she revealed to Robert in her panicked letter of mid-September 1860. Only Katy, who had remained close to her grief-stricken sister during those first years after Elisha's death, had witnessed her eccentricities.

Daily, and sometimes several times a day, Maggie opened the black-draped panels of a shrine to Elisha that bore an eerie resemblance to that of a Catholic saint. The shrine was fashioned in a closet and surrounded by a small engraving of the explorer, the gifts he had given her during their courtship, a map of his wanderings in the Arctic, and other mementos. There, after striking a match and lighting a candle beneath the explorer's flower-bedecked image, the young woman sobbed tearlessly, her cries reaching a sharp pitch before stopping altogether.

Disquieted by Maggie's strange ritual, Katy told no one about it. Nor did she reveal its shameful sequel. "After each exhausting outburst of emotion," wrote Pond in *Time Is Kind,* "Maggie would stumble blindly to the outer room and drink until sleep came with dreams which bore her far away."

Members of the Fox family were hardly strangers to the harmful effects of alcohol. Years before Maggie and Katy's birth, their father, John, had slipped into alcoholism and reformed only after years of separation from his wife, Margaret. Less talked about were his occasional relapses after his last two daughters were born. Moreover, the Fox sisters were independently introduced to alcohol at very early ages. When Maggie and Katy were first giving séances in Rochester's private homes, some of their hosts had offered them alcohol during the dinners following the sittings. Later, they would take the occasional drink at social occasions and formal dinners. But at some point after Elisha's death, Maggie started drinking regularly.

Brandy soon became a familiar friend, one that cured her insomnia and offered her temporary escape from what seemed a cruel and heartless world. Through her reclusive drinking spells, too, Maggie became less troublesome to those around her. Now, instead of sudden outbursts of loud singing and spells of banging on the piano that invariably brought angry protests from irate neighbors, the unhappy twenty-seven-year-old quietly drank herself into a dreamless stupor.

Desperate for funds, Maggie also agreed to accept money from Katy, whose spiritualist practice now provided a comfortable living. Yet for all her success, the ethereal, dreamy-eyed Katy seldom embraced life joyously or whole-heartedly but seemed removed from those around her. Primly dressed, inclined to taciturnity like her father, John, she seemed to the worried Mrs. Fox and Leah to have the makings of a spinster—the Victorian term for an unmarried woman over the age of twenty-five.

Nevertheless, Katy's low voice and pretty face often attracted admirers from the New York Circle and friends of the group. "There was about her a cool remoteness that gave her an air of mystery, an aura of distinction, which drew one's eyes back to her again and again, and made her presence strongly felt in any room she entered," according to *Time Is Kind*.

If anything that aura only served to enhance Katy's busy spiritualist practice, underscoring a distanced personality considered typical of a gifted medium. In contrast to Greeley's original observation of Katy's intelligence, Robert Dale Owen later opined in *Debatable Land,* "She is one of the most simple-minded and strictly impulsive young persons I have ever met: as incapable of framing, or carrying on, any deliberate scheme of imposition as a ten-year old is of administering a government."

Those impulsive tendencies, coupled with the ongoing frustrations of Katy's dreary life which she shared with Maggie during her weekly visits to Barclay Street, may explain, at least in part, why she often joined her sister in drinking bouts.

Nor was alcohol hard to obtain. In the mid-nineteenth century, New York City had more than six thousand licensed liquor stores, beer gardens, taverns, and upscale saloons. Simultaneously, a muted temperance movement that had begun in colonial times with Dr. Benjamin Rush had grown increasingly shrill. "500,000 drunkards are now living in our blessed America, all moving onward to the dreadful verge. What a scene of immolation!" railed Reverend Charles Giles to his parishioners in November 1835.

By 1841 a small but determined group of New Yorkers created a branch of the Washington Temperance Society—so called to symbolize the pure ideals of that Founding Father—and established a mission on Chatham Street. A year later others founded the secretive Sons of Temperance. Drink, especially "demon rum," was regularly denounced by members of the evangelical American Temperance Union.

By the end of the 1840s temperance would be considered such an important American value that showman P. T. Barnum, a former drinker, publicly admitted that he had taken an oath of abstinence. To drive that message home to tourists who flocked to his American Museum, Barnum even offered William Smith's play *The Drunkard* as part of the 25-cent admission. Still another reminder were the era's behavior manuals that advised young women to shun alcohol.

Given the widespread opposition to drink and its often tragic results—poverty, shattered marriages, declining health and well-being—Maggie and Katy's indulgence was a perverse departure from cultural norms. As with their earlier secrets about the rappings, the sisters managed to conceal their binges from their parents and friends.

In contrast to her sisters, Leah now enjoyed a lively existence with her new husband, Daniel Underwood, and their home was often filled with friends and admiring guests. One of their most prominent visitors was the free-thinking Robert Dale Owen, son of the British-born industrialist and social reformer Robert Owen.

Owen embraced progressive causes as well. He taught school and published the journal *New Harmony Gazette* in Indiana. There, too, he worked closely with women's rights advocate Fanny Wright on the radical *Free Enquirer,* famous for its endorsement of abolition, socialism, universal suffrage, birth control, and changes in the marriage and divorce laws. Following a stint in the Indiana Legislature from 1836–38 and a term in the U.S. Congress in the late 1840s, Owen was appointed ambassador to Italy. When he returned, he became an outspoken abolitionist and spiritualist.

By the spring of 1860 Owen had met Leah and Daniel and not only attended their séances, but became a frequent houseguest. In one of his books, *Debatable Land,* he recounted an intriguing encounter with Maggie in Horace Greeley's townhouse. She happened to be visiting when Owen arrived with Leah and David. Not even knowing of Maggie's existence until that day, the reformer innocently invited her to join that séance. Maggie—to Katy, Leah, and Mrs. Fox's surprise—agreed to participate.

"Raps spelled out 'darken.' Lights soon appeared," Owen recalled in *Debatable Land.* "Then came suddenly a tremendous blow on the center of the table, a blow so violent we all started back...a stroke, apparently dealt by a strong man with a heavy bludgeon...repeated five or six times."

Afterward when the gaslights were relit, they saw that the surface of the mahogany dining room table remained unscathed. "I consider it a physical impossibility that by any human agency, blows indicating such formidable power should have been dealt marks on the table," Owen recalled. To that, Leah had an explanation: "Mrs. Underhill afterwards informed me that she had several times in the presence of her sister Margaretta, been greatly alarmed by blows as tremendously violent as those I have described."

❧

Nothing alarmed New Yorkers more than the threatened violence of the approaching Civil War. After the fall of Fort Sumter on April 12, 1861, New York City's citizens, who had initially protested a trade blockade with the South, heartily embraced the Union cause, festooning the city's buildings with bunting and displaying the Stars and Stripes from every available flagpole. Before long an American flag, hung by ship riggers, appeared on the 284-foot spire of Trinity Church. Even the red-brick *New York Herald* building on Newspaper Row flew the colors from the top of its clock tower, albeit only after its anti-war editor, James Gordon Bennett, was chased down the street by a howling mob.

So fervently did New Yorkers support the war that they bravely endured financial hardships from the declining value of Union currency. "I believe my assets to be reduced fifty percent...at least...but I welcome it cordially for it has shown that I belong to a community that is brave, generous and that the city of New York is not sordid and selfish," wrote George Templeton Strong in his diary of April 23.

By April 25, ten days after President Lincoln called for 75,000 volunteers for the Union Army, eight thousand New Yorkers left for the front. Thousands of other men would pass through New York City from New England and upstate New York, turning its streets into a thoroughfare as they marched south for battle. The spectacle of New York's departing volunteers, coupled with weeping farewells from wives and sweethearts, likely touched a chord in Maggie. Poignant as those last embraces were, the volunteer soldiers and their women had a certain advantage over her, knowing at least that their departure might well be permanent. Neither Maggie nor Elisha had been so fortunate.

⁂

The onset of the Civil War had created delays in the mail, but Maggie knew that was not the reason why Robert Kane's payments failed to appear as promised. After still more negotiation over Dr. Bayard's guardianship of Elisha's letters, Robert had agreed that once Maggie ceded them, he would pay her quarterly interest in the sum of $350 on the $5,000 from his brother's trust. Maggie relinquished the letters in 1861, but the promised quarterly payments failed to arrive on time—and several did not appear at all.

Maggie's friends insisted that she adopt a more stringent approach. She was, after all, Elisha's wife. If Maggie would openly admit that she had wed the explorer, Dr. Gray, Ellen Walter, and Elizabeth Ellet implored, she would legally be entitled to dower rights as his widow. Henceforth, Maggie finally agreed to call herself Margaret Fox Kane publicly—a name that only her attorney had used thus far in his letters to Robert.

Maggie's friends also urged more forceful legal action. By late 1861 or early 1862 Elizabeth Ellet had hired a Philadelphia attorney, B. Carroll Brewster, to file a lawsuit in the Orphan's Court of Philadelphia, then the legal venue for widows and parentless children. The lawsuit contended that Maggie was entitled to one half of Elisha's estate.

Horrified, Robert Kane and his co-executor, Thomas, immediately countered that the claim was malicious and untrue. The Kanes' lawyers also asserted that any marriage between Maggie and Elisha—if there was one—was dubious at best. While the records for the case have disappeared from the files at the Orphans Court, the lawsuit dragged on for years, according to the preface to *The Love-Life of Dr. Kane* and newspaper accounts.

In addition to the litigation, one of Maggie's spiritualist friends, Joseph La Fumee of the *Brooklyn Eagle,* agreed to co-author a book with Elizabeth Ellet that would reveal Maggie's side of the story. Written in the names of Elisha and Maggie, the proposed volume was to include a selection of their exchange of letters. La Fumee also agreed to write the preface.

For months Maggie wavered before finally retrieving the letters from Dr. Bayard. Then she procrastinated, sorting half-heartedly through Elisha's letters, weighing the pros and cons of each and debating which ones were most suitable for publication. "She would make her choice with exasperating slowness; in an hour she would reclaim them all, vowing she could not and would not bare her heart before a curious world," reported Pond in *Time Is Kind.*

At last, by May 1862, 134 letters were selected for inclusion and the resultant manuscript was sent off to the printers. Robert suddenly surfaced when the book's imminent publication was announced. There was no reason for such a volume, the attorney nervously insisted. He and his brother Thomas would agree to a final two-part settlement: the first in the sum of $2,000 as reimbursement for Maggie's legal fees, and the second, the long-promised quarterly sums of $350 paid as an annuity out of Elisha's $5,000 trust, which was invested in bonds.

In return, Maggie was obliged to cancel the publication of her book and return Elisha's letters and the manuscript to Dr. Bayard, who would permanently seal and deposit them in a safe. Should the Kanes fail to live up to their side of the bargain, Maggie would have the legal right to reclaim Elisha's letters and the manuscript.

But the letters were Maggie's only remaining solace for her lost love. To give them up seemed a cruel punishment, one that meant she could no longer hold Elisha's letters in her hands, reading and re-reading his endearments in black and white as she had done re-peatedly since his death. Friends reminded her that she still pos-sessed other tokens of Elisha's love—his gifts, an engraving of his image, copies of certain letters, and a collection of his small notes and cards. In the end, since she could not really afford to disagree, Maggie conceded.

On June 9, 1862, the long struggle seemed at last at its end. The Kanes' lawyer issued $350 as the first quarterly payment in their new agreement. In addition, Maggie received $500 against the $2,000 Mrs. Ellet had advanced her in legal fees. The remainder, the Kanes promised, was to be paid to the former medium before year's end.

~❊~

A year after the 1862 settlement, Maggie remained "betrayed and baffled still," as the spiritualistically inclined American novelist William Dean Howells would later remark in one of his poems. Again the Kanes did not pay the promised funds. The case went back to court. But the Civil War, raging just out of sight, was about to come close to Philadelphia.

In June 1863, General Robert E. Lee's Confederate forces had stormed into Maryland. They met Union soldiers on July 1 in a brutal, three-day battle at Gettysburg, Pennsylvania. The Union may have won, but both sides lost enormous numbers of men—some 20,000 Union soldiers and an estimated 23,000 to 28,000 Confederate men. It would be the turning point of the Civil War. It would also serve as an excuse for another year's delay in Maggie's payments.

Ultimately the Kanes reneged on their original offer and asked Maggie to sign a paper agreeing to reduce the promised $2,000 to half that amount, according to *Time Is Kind.* Maggie stubbornly refused. Once again the two sides were polarized, the Kanes threatening to withhold their payments and Maggie once again seeking advice from friends.

Maggie was now thirty years old. Elisha had been dead for seven years. Her days were consumed with him. She had no way to make a living, could not—or had not the inclination to—marry, and was forced to live off the kindness of friends. It is hardly surprising that she turned increasingly to drink.

At last, one bitterly cold and snowy night in December 1864, her secret was discovered when she ran into Horace Greeley on the street. After leaving the *Tribune* office late, the editor had trouble getting a cab and was treading through the drifting snow from Nassau Street to his home on Nineteenth Street. Maggie tried to avoid him but Horace caught up, grabbing her arm and peering anxiously at her through his spectacles in the falling snow.

"Let me go," she protested to her old friend.

"Why, Maggie, don't you know me? It's Mr. Greeley. What is the matter, child?" he asked.

Her answer was nearly as chilling as the night itself. "I am looking for Elisha," she sobbed. "Let me go! I must find him. He is somewhere in this awful storm; I always find him in the snow."

Horace listened in astonishment to the outburst, and then, smelling liquor on her breath, understood. Gently, in his most paternal tone, he finally persuaded Maggie to let him escort her home. What a sad chain of events had occurred since that June day in 1850 when he first set eyes on Maggie and her sisters at Barnum's Hotel on Maiden Lane! How sweet the sparkling-eyed, young woman had then appeared, how hopeful and excited about life—and what a contrast to the dull-eyed, unhappy being weaving so unsteadily upon her feet beside him now!

As Maggie and her old mentor made their way through the

heavy drifts and approached her home on Barclay Street, she again tried to escape Horace. But he caught her and gently steered her back to the snow-covered stoop at number 15. Helping her up the stairs and taking the key from her hands, he opened the door and watched her ascend to her rooms on an upper floor.

Initially Horace Greeley was dumbfounded by his discovery of Maggie's alcoholism. Even the shock of Elisha's untimely death and the Kanes' financial rebuff, harsh though they were, hardly seemed an excuse. Throughout his adult life, the progressive journalist had been a teetotaler who opposed drinking by men—and especially by women. Greeley had, in fact, been one of the leaders of the May 1853 World's Temperance Convention held in New York City.

He was reluctant to bring Maggie's mother such bad news. Horace had been fond of Mrs. Fox, who, for all her provincial ways, had remained a kind and loyal friend, even to his difficult wife, Mary. The editor finally brought himself to mention Maggie's alarming behavior. While wincing as she listened, Mrs. Fox did not seem surprised. "We have known for many months that Maggie was using strong drink," she quietly admitted, according to *Time Is Kind*. "I do not know how she got started, but I think it was when she first went to live alone. She took brandy to make her sleep, Kate [Katy] says."

The worst of it, Mrs. Fox plaintively added, was that no one knew how to help Maggie break the habit. She and Katy had first tasted liquor while they were quite young when well-meaning hosts of their séances offered them champagne and brandy at dinners. Now, Mrs. Fox tearfully observed, she worried that they had acquired a fondness for it—just like her husband, John. "Do you think they got his weakness?" she asked. "I've often feared it, when I saw them taking a glass of wine."

Yes, Katy was drinking too—perhaps even more than Maggie. Like her older sister, Katy was high-strung and prone to nervousness. Yet such traits, after all, had long been considered aspects of the mediumistic personality—or "sensitives" as they were called in the popular vernacular. Only gradually did Mrs. Fox realize why Katy rose so late in the mornings, why she seemed so groggy when she finally did awaken. Horace immediately went to their doctor and friend, Edward Bayard.

To his surprise, the physician was woefully familiar with Maggie's drinking problem. He told Horace he had tried to talk reason to her and Katy for months—but to no avail. Earlier that same morning, in fact, Bayard admitted that he had been summoned to Maggie's rooms on Barclay Street by a worried neighbor because the young woman seemed very ill.

He blamed Maggie's deterioration on the tragic events of her life. When he first met her in the early 1850s, she had been a sweet, trusting young woman. Yet, in the intervening years she had been subjected to so many harsh life situations—and so much public embarrassment—that her spirit had been broken. The prime culprit, Edward Bayard continued, was Elisha Kent Kane. The man had treated Maggie abysmally, ultimately pushing her into desperate emotional and economic straits. True, others might have considered Elisha a heroic explorer in the Arctic, but from his perspective, the man was nothing more than a "gentleman cad." The physician also considered the Kane family's treatment of Maggie reprehensible.

But surely something could be done, Horace insisted, to cure Maggie and Katy? Perhaps, the physician agreed, stressing that he was even more worried about Katy than Maggie. While Maggie drank until she wandered and became incoherent, Katy's behavior under the influence of alcohol was still more alarming. "She drinks till she finds oblivion; she will destroy herself if she is not checked soon," he predicted.

The doctor had already taken the relatively unusual step of finding a suitable nursing home. The treatment center was run by a colleague, George H. Taylor, a graduate of Harvard College and

New York Medical School who had recently returned from still more study in Sweden. Perhaps not coincidentally, Dr. Taylor was also one of Edward Bayard's neighbors, living close to his own home near the Croton Reservoir, now the site of the New York Public Library. Since 1860 the forty-four-year-old Taylor and his wife had been running a small hospital called the Swedish Movement Cure out of two adjacent brownstones at the northeast corner of Thirty-eighth Street and Sixth Avenue. Their specialty, as the dispensary's name suggested, employed various types of massage and even mechanical devices to release nervous tensions and realign the body.

Knowing the treatments would be costly, Horace volunteered to pay for them. There was no need, the doctor assured him. Leah and Daniel Underhill had already agreed to cover their hospital costs. There was only one condition: that neither Maggie nor Katy should know the identity of their benefactors.

⁊❧⳾

On January 5, 1865, the grizzled, septuagenarian John Fox rose early at the Greeley brownstone. He washed, ate breakfast, and took his customary seat in a rocking chair. A few minutes later his wife, Margaret, walked into the room and saw her husband sitting silently, as he often did at that hour. Moments passed before she noticed that John seemed unnaturally still. Drawing closer, she realized that her husband was dead.

Hearing a crash, Katy ran to the entranceway, where she found Mrs. Fox in a faint. After reviving her mother, Katy helped her to a couch and immediately summoned Horace Greeley, Edward Bayard, Maggie, Leah, and Daniel.

They decided that John Fox, who always preferred upstate New York to the city, should be buried in Newark near his son David's home. Mrs. Fox, too distraught to make the trip, would stay at Leah's home with friends. Greeley and Bayard would have to wait to confront Katy and Maggie about their drinking because the next day the sisters would travel to Newark with Leah and their father's coffin.

After a simple funeral, the mourning family gathered at David's home in Arcadia. During the visit the farmer, his wife, Elizabeth, and other relatives began to wonder about Maggie and Katy's behavior, suspecting that something besides grief for their father was troubling them. Leah finally told David that they had become addicted to alcohol. Perhaps the best way to help Maggie and Katy recover, the brother and sister decided, was to separate them. So David invited Maggie to remain in Arcadia with his family until spring. Maggie would not hear of being shut in all winter in upstate New York, with its bitterly cold temperatures, impassable snow banks, and dreary weather. The idea was unthinkable. New York City had long been her home and her small but cherished apartment on Barclay Street served as a sanctuary for her memories and shrine for Elisha.

Maggie packed her bags and traveled with Katy and Leah back to New York. In Syracuse, where the train stopped for half an hour, the two sisters left the car together, returning just a few moments before the warning whistle. Before long, Leah noted, her younger sisters fell asleep. "She knew the reason for their slumber," Pond observed in *Time Is Kind.*

From Leah's perspective, her sisters, especially the headstrong Maggie, must have seemed foolish ingrates with little common sense or ability to care for themselves. It was only by virtue of her own efforts that Maggie and Katy had been afforded such a privileged life—a life that, for reasons she could never fathom, had been met with resentment and disobedience.

◈

Daniel Underhill was more forgiving than his wife. From his perspective, his sisters-in-law were both still young and attractive women: With proper help and temporary respite from the necessity of making a living, he believed, they stood a very good chance of recovery. That was why he had already made private arrangements with Edward Bayard for their care.

"It was in 1865 that Katie was brought by Dr. Bayard, a homeopathic physician residing in Fortieth Street, New York City, to the 'Swedish Movement Cure' of Dr. George H. Taylor," his son William G. Langworthy Taylor recalled in his 1933 memoir, *Katie Fox: Epochmaking Medium and the Making of the Fox-Taylor Record.* Katy's arrival, he noted, "occurred in the heyday of sanitariums, diet reform, water-cures, high thinking and plain living." The Taylors' hospital bore a strong resemblance to a modern spa, emphasizing the principles of diet, physical exercise, massage, and clean living.

"There were many perfectly well persons who boarded [there] on account of its home atmosphere or...took...the mechanical massage as a means of recuperation from the fatigues of business," William Taylor explained.

Home atmosphere or not, Maggie refused to go. An institution with its schedules and regimens was an anathema, all too reminiscent of the daily drill and tight schedule that Mrs. Turner had attempted to enforce upon her years earlier in Crookville.

Instead, in what was undoubtedly a painful meeting with Edward Bayard, Maggie insisted that she would make every effort to abstain, if only to fulfill her promise to Elisha to lead a "pure" life. If she regressed, she promised, she would either seek his help directly or that of her spiritual adviser, Father Quinn. Moreover, Maggie rationalized, she was still engrossed in an unresolved issue over the Kane settlement. As such, she needed ready access to her friends and attorney. Reluctantly, the physician agreed.

One of Maggie's friends, in fact, had taken drastic measures to settle the Kane annuity issue. On January 3, 1865, just a few days before John Fox's death, an anonymous writer sent a letter to Elisha's sixty-nine-year-old mother, Jane Leiper Kane.

In an appeal to the dowager's highest instincts the writer outlined the sad chain of events surrounding Elisha's romance and marriage, as well as Maggie's unsuccessful battle to obtain funds from his estate. The letter writer was intimately knowledgeable about Maggie's situation—and utterly sympathetic to it. In a firm and concise hand, the writer asked the widowed Mrs. John Kane:

Is not this withholding this money from her, a robbery? Is not Mr. R. P. Kane's violation of his own solemn pledge, on the faith of which the poor girl stopped nearly three years since the suit now before your Court—dishonorable? Has not the young girl whose life has been blighted by her love for Dr. Kane—who for between three and four years received his vows as "the only woman he ever loved"—who as his letters testify is "pure as an angel—of refined mind and spotless character"—yet who is now a lonely and helpless mourner—broke down in health, living on the memory of her buried idol—isolated from all friends and early associations. Has she not a claim—a just claim—to be at least saved from want—to be sheltered from undeserved disgrace? It is not her wish to intrude upon you; if it had been, she could have claimed the dower...years ago and could have published the letters; her forbearance shows her delicacy.

Now, the writer insisted, it behooved Jane Leiper Kane—if not her sons—to right the wrongs before Maggie published her son Elisha's love letters.

I have read the letters, madam, and solemnly assure you that their publication will bring a cloud of reproach on the memory of your illustrious son; not that his love was not *pure* to the end...but because Dr. Kane was capable of seeking out, pursuing and betrothing himself to a young girl, then of meanly deserting her afterwards, throwing himself on her generosity; of denying it in public while in private writing to her that he would not give her up—of marrying her secretly and wringing from her a solemn pledge to keep that marriage secret from all but the witnesses till his return; of requiring her to give up all her means of support, and then to save the family pride, offering the pittance to her in such a way that she could be wronged out of it.

The letter, signed, "A friend to both parties," was intercepted by one of the Kanes' lawyers. While Maggie may never have known about the letter, its bullying and sanctimonious tone seems to have had an explosive effect upon the Kanes. By May 1865, the family stopped sending her the promised quarterly annuities.

Again, Maggie waited patiently for a check and finally appealed to her attorney. By early summer 1865 she realized that the annuity had been withheld deliberately and insisted that Dr. Bayard return Elisha's letters. Afterward, as La Fumee observed in the preface to *The Love-Life of Dr. Kane*, "she declared her determination never again to part with a treasure in which her very life was bound up."

Maggie's lawsuit against the Kanes continued. Defense attorneys reminded the court that Maggie's wedding to Elisha had been performed in a "Quaker" or private ceremony without benefit of clergy. The only witnesses were Mrs. Fox, Katy, and a friend. Since those women were naturally sympathetic parties to Maggie's cause, the Kanes' attorneys argued, their depositions about a wedding ceremony could not be taken seriously. Moreover, no civil marriage documents had been filed to confirm the ceremony. The court upheld the Kanes' contention that Maggie and Elisha had not been legally wed. The case was thrown out of court. The decision implied that Maggie was a wanton woman who had co-habited with Elisha without benefit of a legal marriage—an assumption likely to be believed, given the link between spiritualism and free love.

Maggie was devastated. Her friends were outraged. This, they maintained, was yet another example of the Kanes' nefarious strategy to cheat Maggie out of her rightful due. Moreover, the trial had been unfair from the start: Philadelphia, where the case was tried, was not only the home of the late Judge John Kane but also where his son Robert still maintained a law practice.

Tragically, Maggie's life, once filled with friends, admirers, dinners, and outings was, by the summer of 1865, largely confined to memories. Somehow she hung on, maintained probably by friends and Daniel Underhill, who kept her out of the shantytowns and missions where many of Manhattan's indigent women lived. Still mourning the death of her father, trying to abstain from alcohol, and facing what looked like certain impoverishment, Maggie spent her days shuttling between her home, church, and the Underhill townhouse to visit her mother.

Months before John's death, as Maggie confessed in a second memoir, *The Death-Blow to Spiritualism*, Mrs. Fox had been forced to withstand a terrible revelation. In 1864, Maggie and Katy had confessed the truth about the origins of the spiritualist movement. "My poor father and mother...both knew before their death that all we had practiced for so many years was a fraud and a deception," Maggie recalled.

In response, Mrs. Fox had become morbidly depressed—just as she had years earlier when the spirits first rapped in Hydesville. For comfort, the matron had turned even more fervently to the Methodist church, where she prayed for her daughters' souls. "Oh, my dear children, I do hope that you will get out of this sort of life soon," Mrs. Fox had beseeched Maggie and Katy in the months following their confession.

Leah and Daniel had done their best to comfort Margaret. Yet she had declined, lapsing into a cheerful amnesia, or senility. The matron's "tired old brain with its numbed perception, shut out all grief and disappointment...and she passed from usefulness to carefree second childhood," as *Time Is Kind* put it.

By August 3, 1865, her trials were finally at an end. That day Mrs. Fox quietly passed away in Leah and Daniel's home. In a final gesture of kindness, Daniel Underhill offered to have his mother-in-law buried in the Underhill plot in Brooklyn's elegant Greenwood Cemetery.

❧

With Mrs. Fox's death—and Katy's removal to the Swedish Movement Cure Hospital—Maggie was essentially abandoned, deprived of the companionship that had helped shape her life. Her devoted friends, Edward Bayard, Horace Greeley, Elizabeth Ellet, Joseph La Fumee, and Ellen Walter, once again urged Maggie to become self-reliant, to reclaim her dignity—and to assert her marital rights.

By 1865, more women were demanding those rights than ever before. Among the most vocal of those who had joined the fight for suffrage were the nation's female mediums. Many had long since been liberated from men by the money they collected by giving séances and lecture tours. At the first national convention of spiritualists in Chicago in 1864 they had officially resolved "That we recognize perfect and entire equality of rights as between the sexes, including equal property, equal marital…and religious rights, and…reject the absurd pretext that sex, in any instance, whatever, confers the slightest authority."

Now, Maggie's friends suggested, she had an important opportunity to assert herself—to explain her life and the way she had been mistreated—by publishing Elisha's letters. Despite her persistent threats over the years, Maggie had never seriously planned to expose Elisha's letters, and she remained reluctant to consider it. But a chorus of friends pressed her to be courageous. The Kanes, they reminded her, had shown no compunction in tarnishing her reputation. On September 9, 1865, they had even gone so far as to send the Associated Press a telegram calling the story of Maggie's wedding to Elisha a "canard."

Ultimately, Maggie conceded. Carleton Publishers of New York published the long-held manuscript of *The Love-Life of Dr. Kane*.

"Perhaps many will think that no circumstances could justify the publication of the letters contained in this volume. The lady to whom they were addressed has ever held these letters as too sacred for any eyes save her own to rest upon," read the preface. "She has borne poverty and privation, when their publication many years ago might have given her an independence."

The world, the preface continued, "usually sides with the rich, the proud and the powerful," but perhaps "some good will be accomplished in the unquestionable proof afforded of the pure and spotless character of the two persons whose hearts are laid open in this correspondence."

THE HIGHEST RIGHT

The essence of lying is in deception, not in words.
—JOHN RUSKIN, *Pathetic Fallacy*, 1856

ON A DREARY December 10, 1865, four days after the U.S. Congress ratified the Thirteenth Amendment outlawing slavery, the *Rochester Union* distracted its readers from serious matters of state with the announcement of an intriguing new publication. "A book will probably appear within a short time giving the facts in the history of Dr. Kane, the Arctic navigator, which have hitherto been shrouded in mystery," promised the *Rochester Union*.

The *New York Times* announced the appearance of *The Love-Life of Dr. Kane* with far less enthusiasm. "Though the circumstances explained in the preface may afford some slight ground for the publication of these papers," the *Times* haughtily opined on December 15, "we must still regard it as an intrusion of private matters before that many-headed Monster, the Public—the last body in the world that should be selected to exercise the functions of a court of appeals for the redress of individual grievances."

Despite the advance publicity and all of Maggie's anguished deliberations, *The Love-Life of Dr. Kane* proved a great disappointment. The "many-headed monster, the Public" was not particularly interested in the story of Maggie and Elisha's ill-fated romance. Maggie had waited too long. Americans were reeling from President Lincoln's assassination, distracted by the monumental effort to rebuild burnt-out railroads, farms, and cities, and inundated by an avalanche of true-life stories about the 620,000 Americans killed in the Civil War. Maggie, now a nearly forgotten medium, and her romance with an

Arctic explorer, by then eight years dead, could not compete. The proceeds would be too paltry to support her.

The publication of *The Love-Life of Dr. Kane* nevertheless brought renewed expressions of sympathy from former followers and seemed to brighten Maggie's outlook. Indeed, by the spring of 1866, the Fox family thought Maggie seemed more like her old self than she had been in years. "She had come forth from her seclusion and had resumed her music," according to *Time Is Kind.* "Her sweet voice had sounded once again in song. She had shown many hopeful signs of entering into normal life, again, joining her friends in happy comradeship."

At Dr. Taylor's Swedish Movement Cure Hospital, Katy too was recovering. After several months of treatment, Maggie's younger sister was well enough to leave her room and, while still unable to join other clients at the "public table" for meals, participated in some spa activities. Dr. Edward Bayard and Daniel Underhill were happy to hear the optimistic news. Of course they were still paying the bills: Both Maggie and Katy seemed incapable of managing their personal finances. Absently, they left others to figure it out. "They had always accepted it, as they had always done, childishly unconscious of their money, either as to how it came or where it went," Pond reported in *Time Is Kind.*

The frustrating result was that even when Edward Bayard helped Maggie establish a budget, she had difficulty adhering to it. In April 1867, Maggie hoped to visit Isaac and Amy Post in Rochester, but she was so short of cash that she asked them to advance her the money for the trip.

Maggie implied that she had already resumed—or at least decided to resume—her former work as a medium. Writing somewhat obliquely to the Posts, she explained that she was certain that she could quickly repay the nine-dollar loan. "I can make the money in Rochester to return it to you in perhaps less than a week," she promised. What else could that be but her agreement to conduct a séance in Rochester?

Some years later in a *New York World* story, Maggie explained that her decision to resume work as a spiritualist had evolved out of a series of discussions with Father Quinn. The priest had assured her there was no conflict between Catholicism and spiritualism— especially because her financial security depended upon it. For the sake of earning her bread, Maggie could work as a medium "as long as I was in this business and did not believe in it and had to support myself to charge very high prices so that it would at least limit the number of my patrons."

~❦~

Encouraged by what seemed to be signs of Maggie and Katy's permanent recovery, Daniel Underhill decided to subsidize an apartment for his sisters-in-law on Forty-fourth Street, a few blocks from the Swedish Movement Cure Hospital. For several months all seemed to go smoothly: Katy officially resumed her spiritualist practices, while Maggie lived quietly by her side, occasionally giving private séances with her younger sister as well as on her own.

Lulled into believing her younger sisters had recovered, Leah, having avoided Katy and Maggie for months, decided to visit them one summer morning in 1867. Leah arrived at her sisters' home at the requisite calling hour, expecting to congratulate them on their return to health.

At the matron's ring, the door was flung open. There, to Leah's horror, stood Maggie and Katy in rumpled clothes, weaving unsteadily on their feet and bidding her an incoherent welcome. Behind them was a dirty and disheveled parlor reeking from liquor and stale air, the results of a two- or three-day drinking binge.

At Leah's chiding, Katy began crying, while Maggie could no longer hold back her resentment. She excoriated Leah for her domineering control of their lives, for her forceful manipulations of her and her younger sister into mediumship, for ruining their lives.

"The scene that followed was one never to be erased from her memory...a hideous recollection of Maggie's maudlin insolence and Kate's hysterical protests," wrote Pond in *Time Is Kind*. In the aftermath of shrill rebuttals and recriminations, Leah escaped to her waiting carriage, returned home, and took to her bed for weeks.

It would be months, according to Fox family legend, before "The poison of her rage was finally overcome." While Leah would eventually forgive her youngest sister, her long-standing alienation from Maggie would be permanent.

~❦~

The next few years of Maggie's life were clouded by drink and careless record-keeping that left most of her actions unknown. Better chronicled was Katy's return to Dr. Taylor's Swedish Movement Cure Hospital, where the ever-solicitous Taylors attended her. Gradually, she began giving séances to private clients and patients at the hospital.

While Maggie had been preoccupied with her lawsuit again the Kanes, spiritualism's popularity had rebounded during the Civil War. The renewed interest came from mourning mothers, wives, sisters, and other relatives of the soldiers who lost their lives.

Mary Todd Lincoln, the eccentric wife of President Lincoln, became one of spiritualism's strongest advocates. She believed she could reach their dead son, Willie, through séances. Lincoln had remained skeptical but in an ongoing effort to please his wife remained open to the idea of spiritual communication.

In 1861, for instance, after patiently listening to reformist Robert Dale Owen deliver an enthusiastic presentation on spiritualism, President Lincoln, with a glimmer of amusement in his eyes, replied, "Well. For those who like that sort of thing, I should think it is just about the sort of thing they would like."

Just as ambiguously the Chief Executive agreed to accept spiritualist books penned by Maggie's old friend former Wisconsin governor Nathaniel P. Tallmadge. From time to time, he also attended séances with his wife conducted by medium Nettie Colburn Maynard.

Gradually the First Lady became even more adamant in her beliefs in the power of spirits. "He lives, Emilie," she insisted to the nurse of her dead son after a séance. "He comes to me every night and stands at the foot of my bed, with the same sweet, adorable smile he always had."

British-born medium Charles J. Colchester, allegedly the illegitimate son of a duke, was a favorite of Washington congressmen. Out of curiosity, if nothing else, Lincoln invited Colchester for a séance at the White House and seemed to have enjoyed his showmanship. Later, following the President's assassination in April 1865, Colchester moved on to Buffalo, where religious groups, stymied about how to discredit him, eventually accused him of operating as a "sleight-of-hand artist" without a license.

Colchester's trial began August 19, 1865, and ignited the old debate about spiritualism. Predictably, the New York press adopted its usual attitudes: Greeley's *New York Tribune* equivocating, Bennett's *New York Herald* debunking, and William Henry Raymond's *New York Times* urging caution about hasty conclusions. "The practical inference from all this would seem to be, first—however puzzled you may be with spiritualism, however interested in it as a curious development in philosophy, don't trust it," the *New York Times* opined on September 27.

The trial concluded with Judge Hall's decision that Colchester pay a $40 fine plus $473 in legal fees for refusing to prove that he was either a magician or a medium. The next day hundreds of enraged spiritualists assembled at Manhattan's Metropolitan Hall. Infuriated, they staged a "Religio-Political Court of the People" satirizing the judge's decision.

The controversy smoldered for months in the New York press. In 1866, America's famous showman P. T. Barnum, who took a wry pleasure in characterizing himself as the "king of humbugs," published a cautionary book entitled *The Humbugs of the World.* Widely distributed, the impresario's work was meant to distinguish true oddities, such as the ones displayed at his American Museum, from those that were fraudulent.

One of the "humbugs" he denounced was American spiritualism: "The 'spirit rapping' humbug was started in Hydesville, New York, about seventeen years ago by several daughters of a Mr. Fox. The Fox family found that the rapping business would be made to pay; and so they continued it, with varying success, for a number of years." Since then "there has been a constantly increasing demand for 'spiritual wonders,' to meet which numerous mediums have 'developed.'"

Over the years the mediums had developed special types of "spiritual humbuggery." These included mediums who wrote automatically through the spirits, those who telepathically read sealed letters, and those who used "spirit cabinets" through which spirits materialized into human form.

So damning were such accusations that the National Convention of Spiritualists held in Cleveland in September 1867 advised conferees to avoid jumping to conclusions about strange "physical manifestations." A table moving was not necessarily proof of a spiritual presence. Nor was the sound of eerie voices. Enthusiasm for spiritual communication ran so strong that it naturally leant itself to abuse, giving the movement a bad name. For that reason, mediums must be scrupulously honest in their practices.

Six months later, in commemoration of the twentieth anniversary of the spiritualist movement, the National Organization of Spiritualists launched a series of celebrations in various cities around the country. Thousands of supporters attended. One of the most exuberant celebrations was held March 31, 1868, at Rochester's

Corinthian Hall. The Fox sisters' earliest supporters—Amy and Isaac Post, George Willits, and the Reverend A. H. Jervis—appeared on the platform to memorialize that historic night.

"Ladies and Gentlemen—There seems to have been a spontaneous movement throughout this country, in regard to holding an anniversary meeting in commemoration of the advent of modern spiritualism," began keynote speaker Edward Jones. "It is now twenty years since this startling phenomenon made its appearance among us in this city, and in this short space of time it has become known nearly throughout the world. Converts to this faith and philosophy are now numbered by millions. No system of philosophy or religion has ever made such rapid strides...We have reason to hope that the light emanating from the spirit spheres will ultimately dispel the darkness and superstition which have so long enshrouded the world."

That same afternoon another celebration took place in Boston's banner-bedecked Music Hall, where three thousand spiritualists and seven hundred children gathered. The event began with a formal march by members of several spiritualist organizations, escorted by a platoon of police. A rousing band led a parade outside the Music Hall, around Boston Commons, and down several streets before returning to the auditorium. Standing before the audience that evening, Dr. H. F. Gardner introduced one of spiritualism's foremost figures, the Poughkeepsie Seer: "Our friend and brother, Andrew Jackson Davis, who is upon this platform, some years previous to the manifestations in Hydesville, was the subject of spirit control, and in his clairvoyant state predicted that these manifestations would occur at a certain time—which prophecy was fulfilled."

In New York, the celebration was held in Manhattan's Everett Rooms, where guests were lavishly entertained with a series of piano recitals, violin performances, spiritualist readings, and recitations. The speeches were followed by the arrival of Katy and Leah.

Somewhat later, according to a report in the *Banner of Light,*

Maggie arrived as well, her tardiness due, it was tactfully observed, to a prior commitment. In all likelihood Maggie had hesitated to appear at all and had done so at only the last minute, fretting that by promoting the spiritualist cause she was breaking her old promise to Elisha.

⁓❧⁓

Just a few days after the twentieth-anniversary celebrations Horace Greeley finally stopped equivocating. He denounced the movement as a nefarious influence upon the nation's morals. "Men and women... have grown lax in their notions of marriage, divorce and moral purity... the aggregate of insanity and suicide has been increased by spiritualism," he lamented in a widely reprinted *Tribune* story.

Greeley's words mirrored the popular belief that spiritualism led to psychological harm, increasing the likelihood that followers would become suicidal, insane, or vulnerable to alcoholism.

A cadre of the nation's physicians, neurologists, and alienists already were pondering the origins of aberrant mental conditions and their relationship to physical health. Could one abnormal psychological state trigger another? What did a tendency to fall into a trance portend for that individual's subsequent emotional stability? Why were certain individuals—those prone to clairvoyance, telepathy, or hallucinations—identified as "sensitives"?

Theories abounded. In 1868, G. W. Sampson, president of Washington, D.C.'s Columbian College, warned that the mind-body connection was so intense that spiritual experiments could dangerously overload the nervous system. To Sampson, as to many other investigators, the human spirit was key to the health of the body.

The human spirit, British anthropologist Alfred Russell Wallace asserted in an April 1869 *Quarterly Review,* was so powerful that it had overwhelmed the laws of nature and had manifested itself quite independently. "He [man] is, indeed, a being apart, since he is not influenced by the great laws which irresistibly modify all other organic beings," Wallace maintained, denouncing natural selection less than a decade after its introduction.

Wallace, a close associate of Charles Darwin, not only admitted that he believed in spirit power, but that he had conducted scientific experiments on its phenomena: "I have now had every opportunity of fully testing, & which demonstrate the existence of forces & influences not yet recognized by science. This will I know seem to you like some mental hallucination...I am in hopes that you will suspend your judgment for a time till we exhibit some corroborative symptoms of insanity."

Wallace's observation reflected his new theory linking spiritualism to the poorly understood dynamics of the human nervous system. By the 1870s, his theory was challenged by an American investigator, William Hammond, a "professor of disease of the mind and nervous system" in the Medical Department of the University of the City of New York, who asserted that hallucinations had no relationship to the spiritual world. Mediums were not receiving messages from another world, but were "victims of some severe disorder of the nervous system."

By the 1880s that theory would be given even more credence when neurologist George Beard dubbed such susceptible individuals as "neurasthenics," who were vulnerable to disorders such as nervous dyspepsia, insanity, and drunkenness.

While spiritualists hotly refuted that theory and insisted that they possessed extraordinary mental gifts, they agreed that the maintenance of a healthy physical and mental lifestyle was critical for clairvoyance. "Anxiety, care, vexation, disgust, desire, and wish, unfit the mind for control by spirits," the Rochester-based Reverend Dr. Charles C. Hammond had warned readers in his 1852 spiritualist guidebook. "So also does excessive labor, fatigue, disease, surprise, or any other cause which increases the positive condition of the medium."

Similarly, Andrew Jackson Davis—who, by then, had distanced himself from the elaborate and gimmick-oriented spiritualist "manifestations" like spirit cabinets, spirit music, and levitations—had nevertheless stressed the importance of the trance as a means of achieving higher states of clairvoyance. To do so, as Hammond's guide reflected, Davis scrupulously avoided the use of alcohol, believing that purity of mind and mood were the key to higher states of consciousness. Echoing that message was W. H. Evans's warning to readers of his 1865 book *How to Be A Medium:* "Do not indulge in stimulants, nor excessive smoking. Anything which interferes with the proper functioning of the body hinders the right expression of the psychic nature."

≈✧≈

Katy's persistent return to alcoholism did not necessarily seem to impair her spiritual communications, as her caretakers, George and Sarah Taylor at the Swedish Movement Cure Hospital, soon discovered. Repeatedly between 1865 and 1871, after months of abstinence, a seemingly recovered Katy would conduct séances and visit her sister Maggie at her apartment.

Then, for no apparent reason, the slender medium would return to the hospital so inebriated that a despairing Sarah Taylor would rush her out of sight. So skillfully did Sarah minister to Katy that few people ever saw her relapses. "When for a time under the influence of drink (there were reform periods when she was quite trustworthy in this matter) she was hustled off to her room by my mother so that I saw uniformly the smiling, cheerful, patient, Katie," William Taylor recalled in his memoir *Katie Fox: Epoch-making Medium and the Making of the Fox-Taylor Record.*

Simultaneous with Katy's first admission to their hospital, the Taylors were struggling with grief themselves. They had recently lost two of their three children, three-year-old Frankie and eighteen-month-old Leila. While well aware of Katy's reputation as a famous medium, the Taylors avoided eliciting her help.

Nevertheless, one March day in 1869 Katy sent for Sarah, informing her that she had communicated with the spirit of Sarah's deceased grandfather. Remaining skeptical as Katy put herself into a trance, Sarah found herself becoming transfixed with awe as her patient proceeded to reveal one intimate detail after another about her dead children.

Over the next seven or eight months Katy delivered so many other inexplicably accurate messages—sometimes through mirror writing—that Sarah and her husband, George, became convinced that she was psychically gifted. As their son William later recalled, his parents—and everyone else who knew her—felt sure that "Katie was a great medium—all classes of spirits, high and low, elect and damned, could manifest through her channel."

By November 1869 the Taylors were working feverishly to transpose Katy's spirit messages into a standard written form, or diary—later known as *The Fox-Taylor Record* and still considered an authoritative account of the medium's later life. Among the 1,367 communications the couple collected over the next twenty-three years were hundreds of messages from their lost children. Inevitably, many of them reflected Katy's ongoing struggle with alcohol, which the Taylors, in their eagerness to talk with their dead offspring, stoically accepted as a perverse accompaniment to her clairvoyance.

"This is the séance that was held when Katie was dead drunk," Sarah, having thrown aside all pretensions of medical objectivity, recorded in her diary on February 14, 1870. Under the entranced Katy's instruction, after turning off the light and opening the window Sarah opened a drawer, where to her and George's surprise lay a "spirit drawing" of her late son Frankie.

"Drunkenness, like dying, releases evangelical power...," Sarah scrawled in that diary, inadvertently adding another piece to the fierce debate already raging among doctors and psychologists over the relation between alternate states of consciousness and health.

By May 25 her friend Robert Dale Owen managed to extract a promise that Katy would abstain for the next six months. Four days later, during an outing with Maggie, she broke her promise.

"Katie comes back in no condition to work," Sarah recorded on May 29, 1870. "Katie ought to have minded her mother [Mrs. Fox's spirit] and not gone with her sister to that place. We hope she will keep away now."

Implicit in Sarah's notation was the idea that Katy should avoid Maggie because of her bad influence. Yet neither sister was willing to accept the suggestion.

To Maggie, Katy was an increasingly important source of comfort and companionship. Katy, moreover, was the only person who knew everything in their strange history. Alienated from Leah, with her parents dead, Maggie had only her younger sister. It must have seemed unreasonable that the Taylors could so cruelly judge her, that they demanded that Katy keep her distance: They had, after all, never met Maggie and knew nothing about her, except unflattering, mean-spirited rumors.

Katy also clung to Maggie. While she maintained a polite relationship with Leah, Maggie was the only sister she could trust. She would, as Katy told the Taylors, do anything to help Maggie return to her formerly lively and fun-loving self.

In August 1870, learning that Maggie was in the throes of another drinking binge, Katy tried again to help, leaving the hospital to nurse her sister back to sobriety.

But the outcome was sorrowful for both women. "Katie meets Maggie on August 5th, who was fearfully in need of care," Sarah recorded in the diary on August 7. "She remained with her and tried to do for her, but the consequence was she went down under the breakers herself [with drink] instead of gliding smoothly over as she had been doing for four weeks and more. The sea she met in her sister and her sister's surroundings was too much for her frail bark and she returned to us Saturday evening, the sixth, sad, sad."

⚬❧⚬

Maggie was especially desperate as her other friends disappeared. By 1870, the aging Mrs. Walter had moved away because of her health; that same year, Horace Greeley was feverishly crisscrossing the country in a fruitless presidential election against Ulysses S. Grant. And while Drs. Gray and Bayard as well as the devoted Joseph La Fumee continued to call upon Maggie, none of them could rescue her from waves of depression and the demon alcohol.

In 1871, however, both Maggie and Katy rallied. Maggie, by then thirty-eight years of age, gave up drinking and decided to resume conducting séances on a steady basis. She had been assured by Father Quinn that conducting séances was permissible if they were for her self-support. To protect herself from any additional implications of sin, she designed a unique calling card. "So that as few people as possible might be deceived I had on my cards an emphatic disclaimer of any occult inspiration," Maggie explained in her memoir *The Death-Blow to Spiritualism*. On the back of each card the message read, "Mrs. Kane does not claim any spirit power; but people must judge for themselves."

Even among the usually tolerant mediums of organized spiritualism, such a message raised eyebrows. But ultimately it was of little import, especially to curious clients, who regarded Maggie's card as simply another paradox, another aspect of the once-famous medium's mystique. Before long, Maggie's appointment book was again filled with séance appointments.

Still, according to *Time Is Kind*, she never reached her earlier levels of success. Alcoholism and its ravages upon her body were to blame: "The deterioration of her physical organism had brought with it diminution of the esoteric force which once had surged through her but she still had followers, many who believed and relied upon her. At times there were transient flashes of her early strength, brief periods in which she...stood in the sweet dignity of her real self."

By the summer of 1871 other observers felt equally encouraged about Katy. Privately, George Taylor and Edward Bayard surmised that she would never be permanently cured, but admirers Robert Dale Owen and banker Charles Livermore, a longtime client, remained so dazzled by her abilities that they could only blame her habit on Maggie's pernicious influence.

Livermore based his opinion on the rumors he had heard about Maggie—rumors easy enough to believe, especially since he had never set eyes on her before—that she was emotionally unstable, that she had fabricated her marriage to Elisha Kent Kane, that she had taken his brothers to court to extort money from the explorer's estate. Livermore was consequently "determined to remove Kate from all adverse influences, separate her forever, if he could, from the deteriorating companionship of Maggie." But to do so, the banker had to create a subterfuge in the form of an offer to send Katy to London for a visit.

✤

England's capital city was a stronghold of spiritualism. The movement had arrived in London in 1852 through the appearance of Mrs. W. R. Hayden, wife of the Boston editor of the *Star Spangled Banner* magazine. Already a well-known Massachusetts medium, she continued the practice in London. Inevitably the idea of talking with the dead intrigued the great and small, touching writers and thinkers such as Charles Dickens and George Eliot.

A month after Mrs. Hayden's arrival, Dickens published "The Ghost of the Cock Lane Ghost" in his weekly journal *Household Words,* satirizing Mrs. Hayden's raps and suggesting they could only be created by warmed knee joints. By the spring of 1853, nevertheless, Mrs. Hayden had several imitators.

Before long spirit circles appeared in London's drawing rooms and parlors, expanding to Keighley (where followers founded Britain's first spiritualist church), Coventry, Bradford, Nottingham, Belfast, and other towns. By 1855 the nation's first spiritualist publication, the *Yorkshire Spiritual Telegraph and British Harmonial Advocate,* appeared.

Author George Eliot disparaged the movement, declaring that it was "better [to] be occupied with the intestinal worms of tortoises" than with spiritualism. Among those who remained fascinated were Alfred Lord Tennyson and William Makepeace Thackeray, who had witnessed his first séance in 1852 in the New York home of historian George Bancroft. No less enthusiastic were several visual artists, among them painter James Whistler, the Pre-Raphaelite artist-poets Dante Gabriel Rossetti, and his siblings William and Christina.

The decade between 1860 and 1870 was known as the "American Invasion," as Frank Podmore, a relentless investigator of the British Society for Psychical Research, observed in his 1902 history *Mediums of the 19th Century.* American mediums found a huge appreciative audience in Britain. Knowing that, Charles Livermore persuaded Katy that she could join them—especially in light of her talents and history as one of spiritualism's co-founders. She would, the widowed banker predicted, immediately be welcomed as a celebrity.

Katy responded half-heartedly. True, Livermore would pay for her trip and had given her his solemn word that his influential friends would warmly receive her. Yet Katy had compelling reasons to stay in New York. She did not want to abandon Maggie, whom she felt desperately needed her companionship. Maggie also was unenthusiastic about Katy's trip, becoming so upset that she vowed to give up drinking forever if Katy would promise to remain in New York.

Much as Maggie needed Katy, the younger sister clung to the Taylors as emotional buttresses against the temptation to drink. Yet, it was Sarah Taylor who urged Katy to reconsider. England would provide Katy with a refreshing change of scenery.

Ultimately, Katy was persuaded to go, if only to end the argument. Rarely did she take a firm stance on the events that shaped her life. "Kate did not make decisions," as Pond put it in *Time Is Kind.*

∾❊∾

Charles Livermore lost no time in purchasing Katy's steamship ticket for a departure on October 7, 1871. The enthusiastic banker also arranged passage for his cultured, middle-aged cousin Blanche Ogden as a traveling companion and chaperone, as well as providing a generous allowance for Katy's new wardrobe. By late August, every detail of the trip had been completed, including notices to Livermore's London friends about Katy's arrival. Yet as the departure date drew near, she became inexplicably restless and irritable, quarreling with her sponsor, and, to Sarah Taylor's dismay, spending most of her time with Maggie.

As it turned out, Sarah's worries were in vain. True to her promise, Maggie had continued to abstain, her energies engrossed in her busy spiritualist practice. The sisters' last month together was among their happiest: "Maggie was self-supporting now, and her close friends, like Kate's devoted admirers, felt a surge of hope and the strong assurance that good would come of the parting," according to *Time Is Kind.*

Maggie and Katy's two groups of friends, who had each accused the other sister of starting to drink, gathered for Katy's departure.

Sarah would meet Maggie for the first time in the steamship, in fact. Her impression of Katy's sister astonished her. This was not the depraved and careless individual she had envisioned, but instead a petite, discreetly dressed woman who looked considerably younger than her thirty-eight years, who sat in the stateroom chatting sweetly with Katy's friends and smiling politely when they were introduced.

What made the tales of drunken debauchery Sarah associated with Maggie seem impossible were her friends, "persons of obvious refinement. Their manner toward her was that of true respect."

At the last whistle of the steamship, Maggie, Sarah, and other well-wishers embraced Katy and, after rushing down the runway, watched the majestic vessel push away from the shore.

Maggie stood on the pier watching Katy's tiny figure disappear into the distance. She realized that now, for the first time in her life, she was truly on her own.

~~✻~~

"The nurse of full-grown souls is solitude," the nineteenth-century poet and spiritualist James Russell Lowell observed in his poem on Christopher Columbus's famous transatlantic voyage.

In the wake of Katy's 1871 crossing of the Atlantic, Maggie was forced to grapple with that solitude, nursing herself into an independent existence that rested upon her success as a medium. Yet the details of that lonely life were only sporadically preserved because Maggie, as her former mentor Susanna Turner had noted with irritation some eighteen years earlier, was a notoriously poor record-keeper.

Enhancing Maggie's efforts to support herself in those years was spiritualism's ongoing appeal for many Americans. Spiritualism attracted new groups of followers, many of them liberals who were linked with the women's suffrage movement.

Maggie seems to have remained indifferent to the well-publicized lectures that drew suffragettes and liberals to public meetings, forums, and rallies. Having long been mired in the sorrows of her own life that were best soothed by prayer, memories, and alcohol, the once lively and astute medium remained apart, stubbornly apolitical.

Maggie's sister Katy was a close friend of feminist Isabella Beecher Hooker, who had recently moved to New York and to whom Maggie had probably been introduced on at least one occasion. Amy Post remained an active suffragist after her husband Isaac's 1872 death and visited occasionally while on her way to see her Long Island relatives.

Yet Maggie remained uninterested in suffrage, even though she, like many of her more political contemporaries, had suffered so obviously from its absence. Her marked absence from the fiery battle for women's rights of that era suggests that Maggie was unable to look beyond her own troubles to the larger implications of that movement whose birth she and her sisters had inadvertently witnessed twenty-two years earlier. Few women living in the years immediately following the Civil War could ignore the questions that the women's movement had raised about the vote, individual liberties, and the sanctity of the American hearth and home.

Even fewer of them, as Elizabeth Cady Stanton and Susan B. Anthony observed, could frame such questions and attract the attention of the public as effectively as spiritualist Victoria Woodhull, who burst upon the national scene in 1870 as one of the most colorful and radical leaders of the suffrage movement.

Born into a raffish family of ten siblings in Homer, Ohio, in 1838, the divorced and remarried Victoria and her equally beguiling sister Tennessee Claflin—Tennie as she preferred to be known—claimed they had been called to New York in 1868 through a spiritualist vision. By 1869 the Claflin sisters had endeared themselves to the city's rich and powerful, including the aging railroad tycoon Commodore Cornelius Vanderbilt. Victoria and Tennie stunned the vulgar tobacco-spitting railroad king with their clairvoyant pronouncements about the stock market.

Later that year, in an ostentatious display of gratitude, the commodore established Victoria and Tennie in a posh Wall Street brokerage house at 44 Broad Street, instantly transforming them into America's first female brokers. In their dazzling new position, the elegantly dressed sisters became a national sensation overnight.

On February 14, 1870, when the doors to Woodhull & Claflin & Company's custom-designed new offices opened, two of New York City's most colorful characters—"Boss Tweed" of Tammany Hall and gold magnate Jim Fisk—appeared and were nearly stampeded by other celebrities and curiosity seekers. Even more significant were the throngs of women who appeared from every walk of life, clutching parcels and handbags, standing patiently in line to invest their life savings with the two glamorous new brokers.

From there, it was a short step for the ambitious Victoria to exploit her wealth, visibility, and clairvoyance by assuming the presidency of the National Association of Spiritualists. Soon thereafter she was nominated by the Equal Rights Party as the candidate for the U.S. presidential election of 1872.

Yet even with the rising hopes for a new social order promised by Victoria's campaign, national sentiments were not in her favor. The "Bewitching Broker of Wall Street" roared through a raucous series of public appearances, endorsing sexual equality in finance and marriage and more lenient divorce laws, the last of which shattered earlier allegiances within the American Woman Suffrage Association and disillusioned key supporters like Susan B. Anthony.

In an electrifying talk on the stormy night of November 20, 1871, Victoria, baited by an incredulous audience of three thousand at Manhattan's Steinway Hall, made the mistake of linking women's rights to suffrage with free love. When a member of the audience asked if she personally practiced free love, Victoria boldly declared, "Yes! I am a Free Lover. I have an *inalienable, constitutional* and *natural* right to love whom I may, to love as *long* or as *short* a period as I can; to *change* that love *every day* if I please and with *that* right neither *you* nor any *law* you can frame have *any* right to interfere...."

Many listeners were appalled. Others walked out. Newspaper headlines accused Victoria—and the suffrage movement—of endorsing free love. Leaders like Elizabeth Cady Stanton and Isabella Beecher Hooker of the National Suffrage Woman Association stood tough, though, bravely committed to supporting Victoria.

Pitted against Victoria in her unsuccessful bid for the presidency was Maggie's former mentor Horace Greeley. Still idealistic, desperately attempting to heal the scarred nation from the Civil War, the editor had won the nomination from the Democratic party, which finally endorsed his favorite cause—complete amnesty for the South. Ultimately, Horace was defeated, too. Voters enthusiastically elected war hero Ulysses S. Grant as their next president.

Horace died a broken man on November 29, 1872, two short weeks after his defeat. For decades, Maggie's old mentor had urged his readers to embrace a variety of liberal causes—as disparate as Fourierism, temperance, and abolition—that reflected his goal of dealing honestly with one's fellow man. "Do the thing that is the highest right," as he once famously advised Lincoln on the brink of Civil War, "and tell me how I am to second you."

~❄~

In England, just as Sarah Taylor had predicted, Katy's arrival in London had opened her eyes to a new world. She immediately created a sensation. She appeared at her first reception in a flattering blue gown, looking much younger than her thirty-six years. Smilingly modestly as she was introduced to Livermore's friend Benjamin Coleman and his guests, Katy had already won their approval even before she gave an impressive demonstration of her rapped messages later that evening.

Among those who admired her was Henry Jencken, a tall, blond widower born in Germany, naturalized as an English citizen, and a member of the British Bar. Katy had also noticed the handsome forty-nine-year-old barrister but was immediately distracted by introductions and conversations with other guests. Within a few days, Katy was giving séances and swept up into a dizzying schedule of parties and receptions where she was regaled with aperitifs and fine wines.

After several weeks of refusing such temptations, Katy finally gave in, becoming so constantly intoxicated that her concerned chaperone, Blanche Ogden, rushed her off to Paris to dry out. That winter, the twosome discreetly returned to London and once again Katy resumed her role as celebrity medium, often with the enamored Henry Jencken at her side.

Katy wrote cheerfully about her activities to Maggie. She told of hobnobbing with the famous expatriated American medium Florence Guppy; winning admiration from William Harrison, London editor of the *Spiritualist;* and invitations to participate in several séances before the eminent physicist Sir William Crookes. Her happiest news came in April 1872. Katy was strolling through the box-wood gardens of a friend's country house with Henry Jencken when the barrister took Katy's hand in his, confessed his love, and proposed. Brightening for a moment but then turning away, Katy began to weep. She was, she confessed, as a bewildered Henry took her in his arms, addicted to alcohol and thus unfit to return his love. Blithely Henry brushed aside her history, assuring her that it was of little consequence, that he still wanted her for his wife.

⌘

Dressed in a white lace gown, her hair bedecked in a flowered wreath, Katy was wed to Henry Jencken at St. Marylebone Parish Church in London at 11 A.M. on December 14, 1872. After the ceremony, the bride and groom entered a carriage with a milk-white horse and, accompanied by their friends, were driven to a magnificent wedding breakfast at 45 York Place in Putnam Square.

Among the wedding guests, according to reports in the *Spiritualist* and the *New York Herald,* were the spirits who enthusiastically signaled their approval of the match. "As the company, with brimming bumpers, rose to do honor to the toast 'our Spirits Friends,' the heavily laden table was gently raised from the floor and suspended in mid-air for some seconds," observed the *Spiritualist.*

Even to earthly observers Katy's marriage to Henry seemed ideal. The bridegroom was well-respected personally and professionally. Like his parents, who had dabbled in philosophy, light theories, music, and medicine, Henry had long been fascinated by spiritualism. He was, noted the *New York Herald,* "among the first of the professional men of England to publish what he knew about spiritual phenomena at the time when the announcement...produced more ridicule and required more moral courage than at the present time."

From the equally heady perspective of Katy, the only missing ingredient to her wedding was Maggie. Of lesser importance was the absence of Leah and Daniel. Practical considerations—the high cost of transatlantic passage—may have explained Maggie's absence, if not the Underhills'. But almost certainly there was another unspoken reason: Henry was convinced that Maggie had corrupted Katy and led her into alcoholism.

Years later, Katy would insist to a Rochester newspaper reporter that it was spiritualism—not Maggie—that had introduced both of them to strong drink. "We were wined and dined everywhere," Katy recalled. "People would send baskets of champagne to us, and very soon the habit of drinking had become strong with us."

Nevertheless Henry would not be convinced. Being a friend of Benjamin Coleman, who frequently corresponded with American banker Charles Livermore, Henry may well have been biased. Daniel and Leah Underhill, who began a correspondence with Henry soon after his engagement to Katy, also may have implicated Maggie in their letters.

To compensate for the family's absence from the wedding, the newlyweds arranged for a steward on the luxurious *White Star* steamship line to deliver part of the wedding cake to New York.

❦

After returning from a honeymoon on the Continent, Katy Fox Jencken settled happily into her husband Henry's splendid townhouse at London's Brompton Court. Like her wealthy sister Leah, Katy had no thoughts of becoming a lady of leisure following her marriage. Spiritualism was all that she knew, was in her blood by then, and given her husband Henry's avid interest in it, she continued to give séances. And then, shortly after her thirty-eighth birthday, she learned that she was pregnant.

The news, delivered by letter to New York, thrilled Maggie. Denied the chance to become a mother herself, she now wanted to become a doting aunt. Carried along by that excitement, Maggie went shopping, undoubtedly wandering through Manhattan's "Ladies Mile" on lower Broadway, famous for the latest fashions in clothes and home furnishings, and perhaps strolling two streets south to the most luxurious emporiums of all, A. T. Stewart's "Marble Palace," on Sixth Street near Fifth Avenue. Later, back in her solitary apartment. Maggie stitched the fine fabrics she had purchased into tiny garments, trimming them with delicate ribbons.

Several weeks later in London, Maggie's carefully wrapped package, containing her gifts and a congratulatory letter, arrived at Brompton Court. Katy stared at the note and Maggie's sweetly decorated clothes and burst into tears. Then she quickly hid away the garments, knowing that any association with Maggie—including her gifts—was bound to cause unpleasantness between her and Henry. Katy did not dare show him Maggie's letter or reveal who had sent her the infant's layette.

On September 19, 1873, a month before her due date, Katy endured a long, difficult labor that ended with the delivery of a baby boy. She and Henry named him Ferdinand Dietrich Lowenstern. During the birthing, attendants claimed that the labor room had been filled with strange knocking sounds. When the baby appeared with his head draped in a caul—actually the placenta—Katy's attendants were convinced that he had a strong connection to the supernatural.

For centuries before the advent of American spiritualism, superstitious men and women had believed that a child born with a caul had unusual psychic powers. Adding to that view were reports from the baby's anxious nurse, McPherson, that strange sounds—knocks or taps—seemed to emanate from within the nursery. One night, while Katy and Henry attended an event at London's famous Crystal Palace, the nurse claimed that a veiled figure appeared in the nursery and stared at Ferdy, as little Ferdinand was called. At other times, she claimed that shadowy figures loomed over the crib and passed luminous hands over the infant's body.

In December 1873, after Katy brought Ferdy to the seaside resort town of Brighton to escape that city's dank winter air, she wrote Leah that her three-month-old son had distinctly spoken the words "ma-ma, darling ma-ma" when McPherson brought him to her.

"She fairly dropped him on my lap, she was so frightened, and I could not help but laugh at her, though I was startled too. I can hear you laugh heartily at this, but Leah, it is true!," Katy wrote. "…Sometimes light shines out of his precious eyes so bright it cannot be described, and we have all seen a halo 'round his head. It frightens me; I fear he is too pure to live, and I would die without him."

But that was only the beginning. On February 28, McPherson summoned Henry and attorney James Watson, who was visiting, to report that little Ferdy was holding a pencil in his hand. Inexplicably, according to Watson, who witnessed the entire event, the infant wrote a message emanating from his dead wife Susan, suggesting that Henry was well advised "to go back to London" where he would recover his health. On still another occasion, the awestruck Jenckens again watched Ferdy writing—and this time in Greek. The message read "Who believes in me shall live."

On May 8, Henry and Watson published accounts of those events in the spiritualist journal *Medium and Daybreak*. Before long rumors of the child's unusual spiritual powers had spread to London and New York.

By the time the Jenckens arrived back in London they were besieged with invitations from the curious, among them several scientific investigators who wanted to observe Ferdy for themselves. Henry, for all his initial excitement about his presumably gifted son, was a very private man and stubbornly rejected all efforts to have Ferdinand displayed as a child prodigy.

By the summer Katy discovered that she was once again pregnant. Since she still had not shared her first born with her family or seen home since she left, Henry obligingly booked passage for her and Ferdy on the *Helvetia,* which sailed from Dover for New York in November. Their separation, he promised Katy, would be brief—only a few weeks' duration—for he planned to cross the Atlantic in December and join her in Manhattan while they awaited the birth of their second child together.

In anticipation of Katy and Ferdy's arrival, Maggie invited them to stay with her. But again Leah had pre-empted her. For weeks before Katy's departure, letters were sent back and forth across the Atlantic between Henry and the Underhills, at whose home she and her baby were to stay. Their large townhouse, Leah and Daniel explained in those letters, was similar to his at Brompton Court—spacious, well furnished, and fully staffed with servants. Katy and little Ferdy would have quarters of their own, servants to look after them, and a doting aunt and uncle. Most important of all, they lived a safe distance from Maggie and the resultant temptation to drink.

Maggie was disappointed that they were not staying with her. But she welcomed Katy and Ferdy joyously, fussing over him as if he were her own. When Henry was delayed in London on business Maggie was not disappointed, for that meant still more opportunities for visits during Katy's last months of her pregnancy.

Unexpectedly icy blasts of wind and snow swept over Manhattan in mid-December, a harbinger of what would become the coldest winter on record. By January 1875, still more snow, combined with sub-zero temperatures, transformed Manhattan's busy streets into sheets of ice, its Fifth Avenue marble mansions into snow-frosted facades, and the shanties of First Avenue into ragged igloos from which sooty pipes spewed smoke. Around the Battery an eerie silence lay over the whitened docks and harbors, its boats and ships stilled by an impenetrable ice blockade on the Hudson.

Katy's second son was born on a chill January day in 1875 at the Underhill home. Happily, though, the birth, eased by the doctor's use of the new drug chloroform, was less difficult than Ferdinand's arrival. An attractive child, who was named after his father Henry, the new baby seemed as ordinary as his brother Ferdy was extraordinary. To Katy, nevertheless, her second son's arrival was nothing less than a miracle.

"And so we have Katy back again, not Katy alone but Katy with two beautiful children, the blessings that she can see and feel and touch... the little hand," Sarah Taylor noted with pleasure after seeing Katy and her children in April.

Maggie, too, had poured herself into Katy's happiness. To the forty-two-year-old aunt, her nephews seemed an unexpected gift of love.

In May 1875, having been twice delayed in London by court matters, Katy's husband, Henry, finally arrived in New York. It must have been a dreaded meeting on both sides. But Maggie charmed Henry from the moment they met, immediately dispelling his fears. Maggie, too, warmed to her new brother-in-law's wit and charm, unequivocally approving of her sister's match. So fond did the ensuing friendship become during the six weeks of Henry's visit that he invited Maggie to London the following year.

On July 5, 1875, Maggie saw Katy and her family off at the steamship. A year later, true to her promise, she visited her sister, Henry, and their children in London. For Maggie, the visit would remain an appealing memory of a family life that she had been denied.

x,⊕ 13 ⊕x

GREAT MAGNETISM AND REMORSE

When we remember that, from the beginning of the world, some
such possible communication between departed loved and the
beloved on earth has been among the most cherished legends of
humanity, why must we always meet with such phenomena with a
resolute determination to account for them by every...supposition
but that which the human heart most craves?
—HARRIET BEECHER STOWE, "What Shall We Do With Tina?"

AFTER RETURNING to New York from London in 1878, Maggie resumed her spiritualistic practice with renewed energies. She became
so successful that she was eventually called upon by an aging, aristocratic Philadelphian, Henry Seybert. In his youth, the wealthy septuagenarian, a trustee of the University of Pennsylvania, had been an
aspiring mineralogist and by the late 1870s still maintained an active
membership in the scientifically oriented American Philosophical
Society. To show his devotion to his native town of Philadelphia,
Seybert had also donated a clock and bell to that city's Independence Hall in 1876 at the time of America's centennial.

A dilettante who flitted from one scientific discipline to another, Seybert's interests eventually led him to spiritualism. So enthusiastically did he ascribe to its claims that he joined a spirit circle
that met nightly at Philadelphia's Ninth Street to touch the hands
of the allegedly "rematerialized" seventeenth-century spirit Katie
King, the pretty daughter of the English Sir John Morgan.

Following a December 1874 exposé by the *Pennsylvania Inquirer*
revealing that Miss King was actually a living young woman, who
resided at an upscale boarding house where she kept gifts from Sey-

bert, Andrew Jackson Davis, and other prominent believers, the wealthy Philadelphian nevertheless remained convinced about the power of spirits.

Intent on establishing an important spiritualist center, Seybert made Maggie an intriguing offer. If she would agree to reside in his "Spiritual Mansion"—the luxurious home Seybert had newly established in Philadelphia—and conduct séances for his friends and other private clients, he promised her a generous salary. At first, the invitation sounded like an ideal opportunity. Maggie had always enjoyed Philadelphia—except, of course, for her time at the Orphan's Court during her lawsuit against the Kanes. It was in that city, after all, that she had spent some of her happiest days with her beloved Elisha. Moreover, she was weary of her spiritualist practice in Manhattan, its long hours, demanding clients, and uneven pay. Lured by Seybert's offer she agreed, convinced that "the quiet existence...there would be preferable to the daily and distasteful practice of public mediumship," according to *The Death-Blow to Spiritualism.*

Maggie was installed as "the high priestess of this new temple of the unseen entities." And at first she was delighted, finding herself "honored and treated with exalted respect" by Seybert's staff, clients, and friends. As anticipated, Maggie was to raise spirits for her aging patron and his friends in the spirit of scientific inquiry. Gradually, however, the wealthy septuagenarian started asking her to contact spirits of famous historical and religious figures, including, to Maggie's growing distaste, "nearly every martyr and saint in the Protestant calendar, and from the famous sages and rulers of old."

Unhappily but dutifully Maggie attempted to oblige him. Feverishly, incessantly, Seybert agitated for the spirits of still more religious figures, now demanding that she include figures from the Old and New Testaments, among them Elijah, the angel Gabriel, St. Peter, and St. Paul. Maggie balked, frightened by the implications that she was threatening her own salvation as a Catholic. Refusing, indeed revolting "against this mania for the supernatural and the impossible," she came to believe that the old man was exploiting her, using her gifts as an "instrument of pure religious insanity," as she later told her biographer, journalist Reuben Davenport. Soon after that revelation, Maggie resigned. She would return to a more modest but emotionally reconcilable life as a public medium in rented rooms in New York.

⁂

Across the Atlantic scientists were already investigating the link between spiritualism and natural laws, but in a far more measured way than had Seybert. One of the most famous was Sir William Crookes, a distinguished Fellow of England's Royal Society. Trained as a chemist, he was renowned for his 1861 discovery of the element thallium and the radiometer. In 1871, while spiritualism was reaching new levels of popularity in England, Crookes vowed to drive the "worthless residuum of spiritualism" into the ground through scientific investigation.

The challenge proved far more difficult than he anticipated. Using weights, balances, and electro-magnets, Crookes began his ghost-busting efforts by attempting to wrest the secret of table-tipping from mediums. Finding little satisfaction there, Crookes next examined the levitating medium Daniel Douglas Home, who also demonstrated other strange feats, such as elongating his body into impossible lengths and floating in the air—a spectacle which the scientist was ultimately forced to admit he had personally witnessed. Crookes persisted in his studies even after publishing a report in the 1871 *Quarterly Journal of Science* supporting his observations and consequently convincing many of his colleagues that he had gone mad.

In 1874 he investigated Katy Fox Jencken. Stunned by her clairvoyance and finding no rational way to account for it, Crookes ultimately admitted that he had been won over to the validity of spirit communication.

Simultaneously he was observing an attractive English medium, Florence Cook. A teenager from a working-class family, Cook had soared to fame because of her success raising the spirit of Katie King—the same ghost who was reputed to be appearing in Philadelphia.

Like her transatlantic double, that fetching female spirit of London materialized in human form, dressed in white filmy gowns that especially thrilled her male spectators. Night after night Florence Cook was locked and tied into a "spirit cabinet," or large wooden chest. Once she was in a trance, the door to the spirit cabinet was shut. Soon the gauzy face and figure of Katie King materialized before members of the audience, accompanied by the moaning sounds of the still-entranced Miss Cook, who, allegedly, remained tied in the spirit cabinet.

Her performances were a sensation until one memorable séance in December 1873, when audience member William Volckman impulsively reached out, latched onto Katie King's manifestation, and refused to let go.

After a violent struggle, the luminous figure broke away and shut herself into the spirit cabinet. Five minutes later the door to the cabinet was opened, revealing a disheveled Florence Cook, securely fastened to her ropes.

In the midst of the subsequent uproar, the teenage medium, insisting to the newspapers that there had been no fraud, agreed to "offer myself upon the altar of science." As it happened that altar was none other than one owned by the convert Sir William Crookes. After five months of investigation—during which, it was later alleged, the middle-aged scientist and adolescent Miss Cook had an affair upon that altar—the medium announced that she would no longer raise the spirit of the seventeenth-century spirit.

Ultimately it was mental telepathy—the same gift that often dazzled Maggie's clients—that inspired a cadre of independent English investigators to create an organization to systematically study psychic phenomena. Perhaps not coincidentally, one of them, Sir William Barrett, of Dublin's Royal College of Science, had recently thrilled his colleagues with experiments in thought transference at a January 1882 scientific conference. The following month many of them had reconvened to form the British Society for Psychical Research.

The new organization's goal, according to Cambridge professor Henry Sidgwick, who would become the first president of the SPR, as the society was called, was to separate the emotionalism that surrounded spiritualism from scientific inquiry. Sidgwick's group served as a model for Harvard University professor William James, who would later help establish the American Society for Psychical Research, or ASPR.

"We believed unreservedly in the methods of modern science, and were prepared to accept...her reasoned conclusions, when sustained by...experts; but we were not prepared to bow with equal docility to the mere prejudices of scientific men," Sidgwick explained some years later. "And it appeared to us that there was an important body of evidence—tending *prima facie* to establish the independence of soul or spirit—which modern science had simply left on one side with ignorant contempt."

꽃

In Philadelphia, that same "important body of evidence" continued to absorb Henry Seybert so obsessively that shortly before his death in September 1881, the septuagenarian bequeathed $60,000 for a chair in philosophy to the University of Pennsylvania. He also established a matching bequest for a commission mandated to investigate "all systems of morals, religion or philosophy which assume to represent the truth; and particularly of modern Spiritualism."

The ten-member Seybert Commission on Spiritualism convened in Philadelphia in 1883. Soon after its formation, Chairman Horace Howard Furness of Philadelphia invited Maggie to participate in its investigations.

Maggie was ambivalent. It made no sense to cooperate in an investigation supported by a bequest from a man who had treated her so unkindly during his lifetime. Nor would the findings of the Commission—whatever they were, pro or con—likely improve her own financial situation. Maggie accordingly ignored Furness's invitation.

Ten days later Furness politely wrote again, "Since I have not heard from you, I fear that my letter has miscarried, and will therefore repeat it. I am...very anxious, that the 'Seybert Commission' of which I am the chairman, should have an opportunity of investigate the 'Rappings.'"

Ultimately Maggie agreed to an examination but warned Furness that while the raps came through her body, she made no claims to communicate with spirits—just as her calling card indicated. Her plan, as she later told her memoirist Davenport, was to confound the Commission as an act of revenge upon Seybert and his bequest.

In early November 1883, Maggie arrived at Furness's townhouse on Philadelphia's tree-lined West Washington Square. On November 6, the day after an introductory investigation in Furness's dining room, the commissioners asked Maggie to suggest a test that might prove she did not intentionally produce the sounds.

"I could name a great many tests, but they might not be satisfactory to you," Maggie hedged, according to the Commission report. "For instance, the one of standing on glass tumblers where the raps are produced on the floor." While she admitted that she had not performed that test since she was young, the commissioners decided it was worth a try. A few minutes later one of them appeared with four heavy glasses, which he placed in two rows on the carpet.

What came next, preserved so dryly in the Commission report, remains one of the most ludicrous images in the history of spiritualist investigations. In spite of a corset, a long dress, and button-down shoes, Maggie somehow managed to mount the four glass tumblers. While neither her attitude nor facial expression was preserved in the commission's official report, the scene must have been memorable.

"The heels of her shoes resting upon the rear tumblers and the soles upon the front tumblers. The Committee co-operate with the Medium, and, in conformity with her suggestions, all the men clasp hands and form a semi-circle in front of the Medium, the hands of the latter, being grasped by the gentlemen nearest to her on either side," read the report.

Then there was silence. "It may be a few minutes before you will hear any rapping through these glasses," Maggie warned. Yet the moments continued to tick without any results until finally the commissioners moved the glasses to a second position. Gamely, Maggie mounted the four glass tumblers again but after still more silence, the men abandoned the experiment.

Somewhat later that evening, Furness asked a question meant to test Maggie's sincerity. "You have come to the conclusion that they [the raps] are entirely independent of yourself?" Furness inquired hopefully.

"No, I do not know that they are entirely independent of my-self," Maggie replied.

"Under what conditions can you influence them?" Furness persisted.

Maggie's response, according to the Commission report, was garbled, but ultimately interpreted as "I cannot tell."

Again, Maggie mounted the glass tumblers. This time, after a another long delay, the Commissioners heard three raps.

Having placed his hand on Maggie's foot, Commissioner Fur-ness exclaimed, "This is the most wonderful [inexplicable] thing of all, Mrs. Kane, I distinctly feel them in your foot. There is not a particle of motion in your foot, but there is an unusual pulsation."

The next morning, Horace Furness confided in a fellow com-missioner that they believed Maggie's raps were "confined wholly to her person, whether produced by her voluntarily or involuntarily."

Maggie counted her examination as a triumph, if only because she had left the commissioners stymied. Nevertheless, after exami-nations of dozens of other mediums, the Seybert Commission concluded that spiritualist manifestations revealed through raps, slate writings, and full-body materializations were fraudulent.

Still, Furness equivocated about the possibility of life after death. "Although I have been thus thwarted at every turn in my investigations of Spiritualism, and found fraud where I had looked for honesty...Spiritualism, pure and undefiled...must be something far better than Slate Writing and Raps. These grosser physical manifestations can be but the mere ooze and scum cast up by the waves on the...waters of a heaven-lit sea, if it exists, must lie far out beyond."

⅓❦

The raps—what the Seybert Commission dubbed the "mere ooze and scum" of an inchoate spirit world—would remain Maggie's sole means of support. By the mid-1880s the gray-haired Maggie— by then in her fifties—often traveled from town to town, offering séances in hotels and boarding houses or wherever else she could attract clients.

Unhappily, even the small sums of money Maggie collected from her clients did not buy her peace of mind, but instead prompted new waves of guilt. No sooner was a séance over, Maggie told Davenport, than she would be overcome with recrimination. "The next day I would drown my remorse in wine," she said. After she recovered, she began the cycle all over again—returning to her small, overly decorated home, now a second-floor apartment on Manhattan's West Forty-sixth Street, placing more advertisements in the newspapers, conducting séances for her clients.

Yet to those who knew Maggie during the 1880s, the once-beautiful woman remained a compelling, if ailing, personality with an indisputable charisma that fascinated all who met her. One man who met Maggie during that period was a skeptical printer, Commodore Joseph Tooker, who had attended one of her sittings out of sheer curiosity.

"Spirit séances are likely to puzzle," he told the *New York Times* in a February 14, 1886, story. Upon entering Maggie's "pretentiously furnished" home, the printer was ushered into a back parlor. There, the commodore noted, "were several people patiently waiting to interview relatives that had 'gone before.' The medium was a middle-aged and very pale lady who had just risen from a bed of sickness."

While offering no hints about his identity, he was presented as a friend of another guest and felt "fully satisfied" that she did not guess his identity. Contrary to her previous denials about spirit communication, Maggie now, at least according to Tooker's report, openly embraced it. "She prefaced her celestial communications with an expression of full belief in spiritualism," Tooker noted, but explained that "she was ignorant while in a trance condition what she was imparting." After becoming entranced Maggie took on the "appearance of a corpse" and then "took my hands in hers and gracefully sank back into deep thought. She possessed a great magnetism, for the touch of her fingers produced a pricking sensation as if I were holding the hands of an electric battery."

What stunned the commodore most of all was Maggie's telepathic gift. Somehow, he admitted, she was "familiar with the names of my dead relatives and acquaintances." He added, "Her descriptions were very accurate and [the] messages quite as I would anticipate from those she declared were surrounding us."

～✿～

In London, the fifty-nine-year-old Henry Jencken suddenly became ill and died of a stroke on November 26, 1881. Soon after notifying Maggie and Leah of her husband's death, the grieving Katy assured them that she planned to return to Manhattan with her two sons immediately after Henry's estate was settled.

Four years crept by and still Katy had failed to arrive. She was, she wrote from time to time, mired in unanticipated delays involving her late husband's affairs. Maggie was deeply frustrated by her inability to communicate with Katy. While Henry had been a highly respected international lawyer with a "handsome competence" annually received from inherited German properties, the newly widowed Katy was stunned to learn that his allowance could not be transferred to her. Compounding that financial blow was the ethereal Katy's inability to understand the intricacies of Henry's investments.

Having lost touch with Katy, who seems to have moved from Brompton Court in the midst of her financial difficulties without leaving a forwarding address, her old mentors Sarah and George Taylor had sadly concluded that they would never see Katy again.

Then, on the afternoon of July 1, 1885, Sarah saw a woman and boy pass by the Taylors' new residence at the Brantling Hotel on Madison Avenue. "I noticed her face and thought how strongly she resembled Katie, only more fleshy and older," Sarah wrote in her diary. And indeed, she was correct, as Sarah soon learned when Leah, with Katy with her two sons, arrived at her doorstep. "My joy can better be imagined than described. Here was Katie looking well and happy, though ten years older, with two nice healthy looking English boys," Sarah wrote.

By then, Ferdy was a manly-looking twelve-year-old. In contrast, his brother Henry, an epileptic, was frail. As they had years earlier, Katy and her sons lived with the Underhills at their townhouse. But this time the visit was fraught with tensions. Before long, the two sisters were quarreling bitterly over how to discipline the boys—and probably over a new book that Leah had commissioned about the history of spiritualism.

Just before Katy's arrival, Leah, still vibrant at seventy-two, had finished compiling notes, newspaper articles, and other memorabilia of spiritualism for her memoir. The resultant 1885 volume, *The Missing Link in Spiritualism,* credited to Ann Leah Underhill as author, included steel engravings of her and her family along with an account of the role she and her family played in the rise of the spiritualist movement. While *The Missing Link* touched only lightly upon the strained dynamics between Leah and her sisters, those same tensions continued to create disharmony.

This time Katy was at the center. As a mother Katy was both overindulgent and overprotective, according to *Time Is Kind*, making the boys difficult to manage, much to Leah, Daniel, and Maggie's dismay. After quarreling with the Underhills over her sons, Katy rushed off with them to Arcadia that summer to meet their uncle David and his family. Within a few days, even the seasoned father of five grew alarmed at Katy's apparent inability to discipline Ferdy and Henry.

By the fall of 1885, Katy returned to New York and enrolled her sons in public school. Just as Maggie, Leah, Daniel, and David feared, neither boy made a good adjustment—especially Henry, whose health worried Katy so much that she often kept him at home, privy to her séances. Even when Henry felt well, Katy would not let him or Ferdy out of her sight to play with other children. Instead, she insisted, they had to be with her at all times, including at her weekly séances that were open to the public.

To that, Leah strongly objected. It was, after all, no way for children to be raised: They should be in school, engaged in some worthwhile hobby or pursuit, or playing with boys their own age. But at forty-nine years of age, Katy, perhaps for the first time in her life, defied her eldest sister. She would do just as she pleased with her sons, even if no one in her family approved.

By late May 1886—a little less than a year since her arrival in New York—Katy's life began to unravel. During the last weekend of that month, Sarah Taylor reported, Katy had taken her sons to New Jersey to visit English friends. Upon her return, she carefully avoided Sarah and when they finally met the following Tuesday, June 1, Katy seemed upset.

By Wednesday, the mystery was sadly solved. That day, Sarah wrote in her diary that "the Doctor [her husband, George] came over to tell me that Katie was in a miserable saloon, drunk...and [he] had searched her out...It appears that these English friends had induced her to take wine at dinner and when she once got the taste all the rest followed." Most poignant of all, Sarah added, "She had been in this city one year this month and not until now has a drop touched her lips. We are heart sick, for we know so well her old ways."

To help her, Sarah and George attended to Ferdy and Henry and locked Katy in a room at the Brantling Hotel, but somehow she managed to escape. After several agonizing attempts, a solicitous Sarah succeeded in getting Katy sober. "She came to herself, only excessively nervous," the nurse sorrowfully recalled.

Despairingly, Sarah tried to talk reason to Katy, explaining that she had little time left to offer her counsel. For months, the Taylors had planned a European trip and were scheduled to leave that same day, July 2, 1886.

Predictably, Katy's sobriety was short-lived. Within two weeks of the Taylors' departure, she boarded a train, apparently leaving the boys behind with friends, arrived in Rochester, and took a room at the Hotel Brunswick. And for a brief moment she was happy—surrounded by old admirers from her hometown, as well as new followers of spiritualism, all clamoring for séances.

Then, on August 27, a local reporter telegraphed the *New York Herald* the inevitable story. "Policeman Hines...saw Mrs. Jencken on a prominent street here, and followed by a crowd of street gamins hooting at her," reported the *Herald.* "He locked her up and placed a charge of drunkenness against her." After a humiliating night in jail, several of Katy's friends bailed her out and helped her board a train for New York City.

After that public humiliation—met undoubtedly with outrage from Leah and Daniel—Katy established a separate apartment with her sons.

❧

Maggie's relationship with Katy during the next eighteen months was also fractured by arguments over the boys and over Katy's drinking.

At the time Maggie had abstained. Instead, she resorted to drugs to relieve her aches, pains, and other physical ailments. Almost certainly one of these was the wildly popular painkiller laudanum—a mild opium-based drug, which was cheaper than gin and readily prescribed by doctors for a wide range of complaints.

The source of Maggie's ailments has never been clear and was perhaps related to alcoholism, but it left her looking thin and pale. As a Dr. Gustave Wiksell would tell author Mariam Pond of *Time Is Kind* in 1940, he vividly remembered Maggie from a séance he and his wife attended at her home one bright fall day in 1887. His interest had been piqued by a three-line newspaper advertisement about Maggie's séances. The young doctor and his wife "met the little old lady in her large old-fashioned room up one flight."

Deliberately, to avoid giving Maggie any hints about their identities, Dr. Wiksell had neither introduced himself nor his wife. Yet, as soon as the couple were seated, Maggie regarded them gently. "At once [she] began to write with both hands, sheet after sheet, very rapidly, tossing them across the table to me," Wiksell said.

To Dr. Wiksell the pages seemed indecipherable, as if written in some strange hand: Only later did he understand that Maggie had written them backwards. "She smilingly told me to hold it up to a mirror; I then saw in my father's peculiar back-hand a message signed, 'Your loving father, Gustave Wiksell,'" the physician recalled. "This was enough for me, but many more sheets followed, all equally correct in every way."

Afterward, Maggie invited Dr. Wiksell to mentally ask her a question. Simultaneously she suggested he should mutely "request the raps to come anywhere you wish." Silently, the young physician thought of a question and then wished it to be answered by the window, which, he noted, was at least twelve feet away from the séance table where he, his wife, and Maggie sat. "At once came the sharp clear raps on the glass," Dr. Wiksell recalled. "Out of a lifetime of contacts with the people of the spirit world…my séance with Margaretta Fox Kane was in many respects the most satisfactory one of many thousands in over sixty years of experience."

~❧~

By then Maggie's reputation was so strongly established among spiritualists that the following winter she received an invitation from an English admirer, a Dr. H. Wadsworth of 21 Queen Street, inviting her to London. The offer had come with several enticements: a substantial amount of money, comfortable quarters, and an audience of well-heeled guests, all of whom, Dr. Wadsworth assured Maggie, were eager to experience her clairvoyant gifts at first hand.

Initially Maggie was flattered. There was little to prevent her from accepting the offer. It had been years since she had visited London. The money was a certainty. As winter drew to an end, she had not told her younger sister that she had accepted the London doctor's invitation. Perhaps she never had the opportunity. By 1888, Katy had become increasingly flighty and undependable, disappearing for weeks on end on out-of-town trips that were often coupled with alcoholic binges.

Maggie sailed on March 22, 1888. During the twelve-day crossing, she must have had some kind of conversion. Perhaps old guilt reappeared, or the distance from her life prompted self-examination. She had come to a momentous decision. She would neither lie nor prevaricate any longer. When Dr. Wadsworth met her at the pier, she greeted him with an announcement.

"I think too much of you to deceive you," she began. Then she added, "There is nothing to spiritualism, it's a fraud."

Maggie's eccentric behavior was well known in spiritualist circles. That may explain why the astonished physician initially did little more than nod numbly at the famous American's strange outburst. He appreciated Maggie's frankness, Dr. Wadsworth finally said, but still anticipated that she would proceed with the scheduled séances.

≈✻≈

Equally disconcerting to others who knew Maggie was a statement from Katy published on March 27 in the *New York Herald*. She had, according to her version of the story, seen Maggie off on the ship in New York five days earlier, alleging that her sister had sailed to England to give a séance to Queen Victoria. "I saw the invitation. It was signed by a committee of gentlemen, requesting her on behalf of the Queen to visit England," Katy insisted to a *Herald* reporter. "The Queen has lost many friends of late by death, and she is anxious to learn something about them from the other world."

The story, skeptically headlined "The Wildest Story yet about Queen Victoria and the Mediums," played off upon well-known rumors about the sovereign's belief in spiritualism. While the long-grieving royal widow had participated in séances to reach her beloved husband, the late Prince Albert, no evidence has been found to support Maggie's appointment with the queen.

More definitive were accounts suggesting that after Maggie's departure, Katy continued to drink heavily. By Friday, May 4, 1888, her neighbors became so alarmed about her and her neglectful treatment of young Ferdy and Henry that they contacted the Society for the Prevention of Cruelty to Children. Without warning, an agent of that institution appeared at Katy's Manhattan apartment and arrested her for "drunkenness and flagrant neglect of her maternal duties."

Legally the organization, one of many new social and humanitarian causes created after the Civil War, had been empowered to make arrests since 1881. Founded in 1874 by Elbridge T. Gerry—once the New York State Attorney General and former president of the American Society for the Prevention of Cruelty to Animals—his Society for the Prevention of Cruelty to Children had the obligation to remove neglected minors from irresponsible parents and temporarily place them in asylums before assigning them to foster parents.

After spending a sleepless night in the Tombs Police Court, Katy appeared before its officers for a hearing. "In the middle-aged woman with dissipated face and plain and somber attire who stood before the justice," observed the *New York Herald,* "few might have recognized yesterday the bright and handsome Kate Fox, the spiritualistic medium who some twenty years ago, together with her sister Margaret, gained so much celebrity for her allegedly supernatural exhibitions."

From Katy's perspective, the arrests were motivated by spite, the result of a smoldering hate campaign toward all mediums emanating from a recent exposé of Madame Diss De Barr (Della Ann O' Sullivan or Ann O'Delia Salomon as she was variously named) of New York City and her fraudulent production of "spirit pictures."

When Maggie first read the news, she too believed that Katy's arrest was motivated by the wave of anti-spiritualist sentiment sparked by Diss De Barr. The excesses of spiritualism and the preponderance of fraudulent mediums like her had finally turned the tide of public opinion against the movement.

Increasingly through the 1870s and 1880s, spiritualist practitioners had added gimmicks to their séances that were often exposed as hoaxes. Spirit cabinets remained standard equipment. The planchette, a heart-shaped piece of wood brought from France to the United States in 1868, was another piece of mediumistic gear produced in such mass numbers that nearly anyone—including children— could engage in "automatic writing." Another séance feature often exposed as a scam were "apports"—real-life objects such as flowers, jewelry, or even sprays of perfume—that sometimes appeared overhead or dropped into the laps of the members of séance audiences. Equally common, too, was the appearance of "spirit photographs," images of the deceased that could be captured on photographic film.

Exacerbating spiritualism's association with fraud had been the 1874 arrival in New York of an exotically dressed, obese Russian seer, Helen Petrovna Blavatsky—Madame Blavatsky—who attracted an enormous group of followers. First she claimed that she could raise

the spirit of Katie King's father, John. Then, with aid from journalist Henry S. Olcott, she created a mystical brand of spiritualism called
Theosophy. In 1878, a year after writing the bestselling *Isis Unveiled,*
Madame Blavatsky and Olcott left New York for India in search of
more enlightened spiritual guidance. Within six years, her practices
were investigated in India by the British Society for Psychical Research's
Richard Hodgson. Thereafter, she was widely publicized as a hoax.

Another challenge to spiritualism came from Mary Baker Eddy, a
former invalid from New England who had been cured of depression
and other ailments through the healing medium Phineas Parkhurst
Quimby. After Quimby's death in 1866, Eddy again slipped into depression before healing herself by exploring "Christian Science mind-
healing." All disease, she asserted in her 1876 first edition of *Science
and Health,* the bible of her new faith, was a fiction of the soul. Neither disease nor matter existed. Both were creations of the soul which
symbolized the universal mind, or Jesus Christ, at work.

Spiritualism, with its sharp divisions between life and death and
messengers known as mediums, was false and based upon unscien-
tific concepts. "The Science of Christianity is misinterpreted by a
material age, for it is the healing influence of Spirit (not spirits)
which the material sense cannot comprehend—which can only be
spiritually discerned," Eddy maintained. In 1879 she obtained a national charter for the Church of Christ, Scientist. *Science and Health*
was reprinted fifty times, its contents familiar to thousands of former spiritualists who now embraced Christian Science instead.

The most notorious fraud involved Madame Diss De Barr—
the same medium to whom Katy attributed her own arrest and the
seizure of her sons. After a well-publicized trial in a Special Sessions
Court at the Tombs, Diss De Barr was found guilty of defrauding
attorney Luther Marsh of his money through the use of stolen
"spirit paintings."

"The disclosures regarding the notorious Diss De Barr had
offended Mrs. Kane more than anything which had occurred in
Spiritualism in a long time," maintained Maggie's memoirist

Davenport, "for they presented the enforced association of her name and the simple, childish origins of the 'Rochester knockings,' with the gross and revolting frauds which had been their outgrowth...[from the] developed system of Spiritualism."

On May 14, Maggie penned and mailed an extraordinary statement from London to the *New York Herald*. Published on May 27 in New York, Maggie's letter explained that she was currently residing in England. She wrote:

> I presume my absence has added to my darling sister's depressed state of mind. The sad news has nearly killed me. My sister's two beautiful boys referred to are her idols. Spiritualism is a curse. God has set His seal against it! I call it a curse, for it is made use of as a covering for heartless persons...and the vilest miscreants make use of it to cloak their evil doings. Fanatics...ignore the 'rappings'... and rush madly after the glaring humbugs that flood New York. But a harmless 'message' that is given through the 'rappings' is of little account to them; they want the 'spirit' to come to them in full form, to walk before them, to embrace them, and all such nonsense...Like old Judge Edmonds and Mr. Seybert of Philadelphia, they become crazed and at the direction of their fraud 'mediums'...induced to part with all their worldly possessions as well as their common sense...No matter in what form Spiritualism may be presented, it is, has been and always will be a curse and a snare to all who meddle with it. No right minded man or woman can think otherwise."

The letter must have been a great relief. Was it an echo from her long-ago refusal to rap? A burst of frustration from all those years of being forced to elicit the spirits? Or rage at the way spiritualism had contributed to Katy's ruin and her own? Maggie had finally spoken out her own voice without ghostwriters, domineering older sisters, or in the trance voice of the spirits. Suddenly, perhaps for the first time in her life, Maggie was free.

"A Clean Breast of All her Miracles and Wonders"

To say that the spiritualistic world is aroused by the threatened disclosures of Margaretta Fox Kane, one of the originators of the so-called 'mediumistic' manifestations, is to put it very feebly.
—*New York Herald,* September 25, 1888

MAGGIE'S LETTER was only her first grand gesture. Within a few days, Katy sent a telegram despairing over her inability to retrieve her boys from the Juvenile Asylum. The message, delivered to Maggie while attending a banquet at the home of spiritualist H. (probably Hensleigh, a spiritualist advocate in that era) Wedgwood, scion of the famous china company, so thoroughly unnerved her that she sprang into action. "Like a flash it came upon me what I should do," Maggie later told a *New York Herald* reporter. "I left the brilliant party... [and] after I executed my plan I drove to Montague Williams, the London criminal lawyer, and told him of it. He applauded me."

Adding to Maggie's delight was the attorney's assurance that her nephews could not be indefinitely detained in New York. As citizens of England, they had the right to return to their native country. The only condition for their release was the identification of an English member of the Jencken family who would serve as their guardian. And that was something that Maggie had already arranged.

Recalling that Katy's brother-in-law Edward Jencken was traveling in Russia, Maggie had cabled New York's Society for the Prevention of Cruelty to Children that same night in his name. As next-of-kin to Ferdinand and Henry, the alleged Edward Jencken explained in that telegram that he requested their release from the Juvenile Asylum and immediate return to London accompanied by their mother, Katy Fox Jencken. Once the family was reunited, he planned to send young Ferdinand and Henry to school in Brighton.

The next morning to complete the ruse, Maggie, dressed in somber clothes, presented herself to the manager of Edward's fashionable hotel, the Cavendish on St. James Street. Posing as his widow to the sympathetic hotel manager, Maggie managed to get access to his mail. "Not a word of objection, you know. I might have been arrested," she triumphantly recalled to the *New York Herald* several months later.

Having heard about the intentions of Edward Jencken, one of Katy's spiritualist friends, Isabella Beecher Hooker, the feminist and youngest sister of Harriet Beecher Stowe, attempted to have the Jencken boys released in New York. To the sixty-six-year-old Mrs. Hooker, the removal of a child from his mother was an abomination, still one more example in a long list of injustices perpetrated upon the disenfranchised women of America during its hundred-year-old history.

Four months earlier, on March 30, 1888, Isabella had addressed the International Council of Women in Washington, D.C. on that same issue. Asserting that the U.S. Constitution had not actually denied women the right to the vote, she maintained that the document had been deliberately ignored by men, thus disempowering half of the American population. "Herein is the degradation of woman to-day, not only that she cannot have a voice in making the laws and choosing officers to execute the laws, but she is compelled to be taxed, fined, imprisoned, hung even, by the verdict always of her political superiors—her male sovereigns, every one of whom is considered competent to legislate for her and to sit in judgment upon her by court and jury...," Isabella had argued.

Naturally, Isabella believed that Katy stood little chance of regaining custody of her sons against a disapproving court of men. Moreover, as she explained in a July 4, 1888, letter to Edward Jencken, she felt "assured that the abduction of the boys and the arrest of Mrs. Jencken are the result of enmity to spiritualism and a determination on the part of well meaning bigots to crush this 'pestilential heresy.'" In such a climate, she argued, "It seems to me best to use personal influence for the release of the boys rather than the law courts as the community is just now much stirred up by the Diss De Barr case, which has gone against her."

By then, Isabella had already used her personal influence to persuade the superintendent of the Juvenile Asylum to release Katy's sons to her and her attorney husband, John Hooker. Ferdinand, Henry, and Katy were to sail with him to Berlin on July 21. From there, it was a short journey to England.

A jubilant Katy and her boys soon arrived in London, where an equally thrilled Maggie greeted them. "I tell you... I took them in my arms, wasn't I rejoiced? I said to them, 'here's your Uncle Edward, boys,' pointing to myself, and they shouted back 'Hello, Uncle Edward,'" Maggie later told a *Herald Tribune* reporter.

Her nephews' rescue was only the first part of Maggie's campaign to correct the injustices perpetrated by spiritualism. While continuing to give séances in London, Maggie's spiritualist exhibitions now took an unexpected turn. No sooner were her British guests impressed with certain feats than Maggie would reveal how she had accomplished them. Her technique, as she later explained to the *Herald,* was to proceed "to a certain point in the process of delusion and then frankly undeceived [her guests]...convincing them of the ease with which they could be practiced upon." Exactly which feats she detailed and how they were accomplished has not been preserved.

To Maggie's surprise, many members of her audiences expressed gratitude instead of outrage. One of the most thankful was her influential spiritualist friend Hensleigh Wedgwood. As he wrote on July 18:

Dear Mrs. Kane: I am not so much surprised as I might be at what you have revealed to me if I had not already been led to believe that many spiritualistic mediums practice upon the credulous.

The illusion, however, was perfect while it lasted.

You do well to expose these infamous frauds, and I thank you for having enlightened me.

Such exposures were meant to be a dress rehearsal for a far more damaging public confession Maggie planned to give when she returned to the United States. But the thought of telling all in a public setting frightened her, making her so anxious and depressed that she contemplated suicide. "My troubles weighed upon me, and when I was coming over on the *Italy*, I do believe that I should have gone overboard but for the Captain and the doctor and some of the sailors," as she later admitted in *The Death-Blow to Spiritualism*.

Still, the "great decisions of life," as the spiritualist-oriented psychologist Carl Jung observed a half century later, "have as a rule far more to do with the instincts and other mysterious unconscious factors than with conscious will and well-meaning reasonableness."

By the time the *Italy* docked at the piers of the Battery on September 22, Maggie was listening to those instincts. As she walked down the gangplank, a group of reporters spotted her and rushed over to ask her opinion about Diss De Barr's recent exposé. The whole incident was an embarrassment, Maggie observed. Didn't they know that the "spirits never return"? Taken aback, the newsmen pressed for more information. If they wanted to know more, Maggie suggested, they could visit her at home for "an interesting exposure of the fraud."

The next day, having heard about Maggie's offhand remark, James Gordon Bennett dispatched a talented young reporter to Maggie's home. While bylines were not yet included on the pages of the *Herald*, the journalist was probably Reuben Briggs Davenport, who would later ghostwrite Maggie's memoir.

Bennett's instincts soon proved more newsworthy than even he had suspected. After calling at Maggie's "modest little house," the *Herald* reporter recalled that he "was received by a small, magnetic woman of middle age, whose face bears the traces of much sorrow and of a world-wide experience." Although Maggie was "negligently dressed...and not in the calmest possible mood...she knew what she was talking about when, in response to my questions, she told a story of as strange and fantastic a life as has ever been recorded."

For the fifty-five-year-old Maggie, the interview seemed a unique opportunity to rivet the attention of the American public. By doing so, she hoped somewhat naively, she would regain her self-respect. And in that attempt the *Herald* cooperated—if only to sell newspapers. Maggie, the *Herald* reported, while having engaged in "albeit a notorious career [which] has classed her with mountebanks and worse...retained a degree of public respect. Perhaps it is because years ago, she abandoned the art of deception and has since to her intimate friends evinced no ordinary measure of contempt for all who have since practiced it."

During the interview, Maggie had "declared over and over again her intention of balancing the account which the world of humbug-loving mortals held against her, by making a clean breast of all her former miracles and wonders."

Adding to the drama of the confession was Maggie's labile emotions, ranging from relief to bitterness to sorrow, and finally stirring her to such an agitated state that she rose from her chair, began to pace, and then sat down again, covering her face when on the point of tears. At still other moments during that tumultuous interview, "she would seat herself suddenly at a piano and pour forth fitful floods of wild, incoherent melody, which coincided strangely with that reminiscent weirdness which...characterized the scene."

Within a few weeks, Maggie predicted to her stunned listener, she planned to deliver a public lecture that would embarrass the spiritualist community. She would do so to "shame and dumb-found all the spiritualistic frauds who have not yet repented into poverty or exile of their nebulous ways...[and] reveal one after an-other of the methods by which willing believers have been so briskly duped and robbed."

Why, then, the reporter finally asked, if Maggie loathed spiritu-alism, had she continued to practice it?

With that question, all the years of pent-up resentments she held toward Leah exploded in a fiery condemnation. "Another sis-ter of mine," and she coupled the name with an injurious adjective, "made me take up with it. She's my damnable enemy. I hate her. My God! I'd poison her. No, I wouldn't but I'll lash her with my tongue," Maggie exclaimed.

Somewhat later in that extraordinary interview, Maggie ruefully admitted her powerlessness to raise spirits. "No, no the dead shall not return, nor shall any that go down in hell. So says the Catholic Bible, and so say I. The spirits will not come back. God has not or-dered it."

Her exposé, Maggie then added, would focus upon the rap-pings. Then, to illustrate what she meant, the parlor began echoing with knocks—first sounding beneath the journalist's feet, then moving beneath his chair, and finally reverberating under the table upon which he leaned.

Afterward, Maggie led her incredulous interviewer to a door where more raps were heard. Finally, after seating herself at the piano stool, the instrument itself soon resonated with knockings.

"Is it all a trick?" the reporter asked.

"Absolutely. Spirits, is he not easily fooled?"

Rap, rap, rap!

"I can always get an affirmative answer to that question," Maggie remarked.

"...it is as you say, the manner in which the joints of the foot can be used without lifting it from the floor. The power of doing this can only be acquired by practice begun in early youth...and it was my eldest sister who first put the discovery to such an infamous use.

I call it infamous, for it was."

❦

The *Herald* story, published on September 25, 1888, sold thousands of copies and was immediately reprinted in dozens of other newspapers across the nation. As Bennett knew, exposés of spiritualism were bound to be big news—especially when issued by one of the famous Fox sisters. A day later, the *Herald* reported that Maggie's comments had stirred an enormous controversy and created consternation among the nation's spiritualists:

"Several of the mediums said that they could hardly believe their eyes when they read of Mrs. Margaret Fox Kane's determination, and they declared almost unanimously that 'she would not do it if she were in her senses.' They accuse her of excessive indulgence in drink and hint that she is not responsible for what she says."

Beyond such accusations from mediums, Maggie's remarks also horrified thousands who believed in spiritualism. Before long Bennett had dispatched his reporters to exploit the contretemps into a still more heated debate in his pages.

By the following Sunday, September 30, under the triple headlines "Shocked Spiritualists," "But They Make the Best of Mrs. Kane's Exposé," and "Alleging Dipsomania," the *Herald* observed that hundreds of thousands of spiritualism's believers had been set on edge by Maggie's revelations.

"Already it is violently discussed in certain mystical circles," said the *Herald*. Among the first to be interviewed was Mrs. E. A. Wells, a prominent medium of the New York Circle and a participant in the weekly meetings of the spiritualists at Brooklyn's Adelphi Hall. Shocked by Maggie's resolution to expose and embarrass the nation's spiritualists, she dismissed the report as one of the medium's idle threats. Personally, Mrs. Wells added, she had always regarded the Fox sisters with respect because they had been the first to receive messages from the spirit world.

"But do you believe if she made those noises with her feet, as she says, they would sometimes be heard on the ceiling of a room?" Mrs. Wells mused. "No, it cannot be explained by saying that the principle is...the same as...ventriloquism. No, no, she can never convince thoroughly earnest Spiritualists that she produced the rappings by fraud."

Others predicted that whatever Maggie planned to say would have little impact upon the spiritualist movement. Among the most outspoken was well-known Boston medium Helen Fairchild, who pleaded ignorance about the threatened exposure. "I don't believe she can expose any fraud," Fairchild opined. "But if fraud exists, why then I say let it be exposed; the sooner the better. There's no fraud about me, that's very certain, and I've [had] some of the very best people in New York to come here."

Moreover, it was well known that Maggie and Katy were fond of drink. "Maybe she's out of money and thinks the Spiritualists ought to do something for her. I shouldn't wonder," she concluded.

No less blasé and even more damaging were comments made by Maggie's brother-in-law Daniel Underhill, who had agreed only reluctantly to speak with the *Herald* and only because his wife, Leah, was not in the city. Left unsaid was the obvious—that Daniel had insisted that Leah leave town to avoid any adverse publicity from Maggie's brash "confession."

"I have for years helped both Maggie and Katie, and my wife has done everything in the world for them," Daniel told the *Herald* reporter. "We have furnished apartments for Maggie twice. They might both do very well if they would only keep sober. Maggie can be as nice as you please or as vicious as the devil. Several persons have undertaken to manage her, but all have failed."

Reiterating the idea that Maggie was emotionally unbalanced, Daniel added, "I have done so much for her and she has behaved so badly in return that I have given her up now and will have nothing to do with her. She says, she will lecture, does she? Well, I don't believe she ever will. She's incapable of it."

Daniel observed that this was not the first time that Maggie had made such a threat. "She has had such spells before. It is astonishing to me that people have stuck to her and Katie as they have. It is all bosh about revealing the manner of producing the raps. I don't believe she knows how they are produced except that is it done by an occult agency."

Other spiritualists, attending a weekly meeting of the First Spiritual Society of New York in the gaudily painted ballroom of Brooklyn's Adelphi Hall, offered similar opinions. Still, unlike the Society's earlier gatherings of hundreds, only sixty-five people appeared at the hall that Sunday. "The majority of them looked rather blue, and there were but a few quarters, dimes and nickels in the contribution plate," observed the *Herald.* "Few of the prominent mediums were present."

The Society's president, Henry J. Newton, dismissed the poor attendance following reports of Maggie's threatened exposé as coincidental. "Nothing that she could say in that regard would in the least change my opinion nor...of any one else who has become...convinced that there is an occult influence connecting us with an invisible world," Newton blithely maintained. The rappings, he told the *Herald,* were involuntary and emanated from the spirits.

"I have seen Margaret Fox Kane herself, when lying on a bed of sickness and unable to rise, produce rappings in various parts of the room...and upon the ceilings, doors and windows several feet away from her," he claimed. Moreover, "I have seen her produce the same effects when too drunk to realize just what she was doing."

All too often, Newton sharply reminded the *Herald* reporter, the American public seemed to have forgotten that the Shakers of New Lebanon, New York had first experienced similar manifestations in 1832. "These continued in more or less varying phases and gradually developed down to the time when the 'Rochester knockings' in 1847 were first made known, and brought into celebrity by Leah, Margaret and Cathie [Katy] Fox."

⁓❦⁓

Maggie did not respond to the insults. Instead, she seems to have hunkered down, spending her time at home organizing her talk designed to condemn spiritualism and its abuses. Among the most outrageous of those, Maggie had decided to argue, was spiritualism's covert association with free love—something that neither she nor her sisters, nor anyone else involved in the early spiritualist movement, had encouraged.

Such a revelation would sink spiritualism as surely as the mention of free love had scuttled Victoria Woodhull's bid for the presidency of the United States sixteen years earlier, Maggie realized. By the time a *New York Herald* reporter arrived at her home on October 9, Maggie was ready to hint at the subject of her lecture. She told the journalist she had no expectations of financial reimbursement.

"It is known that an overture was made to Maggie Fox suggestive of a money consideration for her silence, and that she rejected it with much indignation," explained the *Herald* in a story the following day. Adding to the story's titillating tone was Maggie's promise of a sensational revelation. "I am going to expose the very root of corruption in this spiritualistic ulcer. You talk about Mormonism!" Maggie exclaimed, alluding to that religion's polygamous practices.

She had, she explained, witnessed immoral behavior during her recent trip to London. On one occasion, she was invited to the home of a wealthy Englishman to observe a materialization, and a naked woman appeared wrapped in luminous paper. At certain other séances "none but the most tried and trusted are admitted... there are shameless goings on that vie with the secret Saturnalia of the Romans."

That afternoon as Maggie was completing her stunning confession, a visitor appeared quite unexpectedly—her sister Katy, who had arrived from England on the *Persian Monarch* with her two teenage sons without any advance notice.

"The sisters at once fell on each other's necks, in an ecstasy of affection and delight at being together once again," observed the astonished *Herald* reporter. "Mrs. Kane had only just been talking of her projected lecture on 'The Curse of Spiritualism' and Mrs. Jencken, who had heard nothing of the proposed exposé, except as it was casually rumored...at the steamship dock, promptly gave her acquiescence."

Seizing the moment, the journalist immediately asked Katy for her opinion about spiritualism. "I do not care a fig for Spiritualism...except so far as the good will of its adherents may affect the future of my boys," she retorted. "They are all I have in this life, and I live or die for them."

Katy's appearance had improved, noted the *Herald*, and she now seemed far more healthy and confident than when her sons were taken by the Society for the Prevention of Cruelty to Children the previous spring. "No matron could bear a more placid and comely expression, and she declares with heartfelt earnestness that she is done forever with her once-besetting-vice."

After urging her a second time to clarify her views on spiritualism, Katy scoffed. "I care nothing for Spiritualism...So far as I am concerned, I am done with it. I will say this, I regard it as one of the very greatest curses that the world has ever known."

What rankled her most of all, she continued, was her sister Leah, the "worst" of the spiritualists. She believed that it was at the malicious instigation of Leah that she had been arrested the previous spring. "I don't know why it is, she has always been jealous of Maggie and me," Katy added. "I suppose because we could do things in Spiritualism that she couldn't."

As a youngster, Katy admitted, she had often wept because of the life she was leading. Now, she added, "The time has...come for

Maggie and I to set ourselves right before the world. Nobody knows at what moment either of us might be taken away. We ought not to leave this base fabric behind us unexposed."

But stories, even those published in the widely circulated New York newspapers, were not proof enough. To disseminate the truth about the origins of spiritualism beyond the metropolitan area, Maggie and Katy agreed to have their history published in a book. Five days after Maggie's confession to the *Herald* reporter, she and Katy signed an agreement with Reuben Briggs Davenport to publish the exposé as *The Death-Blow to Spiritualism.*

"No one who does not love illusion for illusion's sake—better, in other words, than he loves the truth—can, after reading this volume, remain a follower of Spiritualism and its hypocritical apostles," Davenport wrote in the preface.

At the least, the book would challenge the course of spiritualism represented in Leah's *The Missing Link in Spiritualism.* At its best, it would provide a historical memoir of Maggie's perception of her and Katy's lives and entanglement in the spiritualist movement.

∝❧∾

On Sunday, October 21, New Yorkers awoke to a front-page story splashed over four columns in the *World* entitled "Spiritualism Exposed. The Fox Sisters Sound the Death-Knell of the Mediums."

"The severest blow that Spiritualism has ever received is delivered to-day through the solemn declaration of the greatest medium of the world that it is all a fraud, a deception and a lie," trumpeted the *World* in its introductory remarks for the illustrated story.

After describing the highlights of Maggie's life and romance with Elisha Kane, the *World* acknowledged that she felt obliged to make a full confession. "Spiritualists say that I am mad. I have had a life of sorrow. I have been poor and ill, but I consider it my duty, a sacred thing, a holy mission...I want to see the day that it is entirely done away with. After my sister Katie and I expose it, I hope Spiritualism will be given a death blow."

In the meanwhile, Maggie added, "I am waiting anxiously and fearlessly for the moment when I can show to the world, by personal demonstration, that all Spiritualism is a fraud and deception. It is a branch of legerdemain but it has to be closely studied to gain perfection...I trust that this statement coming solemnly from me, the first and most successful in this deception, will break the force of the rapid growth of Spiritualism and prove that it is all a fraud, a hypocrisy and a delusion."

That night at the three-thousand-seat New York Academy of Music, the stage was stripped of the set design for its current production of Denman Thompson's play "Old Homestead." It had been rearranged with "a bare and somber drawing room scene," according to the *New York Times.*

As soon as the Academy doors opened, hundreds of spiritualists, well-to-do men and women, curious onlookers, and a full press corps streamed into the huge, balconied theater to watch Maggie Fox fulfill her promise to denounce spiritualism. Their mood was restive and disruptive, as boisterous as the audience had been nearly forty years earlier at Rochester's Corinthian Hall where Maggie had appeared to prove the existence of spiritualism.

Did Maggie see the parallels between the two appearances—or their ironies? Or was she simply too caught up in the tensions of the moment to think about the past and the circular path her life had inadvertently taken? Whatever Maggie felt has not been preserved. The only accounts of the event are those reported in the newspapers.

"The great building was crowded and the wildest excitement prevailed at times. Hundreds of Spiritualists had come to see the originators of their faith destroy it at one stroke. They were greatly agitated at times and hissed fiercely," observed the *New York Herald* the next morning. Amidst the resulting din, the portly Dr. Cassius M. Richmond appeared on the stage, observing that there had been no miracles in eighteen hundred years and then, in that context, proceeded to discredit Diss De Barr. After demonstrating some tricks of legerdemain common to the spiritualists, Dr. Richmond dramatically stepped back from the footlights.

It was then that Maggie made her appearance on the stage. "She was greeted with cheers and hisses. She put on her glasses, curtsied to the audience, and read slowly and in a voice trembling with emotion her confession," said the *Herald*. In a nearby box sat her sister Katy, applauding her words.

"Thereby stood a black-robed sharp-faced widow working her big toe and solemnly declaring that it was in this way she created the excitement that has driven so many persons to suicide or insanity," said the *Herald*. "One moment it was ludicrous, the next it was weird."

"That I have been mainly instrumental in perpetrating the fraud of Spiritualism upon a too confiding public, many of you already know. It is the greatest sorrow of my life," Maggie admitted. "It is a late day now, but I am prepared to tell the truth; the whole truth and nothing but the truth, so help me God."

At that point, Maggie, the *Herald* noted, stretched her hands upward toward the heavens. "When I began this deception I was too young to know right from wrong. I hope God Almighty will forgive me and those who are silly enough to believe in Spiritualism."

Stepping forward, Dr. Richmond then invited several physicians to the stage in anticipation that they would examine Maggie as she produced the sounds. "Three doctors knelt down, took hold of Mrs. Kane's big toe and assumed a grave air," noted the *Herald*. After they agreed that they had heard rappings produced by Maggie's toe, the trembling woman stood up so that the audience could hear the sounds.

The moment was unforgettable. "There was dead silence. Everybody in the great audience knew that they were looking upon the woman who is principally responsible for Spiritualism, its founder, high priestess and demonstrator," observed the *Herald*. "She stood upon a little pine table with nothing on her feet but stockings. As she remained motionless, loud, distinct, rappings were heard now in the flies, now behind the scenes, now in the gallery."

"Mrs. Kane became excited," observed the *Herald*. "She clapped her hands, danced about and cried:—'It's a fraud! Spiritualism is a fraud from beginning to end! It's all a trick! There's no truth in it!'"

Even that outburst did not quell Maggie's mood. Emboldened by a "whirlwind of applause, she went into the audience, placed her foot upon the shoe of a prominent gentleman and demonstrated a series of raps whose sounds he publicly acknowledged."

By doing so, the *Herald* observed, Maggie had destroyed the credibility of spiritualism for all time.

"It was the general opinion of people who were in the Academy last night that the confession of the founders of Spiritualism and the...exposure of the tricks of mediums ends this form of swindling and that it can never recover from this crushing blow," concluded the *Herald*. "The Spiritualists in the audience almost frothed at the mouth with rage as they left the building and muttered furious threats against their foes."

༈

Several days after Maggie's electrifying appearance at the New York Academy of Music, her old spiritualist friend Joseph La Fumee, co-author of *The Love-Life of Dr. Kane* and a reporter for the *Brooklyn Eagle,* called at her home. Twice she had refused to see the sixty-seven-year-old journalist but on his third attempt she reluctantly admitted him to her parlor, according to *Time Is Kind.* Frustrated but long since accustomed to Maggie's erratic moods, La Fumee took one look at his careworn friend and understood.

Whatever sense of relief she may have felt from the confession at the Academy of Music had already faded and, in its wake, she had begun drinking again. She later blamed her ongoing need for funds and anxiety about obtaining them. But in late October 1888, Maggie was not yet ready to share that with Joseph La Fumee, even though he had repeatedly come to her rescue before.

What worried La Fumee most was his hunch that Maggie had already fallen prey to promoters who would want her to go on a national tour, luring her with promises of fame and fortune. Just a few days earlier, on October 22, the night after Maggie's Academy of Music appearance, La Fumee had attended a meeting of worried fellow spiritualists. They begged him to dissuade Maggie from taking her confessions on the road.

But La Fumee had arrived too late. Proudly, Maggie admitted to her old friend that she had already agreed to a lecture tour. Her manager was the dapper, mustached Frank Stechen, described by the *World* as "a Western theatrical man and manager of a well-known star." He had arranged Maggie's lecture-demonstration at the New York Academy of Music. In fact, as she explained, she was scheduled to leave with Katy in a few days on a tour that would take them to some of America's largest cities.

Delicately, using all the tact that he could muster, La Fumee questioned Maggie about her motives. She was doing so out of personal conviction, Maggie insisted—not out of a need for funds. "I'll get along all right! You need not worry about money. I have plenty of money, right this minute. And I'll make more by showing people how the raps are made than I did telling lies to them!"

Dubious, but trying to understand Maggie's decision, La Fumee asked Maggie to rap for him. She agreed but could only produce raps near her feet—and not across the room. Puzzled, La Fumee asked her to try again. After all, if she could control the raps, he reasoned, why wouldn't she make them echo throughout the parlor as before? But Maggie refused, saying it was too hard.

Many questions surround this incident reported in Pond's account. Was Maggie simply too tired—or too intoxicated—to make the sounds echo in other parts of her room? Had the performance at the Academy of Music strained her feet so much that she could no longer create a reverberation? Or, as the spiritualists would argue, had the spirits abandoned Maggie because of her public condemnation of their existence? Any doubt on the part of witnesses, after all, like those who had participated in the Corinthian Hall committees, the Buffalo doctors, the Harvard professors, and members of the Seybert Commission, was certain to drive away the spirits, as the nation's mediums often reminded their audiences.

❧

In November posters appeared in Rochester announcing that on the fifteenth of that month Maggie and Katy would appear at the Lyceum Theater to demonstrate their raps.

In an appeal to the truth-loving public one poster noted that "Clergyman and laymen should do everything in their power to help these poor women to dispel the darkness and gloom that has come upon our land largely through their influence."

To emphasize that message, a picture of a gravestone appeared in the advertisement's right corner. Upon it were these words:

"Modern Spiritualism Born March 31, 1848 at Hydesville, New York. Died November 15, 1888 at Rochester, NY. Aged 40 years, 7 months and 15 days...born of mischief, gone to Mischief."

The poster also mentioned that "a small Admission Fee will be taken to defray expenses."

While Katy initially participated in the events, her mental condition was so poor, according to an article in the *Rochester Democrat & Chronicle,* that she elicited more pity from her audiences than wonder. "She spoke in a parrot-like way, using the strongest sort of language, of her repentance....She said the same thing over and over, seeming to have learned it by heart," observed the newspaper.

Even so, the reporter, who had managed to obtain an interview with the medium, concluded that "Kate Fox believed in Spiritualism and in her own powers as firmly as ever." Her appearance on the lecture circuit, he opined, was out of pure necessity for "she and her children wanted money, possibly bread, and that in her weakened condition of mind she had taken this way of getting those essentials."

Further proof of Katy's wavering commitment to the confessions was a letter she wrote to an English friend, the medium Mrs. Cottell, in late November 1888 just after her appearance in Rochester.

Reprinted in *Time Is Kind,* the letter suggests that after Maggie's appearance at the Academy of Music, Katy had either disavowed her sister's behavior or supported it merely to save face. "I would have written to you before this but my surprise was so great on my arrival here, of Maggie's exposé of Spiritualism, that I had no heart to write to anyone," Katy wrote. Explaining that the managers of the Academy of Music—not her or Maggie—had made money from the event, some $1,500, Katie ruefully admitted that she wished she had remained with Mrs. Cotell:

"If I had the means I would now return to get out of all this. I think now I could make money in proving the raps were not made with the toes. So many people come to me to ask me about this exposé of Maggie's that I have to deny myself to them." Katy seems to have left the tour after her Rochester appearance. Around that same time, she withdrew from Davenport's book project. The published volume was based solely upon Maggie's comments.

During the winter of 1888–89 Maggie appeared in other cities. That spring she drifted back to New York, becoming a curiously forlorn figure. Her repudiation of spiritualism had briefly lifted her into the public eye and then, just as suddenly, dropped her into the gutter of old news. The nation's mediums, embarrassed by Maggie's public confession, shunned her.

One gray November day in 1889, a little over a year after Maggie's confession at the Academy of Music, she wandered down Manhattan's Sixth Avenue or Columbus, according to the spiritual publication *The Banner of Light,* and happened upon Mary Newton, wife of the president of New York's First Spiritual Society.

"Oh! Mrs. Newton, I do believe the good angels have sent me to you," Maggie said, smiling enthusiastically as she greeted her old acquaintance.

Surprised by Maggie's friendliness, Mary Newton responded politely. What puzzled her most, Mary told her husband, Henry, later that day, was Maggie's desire to renew their friendship. Quite unexpectedly, "she seemed very repentant of the course she had pursued: gave me her address and wished Mr. Newton and myself to call upon her and she would tell us all about it."

The offer was one that Henry felt he could not refuse. "It was our religious duty, as Spiritualists, to stand by Mrs. Kane, especially if she was repentant," he said. "For we, in common with hundreds, yes, thousands could testify to the genuineness of the 'raps' as given through her mediumship." After all, he reminded his wife, their purpose was to convey to living men and women the existence of an "unmistakable individual intelligence" beyond the grave.

By the late 1880s the concept of what spiritualist Henry Newton referred to as an "unmistakable individual intelligence" was also puzzling Harvard University professor of philosophy William James. Years earlier, the psychologist had become acquainted with spiritualism through his social reformer father, Henry, who hobnobbed with Emerson, Alcott, and Thoreau and had embraced the "shifting voices" of Swedenborg, Fourierism, Socialism, and Calvinism while William was growing up.

At Harvard, William James became so intrigued with the relationship between certain psychological types and their claims of spirit communication that in 1885 he helped establish the American Society for Psychical Research (ASPR).

Like the English model founded in 1882 by Cambridge professors Henry Sidgwick and Frederic Myers, the ASPR included a slate of distinguished scientists and investigators. Among its earliest members were academic luminaries, including Simon Newcomb, astronomer of the Naval Almanac Office; George S. Fullerton, a professor of philosophy at the University of Pennsylvania; Edward Pickering, head of the Harvard College Observatory; and William James's student, psychologist G. Stanley Hall.

During the ASPR's first year, James's interest in spiritual communication was heightened by his introduction to a young Boston medium, Leonora Simonds Piper, who his mother-in-law, Mrs. Gibbens, insisted had extraordinary powers of clairvoyance. Skeptical but determined to keep an open mind, James had consequently attended a séance in Mrs. Piper's parlor, which, he noted with relief, was devoid of the usual paraphernalia of late-nineteenth-century séances—spirit cabinets, circles of chairs, bells, and trumpets.

Equally intriguing was Mrs. Piper's utter lack of pretension. Guests were to expect no elaborate side effects, she modestly explained. Nor, she admitted rather ingenuously, did she understand what happened when she went into a trance; sometimes, in fact, members of her séance audience reported that Mrs. Piper's "spirit controls" had been unreliable.

The information that the young medium revealed while entranced was nevertheless so convincing, displaying such intimate knowledge about James and his family, that the psychologist was unnerved. "My impression after this first visit was that Mrs. P. was either possessed of supernormal powers, or knew the members of my wife's family by sight and had by some lucky coincidence become acquainted with such a multitude of their domestic circumstances as to produce the startling impression which she did," James wrote.

To deepen his understanding, the psychologist attended countless séances and sent her many "test subjects," but ultimately remained convinced that Mrs. Piper's "spirit controls" were genuine. "My later knowledge of her sittings and personal acquaintance with her had led me absolutely to reject the latter explanation, and to believe that she has supernormal powers," James concluded.

In one of his most famous essays on psychical research, the psychologist compared Mrs. Piper to a "white crow"—a metaphor for an exception to the norm which, in spite of scientific evidence to the contrary, James believed investigators should never overlook. "If I may employ the language of the professional logic-ship, a universal proposition can be made untrue by a particular instance," he wrote in 1897. "If you wish to upset the law that all crows are black, you must not seek to show that no crows are; it is enough if you prove one single crow to be white."

Between 1885 and 1886 James relentlesly pursued his investigations of Mrs. Piper. In 1887, when Richard Hodgson, fellow researcher and member of the British Society for Psychical Research, arrived in Boston, James asked him to focus upon her almost exclusively.

Paradoxically while Mrs. Piper continued to baffle James, Hodgson, and their colleagues through the late 1880s, Maggie's nearly simultaneous flight into renunciation would deepen the shadow of disbelief that settled over the public concerning the once popular spiritualist movement.

"An Unmistakable Individual Intelligence"

Tis strange—but true; for truth is always
Strange;
Stranger than fiction.
—Lord Byron, from *Don Juan*

By late 1889 Maggie's financial situation had become desperate. Equally distressing was her recognition of her recent mistake. She had intimated as much to Mary Newton during their meeting on Columbus Avenue. Henry Newton and spiritualist C. P. Sykes had responded by calling upon Maggie at her home. What she said was so startling—so contrary to the events at the New York Academy of Music—that the two listeners begged Maggie to repeat it before other witnesses.

She agreed and on November 16, 1889, appeared before the Newtons, their guests, and a stenographer. According to a story in the *Banner of Light,* Maggie recanted her former condemnation of spiritualism.

"For months past I have suffered unspeakable anguish and I now feel the most poignant regret for the ruinous course I was made to follow," she began. "Those charges were false in every particular. I have no hesitation in saying that."

Why, then, Henry Newton asked, had she confessed?

There were several compelling reasons, Maggie claimed. While she was in London in 1888, representatives of the Catholic Church, among them Henry Edward Cardinal Manning, had insisted that she abandon this "wicked work of the devil," or conducting séances.

For months Maggie had resisted the clergy's pleas but in the end, recalling her vows as a Catholic, she had relented. Unmentioned was the arrangement she had worked out years earlier with Father Quinn that justified her need to support herself through spiritualism.

The dire state of Maggie's finances was another factor. "At that time I was in great need of money, and persons who...I prefer not to name, took advantage of the situation, hence the trouble," she claimed. To her despair, the promised funds for her Academy of Music appearance either had not been paid or were far less than anticipated. The result was that Maggie's finances were even more tenuous now than before her public confession. "I have known nothing but calamity, want and suffering since," she said.

Whatever promises Maggie's manager, Frank Stechen, had made, a windfall from the national tour had never materialized or, if it had, he must have hidden the profits. The contract for her national tour was $550 and once it ended, Maggie was left penniless in Boston.

Above all, Maggie insisted that she wanted it understood by her fellow spiritualists that her denunciations at the New York Academy of Music were lies, that her faith in spiritualism was even stronger now than ever before. "When I made those dreadful statements I was not responsible for my words. Now that I have got rid of the terrible incubus which enthralled my every word and action, my belief in the philosophy and the phenomena...of Spiritualism is unshaken. Its genuineness is an incontrovertible fact," Maggie insisted.

Maggie's manner was so earnest that one of her listeners, J. L. O'Sullivan, the U.S. Minister to Portugal, was deeply moved. "If ever I heard a woman speak truth, it was then," he insisted.

While Maggie explained that she did not believe in spiritual materializations, she reminded her listeners that she possessed a unique gift. "There is not a human being on earth can produce the 'raps' the same way as they are made through me," she said, with a hint of her old pride. Desperate for funds, she again planned to appear on the lecture circuit. "I will devote myself entirely to platform work as that will give me a better opportunity to refute the foul slanders uttered by me against Spiritualism."

To underscore her remarkable interview, Maggie wrote an open letter to the public. It read:

128 West Forty-third Street
New York City,
November 16, 1889

To the Public:

The foregoing interview having been read over to me I find nothing contained therein that is not a correct record of my words and truthful expression of my sentiments. I have not given a detailed account of the ways and means which were devised to bring me under subjection, and so extract from me a declaration that the spiritual phenomena as exemplified through my organism were a fraud. But I shall fully atone for this incompleteness when I get upon the platform.

Maggie's interview and letter, published on November 20, 1889, in the *Banner of Light,* was received with only tepid interest. If anything, it seemed to diminish her already shattered reputation, reducing her to an aging eccentric whose retraction of her earlier recantation bordered on the absurd.

Typical of the widespread skepticism was the reaction of spiritualist Isaac Funk, publisher and proprietor of the Funk and Wagnalls publishing house. He had often been impressed by Maggie's raps, including one memorable instance when she telepathically recited a letter folded in his pocket.

After Maggie's recantation of her exposé, though, Funk refused to believe anything she said. His one enduring observation was that by then Maggie was desperate for money—so needy that "for five dollars she would have denied her mother, and would have sworn to anything."

᪤

The few surviving first-person accounts about Maggie after her 1889 recantation suggest that her re-embrace of spiritualism was genuine, that in spite of her previously muddled behavior, she was determined to correct her earlier accusations of a fraudulent spirit world.

During the winter of 1889–90 Maggie appeared at the Shawmut Lyceum of Boston's Wells Memorial Hall. Superficially at least, according to medium Mary T. Longley, the graying, careworn Maggie still radiated refinement and candor—a far cry from Funk's caricature of her as a desperate woman. "I have had the pleasure of listening to her inspired words of spiritual import and exhortation, quietly, gently spoken to adults and children alike," Mrs. Longley wrote.

Several weeks later, on March 31, during the forty-second anniversary celebration of spiritualism, Mrs. Longley was again seated near Maggie on the platform at Wells Memorial Hall. As soon as the famous medium asked the spirits to make their presence known, the hall filled with raps. "She was then in very feeble health," Mrs. Longley recalled, "a subdued, quiet, unassuming little woman, entirely free from any assumption or arrogance or pomposity."

᪤

While Maggie's earlier exposé at the New York Academy of Music did not deliver the intended "death-blow" to the spiritualist movement, it still packed a punch, leaving its aging ringmaster Leah breathless. Leah had sought refuge in Arcadia when Maggie's threatened denunciation hit the newspapers. Still Maggie's astonishing confession, the newspaper coverage, and the chain of protests it elicited from spiritualists caused her untoward anguish. Even after the seventy-four-year-old Leah returned to New York in 1889, cavalierly dismissing the scornful expressions and criticisms that often greeted her in public, she remained depressed. On November 1, 1890, she fell to the floor, the victim of a stroke. Several hours later, with Daniel at her side, Leah passed away.

∼❧∽

Katy did not fare much better. After leaving Rochester and distancing herself from the recantation, she seems to have had little to do with Maggie. Living in Manhattan with her sons, Katy scraped out a living from her séances and the wages that Ferdinand earned as he drifted from job to job. Katy's ongoing alcoholism added to the family's difficulties. But in October 1889 there seemed one hopeful development—Katy's former mentors George and Sarah Taylor returned from Europe.

Life in the spirit world, Katy assured her old friends when they met, while speaking through the spirit of Sarah's uncle Isaac, was far preferable to that of an earthly existence: "I found everything far different, so much more beautiful, so much to draw her here. I found nothing that conflicts with my religious views, nothing but what I have longed for from my boyhood. This is a most beautiful world. Friends we have loved and thought lost are waiting on the margin on the shining shore for their loved ones and seeking to make them happy."

After that session, the Taylors promised to see her again. Then, without warning, Katy disappeared. "The Doctor [George Taylor] called at her lodgings but she had left and he could not learn where she was. We heard nothing from her or of her until this day, nearly a year," Sarah wrote despairingly on February 15, 1892. The resultant letter, giving a shabby address on Columbus Avenue, begged Sarah to visit.

To the nurse's horror, Katy's livid complexion, swollen face, and confused mental state—symptoms of end-stage alcoholism—told everything. Hovering nearby was twenty-year-old Ferdinand, who, having fruitlessly tried to keep Katy from the bottle, tended her with increasingly desperate devotion. Henry's whereabouts were not mentioned.

Neither Katy's spirits, nor those she called up for the Taylors, nor even Ferdinand could seem to help Katy help herself. On July 1, 1892, Sarah Taylor received a telegram from Ferdinand: "Mother is dead. Do come up."

"And so it was! Katie had been on her last spree, had taken her last drink and had by these excesses separated herself from her body," Sarah sadly wrote in her diary that summer day. "The poor abused body lay there stark and stiff but no Katie either sober or drunk was there to claim it...Oh! If I could speak with a go-between without a third-party but alas! I don't know how."

The only sister who still might have served as that go-between was Maggie. But by the summer of 1892 the fifty-nine-year-old Maggie also was failing. Having taken pity on her, Henry and Mary Newton had hosted Maggie in their home for several months, but her heavy drinking—combined with her abuse of pain-killing drugs—soon made her a difficult and, ultimately, untenable guest.

Underscoring Maggie's desperate circumstances was a notice placed in the *Banner of Light* on January 9, 1892, asking followers to contribute to Maggie's care. The result was a paltry $86.80.

What happened to Maggie after she left the Newtons, where she lived and how she survived in the last months of that year, remains shrouded in mystery. What is known, according to a pro-spiritualist pamphlet entitled *Rappings,* was that by the winter of 1892–93, Maggie had become critically ill and lay bedridden in a Ninth Street tenement house.

There, a Mrs. Mellen, a non-spiritualist physician of the Medico Legal Society of New York, attended Maggie for several hours a day. "Mrs. Fox Kane was unable to move hand or foot," the physician recalled. "There was not a closet in the place nor any other hiding place of any kind. And yet the knockings were heard now through the wall, now through the ceiling, and again through the floor."

"They were heard in response to questions the woman put to her guide, as she expressed it," Mrs. Mellen added. "And she was as incapable of cracking her toe-joints at this time as I was."

According to *Time Is Kind*, it was Joseph La Fumee who provided for Maggie in the end and who had her moved from the Ninth Street tenement to the Brooklyn home of her friend Mrs. Emily B. Ruggles.

By the latter part of February 1893, Maggie had slipped into a coma. Two weeks later, on Tuesday night, March 7, as Joseph La Fumee sat by Maggie's side, she opened her eyes and regarded her old friend fondly. Her eyes were "free from all the cloudiness of drugs' reactions, and…wide with joy, a radiant joy that transfigured her."

The end came soon afterward in the early morning hours of March 8 when Maggie slipped quietly away.

~᯦~

By 8 P.M. on March 10 so many spiritualists had pushed their way into Brooklyn's Bradbury Hall for Maggie's funeral that some had to stand in the stairways. "The hall was so densely packed, that it was almost impossible for a man to get in or out," complained the *Brooklyn Eagle*. "There was no ventilation and the place was suffocatingly hot."

In spite of the discomfort, the men and women, who had traveled from as far away as Boston and upstate New York, were determined to attend the ceremony that was meant to be a heartfelt tribute to the surviving founder of the spiritualist movement.

Whatever resentment the spiritualists felt about Maggie's recantation at the New York Academy of Music now seemed entirely forgotten. "Most of the leading Spiritualists were present last night and Mrs. Kane was buried in as complete an odor of Spiritualistic orthodoxy as enveloped her when her sisters Katie and Leah, her rappings, table tippings and other manifestations astonished half the crowned heads of Europe nearly forty years ago," opined the

Eagle. The newspaper added that there was no "suggestion that Mrs. Kane had ever declared her manifestations a humbug and explained that she produced the rappings by dislocating the joint of her great toe."

At the front of the hall, just before a platform, sat Maggie's casket, surrounded by lilies and others flowers. Several prominent mediums, among them Henry and Mary Newton, Mrs. M. A. Gridley, and Miss Annie Burnham of Boston, were seated on the stage.

The next morning, possibly at the suggestion of Maggie's brother, David Fox, her body was laid to rest in the Underhill plot in Brooklyn's stately Greenwood Cemetery. Nearby were the graves of her mother, Katy, Leah, and brother-in-law Daniel.

To the sensitive and thoughtful Joseph La Fumee, who knew Maggie's history nearly as well as his own, her burial in the Underhill plot seemed a final, ironical injustice. A year later, the aging journalist had her casket moved to the La Fumee family plot at Brooklyn's Cypress Hill cemetery.

On November 3, 1893, nine months after Maggie's demise, spiritualists, disgusted with ongoing accusations of fraud and specious imitators, gathered in Washington, D.C. to incorporate the National Spiritualist Association of Churches (NSAC) as a nonprofit religious organization. The organization's goal was to establish spiritualism as a "recorded legitimate religion" in the United States with the right to charter spiritualist churches, state associations, spiritualist camps, and educational institutions.

Headquartered in upstate New York on the grounds of the spiritualist summer colony then known as the Cassadaga Lake Free Association—now the Lily Dale Assembly—NSAC has remained at that location into the present. Today the organization includes about one hundred and fifty spiritualist churches under its charter and has five to seven thousand members whose religion is exclusively spiritualism. Thousands of others, perhaps hundreds of thousands, embrace spiritualism while still practicing other faiths.

A few years after NSAC was established as a legitimate religion, Americans heard rumors about Edgar Cayce, a young man from Kentucky with uncanny healing powers. In 1898 the youth had developed a paralysis of the throat that stymied his doctors, but after falling into a hypnotic trance, he discovered an effective treatment and cure. Before long Cayce had regained his voice, and he soon realized that his gift could be used to heal others. When visitors arrived for a consultation, Cayce placed himself into a hypnotic trance, diagnosed their disease, and recommended a treatment.

Eventually he could even diagnose people without seeing them—merely by learning their names and addresses. By the time of Cayce's death in 1945 he had diagnosed more than thirty thousand people and had hundreds of sworn affidavits attesting to successful cures from physicians and patients.

With the onset of World War I and the deaths of thousands of young men, a new generation of spiritualists appeared. One of the most prominent was Sir Arthur Conan Doyle, author of the Sherlock Holmes detective series, whose pro-spiritualist book *New Revelation* was published in 1917. To Doyle, a member of the British Society for Psychical Research who had recently lost one of his sons and a brother in the war, belief in spiritual communication was a certainty. In November 1916 he had announced in the *Observer* a "new revelation of God's dealing with man which must modify some ill-defined and melancholy dogmas as to the events which follow the death of the body."

The patrician British author appeared before audiences in the United States to promote that idea before returning home to begin writing *The History of Spiritualism.* "It is indeed curious that this movement, which many of us regard as the most important in the history of the world since the Christ episode, has never had a historian from those who were within it," the author wrote in the preface to his 1926 two-volume history. A message from a medium, Doyle insisted, "is a genuine breath from beyond, and yet each intermediary tinges with his or her personality the message which comes through. So, as in a glass darkly, we see this wondrous mystery, so vital and yet so undefined. It is its very greatness which prevents it from being defined."

Of course many Americans remained skeptical. One of the most outspoken was magician Harry Houdini, who agreed in December 1922 to join an investigative panel sponsored by the similarly disgusted editors of *Scientific American.* The subject of their investigation was the Amazing Margery, the blonde, bobbed-haired Mina Crandon, the spiritualist wife of a Boston physician. When Margery was in a trance under the spirit "control" of her brother Walter's spirit, tables lifted and furniture moved. Far more unnerving was the oozing from Margery's mouth or nose of "ectoplasm"—a sticky, plastic-like substance that was supposed to represent partially materialized spirits. During one of Margery's sittings, she exuded an ectoplasm that formed the shape of human hands.

While the press leaked news of Margery's feats to an intrigued American public, the *Scientific American* committee remained silent, unable to reach a decision. Growing impatient, Houdini declared Margery a fraud and quit the panel. By 1925 the rest of the committee followed and *Scientific American* declared the contest closed.

Eighteen months later spiritualism made headlines again, this time on Halloween Eve 1926, when Houdini died from acute appendicitis. After his widow promised a $10,000 reward to anyone who could deliver the secret, coded message through which Houdini had said he would try to reach her after his death, she was besieged with thousands of versions. In 1929 medium Arthur Ford, pastor of the First Spiritualist Church of New York, contacted Bess Houdini and delivered a ten-word message in code—one that Bess swore was true. Two days later, however, the *New York Graphic* claimed that Bess had previously disclosed Houdini's code to Ford—an accusation that the widow vehemently denied in a letter to the *Graphic* columnist Walter Winchell. The controversy continued for months, sparking record crowds of fifty thousand at spiritualist camps like Lily Dale in upstate New York and Camp Chesterfield in Indiana.

While the psychological and scientific community remained dismissive, one notable exception was William McDougall, a Harvard psychology professor who became chairman of the Department of Psychology at Duke University in 1927. His protégé, Dr. Joseph Banks Rhine, decided to test one of spiritualism's manifestations—extrasensory perception, or ESP, the ability to perceive objects and events distant in time and space without normal means of communication.

Beginning in 1927, Rhine engineered a series of groundbreaking studies on ESP at a Duke University laboratory. Using probability statistics and special cards, Rhine examined subjects for telepathy, precognition, and psychokinesis—the mental ability to move objects. The results, which proved the existence of telepathy, were published in a monograph entitled "Extra Sensory Perception," soon followed by Rhine's bestselling book *New Frontiers of the Mind.* Soon ESP became a household word. Magazines like *Time, Reader's Digest, Scientific American,* and *Harper's* touted Rhine as the father of the new science of parapsychology. By 1937 Rhine and McDougall founded the quarterly *Journal of Parapsychology,* whose review of academic studies in parapsychology has continued to the present day.

After World War II, Rhine's disciples established parapsychology laboratories at universities across the country. In spite of his profound influence upon parapsychology—or PSI as it is known today—the field never achieved full acceptance in the American scientific community, even though in 1969 the Parapsychological Association was admitted to and still remains part of the American Association for the Advancement of Science.

A handful of superstar mediums offered themselves for study to help support the field. Among the most celebrated was the Irishborn medium Eileen Garrett. One of her most dramatic feats occurred in 1930. While attempting to raise the spirit of the late Sir Arthur Conan Doyle in London, her "control," or guiding spirit, was interrupted by the arrival of a new spirit calling himself Irwin. Just a day earlier the British had learned about the crash of an experimental dirigible airship in France. Now Irwin gave Mrs. Garrett a dramatic but highly technical account of the crash. A day or so later it was learned that Irwin was the name of the dead captain of that airship and his explanation of the tragedy was accurate.

Like her famous predecessor, Leonora Piper, Mrs. Garrett was so perplexed about her psychic abilities that she spent her life cooperating in scientific experiments. In 1951 Mrs. Garrett moved to Manhattan and founded the Parapsychology Foundation, which was devoted to the study of PSI. As a close friend of Aldous Huxley, author of *Brave New World,* Mrs. Garrett also made contact with his first wife after her death in 1955. Later, she participated in early psychological experiments with LSD and other hallucinogens. The Parapsychology Foundation subsequently contributed to the experimental work of Timothy Leary and Richard Alpert at Harvard and is still in existence today.

While some Americans still consulted mediums and kept spiritual centers like Lily Dale and Camp Chesterfield busy in the summer months, the postwar era had become a time of spiritual desolation. Social critics of the late 1940s and 1950s faulted modernity, with its staccato pace, emphasis on material status symbols, and belief in scientific rationalism and technology. Among the most influential books on the relationship between the spirit and the body were Norman Vincent Peale's 1948 *A Guide to Confident Living* and his 1952 *The Power of Positive Thinking*. "It has been said that thoughts are things, that they actually possess dynamic power…conditions are created by thoughts far more powerfully than conditions create thoughts," as Peale wrote. "This great law… simply stated is that if you think in negative terms you will get negative results. If you think in positive terms you will achieve positive results."

Reminding readers that William James believed that the human brain was only a medium for the soul, which would enter a higher understanding after death, Peale's *The Power of Positive Thinking* reaffirmed the concept of postmortem existence. "I believe there are two sides to the phenomenon known as death—this side where we now live and the other side, where we shall continue to live… We merely change the form of the experience called life and that change, I am persuaded, is for the better."

The idea of a spirit life even extended to certain psychological circles. One of its most outspoken advocates was Dr. Ian Stevenson, former chairman of the departments of psychiatry and neurology at the University of Virginia Medical School, who, after investigating dozens of accounts of reincarnation, published the well-received *Twenty Cases Suggestive of Reincarnation* in 1966.

That same year the iconoclastic James A. Pike, the fifth bishop of the Episcopal Diocese of California, lost his son, Jim, to a suicide in New York City. Two weeks after Jim's death the bishop returned to the flat in Cambridge, England, that he had shared with his son and was struck by the odd sight of books, postcards, and opened safety pins laid out on the floor at a 140-degree angle. A clock that had been stopped for months at 12:15 was now set at 8:19—the English equivalent of the time Jim had died in New York. One morning the bishop's housekeeper awoke to find that part of her bangs had been singed off—a hair style of hers that Jim had critiqued.

In spite of his skepticism, Pike contacted Mrs. Ena Twigg, one of Great Britain's most acclaimed mediums, who assured the bishop in a séance that Jim had accidentally overdosed on drugs. Some weeks later, when Pike had returned to the States, he met medium Arthur Ford, who reported seeing the spirits of Jim and his grandfather behind Pike as he preached a Holy Week sermon at Manhattan's St. Thomas Episcopal church.

On September 3, 1967, the disquieted bishop agreed to appear on Canadian television in Toronto to be videotaped with Ford to see if the medium could again raise Jim's spirit. That night Ford raised Jim's spirit and disclosed information about him only known to the bishop. In response to that first televised séance—a forerunner to TV shows that feature mediums today—Ford received twelve thousand letters. Suddenly spiritualism was beginning to achieve a visibility not seen for nearly a century.

Two years later Swiss-born psychiatrist Elisabeth Kübler-Ross, who spent most of her career working with terminally ill patients, wrote the bestselling *Death and Dying*. Explaining that death was a natural process that should be treated in an open and loving manner, Kübler-Ross's book called attention to death as a gateway to a higher cosmic existence.

In her 1991 book *On Life After Death,* she refined her thoughts still further, assuring readers that "Death is only moving from one house into a more beautiful one...a transition from this life to another existence where there is no more pain and anguish. All the bitterness and disagreements will vanish, and the only thing that lives forever is LOVE."

Advances in medical technology that enabled physicians to resuscitate victims of heart attacks and trauma were underscoring Kübler-Ross's observations. Patients whose hearts had stopped were now describing "near death" experiences that sounded strikingly similar—moving through a tunnel, approaching lights, greetings from loved ones, and feelings of peace and happiness. So extraordinary were these accounts that philosopher-psychiatrist Dr. Raymond Moody collected them into *Life After Life* in 1975. "I am not trying to prove that there is life after death. Nor do I think that a 'proof' of this is presently possible," wrote Moody. Instead he expressed the hope that those who had experienced a near-death experience would "Speak a little more freely, so that a most intriguing fact of the human soul may be more clearly elucidated."

Moody's hopes would eventually be realized. By the early 1990s a spate of bestselling books on near-death experiences like Betty J. Eadie's *Embraced by the Light* and Dr. Melvin Morse's *Transformed by the Light* had appeared, documenting the similarity of near-death experiences. Physicians attributed those impressions and their accompanying emotions to protective chemicals released by the dying brain, but the popularity of such books revealed ongoing American interest in the idea of a postmortem existence.

Another legacy from Maggie Fox and her sisters is the current interest in New Age books, music, meditation, and philosophy. An eclectic network of spiritual advisors, counselors, books, and objects that encompass neo-pagan traditions, Taoism, Hinduism, Wicca, astrology, and crystals, New Age philosophy defies an exact definition. But one theme resonates through its teachings: a conviction that the human spirit endures beyond the grave.

New Age advocates are not alone. In 2003 half of all Americans believed in the existence of paranormal phenomena, according to polls cited by the *New York Times*.

Signs and mystically decorated storefronts announce the continuing presence of clairvoyants, channelers, and psychics in America. Radio and television shows routinely feature interviews with
celebrity mediums like John Edward, Dr. Sylvia Browne, and James
Van Praagh. Today entire sections of bookstores are devoted to spiritualism, mediumship, channeling, and clairvoyance—topics that
point to another existence, possibly a parallel universe, beyond our
physical world of neighborhoods, playgrounds, office buildings,
and highways.

～✤〜

Is telepathy merely a coincidence after all—a complex series of associations, as traditional schools of psychology would have it?

If so, how can we explain those irrational yet memorable in-
stances when we have sensed that a distant loved one is in danger
or on the brink of death?

Must we automatically assume that mediums are either skilled
imposters or victims of split personalities? Can we trust messages
we dream about or hear from a deceased friend or relative—or
should we chalk this up to wishful thinking?

Can the hapless life of Maggie Fox Kane and her extraordinary
gifts be so succinctly explained?

The answers to these questions remain just beyond our grasp
and comprehension in spite of ongoing research in psychology and
parapsychology.

As was done at the time of Maggie's death, scientists and individuals today are still pondering the possibility, if not the certainty,
of the eternal life of the human soul. Like death itself, this remains
one of our greatest mysteries.

ONE OF THE pleasures of writing a nonfiction book is meeting those who are similarly intrigued with your subject and offer suggestions and sources that inevitably enhance the original concept. It is to the individuals named here that I am indebted for that experience while writing *The Reluctant Spiritualist.*

Special thanks to four writer friends, Madeline Weitsman, Phyllis Halterman, Helen Geraghty, and Triss Stein, members of a bimonthly Monday-night writing group who listened to my original concept and offered thoughtful suggestions about its expression. My appreciation also to mystery writers Annette and Marty Meyers, co-authors of a short story about the Fox Sisters, for their suggestions about historical sources. With gratitude also to writers Louise Bernikow, Gail Hornstein, Barbara Goldsmith, and Elizabeth Harlan for their inspiration.

Shirley Iversen, Larry Naukam, Barbara Pearl, and Deborah Jop in the Local History Room of the Rochester Public Library helped me locate information about the Fox sisters and their impact upon the city. Thanks are also due to library staff member Tony Giambra, who searched out various requests in the Local History Room, and Patrick Yengo, who located several newspaper clips at the Bausch & Lomb Library Center.

I am also indebted to Mary Haidvogel of the City Historian's Office of Rochester, who found other obscure but important newspaper stories about the Fox sisters that greatly enhanced my knowledge about their early Rochester years. City Historian Ruth Rosenberg-Naparsteck patiently answered questions about historical Rochester over a period of many months, suggested other contacts, and graciously critiqued sections of the manuscript. Joan

Hunt, president of the Friends of the Mt. Hope Cemetery, provided important insights into the history of that famous burial ground as well as its importance to the city of Rochester.

Ann Salter, executive director of the Rochester Historical Society, and research director Ann Walton helped me understand the social, economic, and religious climate of Rochester during the mid-nineteenth century and located historical materials about Maggie Fox, her sisters, and their community of friends.

Mary Huth, assistant director of Rare Books and Special Collections at the University of Rochester Library, not only enabled my research on the Fox sisters but repeatedly answered questions about the Posts and directed me to other relevant materials there.

Curator Christopher Densmore of the Friends Historical Library at Swarthmore College answered questions, offered suggestions for sources, and sent along materials related to the yearly meetings of the Friends of Human Progress. My appreciation also to archivist Pat O' Donell for locating a key letter from the Post Family Collection.

I am also grateful to assistance from the spiritualist community of Lily Dale in western New York, especially Sharon Snowman and Joyce La Judice. Nor can I forget Ron Nagy of that community, who showed me some of the Fox sisters' memorabilia—including the famous Hydesville peddler's trunk—and invited me to a service at the spiritualist church. Cosie Allen, director of the Morris Pratt Institute of Milwaukee and a board member of the National Spiritualist Association of Churches, also suggested various books and articles.

The manuscript also greatly benefited from a trip I made to the site of the original Fox family farmhouse on Hydesville Road at the invitation of Bob Hoeltzel, historian for the town of Arcadia. Sadly, Bob passed away in 2003 before this book was published. Through him I met Don and Sue Tierson, who invited me to visit their home in Arcadia, which was the original farmhouse of David Fox.

I am grateful to Charles Cowing, chairman of the Elisha Kent Kane Historical Society, who graciously opened the doors of the Masonic Hall dedicated to that Arctic explorer, suggested relevant sources, and critiqued sections of the manuscript. Through him I met Dr. Kane's great-great-grandnephew, John Rhein III, who provided me with valuable information about his family and his famous explorer relative. Still another Kane expert is Arctic collector and writer Douglas Wamsley, who provided me with an important pamphlet as well as articles on Sir John Franklin and who reviewed the Arctic exploration parts of the manuscript.

With special appreciation to Rob Cox, keeper of manuscripts of the American Philosophical Society, and staff associates Anne Harney and Valerie-Anne Lutz for their professional enthusiasm and personal kindness during my research in the Elisha Kent Kane Papers.

I am also grateful to the dedicated staff of the New York Public Library at Forty-second Street, especially Wayne Furman, Office of Special Collections, and librarians Stewart Bodner and David Smith, who went out of their way to help me find books and locate difficult source materials. With appreciation also to Eileen and Lisette Coly, the latter being the executive director of the Parapsychology Foundation. A special thanks to Dr. Carlos Alvarado, director of research, who helped me find several rare books on spiritualism. I am indebted to John Dorsey in the Research Office of the Boston Public Library. Nor can I forget the kindness of Librarian Dina Malgeri of the Malden, Massachusetts Public Library, who found a quiet place for me to work while I spent a week in my hometown.

Richard Nicholson, historic preservation planner of the city of Albany, Brian Buff, executive director of the Albany County Historical Association, and especially City Historian Virginia Bowers provided valuable background information on that city during the time of the Fox sisters' visit. Thanks are also due to Ruth Sweet and Laurie Burns at the Troy Public Library and to Cynthia Van Ness of the Buffalo and Erie County Library.

Neil Robertson, a great-great-grandnephew of Henry Jencken, who lives in New Gisbourne, Australia, sent me important background information about his family. In Ontario, Canada, genealogist Glen Atwell collaborated with fellow genealogists to trace the roots of the Foxes and Kanes.

Special thanks to Kenneth Silverman, author of a biography on Houdini, for his repeated encouragement about the life of Maggie Fox and her era. I am also indebted to Dorothy O. Helly and Polly Howells of the Women Writing Women's Lives Seminar of the City University of New York on two counts: first, for their invitation to present an early version of the manuscript to our seminar in 2003, and secondly, for their thoughtful comments about sections of the manuscript.

For research assistance I am particularly indebted to my friend writer-researcher Linda Selman, who has so generously given of her time; to the suggestions of Joel Wiener; and to the efforts of Kathy Feeley, Megan Elias, and Jacob Kramer.

A book is only as good as its original concept and thus it is my literary agent, Patty Moosbrugger, to whom I am deeply indebted for her inspiration, encouragement, and ongoing support for my work.

My editor, Andrea Schulz, has been an enthusiastic advocate for the book from the start, providing invaluable editorial advice, support, and kindness as the manuscript has progressed from proposal to final draft to publication. Her astute perception and thoughtful reflection led me to shape it in ways that made it an exciting professional endeavor.

For his keen interest, devotion, and faith in this project, for all the large and small ways that enable an author's work, I especially thank my dear husband, Bill, whose patience and kindnesses have so warmed the writing of these pages.

CHAPTER ONE

"a great fancy," "Spiritualism Exposed," *New York World,* October 21, 1888, page 1.

"Oh Amy it is a very gloomy day...to sleep without it." Margaretta Fox to Amy Post, August 21, 1847, The Isaac and Amy Post Family Papers, University of Rochester.

"simple, gentle and true-hearted," Davenport, *The Death-Blow to Spiritualism,* page 84.

"Until first suggested to us by our mother...had never entered our heads," Ibid., page 93.

"we could do it with hardly an effort." Davenport, *The Death-Blow to Spiritualism,* page 22.

"with one hand hidden...we would have done." Davenport, *The Death-Blow to Spiritualism,* page 98.

"It was not very loud...we were in bed." Lewis, *A Report of the Mysterious Noises Heard in the House of Mr. John D. Fox in Hydesville, Arcadia, Wayne County,* page 5.

On the girls' ability to move furniture through vibrations at the Hydesville farmhouse, see Underhill, *The Missing Link in Modern Spiritualism,* page 7, and Cadwallader, *Hydesville in History,* page 25.

"Mr. Split-foot, do as I do." Underhill, *The Missing Link in Modern Spiritualism,* page 7, and Cadwallader, *Hydesville in History,* page 26.

"O, mother, I know what it is....somebody trying to fool us." Underhill, *The Missing Link in Modern Spiritualism,* page 7, and Cadwallader, *Hydesville in History,* page 25.

"Three more emphatic raps were given...my youngest child." Underhill, *The Missing Link in Modern Spiritualism,* page 7, and Cadwallader, *Hydesville in History,* page 25.

"Is it a spirit?...make two raps." Underhill, *The Missing Link in Modern Spiritualism,* page 7, and Cadwallader, *Hydesville in History,* page 27.

"Will you continue to rap...loud in the affirmative." Underhill, *The Missing Link in Modern Spiritualism,* page 8, and Cadwallader, *Hydesville in History,* page 27.

"clinging to each other and trembling...than she had supposed." Davenport, *The Death-Blow to Spiritualism,* page 22.

"good honest people," "Spiritualism Exposed," *New York World,* October 21, 1888, page 1.

"The two broods of children had distinctive characteristics," Davenport, *The Death-Blow to Spiritualism,* page 82.

On the movements of the Fox family in Rochester, see Pressing, *Rappings That Startled the World,* page 21, and Pond, *Time Is Kind,* pp. 7–8.

"Mr. Fish discovered when too late…on business to the West," Underhill, *The Missing Link in Modern Spiritualism,* page 31.

"first inland boom town," Johnson, *A Shopkeeper's Millennium,* page 33.

"activity and eager life…never passed away." Barnes and Ryan, "Rochester Recollected: A Miscellany of Eighteenth and Nineteenth Century Descriptions," *Rochester History,* Vol. XLI, page 31.

"I do not know of any…natural means." Lewis, *A Report of the Mysterious Noises Heard in the House of Mr. John D. Knox in Hydesville, Arcadia, Wayne County,* page 9.

"Soon it went so far…went right on." Davenport, *The Death-Blow to Spiritualism,* page 92.

"a sound like the falling…unable to solve." Lewis, *A Report of the Mysterious Noises Heard in the House of Mr. John D. Fox in Hydesville, Arcadia, Wayne County,* pp. 15–16.

On Duesler's idea using numbered letters of the alphabet for spirit communication, see Webb, *Spiritualism,* "Peddler's Protest," *New York History,* April 1943, page 230.

"after I got up stairs…I have heard." Lewis, *A Report of the Mysterious Noises Heard in the House of Mr. John D. Fox in Hydesville, Arcadia, Wayne County,* pp. 14–15.

"We could not lower…any human agency." Ibid., page 29.

"Poor Bell…as a murderer." "Spiritualism Exposed," *New York World,* October 21, 1888, page 1.

"'never known anything against him'…he was suspected." Pressing, *Rappings That Startled the World,* page 63.

"I had been…into that room." Lewis, *A Report of the Mysterious Noises Heard in the House of Mr. John D. Fox in Hydesville, Arcadia, Wayne County,* page 35.

"something had been moving…all over her." Ibid., page 33.

"I do not believe in…must be the matter." Ibid., pp. 33–34.

"an almost entire human…communication with the spirit." *The Boston Journal,* November 23, 1904, and Cadwallader, *Hydesville in History,* pp. 22–23.

CHAPTER TWO

"Hundreds have visited...it will be ascertained soon." Lewis, *A Report of the Mysterious Noises Heard in the House of Mr. John D. Fox in Hydesville, Arcadia, Wayne County,* page 10.

"She [her mother] used to say when...of my dear children?'" Davenport, *The Death-Blow to Spiritualism,* page 92.

"pale and worn-looking...of all her trouble." Ibid., pp. 98–99.

"When he would be kneeling...that jigging stops." Ibid., page 97.

"We have spent several days...country, or any other." Lewis, *A Report of the Mysterious Noises Heard in the House of Mr. John D. Fox in Hydesville, Arcadia, Wayne County,* pp. 3–4.

"Is your mother's name Margaret?...what has happened?" Underhill, *The Missing Link in Modern Spiritualism,* page 31.

On infant mortality rates in cities, see McVeigh, *An Early History of the Telephone, 1664–1865,* Public Health, 19th Century, http://www.ilt.columbia.edu/projects/bluetelephone, html/health.html.Edu/.

On mortality and birth rates for adults, see "Expectation of Life at Specified Age by Sex, Massachusetts, 1850 to 1979," Series B pp. 126–135 and Series 5–10 page 56, and "Birth Rate Total for Women 15–44," page 49, from *Statistical History of the United States: From Colonial Times to the Present, U.S. Bureau of the Census,* intro. Ben J. Wattenberg, 1970.

"reason and conscience...truth and light." Branch, *The Sentimental Years: 1836–1860,* page 326.

"What is popularly called 'Transcendentalism'...an appearance." Emerson, "The Transcendentalist," *The Dial: A Magazine for Literature, Philosophy and Religion,* Vol. III, pp. 297–299.

"It is an extraordinary era...outstripped human belief." Marx, *The Machine in the Garden,* page 214.

"We found the cars...patriotic enthusiasm." Greenwood, *Greenwood Leaves,* page 358.

"I should be surprised if among...impetuously toward Heaven." De Tocqueville, *Democracy in America,* p. 507.

"It is a truth that spirits commune...will be established." Davis, *The Principles of Nature,* page 676.

"I perceive that all spirits...without distinction," Ibid., page 655.

"spirit leaves the human form...love of heaven," Ibid., page 658.

"the infinite vortex of Love...Sun of the Divine." Ibid., page 672.

"As there is a spirit in every...live or think at all." Toksvig, *Emanuel Swedenborg: Scientist and Mystic,* page 225. For another explanation of Swedenborg's mystic philosophy, see Cox, *Body and Soul,* pp. 12–15.

"completely broken down...could all die." Underhill, *The Missing Link in Modern Spiritualism,* page 32.

"we could put a stop to the disturbance." Ibid., page 32.

"cold and calculating brain," Davenport, *The Death-Blow to Spiritualism,* page 103.

"Some idea of the profit...very promptly." Ibid., pp. 102–103.

"undress and show her...as in childhood." Ibid., page 103.

"as if a pail of bonnyclabber...upon the floor." Underhill, *The Missing Link in Modern Spiritualism,* page 33.

"We could hear...with a bang." Ibid., page 37.

"Flat foot, can you dance the Highland fling?" Ibid., page 38.

"shower of slippers...thrust he made," ibid., page 39.

"Of course we slily...hoydenish tricks." Davenport, *The Death-Blow to Spiritualism,* page 113.

"To be with Christ is better far." Underhill, *The Missing Link in Modern Spiritualism,* page 41.

"The public...conscious of being deceived." Cook, *The Arts of Deception,* page 16.

"suffering under some psychological delusion." Ibid., page 44.

"sustain this family...should be benefited," Ibid., page 45.

"Oh Stephan, who is dead?...warning of death all night." Ibid.; *The Missing Link in Modern Spiritualism,* page 46.

"I looked in the door...for man to do it." Isaac Post to Joseph & Mary Post, Post Family Papers, SC 176, Friends Historical Library, Swarthmore College.

For more details on Amy and Isaac Post, see Hewitt, "Amy Kirby Post," *The University of Rochester Library Bulletin;* Hewitt, *Women's Activism and Social Change,* Vol. 37, pp. 61–64; Wellman, "The Seneca Falls Women's Rights Convention: A Study of Social Networks," 1991 *Journal of Women's History,* Vol. 3, No. 1; and The Isaac and Amy Post Family Papers, University of Rochester.

"Isaac, my son...thee no harm." Parker, *Rochester: A Story Historical,* pp. 268–269.

"condemning the whole affair...evidence of truth." Webb, *Spiritualism: Peddler's Protest,* pp. 235–236.

"Will the Spirit please move...strength of a man." Ibid., pp. 237–238.

"As to the rappings heard...seems to spread fast." George Willets to Isaac Post, October 23, 1848, The Isaac and Amy Post Family Papers, University of Rochester.

On the close social networks uniting feminism and spiritualism, see Wellman, "The Seneca Falls Women's Rights Convention: A Study of Social Networks," *Journal of Women's History*, Spring 1991, Vol. 3, No. 1; Hewitt, "Amy Kirby Post," *The University of Rochester Library Bulletin*, Vol. 37, 1984; Goldsmith, *Other Powers: The Age of Suffrage Spiritualism and the Scandalous Victoria Woodhull*, pp. 29–31; Braude, *Radical Spirits: Spiritualism and Women's Rights in Nineteenth Century America*, pp. 58–61; and Becker, *A History of the Village of Waterloo, New York*, page 152.

On the controversies surrounding the McClintock's "spirit table" and its association with the call for women's rights, see Braude, *Radical Spirits: Spiritualism and Women's Rights in Nineteenth Century America*, Chapter 3, note #7, pp. 38–39; Rossi, *The Feminist Papers*, page 413; and Becker, *The History of the Village of Waterloo, New York*, pp. 152–154.

"Spiritualism as usual [being] the principle topic…" DuBois, Ellen Carol, ed. *Elizabeth Cady Stanton/Susan B. Anthony, Correspondence, Writings, Speeches*, pp. 76–77.

"a change came over…sickly-looking man," Underhill, *The Missing Link in Modern Spiritualism*, page 47.

"heavy artillery"…"pleasant little cottage," ibid., pp. 48–50.

"Dear Friends, you must…watch over you." Ibid., pp. 48–49.

"good friends…friends in heaven," Ibid., page 51.

"I was enabled to…with more powers." Matilda Rushmore to Isaac Post, January 28, 1849, The Isaac and Amy Post Family Papers, University of Rochester.

"tried hard to convince her younger sisters…dreadfully wicked." Davenport, *The Death-Blow to Spiritualism*, pp. 127–128.

"Katie and I were led around like lambs." "Spiritualism Exposed," *New York World*, October 21, 1888, page 1.

CHAPTER THREE

"Immortality: I notice…what you know." Emerson, *Journals of Ralph Waldo Emerson*, Vol. III, page 20.

"There is a soul at the center…to teach us faith." Emerson, *The Essential Writings of Ralph Waldo Emerson*, page 176.

"excessive determination to form," Emerson, "Swedenborg, or the Mystic." *The Collected Works of Ralph Waldo Emerson*, Vol. IV, page 67.

"Swedenborgianism Americanized." Carroll, *Spiritualism in Antebellum America*, page 53.

For the life of Anton Mesmer, his disciples, the evolution of hypnosis, and its relationship to spiritualism, see Fuller, *Mesmerism and the American Cure of Souls*, pp. 8–33; Moore, *In Search of White Crows*, pp. 9 & 15; and Carroll, *Spiritualism in Antebellum America*, pp. 108–109.

"The most important facts...each other." Bush, *Mesmer and Swedenborg*, page 1.

On the relationship between the spiritualist trance and the Victorian ideal of feminine passivity, see Braude, *Radical Spirits*, pp. 88–91, and Moore, "The Spiritualist Medium: A Study of Female Professionalism in Victorian America," *American Quarterly*, Vol. 27, No. 2, pp. 204–205.

"Electricity and Magnetism...this intercommunication," Underhill, *The Missing Link in Modern Spiritualism*, page 55.

"Frequently our friends...a portion of our vitality," Ibid., page 53.

"In all of our séances...by signals she gave us." Davenport, *The Death-Blow to Spiritualism*, page 127.

"Many of our visitors were anxious...give the signal 'done.'" Underhill, *The Missing Link in Modern Spiritualism*, pp. 52–53.

"of evil origin, unnatural, perplexing, and tormenting." Ibid., page 55.

"These young women...if they deceive everybody." "A Ghost!" *Rochester Daily Democrat*, November 11, 1848.

"How then...thumping on a table." "The 'Spiritual' Humbug," *Daily Advertiser*, May 3, 1850.

"What shall we do?...exhibition of spiritualism." Underhill, *The Missing Link in Modern Spiritualism*, page 52.

"pocketed," "Spiritualism Exposed," *The World*, October 21, 1888.

"When I look back on...pleasure in it." Ibid.

"Our whole family was, at that time...rod of iron." Davenport, *The Death-Blow to Spiritualism*, page 234.

"I have feared that woman...mixture of terrorism and cajolery." Ibid., pp. 232–233.

"No, you cannot go...get the sounds," Underhill, *The Missing Link in Modern Spiritualism*, page 59.

"They came in with the...long absent friends." Ibid., page 60.

"Hire Corinthian Hall." Ibid., pp. 60–62.

"The citizens of Rochester...truly wonderful manifestations." "Wonderful Phenomena at Corinthian Hall," *Rochester Daily Advertiser*, November 14, 1849.

"the best possible humor," "A Ghost!," *Rochester Daily Democrat*, November 11, 1849.

"We venture to agree...the GHOST was there." Ibid.

"During [Capron's] relation...distinctly heard," "Singular Revelations. Communications with Spirits in Western New York," *New York Weekly Tribune*, December 8, 1849.

"the irrepressible awe...the spirit of mirth." "A Ghost!," *Rochester Daily Democrat*, November 16, 1849.

"a committee of five...companions of the goblin." Ibid.

"though the feet were not moved,... *it could be done.*" "Singular Revelations. Communications with Spirits in Western New York," *New York Weekly Tribune,* December 8, 1849.

"seemed to fall like a thunder bolt...favorable, character." Ibid.

"I was at that time...look out for deception." Edmonds and Dexter, *Spiritualism,* page 13.

"As I entered the room...machinery, I imagined." Edmonds, *Letters and Tracts on Spiritualism,* pp. 154–155.

"there was no probability...made by machinery." "Singular Revelations. Communications with Spirits in Western New York," *New York Weekly Tribune,* December 8, 1849.

"When they were standing...wall and the floor distinctly." "Singular Revelations. Communications with Spirits in Western New York," *New York Tribune,* December 8, 1849, page 6.

"Do not go to the Hall...will be mobbed." Underhill, *The Missing Link in Modern Spiritualism,* page 70.

"We will go by ourselves...expect to be killed." Hardinge, *Modern American Spiritualism,* page 557.

"But stamping, shrieking, and all kinds...to desist." Ibid.

"mob of ruffians...over his dead body." Hardinge, *Modern American Spiritualism,* page 46.

"the wary and eagle-eyed...opportunity of investigation," Underhill, *The Missing Link in Modern Spiritualism,* page 113.

"It is difficult to understand...thumping the wall." "Spiritual Communications," *New York Weekly Tribune,* December 15, 1849, page 6.

"The people came from...not what to do." Underhill, *The Missing Link in Modern Spiritualism,* page 101.

"On the 20th of February...sentence I uttered," Hardinge, *Modern American Spiritualism,* page 51.

"The séances of the Misses Fox...of the visitors." Ibid., page 52.

"aspostolic letters...worse spelling." Ibid.

"Now I am ready, my friends...Benjamin Franklin." Hardinge, *Modern American Spiritualism,* pp. 53–54.

"Western New York...doctrines of Spiritualism." Pressing, *Rappings That Startled the World,* page 40.

"humbug and a counterfeit...at the bottom of it." "Those Rochester Rappings," *New York Tribune,* March 6, 1850. On January 3, 1850, Horace Greeley visited Rochester and gave a lecture at that city's Athenaeum. See "The Athenaeum," *Rochester Daily Democrat,* January 1, 1850.

CHAPTER FOUR

"timely warning saved...consumed by the flames," Capron, *Singular Revelations,* page 61.

"Prof. Loomis has...by mechanical means." Hardinge, *Modern American Spiritualism,* page 66.

"We question whether...see the 'ghost.'" "Mysterious Knockings Explained," *Rochester Daily Advertiser,* January 17, 1850, page 2, column 2.

"When that remarkable book...through our [previous] columns." "That Rochester Knocking," *New York Daily Tribune,* January 18, 1850, page 1.

"formed into an experimental...the spirit world." Hardinge, *Modern American Spiritualism,* page 60.

"the undersigned...writers have adopted." Dewey, *History of the Strange Sounds or Rappings,* page ii.

"proper sphere." On the Victorian ideal of true womanhood see Branch, *The Sentimental Years,* pp. 204–205.

"I regret this...defenders in the United States." Elias Wilkinson Capron to Margaret Rutan Fox, February 10, 1850, Isaac and Amy Post Family Papers, University of Rochester Library.

On the strange events at the Phelps household, see Phelps, *Chapters From a Life,* pp. 6–7; Hardinge, *Modern American Spiritualism,* page 63; Goldfarb, *Spiritualism and Nineteenth-Century Letters,* pp. 32–33.

"by raps and movements of a cradle," Hardinge, *Modern American Spiritualism,* pp. 164–165.

"greatly astonished by the evidence they received." Underhill, *The Missing Link in Modern Spiritualism,* page 115.

"The hall was crowded...our triumphant success." Ibid., page 116.

"*elite* of Albany...would be pleased," ibid., page 118.

"A strong army...subsequent public career." Ibid., page 119.

"We really hope...and expose them." "The Mysterious Noises," *Troy Daily Whig,* May 25, 1850, page 2.

"Those who have heard...is as great as ever." *Troy Daily Whig,* May 29, 1850, page 2.

"A murmur arose...handsome and prosperous." Underhill, *The Missing Link in Modern Spiritualism,* page 121.

"We maintain *equality of rights*...world, herself or her God." *Proceedings of the Yearly Meeting of Congregational Friends,* 1850, pp. 14–15.

"Mediums decried the 'body...not a curse.'" Ibid., page 119.

On New York Harbor of the late 1840s, see Ellis, *The Epic of New York City*, pp. 259–260; Grafton, *New York in the Nineteenth Century*, page 230; and Burrows and Wallace, *Gotham*, pp. 737 & 744.

"half intoxicated," Davenport, *The Death-Blow to Spiritualism*, page 130.

"not [to] be confounded...by that name." Underhill, *The Missing Link in Modern Spiritualism*, page 128.

The hotel on the corner of Broadway and Maiden Lane, or at 176 Broadway, was listed in *Doggett's New York City Directory 1850*, page 132, as owned by A. S. Barnum in 1850–51. A year later it was renamed the Howard House by new proprietors Clark & Bailey.

"an encyclopedic synopsis...this curious world," Dennett, *Weird and Wonderful: The Dime Museum in America*, page 27.

"Everyone is open to deception...region of mystery." Ibid., page 30.

"He thought the world...in his day." Maihafere, *The General and the Journalists*, page 128.

"to the worst appetites...from the spiritual world." "The Little Lights at the North—Retrospective Pictures and Present Frames of Mind—Bowen, Beecher, Garrison and Greeley," *New York Herald*, February 5, 1850, page 2.

"There is something...kindred psychologic phenomenon." "Those Rochester Rappings," *New York Tribune*, March 6, 1850, page 1.

For details on the appearance and dress of the Fox sisters on first meeting Horace Greeley, see Pond, *Time Is Kind*, pp. 54–55.

"keep the rabble away," Underhill, *The Missing Link in Modern Spiritualism*, page 128.

"I called upon them...nor enlightened thereby." Greeley, *The Autobiography of Horace Greeley*, page 234.

"stout lady of the ordinary...unexplained visitations." Corner, *Doctor Kane of the Arctic Seas*, page 111. From Willis, *Home Journal*, cited by Pattee, *The Feminine Fifties*, page 241.

"obvious symptoms of impatience...other quarters of the room." "An Evening with the 'Spirits'—New York," *New York Tribune*, June 8, 1850. Also reprinted in Hardinge, *Modern American Spiritualism*, pp. 64–65.

"were struck...liking of all present." Corner, *Doctor Kane of the Arctic Seas*, pp. 111–112.

"We are as much...incomings or outgoings." "An evening with the 'Spirits'—New York," *New York Tribune*, June 8, 1850. Also reprinted in Hardinge, *Modern American Spiritualism*, page 65.

"impression seemed to be...to the present age." "The Knockers," *New York Herald*, June 8, 1850.

"It is lamentable...twelve great philosophers." "The Rochester Knockers and the Savans," *New York Herald,* June 17, 1850.

"the Rochester knockings...vocation and the like." Strong, *The Diary of George Templeton Strong, The Turbulent Fifties,* pp. 15–16.

"like a knocking...when we came away." "To all our Readers and Correspondents," *Holden's Dollar Magazine,* Vol. VI, No. III, September 1, 1850, pp. 573–574.

"When manifestations and communications...constantly in attendance." Underhill, *The Missing Link in Modern Spiritualism,* page 54.

"anxiety, care...positive against it." Hammond, *Light from the Spirit World,* page 238. On Hammond's earlier acquaintance with the Fox sisters, see Dewey, *History of the Strange Sounds or Rappings,* pp. 27–32.

"The Rochester Knockings at Barnum's Hotel," Underhill, *The Missing Link in Modern Spiritualism,* page 128.

"You are the lions of New York." Ibid.

"There, along with much...well have been cognizant." Greeley, *The Autobiography of Horace Greeley,* p. 234.

"We are convinced...being connected with them." Langworthy, *Katie Fox and the Making of the Fox-Taylor Record,* p. 59. See also Pressing, *Rappings That Startled the World,* pp. 12–14.

"I am sure it...so interesting." October 7, 1850 letter from Horace Greeley to Colonel Thomas L. Kane, Horace Greeley Papers, Manuscripts and Archives Division, The New York Public Library.

CHAPTER FIVE

"casawrecks." For details on these and other gifts the Fox sisters brought to Arcadia, see Pond, *Time Is Kind,* pp. 64–65.

"tiresome...with all kinds of people." Maggie Fox to Elisha Kane, 1853, Elisha Kent Kane Papers, American Philosophical Society.

"Mrs. Fox and her three... *integrity and good faith.*" Hardinge, *Modern Spiritualism,* page 71: *New York Tribune,* September 30, 1850.

"more and more confirmed...spiritual world by 'rappings.'" October 7, 1850 letter from Horace Greeley to Colonel Thomas L. Kane, Horace Greeley Papers, The New York Public Library, Manuscripts and Archives Division.

"John, it is impossible...leave my mother?" Cathy Fox to "My Dear Friend," October 26, 1850, The Isaac and Amy Post Family Papers, University of Rochester Library.

"We are endeavoring...nothing but discomfiture." Underhill, *The Missing Link in Modern Spiritualism,* pp. 123–127.

"crowded séances..." Ibid., page 166.

"retrogression to the dark ages." Fornell, *The Unhappy Medium,* page 21.

"On carefully observing…, without fatigue." Letter to the Editor, Buffalo *Commercial Advertiser,* February 17, 1851. The theory was later described in "Discovery of the Source of the Rochester Knockings." *Buffalo Medical Journal,* Vol. VI (March 1851), 628–642.

"new and comical knee-joint theory." Underhill, *The Missing Link in Modern Spiritualism,* page 171.

"The Spirits 'did not choose…emanate from the knee-joint." Ibid., pp. 175–176.

"a far more satisfactory test,…a foot from the floor." Underhill, *The Missing Link in Modern Spiritualism,* page 191; *The Commercial Advertiser,* March 14, 1851.

"tell your readers…almost ceaseless operation." Ibid., page 189. See also Leah's explanation for Mrs. Patchen's discomfort upon attempting to simulate that experiment on pages 176–177.

"very hard work to do…could nearly always guess right." Maskelyne, *Modern Spiritualism,* page 24.

"If you ladies had passed…may say against me." Underhill, *The Missing Link in Modern Spiritualism,* page 223.

On the impact of Mrs. Culver's confession, see Hardinge, *Modern American Spiritualism,* page 70.

"Mr. Burr pretty effectually…annihilate the rappers." "The Knockings," *Rochester Daily Democrat,* May 2, 1851.

"There are to be Rapping times…progress to the people." "Spirits Coming," *Cleveland Plain Dealer,* May 5, 1851, page 1.

"at the outset…imputation of humbug." "Burr and Blue Devils," *Cleveland Plain Dealer,* May 6, 1851, page 1.

"the spiritualists have…all their own way." "Which Has It?—Are the Rappers Knocked, or the Knockers Rapped." *Cleveland Plain Dealer,* May 7, 1851, page 1.

"Mrs. Fish and the pretty Margaretta…the Forest City." "Rival Rappers," *Cleveland Plain Dealer,* May 8, 1851.

"Notwithstanding the burlesques…some of its best minds." Hardinge, *Modern American Spiritualism,* page 297.

"Mrs. Kedzie's coming…upon my Shoulders." Ann Leah Fish to Amy Post, July 22, 1851, The Isaac and Amy Post Family Papers, University of Rochester Library.

"Maggie could not be persuaded to go further." Underhill, *The Missing Link in Modern Spiritualism,* page 223.

"Welcome to the Fox family." Ibid., page 228.

"almost hooted and pelted out of the State." Ibid., page 225.

"Calvin is feeble...fear for his life." Ann Leah Fish to Amy Post, July 22, 1851, The Isaac and Amy Post Family Papers, University of Rochester Library.

"Dear Mother and Leah...tolerable comfort," Underhill, *The Missing Link in Modern Spiritualism*, pp. 229–230.

"We have many friends here...spiritual communication." Katy Fox to Amy Post, October 30, The Isaac and Amy Post Family Papers, University of Rochester Library.

"Invitations and appeals...hear for themselves." Underhill, *The Missing Link in Modern Spiritualism*, page 250.

"kiss the little ones...as he returns." Margaretta Fox to Mrs. Greeley, August 23, 1851, Greeley Manuscript Collection, The New York Public Library, Manuscripts and Archives Division. On April 11, 1851, Horace Greeley sailed on the *Baltic* to England see Prince Albert's World Exposition at the Crystal Palace in Hyde Park, met with Parliament to protest taxes on newspaper advertisements, and then traveled to Paris and Switzerland, returning to New York in September 1851.

CHAPTER SIX

"rolled back the stone from the door of the sepulcher." Hardinge, *Modern American Spiritualism*, page 73.

"1. That the Divine Author...intercourse with the world of spirits." Ibid., page 74.

On the distinctions between Andrew Jackson Davis's "harmonial" philosophy and spiritualism, see Braude, *Radical Spirits*, pp. 33–35, 181–182, and Cox, *Body and Soul*, pp. 5–21, 79–80.

On the new spiritualist publications, see Podmore, *Mediums of the 19th Century*, pp. 202–205; Hardinge, *Modern American Spiritualism*, page 85; and Goldfarb, *Spiritualism and Nineteenth-Century Letters*, pp. 35–39.

"a fine clairvoyant physician," Hardinge, *Modern American Spiritualism*, page 166.

On the growth of the New York Circle in 1851–52 and stories from its guests, see Hardinge, *Modern American Spiritualism*, pp. 71–86.

"Your father is dead...reformatory and scientific movement." Ibid., pp. 81–82.

"first-rate excellence," Underhill, *The Missing Link in Modern Spiritualism*, page 252.

"fine three-story house," Anonymous, *The Rappers*, page 18.

"the most fashionable part of our rapidly increasing city," Burroughs and Wallace, *Gotham*, page 715.

"Our rooms were frequented...became our most intimate friends." Underhill, *The Missing Link in Modern Spiritualism*, page 268.

For details on the Fox sisters' first year in New York on West Twenty-sixth Street, the séance schedule, and Maggie and Katy's attempts to finish their schooling, see Pond, *Time Is Kind*, pp. 102–105.

"An invasion of armies can be resisted, but not an idea whose time had come." *Bartlett's Quotations*, page 427, from *Histoire d'un Crime*, 1852, alternately translated, "We resist the invasion of armies, but we do not resist the invasion of ideas," Hugo, *Poems: History of a Crime*, page 161.

"The developments of this spiritual school...worth investigating." Strong, *The Diary of George Templeton Strong, The Turbulent Fifties, 1850–1859,* page 93.

"The communications are mainly...obtain answers." Underhill, *The Missing Link in Modern Spiritualism,* page 262.

An announcement of Maggie's arrival with Mrs. Fox on October 9, 1852, at the Union Hotel appears in the *Philadelphia Evening Bulletin* of that same date.

While Kane and Fox's *The Love-Life of Dr. Kane* states that Maggie and her mother stayed at Webb's Union Hotel and is confirmed by an announcement in the *Philadelphia Evening Bulletin,* a second notice appeared on October 30 and November 1, 1852, announcing that the "Rochester Knockings" would offer séances to the public at the Utah House hotel three times a day. Maggie and Mrs. Fox may thus have moved to the second hotel on that date even while unmentioned in the memoir.

"prominent and fashionable people...daily in attendance." Kane and Fox, *The Love-Life of Dr. Kane,* page 23.

On the creation of Philadelphia spirit circles, see Hardinge, *Modern American Spiritualism,* page 60.

See Pond, *Time Is Kind,* pp. 107–108, for descriptions of the excitement caused by Maggie's arrival in Philadelphia.

"I beg your pardon...are shown?," Kane and Fox, *The Love-Life of Dr. Kane,* p. 23; see also Pond, *Time Is Kind,* pp. 107–110.

"One of the very first things...lady's should be." Ibid., page 63.

"pleased with his manners and conversation." Ibid., page 26.

"This is no life for you, my child." Ibid.

"his brotherly tenderness for her interests," ibid., page 35.

"had a way of looking...steel-spring under pressure." Elder, *Biography of Elisha Kent Kane,* page 250.

On Kane's family background, see Mirsky, *Elisha Kent Kane and the Seafaring Frontier,* pp. 13–16, and Corner, *Doctor Kane of the Arctic Seas.*

"I thank God, I...does not startle at words." Corner, *Doctor Kane of the Arctic Seas,* page 14.

On the "cult of true womanhood," see Cott and Pleck, *A Heritage of Her Own: Toward a New Social History of American Women,* page 190.

"sat simpering behind...a teapot." Elisha Kane to Eliza Leiper, April, May 1853, Elisha Kent Kane Papers, American Philosophical Society.

"Were you ever in love?...Ask the spirits." Kane and Fox, *The Love-Life of Dr. Kane,* page 27.

"Dr. Kane will call at...an afternoon drive." Ibid.

"Elisha, if you must...die in harness." Elder, *Biography of Elisha Kent Kane,* page 37.

On Kane's early adventures as a naval captain, see Corner, *Doctor Kane of the Arctic Seas,* pp. 33–70, and Elder, *Biography of Elisha Kent Kane,* pp. 29–145.

For details on the Franklin voyage, see Elder, *Biography of Elisha Kent Kane,* pp. 146–165; Corner, *Doctor Kane of the Arctic Seas,* pp. 71–76.

"No service...of the Northwest Passage." Mirsky, *Elisha Kent Kane and the Seafaring Frontier,* page 50.

"I cannot rejoice...period, perhaps forever." Corner, *Doctor Kane of the Arctic Seas,* pp. 81–82.

"Passage to the Pacific," Mirsky, *Elisha Kent Kane and the Seafaring Frontier,* page 40. See Mirsky, page 109, on the similarity between Tennyson's belief and Kane's determination to have his name placed on the Arctic map.

"Might he ask Miss Fox...before his departure?" Kane and Fox, *The Love-Life of Dr. Kane,* page 27.

"The day is so beautiful...your own hour." Ibid., page 29.

"If you have any messages...of the enclosed note." Ibid., pp. 28–29.

"A very pleasant...several of our meetings." Pond, *Time Is Kind,* page 116.

"this would not be very...on the boat." Kane and Fox, *The Love-Life of Dr. Kane,* pp. 30–31.

"Kiss Katy for me...her own." Ibid., page 52.

"call with Mrs. Patterson...dress warmly." Ibid., page 29.

"Weary!...live and die forlorn." Ibid., page 30.

"Although I am still skeptical...accompanying trifle," ibid., page 31.

"he again spoke...was an utter impossibility." Ibid., pp. 32–33.

"Like you, it must not...high position in society." Ibid., page 42.

"Miss Fox, Elisha loves you. I can see that!" Ibid., page 37.

"the future Mrs. Kane." Ibid., page 39.

"Here, Margaret,...godsend," ibid., pp. 36–37.

"love on," Ibid., page 77.

"I would do anything." Maggie Fox to E. K. Kane, n.d., Elisha Kent Kane Papers, Fox-Kane Correspondence, In re schooling, 1853.

"I feel that I have...these sounds." Ibid.

"laughing girl...Preacher." Kane and Fox, *The Love-Life of Dr. Kane,* pp. 40–41.

"What pretty girl was that...with you?" Ibid., page 43.

"Wrap my letters...me from coming." Ibid., pp. 43–44.

"write to me letters...me your movements." Ibid., page 44.

"Do not be afraid...my contradiction." Ibid., page 45. For details of the events leading up to that letter, see also Pond, *Time Is Kind,* pp. 124–125.

"I am delighted...thanks for the music." Kane and Fox, *The Love-Life of Dr. Kane,* page 46.

On the story about the suicide, see "Melancholy Suicide," *New York Herald,* January 8, 1853, page 4.

"Your sister's name...suspected deceit." Kane and Fox, *The Love-Life of Dr. Kane,* pp. 46–47.

"I cannot get away...Maggie Fox of the Spirit Rappings." Ibid., pp. 47–49.

"I will see you, if time...you both with respect." Ibid., page 49.

CHAPTER SEVEN

"flared in a torrent of protest," Pond, *Time Is Kind,* page 125.

"He is a vain...Maggie turn from us all!" Ibid., page 125.

"Why do you not write...of old times?" Kane and Fox, *The Love-Life of Dr. Kane,* page 51.

"to meet the great men," Corner, *Doctor Kane of the Arctic Seas,* page 116.

"Oh dear Maggie, when I...he alone has no coldness." Kane and Fox, *The Love-Life of Dr. Kane,* pp. 51–52.

"All the warmth and affection...you know who." Ibid., pp. 53–55.

"You will forgive me...engagement during the day." Ibid., page 56.

"thorough-going, but reasonable spiritualist," Anonymous, *The Rappers,* page 107.

"True feminine genius is ever...perpetual childhood." Greenwood, *Greenwood Leaves: A Collection of Sketches and Letters,* pp. 310–311.

"You thought strange...over Maggie and me." Katy Fox to Elisha Kane, n.d., Elisha Kent Kane Papers, American Philosophical Society.

"Do say when I can see...gone for a week." Kane and Fox, *The Love-Life of Dr. Kane,* page 57.

"Dear, dear Maggie...Do, dear Maggie, do!" Ibid., pp. 57–58.

"cute, cunning dissembler...with a pretty face." Ibid., page 66.

"full of energy, intelligence...better than the '*rappers.*'" Ibid., page 60. For more detail on Kane's lectures in Boston, see Mirksy, *Elisha Kent Kane and the Seafaring Frontier,* page 110.

"When I think of you, dear darling...so much difference." Ibid., page 62.

"asked no questions," Pond, *Time Is Kind,* page 129.

"One an under-handkerchief...wherever she is." Kane and Fox, *The Love-Life of Dr. Kane,* pp. 62–63.

"How does Washington come on?...your friend comes." Ibid., page 64.

"Maggie, I am sick...the world of love!" Ibid., pp. 65–66.

"Nothing is left me...for my departure." Mirsky, *Elisha Kent Kane and the Seafaring Frontier,* page 113.

"I am grieved to hear...before you go to the Arctic." Kane and Fox, *The Love-Life of Dr. Kane,* pp. 68–69.

"Dear Miss Incomprehensible Kate,...help you and Maggie?" Ibid., pp. 70–72.

"I am very anxious...not many believers?" Katy Fox to Elisha Kane, n.d., Elisha Kent Kane Papers, American Philosophical Society.

"Your letter was received this morning;...As ever, your Maggie." Kane and Fox, *The Love-Life of Dr. Kane,* page 74.

"I saw that you loved...in the other, never." Ibid., pp. 78–79.

"worrying the [Naval] Department...his telegraph flying." Elder, *Biography of Elisha Kent Kane,* page 175.

"Dearest Pet: Come out...fluttering bird. Come!" Kane and Fox, *The Love-Life of Dr. Kane,* page 81.

"tumbledown hair...disarranged locks and wet forehead." Ibid., pp. 82–83.

"I have been thinking over...fits of low spirits." Fox-Kane Correspondence: In re Schooling 1853, Elisha Kent Kane Papers, American Philosophical Society.

"refined, educated, conscientious woman," Kane and Fox, *The Love-Life of Dr. Kane,* page 94.

"Very, very sorry, dear darling...should be your home." Kane and Fox, *The Love-Life of Dr. Kane,* pp. 83–84.

"Listen, Maggie; instead...lady abbess, a *schoolmistress.*" Ibid., page 88.

"I am sick of this life...from our rooms." Pond, *Time Is Kind,* pp. 136–137; see also Underhill, *The Missing Link in Modern Spiritualism,* pages 270–271.

"very interesting girl," Corner, *Doctor Kane of the Arctic Seas,* page 122.

"Bear up, dear little...before the Tigress." Elisha Kane to Maggie Fox, Elisha Kent Kane Papers, American Philosophical Society, Folder 1, 1853; Kane and Fox, *The Death-Blow to Spiritualism,* page 226.

"Mother has been perfectly willing...not even see Leah." Maggie Fox to Elisha Kent Kane, n.d., Fox-Kane Correspondence, In re schooling 1853, Elisha Kent Kane Papers, American Philosophical Society; Corner, *Doctor Kane of the Arctic Seas,* page 122.

"After mature deliberation...to [you to] make the selection [of the school]." Mrs. Margaret Fox to E. K. Kane, Elisha Kent Kane Papers, American Philosophical Society, Folder 1, 1853.

"I have had but one...self sacrificing friend & lover." Elisha Kent Kane to Maggie Fox, n.d., Elisha Kent Kane Papers, American Philosophical Society.

"relief of my dear husband...lasting obligations to you." Leah Kane to Elisha Kent Kane, April 12, Elisha Kent Kane Papers, American Philosophical Society. "The note that he sent her $75 without acknowledgment" appears on the back of that letter.

"I have been inquiring... *in you*," Elisha Kane to Maggie Fox, March 17, 1853, Elisha Kent Kane Papers, American Philosophical Society.

"My opinion is decidedly...dispositions & religion." Eliza Leiper to Elisha Kent Kane, April 4, 1853, Elisha Kent Kane Papers, American Philosophical Society.

"Through her influence...money comes from," Kane and Fox, *The Love-Life of Dr. Kane,* page 93.

"unfortunate conversations with 'spirits'...cause her to withdraw." Elisha Kane to Eliza Leiper, May 1, 1853, Elisha Kent Kane Papers, American Philosophical Society.

"There, dear Maggie...by the whole house." Kane and Fox, *The Love-Life of Dr. Kane,* page 101.

For details on Kane's rheumatic attack of late April 1853, see Corner, *Doctor Kane of the Arctic Seas,* pp. 120–121, and Elder, *Biography of Elisha Kent Kane,* pp. 180–181.

"three weeks of helplessness on my beam ends." Elder, *Biography of Elisha Kent Kane,* page 180.

"You have heard of my attack...blessings of home." Elisha Kane to Eliza Leiper, May 1, 1853, Elisha Kent Kane Papers, American Philosophical Society.

"cannot possibly come." Elisha Kane to Maggie Fox, Elisha Kent Kane Papers, American Philosophical Society.

"Don't rap for Mrs. Pierce...very-very sick." Kane and Fox, *The Love-Life of Dr. Kane,* page 114.

"If that belonged...should be yours." Ibid., page 116.

"not so well...original phenomenon!" Pond, *Time Is Kind,* page 40.

"I will be true...corpse before you." Kane and Fox, *The Love-Life of Dr. Kane,* page 131.

"perfectly well...Yours Evermore, Maggie." May 16, 1853, Maggie Fox to Elisha Kane, Elisha Kent Kane Papers, American Philosophical Society.

"large, well-chosen library," Kane, *Arctic Explorations,* page 10.

"No one knows as...value of foresight." Mirsky, *Elisha Kent Kane and the Seafaring Frontier,* page 111.

"leave after me a name and a success." Kane and Fox, *The Love-Life of Dr. Kane,* page 48.

"the winning grace...look and movement," ibid., page 24.

"If my to-morrow be clear...soothe me to sleep." Ibid., pp. 139–140.

"excited murmurs and glances,...famous native son." Pond, *Time Is Kind,* page 147.

"Pet, lamb, in a few days...to be eternal?" Kane and Fox, *The Love-Life of Dr. Kane,* page 110.

"When you come back...my heart in it." Pond, *Time Is Kind,* page 147.

"her body wracked with sobs," ibid., page 147.

"very tastefully...a most inviting entrance." Kane and Fox, *The Love-Life of Dr. Kane,* pp. 149–150.

"It was as if...the cold exterior," Pond, *Time Is Kind,* page 148. For more details, see also pages 148–149 and Kane and Fox, *The Love-Life of Dr. Kane,* pp. 151–152.

"When I think of our parting...live for each other." Kane and Fox, *The Love-Life of Dr. Kane,* pp. 150–151.

"and in how disconsolate...have a last parting." Ibid., page 151.

"how deep and sincere...for her young charge." Ibid., page 153.

"our little bird...nestle in your bosom." Ibid., page 152.

CHAPTER EIGHT

"an object of intense curiosity," "The Arctic Expeditions," *New York Herald,* June 1, 1850.

"As the vessel passed...his rheumatic attack." Kane and Fox, *The Love-Life of Dr. Kane,* page 155.

"may expect to hear from them," ibid., page 155.

"Just standing out to sea...you were unhappy." Ibid., page 157.

"subdued look of a broken-down invalid...well or vigorous." Elder, *Biography of Elisha Kent Kane,* page 276.

"very dear friend to me...a number of questions about you." Maggie Fox to Elisha Kane, Elisha Kent Kane Papers, American Philosophical Society.

"quiet old country house... *never sleep within her house.*" Kane and Fox, *The Love-Life of Dr. Kane,* pp. 160–161.

"seemed stronger...alacrity of a well man." Corner, *Doctor Kane of the Arctic Seas,* page 125.

"never lost a minute...difficult to accomplish much." Kane and Fox, *The Love-Life of Dr. Kane,* page 169.

On details about Mrs. Ellen Walter's attentions to Maggie of 1853–55, see Pond, *Time Is Kind,* pp. 153–158.

"If my advice were asked...pursuing at Mrs. Turner's." Kane and Fox, *The Love-Life of Dr. Kane,* page 162.

"I am very lonely...one hour every day." Maggie Fox to Cornelius Grinnell, n.d., Elisha Kent Kane Papers, American Philosophical Society.

"suffered from a severe illness brought on by mental disquiet." Kane and Fox, *The Love-Life of Dr. Kane,* page 164.

"brain fever...a long and carefully supervised rest." Pond, *Time Is Kind,* page 154.

"struck down with such a malady...for lost time." Kane and Fox, *The Love-Life of Dr. Kane,* page 164.

"Not having received any communication...high minded friend," Ibid., pp. 165–166.

"very much distressed...inclination nor the strength." Ibid., pp. 166–167.

"one word to wound...Mr. Turner heartily joins." Ibid., pp. 168–169.

"I thought yours to the Doctor...shine all the brighter." Ibid., page 170.

"You should therefore...or early Friday morning." Ibid., pp. 171–172.

"We do not expect to hear...September or October." Ibid., page 172.

"shelf of ice...tongues of worn-down rock." Kane, *Arctic Explorations,* page 56.

"some apprehensions...liberation." Ibid., page 52.

"swollen, haggard...our homeward march." Ibid., pp. 105–109.

"The week that followed...dreadful premonitions of tetanus." Ibid., page 117.

For details on Kane's adventures in the Arctic between July 1853 and April 1854, see Kane, *Arctic Explorations,* pp. 5–136. Also Corner, *Doctor Kane of the Arctic Seas,* pp. 125–156.

"Dear dear Maggie: In the midst of ice...its quiet loveliness." Kane and Fox, *The Love-Life of Dr. Kane,* pp. 175–176.

"we may look for the Doctor...of the lost ones." Ibid., page 177.

"no tidings yet of the Doctor...winter in the Arctic regions." Ibid., page 178.

"Never, dear brother,...well aged and worn." Corner, *Doctor Kane of the Arctic Seas,* page 170.

For details on Elisha's adventures in the Arctic during late 1854 and early 1855, see Kane, *Arctic Explorations,* pp. 209–433, and Elder, *Doctor Kane of the Arctic Seas,* pp. 155–208.

"I know it is a hazardous...an incumbent duty." Kane, *Arctic Explorations,* page 168.

"further attempt to penetrate to the south...hopeless." Ibid., page 177.

"We have managed...domestic wheel of shipboard." Ibid., page 295.

"early departure," ibid., pp. 308–309.

"not only cheered the dispirited...cause for complaint." Corner, *Doctor Kane of the Arctic Seas,* page 214.

"Our boats are at the open water...our nostrils and our hearts." Ibid., page 387.

On details of the Kane Rescue Mission, see "The Hartstein Arctic Expedition," *New York Herald,* June 1, 1855, page 1; "Departure of the Kane Expedition," *New York Times,* June 1, 1855; and Corner, *Doctor Kane of the Arctic Seas,* pp. 220–222.

"If the Doctor returns...in October following." Kane and Fox, *The Love-Life of Dr. Kane,* page 182.

"I trust in kind Providence...improve in every hour." Ibid., pp. 183–184.

"I really feel sorry...moment was doubly precious." Ibid., page 184.

"to commence again...right good earnest." Ibid., page 185.

"My eyes never looked...open to us a way." Kane, *Arctic Explorations,* page 409.

"All of them...hunger-stricken men." Ibid., page 411.

"tortuous but romantic travel through a misty atmosphere," ibid., pp. 412–415.

On Kane's entrance to Melville Bay, see Kane, *Arctic Explorations,* page 424.

"It is six o'clock...be a dream?" Ibid., page 429.

"all manner of kindness...the Danes of Upernavik." Ibid., page 431.

"The men in the boat...the first identified." Corner, *Doctor Kane of the Arctic Seas,* page 223.

On Mrs. Fox's reaction to Maggie's desire for beautiful new clothes, see Pond, *Time Is Kind,* page 158.

"Few events within the range of possibility...his exploring party." "Return of Dr. Kane," *New York Daily Tribune,* October 12, 1855, page 1.

"The Doctor has improved...a hand with a hearty grip." "Dr. Kane Home Again," *New York Times,* October 12, 1855. See also Corner, *Doctor Kane of the Arctic Seas,* page 224.

"almost absurd. I have grown like a walrus." Elder, *Biography of Elisha Kent Kane,* page 215. Self-portraits of Elisha Kent Kane before and after his journey through the courtesy of John Rhein III, great-grandnephew of Elisha Kent Kane, indicate that he also lost his hair during that journey. On Kane's return, see also "Return of Dr. Kane," *New York Times,* October 13, 1855, page 4, col. 1; "The Last of the Arctic Explorers," *New York Daily Tribune,* October 13, 1855, pp. 4–5; "Second Grinnell Expedition," *New York Times,* October 16, 1855, pp. 1–2; "The Arctic Voyagers," *New York Times,* October 18, 1855, page 2.

"such a welcome as comes only from the depths of his heart." "The Arctic Expeditions," *New York Herald,* October 12, 1855; see also Corner, *Doctor Kane of the Arctic Seas,* page 224.

On Maggie and Ellen Walter's behavior while awaiting Elisha's arrival, see Kane and Fox, *The Love-Life of Dr. Kane,* pp. 191–192.

"It was all a mistake...not Dr. Kane!" Ibid., page 193.

"she is above stairs...completely broken down." Ibid., page 194.

"the same as when we parted...engagement had subsisted, etc. etc." Ibid., page 195.

"Do it for me, Maggie!...said in the carriage," ibid., page 196.

"bade him clear...for your sake!" Ibid., page 197.

"A gentleman of this city...school in Philadelphia." *Troy Daily Whig*, October 19, 1855; "Dr. Kane to Marry One of the Fox Girls," *Rochester Democrat Union*, October 22, 1855. See also *New York Herald*, October 26, 1855, and *New York Evening Post*, October 31, 1855. Cited also in Corner, *Doctor Kane of the Arctic Seas*, page 232.

"without a shadow of foundation," "Dr. Kane," *New York Times*, November 1, 1855. See also Corner, *Doctor Kane of the Arctic Seas*, page 232.

"this contradiction...furious in the Kane interest." Kane and Fox, *The Love-Life of Dr. Kane*, page 218. See also *New York Evening Post*, October 31, 1855, *New York Times*, November 20–21, 1855.

"We wish the several journals...these two people?" "Dr. Kane's Prospects," *New York Daily Tribune*, November 6, 1855. See also Kane and Fox, *The Love-Life of Dr. Kane*, page 216.

"I cannot tell you how unhappy...this disturbance and meddling." Kane and Fox, *The Love-Life of Dr. Kane*, page 222.

"liberal-kind-hearted...noble liberality of the Kane family." Ibid., page 217; "Dr. Kane," *The Pennsylvanian*, November 19, 1855.

"Promise me once more...as your own sister." Kane and Fox, *The Love-Life of Dr. Kane*, pp. 205–206.

"a young lady whom...a continuance of his attentions." Ibid., page 208.

"Mrs. Gray has just left...world will censure her." Mrs. Fox to Elisha Kent Kane, December 6, 1855, Elisha Kent Kane Papers, American Philosophical Society.

"unless he heard it...Margaret's own lips," Kane and Fox, *The Love-Life of Dr. Kane*, page 209.

"discarded lover...wretched in such a way!" Ibid., page 214.

"I have seen you...and cannot be changed." Ibid., pp. 210–211.

"As to your dear generous...them and for you." Ibid., pp. 212–213.

CHAPTER NINE

"Table moving has got into...the same reason." Strong, *The Diary of George Templeton Strong, The Turbulent Fifties 1850–1859*, page 125.

"It is surely one...moral tone of the age." Ibid., pp. 244–245.

"Its influence is wider, stronger...as well as the ignorant." "The Free Love System," *New York Times*, September 8, 1855.

"began to speak orally... spiritual pyrotechnics," Carroll, *Spiritualism in Antebellum America,* page 127.

"a young and interesting girl of a highly-respectable family," Hardinge, *Modern American Spiritualism,* page 104.

"admirable mediums... tipping medium," ibid., pp. 149–150.

"grand spiritual circle... circle on that table!" *The Rappers,* pp. 48–49.

"rat-revelation, the gospel that comes... in the table-drawer." Wilson, "Emerson and the 'Rochester Rappings,'" Memoranda and Documents, *The New England Quarterly,* June 1968, page 248.

"such a powerful medium... a pack of too affectionate dogs," Strong, *The Diary of George Templeton Strong, The Turbulent Fifties, 1850–1859,* page 92.

"idiots, inspired by the cracking of a restless board," Wilson, "Emerson and the 'Rochester Rappings,'" Memoranda and Documents, *The New England Quarterly,* June 1968, page 249.

"act of duty to his fellow... called Spiritualism," Hardinge, *Modern American Spiritualism,* page 115.

On Hare's experiments with the "spiritoscope," see ibid., pp. 115–119. For more details about his experiments, see "Hare on Spirits," *New York Times,* November 24, 1855, page 1; Cox, *Body and Soul,* pp. 146–151, 155–161; Kerr, *Mediums, and Spirit-Rappers and Roaring Radicals,* pp. 44–46, 73 & 78; Carroll, *Spiritualism in Antebellum America,* pp. 28, 69–71; and Fornell, *The Unhappy Medium,* pp. 31–33.

"The professor spends some hours... a look of painful pity." "Spiritualism and Science." *New York Tribune,* August 26, 1856.

"For the first four or five months... of any person present." Edmonds and Dexter, *Spiritualism,* page 11.

"was a phenomenon... much to say," Strong, *The Diary of George Templeton Strong, The Turbulent Fifties, 1850–1859,* page 133.

On the estimates of spiritualists about their numbers, see McCabe, *Spiritualism: A Popular History from 1847,* page 65.

"The petitioners represent that... for that purpose." Davenport, *The Death-Blow to Spiritualism,* pp. 152–154.

"pleasant debate... material and spiritual worlds." *The Rappers,* page 168.

For other interpretations of the April 1854 petition to Congress, see Hardinge, *Modern American Spiritualism,* pp. 129–135. Note that while *The Rappers,* Hardinge's *Modern American Spiritualism,* and McCabe's *Spiritualism: A Popular History* on page 66 place the number of petitioners at 15,000, Braude, in *Radical Spirits,* limits it to 13,000.

"Your pulpits—and we speak... subject for yourselves." "Address of the Society for the Diffusion of Spiritual Knowledge to the Citizens of the United States," *The*

Charter and By-laws of the Society for the Diffusion of Spiritual Knowledge with the List of Officers for the Year 1854, page 7.

"the earliest and most experienced in the investigation," Carroll, *Spiritualism in Antebellum America,* page 55.

"Clergymen, formerly preachers...deeply infiltrated." "The Free Love System," *New York Times,* September 8, 1855.

"believed that each man or woman...her spiritual affinities." "The 'Free Love' Movement," *New York Tribune,* October 16, 1855.

"breaks no man's leg...his pocket," "Free Love," *New York Tribune,* October 24, 1855.

"We do not know...ruin of thousands." Ibid.

"nearly all mediums...extra-marital relations." Hatch, *The Hatch Divorce Case,* page 12.

"a fine-looking woman...after spiritual knowledge." Anonymous, *The Rappers,* page 19.

"very young...intellectual character," Ibid., page 138.

"Do avoid 'spirits'...Say so to Kate." Ibid., pp. 201. Kane and Fox, *The Love-Life of Dr. Kane,* p. 201.

On Elisha's discussions with his publisher, see Elder, *Biography of Elisha Kent Kane,* page 216. See also Corner, *Dr. Kane of the Arctic Seas,* pp. 230–239.

"A letter was addressed...respect my feelings." Kane and Fox, *The Love-Life of Dr. Kane,* p. 225.

"slightest objection...half a gentleman," ibid., page 226.

"more popular and gaseous...It is a sacrifice." Corner, *Doctor Kane of the Arctic Seas,* page 235.

"Although a mere trifle...brotherly interest in your welfare." Kane and Fox, *The Love-Life of Dr. Kane,* pp. 226–227.

"My own Maggie,—you are again mine...all in all to him." Ibid., page 228.

"I will wear our locket...save me from evil." Ibid., page 230.

"I know I ought to be in Philadelphia...cannot bear to leave." Ibid., page 233.

"in our quiet city...like a boy in his holiday time." Ibid., page 245.

"Then you are doomed...you stay so long!" Ibid., page 243.

"Here—take mine—pet lamb." Ibid., page 232.

"as a sort of sanctuary...seek a shelter?" Ibid., page 236.

"Maggie, Maggie, if you are ever tempted...sweet thoughts, distress me." Ibid., page 239.

"Authordom has again overdone me...take a spell [a rest] soon." Corner, *Dr. Kane of the Arctic Seas,* page 236.

"With little spirit of congratulation...without capacity to enjoy it." Ibid., page 236.

"I get weaker every day...not stand it." Ibid., page 237.

"You must remember...if brought to it." Kane and Fox, *The Love-Life of Dr. Kane,* page 254.

"With you, my dearest...I worship you." Maggie Fox to Elisha Kane, August 15, 1856, Elisha Kent Kane Papers, American Philosophical Society.

"Three more distracted girls...cars again without us." Kane and Fox, *The Love-Life of Dr. Kane,* pp. 254–255.

"I myself am very sick...hasten to New York." Ibid., pp. 255–257.

"Without you all is darkness...ten thousand kisses." Ibid., pp. 258–259.

"I wish to see you again...free happy girl." Maggie Fox to Elisha Kent Kane, n.d., Elisha Kent Kane Papers, American Philosophical Society.

"They will all know now...for my betrothed." Kane and Fox, *The Love-Life of Dr. Kane,* page 263.

"Is it possible...pensive and looking down." Ibid., page 267.

"Dearest Pet...into a wild boar." Elisha Kent Kane to Maggie Fox, "Written the morning after the Declaration," n.d., Elisha Kent Kane Papers, American Philosophical Society; see also Kane and Fox, *The Love-Life of Dr. Kane,* page 268.

"If I send for you, Maggie...what I have told you!" Kane and Fox, *The Love-Life of Dr. Kane,* page 269.

"Such a declaration...consent to this Maggie?" Ibid., pp. 269–271.

"It is very clear that the marriage...not followed by cohabitation." Ibid., page 269.

"Will seven o'clock find you at home?" Ibid., page 272.

"Dear Wife...I'll be with you." Ibid.

"Maggie, what if I should die...that kills me!" Ibid., page 273.

"Remember, Morton—take good care of the Doctor." Ibid., page 273.

"It is for you...I go, or stay?" Ibid., pp. 275.

For the details of Elisha Kane's voyage to England, see Corner, *Doctor Kane of the Arctic Seas,* pp. 245–249.

"I have just time...believe me always as of old." Kane and Fox, *The Love-Life of Dr. Kane,* page 276.

"She comes here daily...if she could, even now." Elisha Kent Kane to John Kintzing Kane, Elisha Kent Kane Papers, American Philosophical Society. Also Corner, *Dr. Kane of the Arctic Seas,* page 246.

"I cannot tell you how unhappy...by Dr. Kane's illness." Corner, *Doctor Kane of the Arctic Seas,* pp. 248.

"My inability to throw...wretched land of fogs." Elder, *Biography of Elisha Kent Kane,* page 235. Also Corner, *Dr. Kane of the Arctic Seas,* page 248.

"My heart is bad, bad...your noble son." Henry Grinnell Letter of November 28, 1856, to Judge K. Kane, Elisha Kent Kane Papers, American Philosophical Society.

"Dear Tutie: I am quite sick...American Consul, Havana." Kane and Fox, *The Love-Life of Dr. Kane,* page 277.

"Newsboys shouted...anguish to my ears!" Davenport, *The Death-Blow to Spiritualism,* page 37.

"Your welcome little note...In love yours faithfully Margaret." Kane and Fox, *The Love-Life of Dr. Kane,* pp. 277–278.

"Why have you not written?...awful imaginings!" Ibid., page 279.

"Dr. Kane is dying...departing very hard." "Dangerous Condition of Dr. Kane," *New York Tribune,* February 17, 1857.

CHAPTER TEN

On the funeral solemnities surrounding the death of Dr. Kane, see Corner, *Doctor Kane of the Arctic Seas,* pp. 250–257; Elder, *Biography of Elisha Kent Kane,* pp. 246–248, 307–383, and Kane, *Arctic Explorations,* pp. lvii–lix.

"The remains of the chivalrous...honors in Independence Hall." "The Remains of Dr. Kane," *Philadelphia Public Ledger,* February 23, 1857.

"To the Memory of Dr. Kane from Two Ladies," Corner, *Doctor Kane of the Arctic Seas,* page 256.

"A few days after...move to 35 East 19th Street." Mrs. Fox to Mr. Robert Kane, n.d., from 50 East 22nd Street, Elisha Kane Papers, American Philosophical Society.

"I know the Doctor must...the last, long farewell." Kane and Fox, *The Love-Life of Dr. Kane,* page 283.

"My dear Mr. Kane...more than all." Margaret Fox to Robert Kane, Thursday evening, 1858, Elisha Kent Kane Papers, American Philosophical Society.

"write a memoir of the man...sake of his fame!" Elder, *Biography of Elisha Kent Kane,* pp. 3–4.

"not giving more copious extracts...real characters." "Life of Dr. Kane," *New York Times,* January 23, 1859, page 2.

"a deep undercurrent in the navigator's life,...added to the biography." Fornell, *The Unhappy Medium,* page 59.

On the scandal surrounding Elizabeth Ellet, Edgar Allan Poe, and Fanny Sargent Osgood, see Silverman, *Edgar A. Poe,* pp. 288–293.

"Her distress and feeble health...some good lawyer." Mrs. E. F. Ellet to Robert Kane, December 1, 1858, Elisha Kent Kane Papers, American Philosophical Society.

"her opinions of persons...like me to do this?" Kane and Fox, *The Love-Life of Dr. Kane,* page 284.

"She is a very interesting...his last moments." Ibid., pp. 285–286.

"This is the first time...you or your mother." Maggie Fox to Cornelius Grinnell, April 21, 1858, Elisha Kent Kane Papers, American Philosophical Society.

"Come and tell *all*...letters bring them." Margaret Fox to R. P. Kane, May 18, 1858, Elisha Kent Kane Papers, American Philosophical Society.

"You know the Doctor's memory...them to be published." Margaret Fox to R. P. Kane, May 28, 1858, Elisha Kent Kane Papers, American Philosophical Society.

"When instead of responding...wrongdoing on your part." Mrs. E. F. Ellet to Robert Kane, May 18, 1858, Elisha Kent Kane Papers, American Philosophical Society.

"long sweet interview...I shall forgive." Margaret Fox to R. P. Kane, August 31, 1858, Elisha Kent Kane Papers, Fox-Kane Correspondence (bundled by R. P. Kane), folder 1, 1853, 1858, American Philosophical Society.

"She has suffered...astray as she did [with] Mrs. [Ellet]." Horace Greeley to Robert Kane, August 31, 1858, Elisha Kent Kane Papers, American Philosophical Society.

"I have read your letter...Greeley and Father Quinn." Robert Kane to Maggie Fox, September 3, 1858, Elisha Kent Kane Papers, American Philosophical Society.

"I am inclined to think...these bad people." Robert Kane to Mrs. Grinnell, September 22, 1858, Elisha Kent Kane Papers, American Philosophical Society.

"two gentleman of our city...some provision to her," Robert Kane to Mrs. Henry Grinnell, September 23, 1858, Elisha Kent Kane Papers, American Philosophical Society.

"These trusts [were] expressed...bequest was declared." Last Will and Testament of Elisha Kent Kane, Elisha Kent Kane Papers, American Philosophical Society.

"I still find her...timid to say this." Father Quinn to R. P. Kane, October 18, 1858, Elisha Kent Kane Papers, American Philosophical Society.

"We will pay $500...able to answer." Underhill, *The Missing Link in Modern Spiritualism,* pp. 300–301.

"It was the unanimous opinion...or disproved by it." Ibid., page 312.

"mostly persons of original...experience of mankind." Fornell, *The Unhappy Medium,* page 67.

"Hearing such wonderful stories...sister in the spirit world." "Suicide of a Spiritualist," *New York Daily Tribune,* December 1, 1856.

"raps had grown tremendously strong...frightening in their force." Pond, *Time Is Kind,* page 176.

"I questioned it about...great precision." Strong, *The Diary of George Templeton Strong, The Turbulent Fifties, 1850–1859,* page 390.

"fell eight or ten percent in a day...four of the afternoon." "The New York Stock Board," *Harper's Weekly,* Vol. 1857, September 12, 1857, page 577.

"We seem foundering...gaunt and desperate." Strong, *The Diary of George Templeton Strong, The Turbulent Fifties, 1850–1859*, page 358.

"I never used anything...wavered in opinion." Underhill, *The Missing Link in Modern Spiritualism*, pp. 283–288.

"There had been no romance...culminated that way." Pond, *Time Is Kind*, page 190.

"He thought I had done...retire from public séances." Underhill, *The Missing Link in Modern Spiritualism*, page 293.

"Now that you are rich, why don't you save your soul?" Davenport, *The Death-Blow to Spiritualism*, page 234.

"I have, I believe,...no estate of the late Doctor Kane." Robert P. Kane to Reverend Quinn, January 7, 1859, Elisha Kent Kane Papers, American Philosophical Society.

"It is very sad...—how useless." Maggie Fox to Robert P. Kane, January 7, 1859, Elisha Kent Kane Papers, American Philosophical Society.

"One passage of that letter...consider it a wrong." Maggie Fox to Robert P. Kane, January 17, 1859, Elisha Kent Kane Papers, American Philosophical Society.

"At that hour I wrote...love and respect him." Maggie Fox to Robert P. Kane, January 22, 1859, Elisha Kent Kane Papers, American Philosophical Society.

CHAPTER ELEVEN

"Please inform Mr. Kane...what to depend upon." Maggie Fox to Father Quinn, April 6, 1860, Elisha Kent Kane Papers, American Philosophical Society.

"It has Willlie's name...the kindness eternally." Maggie Fox to Robert Kane, April, 1860, Elisha Kent Kane Papers, American Philosophical Society.

"Mr. Kane, I am afraid...Do not wait." Maggie Fox to Robert Kane, September 15, 1860, Elisha Kent Kane Papers, American Philosophical Society.

"As for accepting one penny...with no stain." Maggie Fox to Father Quinn, April 5, 1860, Elisha Kent Kane Papers, American Philosophical Society.

"She would like to have...act justly and wisely." Dexter C. Hawkins to Robert K. Kane, November 20, 1860, Elisha Kent Kane Papers, American Philosophical Society.

"I do not see...contents to others." Robert K. Kane to Dexter C. Hawkins, December 1, 1860, Elisha Kent Kane Papers, American Philosophical Society.

"seems to have withdrawn...prevent such a misfortune." Robert Kane to Father Quinn, December 10, 1860, Elisha Kent Kane Papers, American Philosophical Society.

"If I do not hear from you...assistance of your courts." Dexter Hawkins to Robert Kane, December 20, 1860, Elisha Kent Kane Papers, American Philosophical Society.

"After each exhausting...bore her far away." Pond, *Time Is Kind*, pp. 217–218.

"There was about her...any room she entered." Pond, *Time Is Kind*, pp. 193–194.

"She is one of the most...administering a government." Taylor, *Katie Fox: Epochmaking Medium and the Making of the Fox-Taylor Record*, page 97. See also Owen, *The Debatable Land Between This World and the Next, With Illustrative Narrations*, page 498.

"500,000 drunkards are now...scene of immolation!" Branch, *The Sentimental Years*, pp. 231–232.

"Raps spelled out...those I have described." Pond, *Time Is Kind*, page 198.

"I believe my assets...not sordid and selfish." Strong, *The Diary of George Templeton Strong*, page 207.

The Orphan's Court at the City Hall of Philadelphia recently explained that records of the Fox-Kane trial are missing and seem to have been for years, perhaps decades.

"She would make...before a curious world." Pond, *Time Is Kind*, page 219.

"betrayed and baffled still," Howells, *A Thanksgiving*; also Rickert & Paton, eds., *American Lyrics*, page 286.

"Let me go...find him in the snow." Pond, *Time Is Kind*, page 221. Pond's book is the only record of an encounter between Horace Greeley and Maggie. Greeley's subsequent arrangements with Dr. Bayard, however, confirm his awareness of Maggie and Katy's alcoholism.

On the controversial World Temperance Convention of 1853, see "World Temperance Convention," *New York Herald*, May 13, 1853.

"We have known...glass of wine." Pond, *Time Is Kind*, pp. 223–224.

"gentleman cad," Pond, *Time Is Kind*, pp. 225.

"She drinks till...not checked soon." Pond, *Time Is Kind*, pp. 226.

"She knew the reason for their slumber." Pond, *Time Is Kind*, pp. 228.

"It was in 1865...plain living." Taylor, *Katie Fox: Epochmaking Medium and the Making of the Fox-Taylor Record*, pp. 139–140.

"There were many perfectly...from the fatigues of business." Taylor, *Katie Fox: Epochmaking Medium and the Making of the Fox-Taylor Record*, page 140.

"Is not this withholding...friend to both parties," anonymous letter of January 3 from Philadelphia to Jane Leiper Kane from "a friend to both parties," Elisha Kent Kane Papers, American Philosophical Society.

"she declared her determination...life was bound up," Fox and Kane, *The Love-Life of Dr. Kane*, page x.

"My poor father...this sort of life soon." Davenport, *The Death-Blow to Spiritualism*, page 236.

"tired old brain...to care-free second childhood." Pond, *Time Is Kind*, pp. 230–231.

"That we recognize...slightest authority." "The Spiritual Convention," *New York Times,* August 22, 1864.

On the Kanes' accusation that Maggie's engagement to Elisha was a "canard," see "A Canard about Dr. Kane," *New York Tribune,* September 11, 1864.

"Perhaps many will think...in this correspondence." Kane and Fox, *The Love-Life of Dr. Kane,* page x.

CHAPTER TWELVE

"A book will probably appear...shrouded in mystery." "A Story About Dr. Kane," *Rochester Union,* reprinted in *New York Times,* December 10, 1865.

"Though the circumstances...individual grievances." "The Love-Life of Dr. Kane," *The New York Times,* December 15, 1865.

"She had come forth...happy comradeship." Pond, *Time Is Kind,* page 232.

"They had always accepted...came or where it went." Pond, *Time Is Kind,* page 232.

"I can make...less than a week." Margaret Fox Kane to Mr. & Mrs. Post, April 11, 1867, The Isaac and Amy Post Family Papers, University of Rochester.

"as long as I was in this business...number of my patrons." "Spiritualism Exposed," *The World,* October 21, 1888.

"The scene that followed...was finally overcome." Pond, *Time Is Kind,* page 234.

"Well. For those who like...they would like." Sandburg, *Abraham Lincoln: The War Years,* Vol. II, page 306. See also Fornell, *The Unhappy Medium,* page 118.

"He lives, Emilie...he always had." Sandburg, *Abraham Lincoln: The War Years,* Vol. II, page 261.

On Lincoln's additional involvement with spiritualism, see Sandburg, *Abraham Lincoln: The War Years,* Vol. III, pp. 303–345; Maynard, *Was Abraham Lincoln a Spiritualist?: Or Curious Revelations From the Life of a Trance Medium;* Lamon, *Recollections of Abraham Lincoln,* pp. 110–122; and Fornell, *The Unhappy Medium,* pp. 118–123.

"The practical inference...don't trust it." Fornell, *The Unhappy Medium,* page 132. For more details on the Colchester case, pp. 124–132.

"The 'spirit rapping' humbug...spiritual humbuggery." Barnum, *The Humbugs of the World,* pp. 82–84.

"Ladies and Gentleman...enshrouded the world." Hardinge, *Modern American Spiritualism,* page 555.

"Our friend and brother...which prophecy was fulfilled." "Anniversary of Modern Spiritualism," *Banner of Light,* April 18, 1868, in Hardinge, *Modern American Spiritualism,* page 554.

"Men and women...increased by spiritualism." "Spiritualism," *Union Advertiser,* April 20, 1868, page 2, column 1, reprinted from *New York Tribune.*

"He [man] is, indeed,...symptoms of insanity." Browne, *Charles Darwin, the Origin and After—The Years of Fame,* pp. 318–319.

"professor of disease of the mind...of the nervous system." Moore, *In Search of White Crows,* page 136. For additional details on the mind-body controversy of the 1850s–1870s, see Moore, *In Search of White Crows,* pp. 134–137, and Lutz, *American Nervousness: 1903,* pp. 3–7.

On "neurasthenics" and the stages of neurasthenia, see George M. Beard's chart, "Evolution of Nervousness," in Lutz, *American Nervousness: 1903,* page 5.

"...Anxiety, care, vexation,...condition of the medium." Hammond, *Light from the Spirit World,* page 248.

"Do not indulge in stimulants,...the psychic nature." Evans, *How To Be A Medium,* page 107.

"When for a time...cheerful, patient, Katie." Taylor, *Katie Fox: Epochmaking Medium and the Making of the Fox-Taylor Record,* page 99.

"Katie was a great...manifest through her channel." Ibid., page 273.

"This is the séance...dead drunk." Ibid., page 164.

"Drunkenness...evangelical power," ibid.

"Katie comes back...keep away now." Ibid., page 155.

"Katie meets Maggie...the sixth, sad, sad." Ibid.

"So that as few...judge for themselves." Davenport, *The Death-Blow to Spiritualism,* page 236.

"The deterioration...her real self." Pond, *Time Is Kind,* page 242.

"determined to remove Kate from...deteriorating companionship of Maggie." Pond, *Time Is Kind,* page 244.

On the English reaction to Mrs. Hayden's visit and the subsequent spiritualistic craze, see Goldfarb, *Spiritualism and Nineteenth-Century Letters,* pp. 68–114; Porter, *Through a Glass Darkly;* and McHargue, *Facts, Frauds, and Phantasms,* pp. 88–95.

"better [to] be occupied...worms of tortoises," Goldfarb, *Spiritualism and Nineteenth-Century Letters,* page 111.

"American Invasion," Podmore, *Mediums of the Nineteenth Century,* Vol. 2, page 47.

"Kate did not make decisions." Pond, *Time Is Kind,* page 244.

"Maggie was self-supporting...come of the parting." Ibid., page 245.

"persons of obvious refinement...true respect." Ibid., page 246.

"The nurse of full-grown souls is solitude." Lowell, *The Complete Poetical Works of James Russell Lowell,* page 76.

"Yes! I am a Free Lover…have *any* right to interfere," Stern, *The Victoria Woodhull Reader,* page 23.

"Do the thing that is…to second you," Van Deusen, *Horace Greeley,* page 279.

On Katy's letters to Leah and Maggie about her English trip, see Pond, *Time Is Kind,* pp. 262–263.

On Henry Jencken's proposal, ibid., pp. 265–270.

"As the company, with brimming…for some seconds." Ibid., page 270.

For an account of Henry Jencken's life and interest in spiritualism, I am indebted to Neil Robertson per courtesy his relatives' private memoir, *Grandmother's Story: A Look at the Past: Memoirs of Amalie Christine Jencken.* On Jencken's involvement with medium D. D. Home, see McHargue, *Facts, Frauds, and Phantasms,* pp. 86–108; Kerr, *Mediums and Spirit-Rappers and Roaring Radicals,* pp. 60–62, 98; Goldfarb, *Spiritualism and Nineteenth-Century Letters,* pp. 77–81, 84, 92, 105–109; and Moore, *In Search of White Crows,* page 109.

"among the first…than at the present time." Jackson, *The Spirit Rappers,* page 184.

"We were wined…strong with us." "Spirits Led her to Drink," *Democrat and Chronicle,* May 7, 1888.

"ma-ma, darling ma-ma…die without him." Pond, *Time Is Kind,* pp. 275–276.

For details on the infant Ferdinand's spiritual powers, see ibid., pp. 276–277, and Underhill, *The Missing Link in Modern Spiritualism,* pp. 464–470.

"to go back to London," Underhill, *The Missing Link in Modern Spiritualism,* page 469.

"Who believes in me shall live." Ibid., page 470.

"And so we have Katy…the little hand." Fox-Taylor, *Fox-Taylor Automatic Writing, 1869–1892,* page 283.

CHAPTER THIRTEEN

"the quiet existence…practice of public mediumship." Davenport, *The Death-Blow to Spiritualism,* page 165.

"the high priestess…pure religious insanity," ibid., pp. 164–166.

"worthless residual of spiritualism," McHargue, *Facts, Frauds, and Phantasms,* page 105. On Crooke's opinion about Katy Fox Jencken, see *Quarterly Journal of Sciences,* 1874, Vol. IV, p. 83.

"offer myself upon the altar of science," Jackson, *The Spirit Rappers,* page 127.

On Henry Sidgwick's early experiments in spiritualism, see "Henry Sidgwick and Psychical Research," *Proceedings of the Society for Psychical Research,* Vol. XLV, page 138.

"We believed unreservedly…with ignorant contempt." Goldfarb, *Spiritualism and Nineteenth-Century Letters,* page 129.

"all systems of morals,...of modern Spiritualism." Davenport, *The Death-Blow to Spiritualism,* page 167.

"Since I have not heard...investigate the 'Rappings'." Ibid., pp. 169–170.

"I could name...produced on the floor." *The Seybert Commission on Spiritualism,* page 37.

"The heels of her shoes...through these glasses." Ibid., page 39.

"You have come...unusual pulsation." Ibid., pp. 42–47.

For a secondary account of the Seybert Commission proceedings, see Davenport, *The Death-Blow to Spiritualism,* page 177.

"confined wholly...voluntarily or unvoluntarily." *The Seybert Commission on Spiritualism,* pp. 47–48.

"Although I have been...far out beyond." Ibid., page 159.

"The next day...remorse in wine." Davenport, *The Death-Blow to Spiritualism,* pp. 35–36.

"Spirit séances are likely...were surrounding us." "Tricks of the mediums," *New York Times,* February 14, 1886.

"handsome competence." For a full account in an undated *New York Herald* reference, see Jackson, *The Spirit Rappers,* pp. 183–184.

"I noticed her face...English boys." Taylor, *Fox-Taylor Automatic Writing, 1869–1892,* page 293.

On Katy's arguments with the Underhills, Maggie, and David over her boys, see Pond, *Time Is Kind,* pp. 287–289.

"the Doctor [her husband, George] came over...only excessively nervous." Taylor, *Fox-Taylor Automatic Writing, 1869–1892,* page 364.

"Policeman Hines...drunkenness against her." "Kate Fox Locked Up," *New York Herald,* August 29, 1886, page 6.

"met the little old lady...sixty years of experience." "One hour with Margaretta Fox Kane," Pond, *Time Is Kind,* page 330.

"I think too much...it's a fraud." *New York Herald,* September 25, 1888, cited in Fornell, *The Unhappy Medium,* page 176.

"I saw the invitation...the other world." "Royalty and Spirit Rapping, The Wildest Story Yet About Queen Victoria and the Mediums," *New York Herald,* March 28, 1888.

"drunkenness...her maternal duties." "The Spirits Too Much for Her," *New York Herald,* May 5, 1888, page 4.

"In the middle-aged...supernatural exhibitions." Ibid. See also "Spirits Led Her to Drink," *Democrat and Chronicle,* May 7, 1888, reprinted from *New York World,* May 5, 1888.

"spirit pictures." On the trial of Madam Diss De Barr, see "Her Brother Her Accuser," *New York Times,* April 19, 1888.

"Christian Science mind-healing," Eddy, *Science and Health,* xi.

"The Science of Christianity...spiritually discerned." Ibid., page 98.

"The disclosures...system of Spiritualism." Davenport, *The Death-Blow to Spiritualism,* page 29.

"I presume my absence has...man or woman can think otherwise." "The Curse of Spiritualism," *New York Herald,* May 27, 1888; *The Death-Blow to Spiritualism,* page 30.

CHAPTER FOURTEEN

"Like a flash...applauded me." "God Has Not Ordered it," *New York Herald,* September 24, 1888.

"Not a word...have been arrested." Ibid.

"Herein is the degradation...court and jury..." *Votes for Women: Selections from the National America Woman Suffrage Association Collection, 1894–1921,* in Hooker, *The Constitutional Rights of the Women of the United States: An Address Before the International Council of Women, Washington, D.C. March 30, 1888,* page 16.

"It seems to me...gone against her." "Maggie's Queer Story," *New York Herald,* September 25, 1888, page 4.

"I tell you...'Hello, Uncle Edward.'" "God Has Not Ordered it," *New York Herald,* September 24, 1888.

"to a certain point...be practiced upon." "Maggie's Queer Story," *New York Herald,* September 25, 1888, page 4.

"Dear Mrs. Kane: I am not so much...having enlightened me." Davenport, *The Death-Blow to Spiritualism,* pp. 49–50.

"My troubles weighed...some of the sailors." Ibid., page 34.

"great decisions of life...well-meaning reasonableness." Jung, *Modern Man in Search of a Soul,* page 69.

"spirits never return...an interesting exposure of the fraud." "God Has Not Ordered it," *New York Herald,* September 24, 1888; Fornell, *The Unhappy Medium,* page 177.

"modest little house...ever been recorded." "God Has Not Ordered it," *New York Herald,* September 24, 1888.

"albeit a notorious career...not ordered it." Ibid.

"Is it all a trick?...infamous, for it was." Ibid.

"Several of the mediums...for what she says." "Maggie's Queer Story," *New York Herald,* September 25, 1888, page 4.

"Already it is violently discussed...shouldn't wonder." "Shocked Spiritualists," *New York Herald,* September 30, 1888, page 4.

"I have for years...done by an occult agency." Ibid. For additional information on Daniel's suggestion that Leah travel to David Fox's home during the exposé, see Pond, *Time Is Kind,* page 297.

"The majority of them...Margaret and Cathie [Katy] Fox." "Newton Says She Lies," *New York Herald,* October 1, 1888 pp. 5–6.

"It is known that...of the Romans." "And Katy Fox Now," *New York Herald,* October 10, 1888, page 3. The article is also reprinted without a date or reference in Davenport, *The Death-Blow to Spiritualism,* page 50, pages 54–58.

"The sisters at once fell...behind us unexposed." Ibid.

"No one who does not love...and its hypocritical apostles." Davenport, *The Death-Blow to Spiritualism,* page v.

"The severest blow...hypocrisy and a delusion." "Spiritualism Exposed," *The World,* October 21, 1888.

"a bare and somber drawing room scene," "Done with the Big Toe," *New York Times,* October 22, 1888.

"The great building...furious threats against their foes." "Spiritualism's Downfall," *New York Herald,* October 22, 1888, page 5.

"a Western theatrical...well-known star," "Spiritualism Exposed," *The World,* October 21, 1888.

"I'll get along...lies to them!" Pond, *Time Is Kind,* pp. 303–304.

"Clergymen and laymen...defray expenses." *"Lyceum Theatre, Thursday Evening November 15, 1888, The Mother of Modern Spiritualism Kate Fox!"* Broadside, Manuscripts and Archives Division, New York Public Library.

"She spoke in a parrot-like...getting those essentials." Jackson, *The Spirit Rappers,* pp. 212–213.

"I would have written...deny myself to them." Pond, *Time Is Kind,* page 314.

"Oh! Mrs. Newton, I do believe...individual intelligence," copy of statement made by Mrs. Margaret Fox Kane, November, 1889, *Banner of Light,* Saturday, March 25, 1893, page 11.

"shifting voices," Feinstein, *Becoming William James,* page 86.

"My impression after this...has supernormal powers." James, "Certain Phenomena of Trance," Proceedings of the SPR, 6, (1890), page 652. Reprinted in James, *The Works of William James,* page 81.

"If I may employ...single crow to be white." James, "What Psychical Research Has Accomplished," *The Will to Believe & Other Essays in Popular Philosophy,* page 236.

CHAPTER FIFTEEN

"For months past I have suffered...in saying that." "Mrs. Kane's Recantation," copy of statement made by Mrs. Margaret Fox Kane, November 1889, *Banner of Light,* March 25, 1893, pp. 11–13.

"wicked work of the devil." ibid., page 6.

"At that time I was...want and suffering since." Ibid., page 13.

"When I made...an incontrovertible fact." Ibid., page 6.

"If ever I heard...it was then." Doyle, *The History of Spiritualism,* Vol. 1, page 110.

"There is not a human being...against Spiritualism." Copy of statement made by Mrs. Margaret Fox Kane, November 1889, *Banner of Light,* March 25, 1893, page 6.

"128 West Forty-third Street...when I get upon the platform." Ibid., page 8.

"for five dollars she would...sworn to anything." Pressing, *Rappings That Startled the World,* page 75. See also Doyle, *The History of Spiritualism,* p. 110.

"I have had the pleasure...arrogance or pomposity." Cadwallader, "Last Days of Margaret Fox Kane, *Hydesville in History,* page 57.

"I found everything...to make them happy." Taylor, *Fox-Taylor Automatic Writing 1869–1892,* page 379.

"The Doctor [George Taylor] called...this day, nearly a year." Ibid., page 397.

"Mother is dead...I don't know how." Ibid., page 400.

On Maggie's brief stay at the home of Mary and Henry Newton, see Brandon, *The Spiritualists,* page 230.

On the contributions solicited in *Banner of Light* on January 9, 1892, see Moore, "The Spiritualist Medium: A Study of Female Professionalism in Victorian America," *American Quarterly,* Vol. 27, No. 2, 1958, 219.

"Mrs. Fox Kane was unable...as I was." Pressing, *Rappings That Startled the World,* pp. 75–76.

See Fornell, *The Unhappy Medium,* page 181, for a report of Maggie's last days at the home of Mrs. Emily B. Ruggles. See also Brandon, *The Spiritualists,* page 230, for more details.

"free from all the cloudiness...transfigured her." Pond, *Time Is Kind,* page 325.

"The hall was so densely...joint of her great toe." "Margaret Fox Buried," *Brooklyn Eagle,* March 11, 1893, page 5.

EPILOGUE

"recorded legitimate religion," National Spiritualist Association of Churches, *Why NSAC,* page 2. See also National Spiritualist Association of Churches, *By Laws,* October 10, 2003.

On Edgar Cayce's life, Sugrue, *There is a River,* page viii; Stearn, *Edgar Cayce, The Sleeping Prophet*; "Illiterate Man, Becomes a Doctor When Hypnotized— Strange Power Shown by Edgar Cayce Puzzles Physicians," *New York Times,* October 9, 1910.

"new revelation of God's dealing...death of the body." Brandon, *The Spiritualists,* pp. 218–219.

"It is indeed curious...historian from those who were within it." Doyle, *The History of Spiritualism,* Vol. 1, page vii.

"is a genuine breath...from being defined." Ibid., pp. 118–19.

On Houdini's clashes with Doyle, his involvement with the *Scientific American* committee, and Mina Crandon, see Silverman, *Houdini,* pp. 290–297, 322–345, 376–384, 391; Brandon, *The Spiritualists,* pp. 167–189.

"control...ectoplasm." For this and other details on the *Scientific American* committee's investigation of Mina Crandon, see Silverman, *Houdini,* p. 313–340; McHargue, *Facts, Frauds, and Phantasms,* pp. 193–204.

On Bess Houdini's encounter with Arthur Ford, see Spragett, *Arthur Ford: The Man Who Talked with the Dead,* pp. 150–162, and McHargue, *Facts, Frauds, and Phantasms,* pp. 242–245.

On Rhine, see Brandon, *The Spiritualists,* pp. 94–95, 278, 291; McHargue, *Facts, Frauds, and Phantasms,* pp. 240–241; and Rhine, *Extra Sensory Perception* and *New Frontiers of the Mind.*

On Eileen Garrett's life, see Angoff, *Eileen J. Garrett and the World Beyond the Senses*; on her friendship with Huxley, pp. 25–27; Garrett, *Eileen J. Garrett: Adventures in the Supernatural,* especially pages 181–186; and McHargue, *Facts, Frauds, and Phantasms,* pp. 247–255. I am also indebted to Mrs. Garrett's daughter Eileen Coly and her granddaughter, Lisette Coly, Executive Director of the Parapsychology Foundation, for additional insights about the medium.

"It has been said...will achieve positive results." Peale, *The Power of Positive Thinking,* page 166.

"I believe there...is for the better." Ibid., page 210.

On Jim Pike's death and the bishop's spiritualist experiences, see Pike, *The Other Side,* pp. 65–131, and McHargue, *Facts, Frauds, and Phantasms,* pp. 228–257. On Arthur Ford's televised encounter with Bishop Pike, see "Arthur (Augustus) Ford," in Mellon, *Encyclopedia of Occultism and Parapsychology.*

"Death is only moving...more beautiful one," Kübler-Ross, *On Life After Death,* page 10.

"a transition from this life...forever is LOVE." Ibid., page 82.

"I am not trying to...more clearly elucidated." Moody, *Life After Life,* page 10.

PAMPHLETS

Cadwallader, M.E. *Hydesville in History.* Chicago, Ill.: The Progressive Thinker Publishing House, 1917.

Capron, Eliab W. and Barron, Henry D. *Singular Revelations: Explanation and History of the Mysterious Communion with Spirits Comprehending the Rise and Progress of the Mysterious Noises in Western New York, Generally Received as Spiritual Communications,* 2nd ed. Auburn, N.Y.: Capron and Barron, 1850.

Davis, Paulina, *A History of the National Woman's Rights Movement for Twenty Years, with the proceedings of the Decade Meeting held at Apollo Hall, October 20, 1887, from 1850 to 1870, with an Appendix Containing the History of the movement during the winter of 1871 in the National Capitol,* New York: Journeymen Printers' Cooperative Association, 1871; also New York: Kraus, reprint, 1971.

Dewey, D. M. *History of the Strange Sounds, or Rappings, Heard in Rochester and Western New York, and Usually Called the Mysterious Noises!* Rochester: D. M. Dewey, 1850.

Lewis, E. E. *A Report of the Mysterious Noises Heard in the House of Mr. John D. Fox in Hydesville, Arcadia, Wayne County, Authenticated by the Certificates and Confirmed by the Statements of the Citizens of that Place and Vicinity.* Canandaigua: Published by E. E. Lewis, 1848.

National Spiritualist Association of Churches. *Why NSAC.* Lily Dale, N.Y.

National Spiritualist Association of Churches. *Foundation Facts Concerning Spiritualism as a Religion,* Lily Dale, New York, Revised 1999.

Pressing, R. G. *Rappings That Startled the World: Facts about the Fox Sisters.* Lily Dale, N.Y.: Dale News Inc., n.d.

ARTICLES

Albanese, Catherine L. "On the Matter of Spirit: Andrew Jackson Davis and the Marriage of God and Nature," *Journal of the American Academy of Religion,* Vol. 60, Spring 1992.

Barnes, Joseph W. and Ryan, Pat M., eds. "Rochester Recollected: A Miscellany of Eighteenth and Nineteenth Century Descriptions," *Rochester History,* Vol. XLI, January and April 1979, 31.

Broad, C. D. "Henry Sidgwick and Psychical Research." *Proceedings of the Society for Psychical Research,* Vol. XLV. London: Society for Psychical Research, 1938.

Cronise, Adelbert. "The Beginnings of Modern Spiritualism in and Near Rochester," The Rochester Historical Society, Publication Fund Series, Vol. V. Rochester, N.Y.: 1926.

"Discovery of the Source of the Rochester Knockings," *Buffalo Medical Journal*, Vol. VI, March 1851, 628–642.

Edmonds, John W. "Judge Edmonds on 'Spiritualism,'" *Nation*, Vol. I, September 7, 1865, 295–296.

Emerson, Ralph Waldo. "The Transcendentalist," *The Dial: A Magazine for Literature, Philosophy and Religion*, Vol. III. Boston and London: B. P. Peabody, 1843.

Felton, C. C. "The Delusion called Spiritualism," *Living Age*, 1855, Vol. 54, 670.

Hewitt, Nancy. "Amy Kirby Post," *The University of Rochester Library Bulletin*, Vol. 37, 1984.

Jackson, Herbert G. "Corinthian Hall's Rap Fest," *Democrat & Chronicle*, January 9, 1972.

Kane, Margaret Fox. "Statement made by Mrs. Margaret Fox Kane, November, 1889," *Banner of Light*, March 25, 1893.

Lawton, George. "The Drama of Life After Death: A Study of the Spiritualist Religion," *Dictionary of American Biography*. New York: Henry Holt and Company, 1932, 500.

Littell, E. "The Free Love System," *Littell's Living Age*, 2nd Series, Vol. 4, July, August, September 1855. Boston: Littell and Sons, Company.

McKelvey, Blake. "The Rochester Area in American History," *Rochester History*, Vol. XXI, January 1959.

Moore, Laurence. "Spiritualism and Science: Reflections of the First Decade of the Spirit Rappings," *American Quarterly*, Vol. 24, October 1972, 474–500.

Moore, Laurence. "The Spiritualist Medium: A Study of Female Professionalism in Victorian America," *American Quarterly*, Vol. 27, No. 2, 1958, 219.

"Mrs. Kane's Recantation," *The Banner of Light*, Parts I and II, March 25, 1893.

Phelps, William Lyon. "Robert Browning on Spiritualism," *Yale Review*, New Series, Vol. XXIII, 125–38.

Pond, Charles F. "History of the Third Ward," *Publications of the Rochester Historical Society*, Publication Fund Series, Volume One, 1922.

Ryan, Pat. M. "Rochester Recollected: A Miscellany of Eighteenth- and Nineteenth-century Descriptions," ed. Joseph W. Barnes, *Rochester History*, Vol. XLI, January and April 1979.

Spicer, Henry. "Spiritualist Manifestations," *Littell's Living Age*, 2d Series, Vol. 1, June 1853, 807–820.

"Spiritualism: A Cure for Insanity," *The Spiritual Telegraph*, Vol. VI, Summer 1854, 1855.

Taylor, Bayard. "The Confessions of a Medium," *Atlantic Monthly*, No. XXXVIII, December 1860, pp. 699–714.

"The Boston Exclusives Again," *Woodhull and Claflin's Weekly*, October 28, 1871.

"The New York Stock Board," *Harper's Weekly*, Vol. 1857, September 12, 1857.

"To all our Readers and Correspondents," *Holden's Dollar Magazine*, Vol. VI, No. III, September 1, 1850, pp. 573–574.

Truesdale, Dorothy S. "American Travel Accounts of Early Rochester," ed. Blake McKelvey, *Rochester History*, Vol. XVI, April 1954.

Webb, Wheaton Phillips. *Spiritualism: Peddler's Protest, New York History,* April 1943.

Wellman, Judith. "The Seneca Falls Women's Rights Convention: A Study of Social Networks," *Journal of Women's History,* 1991, Vol. 3, No. 1.

Wilson, John B. "Emerson and the 'Rochester Rappings'": Memoranda and Documents, *The New England Quarterly,* June 1968, Vol. XLI, No. 2.

NEWSPAPER ARTICLES

"A Canard about Dr. Kane," *New York Tribune,* September 11, 1864.

"A Ghost!" *Rochester Daily Democrat,* November 11, 1849.

"And Katy Fox Now," *New York Herald,* October 10, 1888, page 3.

"Arrival Extraordinary," *Rochester Daily Advertiser,* August 6, 1847, page 2.

"A Story About Dr. Kane," *Rochester Union,* reprinted in *New York Times,* December 10, 1865.

"Barnum of the New York Museum," *Rochester Daily Advertiser,* August 4, 1848, page 3.

"Barnum's Panorama," *Rochester Daily Advertiser,* August 22, 1848, page 2.

"Burr and Blue Devils," *Plain Dealer,* May 6, 1851, page 1.

"Dangerous Condition of Dr. Kane," *New York Tribune,* February 17, 1857.

"Departure of the Kane Expedition," *New York Times,* June 1, 1855, 1.

"Done with the Big Toe," *New York Times,* October 22, 1888.

"Dr. Kane," *New York Times,* November 1, 1855.

"Dr. Kane," *The Pennsylvanian,* November 19, 1855.

"Dr. Kane Home Again," *New York Times,* October 12, 1855.

"Dr. Kane's Prospects," *New York Daily Tribune,* November 6, 1855.

"Dr. Kane to Marry One of the Fox Girls," *Rochester Democrat Union,* October 22, 1855.

"Fearing Their Enemies" *New York Herald,* October 10, 188, page 3.

"Free Love," *New York Tribune,* October 24, 1855.

"God Has Not Ordered it," *New York Herald,* September 24, 1888.

"Hare on Spirits," *New York Times,* November 24, 1855, page 1.

"Her Brother Her Accuser," *New York Times,* April 19, 1888.

"Illiterate Man, Becomes a Doctor When Hypnotized—Strange Power Shown by Edgar Cayce Puzzles Physicians," *New York Times,* October 9, 1910.

"Kate Fox Locked Up," *New York Herald,* August 29, 1886, page 6.

"Maggie's Queer Story," *New York Herald,* September 25, 1888, page 4.

"Margaret Fox Buried," *Brooklyn Eagle,* March 11, 1893, page 5.

"Melancholy Suicide," *New York Herald,* January 8, 1853, page 4.

"Miss Cora Hatch, the Eloquent Medium of the Spiritualists," *Frank Leslie's Illustrated Newspaper,* May 9, 1857, page 358.

"Mrs. Isabella Hooker Deceived/How the Jencken Boys Were Released—Katie Gets Alms of $15,000," *New York Herald,* September 25, 1888, page 4.

"Mysterious Knockings Explained," *Rochester Daily Advertiser,* January 17, 1850.

"Newton Says She Lies," *New York Herald,* October 1, 1888 pp. 5–6.

"Police," *Rochester Daily Democrat,* August 9, 1841.

"Price Reduced. Wonderful Phenomena at Corinthian Hall," *Rochester Daily Democrat*, November 17, 1849.

"Return of Dr. Kane," *New York Daily Tribune*, October 12, 1855, page 1.

"Return of Dr. Kane," *New York Times*, October 13, 1855, page 4.

"Rival Rappers," *Plain Dealer* May 8, 1851.

"Royalty and Spirit Rapping," *New York Herald*, March 28, 1888.

"Second Grinnell Expedition," *New York Times*, October 16, 1855, pp. 1–2.

"Shocked Spiritualists," *New York Herald*, September 30, 1888, page 4.

"Singular Revelations. Communications with Spirits in Western New York," *New York Weekly Tribune*, December 8, 1849.

"Sketches of Lectures, Spiritualism," *New York Tribune*, November 24, 1855.

"Spirits Coming," *Plain Dealer*, May 5, 1851, page 1.

"Spirits Led Her to Drink." *Democrat and Chronicle*, May 7, 1888.

"Spiritual Communications," *New York Weekly Tribune*, December 8, 1849.

"Spiritualism," *New York Times*, April 1, 1868.

"Spiritualism," *Union Advertiser*, April 20, 1868, page 2.

"Spiritualism: A Cure for Insanity," *The Spiritual Telegraph*, Vol. VI, Summer 1854, 1855, page 233.

"Spiritualism and Science," *New York Tribune*, August 26, 1856.

"Spiritualism Exposed," *New York World*, October 21, 1888.

"Spiritualism's Downfall," *New York Herald*, October 22, 1888, page 5.

"Spiritualism on the Right Rope—Sabbath-day Pastimes," *New York Times*, July 5, 1866.

"Spiritual Manifestations," *New York Times*, September 13, 1867.

"Suicide of a Spiritualist," *New York Daily Tribune*, December 1, 1856.

"That Rochester Knocking," *New York Daily Tribune*, January 18, 1850.

"The Arctic Expedition," *New York Times*, June 1, 1855.

"The Arctic Expeditions," *New York Herald*, October 12, 1855.

"The Arctic Voyagers," *New York Times*, October 18, 1855, page 2.

"The Athenaeum," *Rochester Daily Democrat*, January 1, 1850.

"The Curse of Spiritualism," *New York Herald*, May 27, 1888.

"The 'Free Love' Movement," *New York Tribune*, October 16, 1855.

"The Free Love System," *New York Times*, September 8, 1855.

"The Hartstein Arctic Expedition," *New York Herald*, June 1, 1855, page 1.

"The Knockers," *New York Herald*, June 8, 1850.

"The Knockings," *Rochester Daily Democrat*, May 2, 1851.

"The Little Lights at the North—Retrospective Pictures and Present Frames of Mind—Bowen, Beecher, Garrison and Greeley," *New York Herald*, February 5, 1850, page 2.

"The Love-Life of Dr. Kane," *New York Times*, December 15, 1865.

"The Remains of Dr. Kane," *Philadelphia Public Ledger*, February 23, 1857.

"The Rochester Knockers and the Savans," *New York Herald*, June 17, 1850.

"The Rochester Mystery," *New York Herald*, February 6, 1850, page 2.

"The Spirits Too Much for Her," *New York Herald*, May 5, 1888, page 4.

"The Spiritual Convention," *New York Times*, August 22, 1864.

"The 'Spiritual Humbug,'" *Daily Advertiser,* May 3, 1850.

"Those Rochester Rappings," *New York Tribune,* March 6, 1850, page 1.

"Tricks of the mediums," *New York Times,* February 14, 1886.

"U.S. Arctic Expedition," *New York Tribune,* October 12, 1855.

"Which Has It?—Are the Rappers Knocked, or the Knockers Rapped," *Cleveland Plain Dealer,* May 7, 1851, page 1.

"Who Killed Cock Robin?" *Cleveland Plain Dealer,* May 12, 1851.

"Wonderful Phenomena at Corinthian Hall," *Rochester Daily Advertiser,* November 14, 1849, page 2.

"World Temperance Convention," *New York Herald,* May 13, 1853.

BOOKS

Alcott, William A. *The Young Woman's Guide to Excellence.* New York: Clark, Austin & Smith, 1852.

Alderson, William T. *Mermaids, Mummies and Mastodons: The Emergence of the American Museum.* Washington, D.C.: American Association of Museums, 1992.

Angoff, Allan. *Eileen J. Garrett and the World Beyond the Senses.* New York: William Morrow & Company, Inc., 1974.

Anthony, Katharine. *Susan B. Anthony: Her Personal History and Her Era.* Garden City, N.Y.: Doubleday, 1954.

Barkun, Michael. *Crucible of the Millennium: The Burned-over District of New York in the 1840s.* Syracuse, N.Y.: Syracuse University Press, 1986.

Baker, Jean H. *Mary Todd Lincoln: A Biography.* W. Norton & Company, 1987.

Ballou, Adin. *Ballou's Pictorial.* Boston, Mass.: M. M. Ballou, 1855–1859.

Barnum, P. T. *The Humbugs of the World.* New York: Carleton Publisher, 1866.

Bartlett, John. *Familiar Quotations,* Sixteenth Edition. Boston, New York, London: Little Brown and Company, 1992.

Beard, George, M. *American Nervousness.* New York: G. P. Putnam's Sons, 1881.

Becker, John E. *The History of the Village of Waterloo, New York: and thesaurus of related facts.* Waterloo, N.Y.: Waterloo Library and Historical Society, 1949.

Branch, E. Douglas. *The Sentimental Years: 1836–1860.* New York & London: D. Appleton-Century Company, 1934.

Brandon, Ruth. *The Spiritualists: The Passion for the Occult in the Nineteenth and Twentieth Centuries.* New York: Knopf, 1983.

Braude, Ann. *Radical Spirits: Spiritualism and Women's Rights in Nineteenth Century America,* Second Edition. Bloomington and Indianapolis: Indiana University Press, 2001.

Brittan, Samuel B., ed. *The Spiritual Telegraph,* Vol. VI. New York: Partridge & Brittan, 1855.

Browne, Janet. *Charles Darwin, The Origin and After—The Years of Fame.* New York: Knopf, 2002.

Browning, Elizabeth Barrett. *Elizabeth Barrett Browning: Letters to her Sister, 1846–59.* Edited by Leonard Huxley, L.L. D. New York: E.P. Dutton and Company, Inc., 1929.

Browning, Robert. *The Complete Poetical Works of Robert Browning.* New York: The Macmillan Company, 1915.

Browning, Robert. *The Poems of Browning,* ed. John Woolford and Daniel Karlin. London & New York: Longman, 1991.

Buhle, Mari Jo and Buhle, Paul. *The Concise History of Woman Suffrage: Selections from the Classic Work of Stanton, Anthony Gage and Harper.* Urbana: University of Illinois Press, 1978.

Burrows, Edwin G. and Wallace, Mike. *Gotham: A History of New York City to 1898.* New York and Oxford: Oxford University Press, 1999.

Bush, George. *Mesmer and Swedenborg.* New York: J. Allen, 1847.

Byron, Lord. *The Complete Poetical Works.* Edited by Jerome J. McGann and Barry Weller. Vol. VI. Oxford: Clarendon Press, 1991.

Campbell, Joseph. *The Portable Jung.* New York: Viking Press, 1971.

Capron, Eliab W. and Barron, Henry D. *Singular Revelations: Explanation and History of the Mysterious Communion With Spirits Comprehending the Rise and Progress of the Mysterious Noises in Western New York, Generally Received as Spiritual Communications,* Second Edition. Auburn, N.Y.: Capron and Barron, Fowler & Wells, 1850.

Carpenter, William B. *Mesmerism, Spiritualism, etc. Historically and Scientifically Considered.* New York: D. Appleton, 1877.

Carroll, Brett. *Spiritualism in Antebellum America.* Bloomington: Indiana University Press, 1997.

Charet, F. X. *Spiritualism and the Foundations of C.G. Jung's Psychology.* Albany: State University of New York Press, 1993.

Cheney, Ednah D., ed. *Louisa May Alcott: Her Life, Letters and Journals,* Boston: Roberts Brothers, 1889.

Child, Lydia Maria. *Lydia Maria Child, Selected Letters, 1817–1880.* Milton Meltzer, Patricia G. Holland, and Francine Krasno, eds. Amherst: The University of Massachusetts Press, 1982.

Churchill, Allen. *The Upper Crust: An Informal History of New York's Highest Society.* Englewood Cliffs, N.J.: Prentice-Hall, 1970.

Cook, James W. *The Arts of Deception: Playing with Fraud in the Age of Barnum.* Cambridge, Mass.: Harvard University Press, 2001.

Corner, George W. *Doctor Kane of the Arctic Seas.* Philadelphia: Temple University Press, 1972.

Cott, Nancy F. and Pleck, Elizabeth H. *A Heritage of Her Own: Toward a New Social History of American Women.* New York: Simon & Schuster, 1979.

Cox, Rob. *Body and Soul: A Sympathetic History of American Spiritualism.* Charlottesville & London: University of Virginia Press, 2003.

Cross, Whitney. *The Burned-over District: The Social and Intellectual History of Enthusiastic Religion in Western New York, 1800–1850.* Ithaca, N.Y.: Cornell University Press, 1950.

Davenport, Reuben Briggs. *The Death-Blow to Spiritualism.* New York: Arno Press, 1976, reprinted from edition by Samuel Stodder, New York, 1888.

Davis, Andrew Jackson. *The Philosophy of Spiritual Intercourse.* New York: Fowler and Wells, 1851.

Davis, Andrew Jackson. *The Principles of Nature, Her Divine Revelations and a Voice to Mankind,* Eighth Edition. New York: S. S. Lyon and W. Fishbough, 1851.

Dennett, Andrea Stulman. *Weird and Wonderful: The Dime Museum in America.* New York: New York University Press, 1997.

De Tocqueville, Alexis. *Democracy in America,* trans. George Laurence. New York: Harper and Row, 1966.

Devereux, George. *Psychoanalysis and the Occult.* New York: International Universities Press, Inc., 1953.

Dewey, D. M. *History of the Strange Sounds or Rappings, Heard in Rochester and Western New York and Usually Called The Mysterious Noises! Which Are Supposed by Many to Be Communications From the Spirit World Together With All the Explanation That Can As Yet Be Given Of the Matter.* Rochester, N.Y.: D.M. Dewey, Arcade Hall, 1850.

Dixon, Hepworth. *Spiritual Wives,* Vols. 1 & 2. London: Hunt and Blackett, 1868.

Doherty, Robert. *The Hicksite Separation: A Sociological Analysis of Religious Schism in Early Nineteenth Century America.* New Brunswick, N.J.: Rutgers University Press, 1967.

Doyle, A. C. *The History of Spiritualism,* Vols. 1 & 2. New York: George H. Doran Company, 1926.

Dubois, Carol, ed. *Elizabeth Cady Stanton/Susan B. Anthony, Correspondence, Writings, Speeches.* New York: Schocken Books, 1981.

Edmonds, John W. and Dexter, George T., M.D. *Spiritualism.* New York: Partridge & Brittan, 1853.

Edmonds, Judge. *Letters and Tracts on Spiritualism.* Edited by J. Burns. London: J. Burns, Progressive Library and Spiritual Institution, 1875.

Elder, William. *Biography of Elisha Kent Kane.* Philadelphia: Childs & Peterson, 1858.

Ellett, Elizabeth. *The Women of the American Revolution.* Williamstown, Mass.: Corner House, 1980, reprinted from Baker and Scribner, 1848–1850.

Ellis, Edward. *The Epic of New York City: A Narrative History.* New York: Old Town Books, 1966.

Emerson, Ralph Waldo. *Selected Writings of Ralph Waldo Emerson.* Edited by Brooks Atkinson. New York: The Modern Library, 1992.

Emerson, Ralph Waldo. *The Collected Works of Ralph Waldo Emerson,* Vol. IV. Cambridge, Mass.: Belknap Press, Harvard University Press, 1987.

Emerson, Ralph Waldo. *The Essential Writings of Ralph Waldo Emerson.* New York: The Modern Library, 2000.

Emerson, Ralph Waldo. *Journals of Ralph Waldo Emerson.* Edited by Edward Waldo Emerson and Waldo Emerson Forbes. Vols. III & VI. Boston: Houghton Mifflin, 1909–1914.

Evans, W. H. *How to Be A Medium.* Philadelphia: D. McKay, 1935.

Feinstein, Howard M. *Becoming William James.* Ithaca, N.Y.: Cornell University Press, 1984.

Fleming, Fergus. *Ninety Degrees North: The Quest for the North Pole.* New York: Grove Press, 2001.

Ford, Arthur, in collaboration with Marguerite Harmon Bro. *Nothing so Strange: The Autobiography of Arthur Ford.* London: Psychic Press, 1966.

Fornell, Earl Wesley. *The Unhappy Medium: Spiritualism and the Life of Margaret Fox.* Austin: University of Texas Press, 1964.

Freud, Sigmund. *Psychoanalysis and the Occult, Containing Papers by Dorothy T. Burlingham,* edited by Devereux. New York: International Universities Press, 1953.

Fuller, Robert C. *Mesmerism and the American Cure of Souls.* Philadelphia: University of Pennsylvania Press, 1982.

Gabriel, Mary. *Notorious Victoria. The Life of Victoria Woodhull Uncensored.* New York: Algonquin Books 1998.

Garrett, Eileen J. *Eileen J. Garrett: Adventures in the Supernatural.* New York: Helix Press, 2002.

Gauld, Alan. *The Founders of Psychical Research.* London: Routledge, 1968.

Godey's Lady's Book, ed. L. A. Godey with Sarah J. Hale. New York: The Godey Company, 1837–77.

Goldfarb, Russell M. and Goldfarb, Clare R. *Spiritualism and Nineteenth-Century Letters.* Rutherford, Madison, Teaneck, N.J.: Fairleigh Dickinson University Press; London: Associated University Presses, 1978.

Goldsmith, Barbara. *Other Powers: The Age of Suffrage, Spiritualism, and the Scandalous Victoria Woodhull.* New York: Alfred A. Knopf, 1998.

Grafton, John. *New York in the Nineteenth Century: 37 engravings from Harper's Weekly and Other Contemporary Sources,* Second Edition. New York: Dover Publications, 1977, 1980.

Greeley, Horace. *The Autobiography of Horace Greeley: Recollections of a Busy Life.* New York: E. B. Treat, 1872.

Greeley, Horace. *Recollections of a Busy Life.* New York: J.B. Ford and Company, 1868.

Greenwood, Grace. *Greenwood Leaves: A Collection of Sketches and Letters.* Boston: Ticknor, Reed, and Fields, 1850.

Hammond, Charles. *Light from the Spirit World. Comprising a series of articles on the condition of spirits, and the development of mind in the rudimental and second spheres. Being written wholly by the control of spirits.* Rochester, N.Y.: W. Heughes, 1852.

Hardinge, Emma. *Modern American Spiritualism: A Twenty Year's Record of the Communion Between Earth and the World of Spirits,* Fourth Edition. New York: 1870.

Hare, Robert. *Experimental Investigation of Spirit Manifestations: Demonstrating the Existence of Spirits and Their Communication with Mortals.* New York: Partridge and Britten, 1855.

Harris, Neil. *Humbug: The Art of P. T. Barnum.* Chicago: University of Chicago Press, 1973.

Hatch, Benjamin. *Spiritualists' Inequities Unmasked and the Hatch Divorce Case.* New York: 1859.

Hawthorne, Nathaniel. "The Blithedale Romance," *The Centenary Edition of the Works of Nathaniel Hawthorne.* Ohio State University Press: 1964.

Hewitt, Nancy, A. *Women's Activism and Social Change: Rochester, N.Y. 1822–1872.* Ithaca, N.Y.: Cornell University Press, 1984.

Hooker, Isabella Beecher. *The Constitutional Rights of the Women of the United States: An Address Before the International Council of Women, Washington, D.C., March 30, 1888.* Washington, D.C.: Fowler & Miller Co., 1888.; reproduced by Research Publications, New Haven, CT: 1977, History of Women, Reel 455, 3372.

Howells, W. D. *The Undiscovered Country.* Boston: Houghton Mifflin & Co., 1880.

Howells, W. D; James, Henry; Bigelow, John; Higginson, Thomas Wentworth; Alden, Henry M.; Thomson, William Hanna; Ferrero, Guglielmo; Howe, Julia Ward; and Phelps, Elizabeth Stuart. "Is There a Life after Death," in *After Days, Thoughts on the Future Life.* New York and London: Harper and Brothers, 1910.

Hugo, Victor. *Poems: History of A Crime.* Boston: Aldine, n.d.

Hyslop, James H. *Contact With The Other World.* New York: The Century Co., 1919.

Jackson, Herbert G. *The Spirit Rappers.* Garden City, N.Y.: Doubleday, 1972.

James, William. *Essays in Psychical Research.* Cambridge, Mass. and London, England: Harvard University Press, 1986.

James, William. *The Varieties of Religious Experience: A Study in Human Nature; being the Gifford lectures on natural religion delivered at Edinburgh, in 1901–1902.* New York and London: Longmans, Green and C., 1902.

James, William. *The Varieties of Religious Experience.* New York: Touchstone, Simon & Schuster Inc., 1997.

James, William. *The Will to Believe & Other Essays in Popular Philosophy.* Cambridge, Mass. and London, England: Harvard University Press, 1979.

James, William. *The Works of William James.* Edited by Frederick Burkhartdt and Fredson Bowers. Cambridge, Mass. and London, England: Harvard University Press, 1986.

James, William. *The Writings of William James: A Comprehensive Edition,* ed. John J. McDermott. Chicago and London: The University of Chicago Press, 1997.

Johnson, Paul E. *A Shopkeeper's Millennium: Society and Revivals in Rochester, New York 1815–1837.* New York: Hill and Wang, 1978.

Jung, Carl. *Modern Man in Search of a Soul.* London: Kegan, Paul Trench, Trubner & Co. Ltd: Harcourt Brace and Company, 1956.

Kane, Elisha Kent. *Arctic Explorations: The Second Grinnell Expedition In Search of Sir John Franklin 1853, 54, 55.* Chicago: R. R. Donnelley & Sons Company, 1996.

Kane, Elisha K. and Fox, Margaret. *The Love-Life of Dr. Kane.* New York: Carleton, Publisher, 1866.

Karden, Allan. *Experimental Spiritism: The Book on Mediums.* York Beach, Me.: S. Weiser, 1978.

Kerr, Howard. *Mediums and Spirit-Rappers and Roaring Radicals: Spiritualism in American Literature 1850–1900*. University of Illinois Press, 1972.

Kübler-Ross, Elisabeth. *On Life After Death*. Berkeley, Calif.: Celestial Arts, 1991.

Kübler-Ross, Elisabeth. *On Death and Dying*. New York: Collier Books, Macmillan Publishing Company, 1970.

Lamon, Ward Hill. *Recollections of Abraham Lincoln 1847–1865*. Edited by Lamon Dorothy Teillard. Lincoln, Neb. and London, England: University of Nebraska Press, 1994.

Lathrop, Rose Hawthorne. *Memories of Hawthorne*. New York: Houghton Mifflin and Company, 1897.

Lewis, R.W. *The Jameses: A Family Narrative*. New York: Farrar, Straus and Giroux, 1992.

Longfellow, Henry Wadsworth. *The Poems of Longfellow*. New Haven: Yale University Press, 1913.

Lowell, James Russell. *The Complete Poetical Works of James Russell Lowell*. Boston and New York: Houghton Mifflin & Company, 1899.

Lutz, Tom. *American Nervousness: 1903: An Anecdotal History*. Ithaca, N.Y.: Cornell University Press, 1991.

MacLaine, Shirley. *Out on a Limb*. Toronto and New York: Bantam Books, 1983.

Maihafer, Henry J. *The General and the Journalists: Ulysses S. Grant, Horace Greeley and Charles Dana*. Washington, D.C.: Brassey's, 1998.

Marks, David and Kammann. *The Psychology of the Psychic*. Buffalo, N.Y.: Prometheus Books, 1980.

Marvin, R. *The Philosophy of Spiritualism and the Pathology and Treatment of Mediomania: Two Lectures*. New York: Asa Butts, 1874.

Maskelyne, John Nevill. *Modern Spiritualism: A Short Account of its Rise and Progress with some exposures of so-called spirit media*. New York: Scribner, Welford and Armstrong, 1906.

Marx, Leo. *The Machine in the Garden: Technology and the Pastoral Ideal in America*. London and New York: Oxford University Press, 1964.

Mather, Cotton. "The Devil in New England," *The Wonders of the Invisible World Being An Account of the Tryals of Several Witches Lately Executed in New England*. Boston: Reprinted in London for John Dunton of the Raven in the Poultry, 1693.

Maynard, Nettie Colburn, *Was Abraham Lincoln a Spiritualist?: Or Curious Revelations From the Life of a Trance Medium*. Philadelphia: R.C. Hartranft, 1891.

McDermott, John J., ed. *The Writings of William James: A Comprehensive Edition*. Chicago and London: The University of Chicago Press, 1967, 1977.

McGoodan, Ken. *Fatal Passage: The Story of John Rae, the Arctic Hero Time Forgot*. Carroll & Graf Publishers.

McGuire, William, and R. F. C. Hull, eds. *C. G. Jung Speaking—Interviews and Encounters*. Princeton, N.J.: Princeton University Press, 1977.

McHargue, Georgess. *Facts, Frauds and Phantasms: A Survey of the Spiritualist Movement*. Garden City, N.Y.: Doubleday & Company, 1972.

McKay, Ernest A. *The Civil War and New York City*. Syracuse, N.Y.: Syracuse University Press, 1990.

McKelvy, Blake, *Rochester: The Water-Power City, 1812–1854*. Cambridge University Press, 1945.

Melville, Herman. *Moby-Dick*. Evanston and Chicago: Northwestern University Press and Newberry Library, 1988.

Meyers, Donald B. *The Positive Thinkers: A Study of the American Quest for Health, Wealth and Personal Power from Mary Baker Eddy to Norman Vincent Peale*. Garden City, NY: Doubleday & Company, Inc., 1965.

Myers, W. H. *Human Personality and Its Survival of Bodily Death*. New York: Longmans, Green and Co., 1903.

Mirsky, Jeanette. *Elisha Kent Kane and the Seafaring Frontier*. Boston: Little, Brown and Company, 1954.

Moody, Raymond A. *Life After Life*. Atlanta: Mockingbird Books, 1975.

Moore, R. Laurence. *In Search of White Crows: Spiritualism, Parapsychology, and American Culture*. New York: Oxford University Press, 1977.

Morse, Edward Lind, ed. *Samuel F. B. Morse: His Letters and Journals*, 2 volumes. Boston: Houghton Mifflin and New York: Riverside Press, 1914.

Murphy, Gardner. *Challenge of Psychical Research: A Primer of Parapsychology, with the Colloboration of Laura A. Dale*. New York: Harper: 1961.

Nelson, Geoffrey. *Spiritualism and Society*. New York: Schocken Books, 1969.

Oates, Stephan B. *Abraham Lincoln: The Man Behind the Myths*. New York: Harper & Row Publishers, 1984.

Odell, George C. D. *Annals of the New York Stage*, Vol. V. New York: Columbia University Press, 1931.

Owen, Alex. *The Darkened Room: Women, Power and Spiritualism in Late Nineteenth Century England*. London: Virago, 1989.

Owen, Robert Dale. *Footfalls on the Boundary of Another World*. New York: G.W. Carleton & Co., 1872.

Owen, Robert Dale. *The Debatable Land Between This World and the Next, with Illustrative Narrations*. London: G.W. Carleton & Co, 1872.

Parker, Jenny Marsh. *Rochester: A Story Historical*. Rochester, N.Y.: Scrantom, Wetmore & Company, 1884.

Parker, Theodore. *A Discourse of Matters Pertaining to Religion*. New York: Arno Press, 1972.

Peale, Norman Vincent. *The Power of Positive Thinking*. Englewood Cliffs, N.J.: Prentice-Hall, 1952.

Peale, Norman, Vincent. *Stay Alive All Your Life*. Englewood Cliffs, N.J.: Prentice-Hall, 1957.

Pearsall, Ronald. *The Table-Rappers*. New York: St. Martin's Press, 1972.

Perry, Ralph Barton. *The Thought and Character of William James*. New York: G. Braziller, 1954.

Phelps, Elizabeth Stuart. *Chapters From a Life*. New York: Arno Press, 1980.

Pidgeon, Charles F. *Revelations of a Spirit Medium*. New York: Arno Press, 1974, reprinted from 1922.

Pike, James A., with Kennedy, Diane. *The Other Side: An Account of My Experiences with Psychic Phenomena*. Garden City, N.Y.: Doubleday, 1968.

Podmore, Frank. *Mediums of the 19th Century,* Vols. 1 & 2. New Hyde Park, N.Y.: University Books, Inc., 1963.

Poe, Edgar Allan. *The Complete Tales and Poems of Edgar Allan Poe.* New York: Dorset Press, 1989.

Pond, Marianne Buckner. *Time Is Kind: The Story of the Unfortunate Fox Family.* New York: Centennial Press, New York, 1947.

Porter, Katherine H. *Through a Glass Darkly: Spiritualism in the Browning Circle.* Lawrence: University of Kansas Press, 1958.

Post, Isaac. *Voices from the Spirit World, Being Communications from Many Spirits, by the hand of Isaac Post, Medium.* Rochester, N.Y.: C.H. McDonell, 1852.

Rhine, Joseph B. *New Frontiers of the Mind: The Story of the Duke Experiments.* New York: Farrar & Rinehart, 1937.

Richardson, Robert D., Jr. *Emerson: The Mind on Fire.* Berkeley, Los Angeles, and London: University of California Press, 1995.

Richardson, Robert D., Jr. *Henry Thoreau: A Life of the Mind.* Berkeley, Los Angeles, and London: University of California Press, 1986.

Rickert, Edith and Paton, Jessie, eds. *American Lyrics.* Garden City, N.Y.: Doubleday, Page & Company, 1912.

Rossi, Alice S. *The Feminist Papers: From Adams to de Beauvoir.* Edited and with introductory essays by Alice S. Rossi. New York: Columbia University Press, 1973.

Rourke, Mayfield. *Triumphs of Jubilee: Henry Ward Beecher, Harriet Beecher Stowe, Lyman Beecher, Horace Greeley, P. T. Barnum.* New York: Harcourt, Brace, 1927.

Rugoff, Milton. *The Beechers: An American Family in the Nineteenth Century.* New York: Harper & Row, 1981.

Rule, B. J. *Polar Knight: The Mystery of Sir John Franklin.* New Smyrna Beach, Fla.: Luthers, 1998.

Sachs, Emanie. *The Terrible Siren: Victoria Woodhull.* New York: Harper & Brothers Publishers, 1928.

Sagan, Carl. *The Demon-Haunted World: Science as a Candle in the Dark.* New York: Random House, 1996.

Sandburg, Carl. *Abraham Lincoln: The War Years.* 4 vols. New York: Harcourt Brace, 1939.

Sears, Hal D. *The Sex Radicals: Free Love in High Victorian America.* Lawrence: Regent Press of Kansas, 1977.

Seldes, Gilbert. *The Stammering Century.* New York: The John Day Company, 1928.

Silverman, Kenneth. *Edgar A. Poe: Mournful and Never-Ending Remembrance.* New York: HarperCollins, 1996.

Silverman, Kenneth. *Houdini: The Career of Ehrich Weiss.* New York: HarperCollins, 1996.

Silverman, Kenneth. *Lightning Man: The Accursed Life of Samuel F. B. Morse.* New York: Knopf, 2003.

Spence, Lewis. *The Encyclopedia of the Occult.* London: Bracken Books, 1988.

Spicer, Henry. *Sights and Sounds: The Mystery of the Day Comprising an Entire History of the American "Spirit" Manifestations.* London: Thomas Bosworth, 1853.

Spraggett, Alan. *Arthur Ford: The Man Who Talked with the Dead.* New York: New American Library, 1973.

Stanton, Elizabeth Cady; Anthony, Susan B.; and Gage, Joslyn Matilda, eds. *History of Women Suffrage*, Vols. 1–3, Second Edition. Rochester, N.Y., London, and Paris: Charles Mann, 1889.

Stern, Madeleine B. *The Victoria Woodhull Reader.* Weston, Mass.: M & S Press, 1974.

Stoddard, Henry Luther. *Horace Greeley: Printer, Editor, Crusader.* New York: G.P. Putnam's Sons, 1946.

Strong, George Templeton. *The Diary of George Templeton Strong*, Vols. 1–4. Edited by Allan Nevins and Milton Halsey Thomas, New York: The Macmillan Company, 1952.

Sugrue, Thomas. *There is a River: The Story of Edgar Cayce.* New York: H. Holt and Company, 1945.

Taves, Ann. *Fits, Trances and Visions: Experiencing Religion and Explaining Experience from Wesley to James.* Princeton, N.J.: Princeton University Press, 1999.

Taylor, Eugene. *William James on Exceptional Mental States.* New York: Scribner's, 1983.

Taylor, Paul E. *A Shopkeeper's Millennium: Society and Revivals in Rochester, New York 1815–1837.* New York: Hill and Wang, 1978.

Taylor, W. G. Langworthy. *Fox-Taylor Automatic Writing, 1869–1892.* Edited by Sarah E. L. Taylor. Boston: Bruce Humphries, 1936, 1932.

Taylor, William George Langworthy. *Katie Fox: Epochmaking Medium and the Making of the Fox-Taylor Record.* New York: G.P. Putnam's Sons, 1933.

Tennyson, Alfred Lord. *The Works of Tennyson.* Edited by Hallam Lord Tennyson. New York: AMS Press, 1970.

The Rappers; or, the mysteries, fallacies, and absurdities of spirit-rapping, table-tipping, and entrancement. By a searcher after truth. New York: H. Long & Brother, c. 1854.

Tilton, Theodore. *Victoria C. Woodhull: A Biographical Sketch.* New York: Office of the Golden Age, 1871.

Toksvig, Signe. *Emanuel Swedenborg: Scientist and Mystic.* New York: Swedenborg Foundation, 1983.

True Politeness: A Hand-book of Etiquette for Ladies by an American Lady. New York: F.A. Leavitt, 1840–48.

Underhill, Ann Leah. *The Missing Link in Modern Spiritualism.* New York: Arno Press, 1976.

Vanderhoof, E.W. *Historical Sketches of Western New York.* Buffalo, N.Y.: The Matthew Northrup Works, 1907.

Van Deusen, Glyndon G. *Horace Greeley, Nineteenth Century Crusader.* Philadelphia: University of Pennsylvania Press, 1953.

Von Hartmann, Eduard. *The Philosophy of the Unconscious.* London: Trubner & Co., 1884.

Walz, Jay and Walz, Audrey. *The Undiscovered Country.* New York: Duell, Sloan and Pearce, Inc., 1958.

Washington, Peter. *Madame Blavatsky's Baboon: Theosophy and the Emergence of the Western Guru.* London: Secker & Warburg, 1993.
Whitman, Walt. *Leaves of Grass.* Toronto, New York, London, and Sydney: Bantam Books, 1983.
Whyte, William H. *The Organization Man.* New York: Simon & Schuster, 1956.
Wicker, Christine. *Lily Dale: the true story of the town that talks to the dead.* San Francisco: HarperSan Francisco, 2003.
Wilson, Colin. *The Occult.* New York: Vintage Books, 1973.
Wineapple, Brenda. *Hawthorne: A Life.* New York: Knopf, 2003.
Woodruff, Charles S., M.D. *Legalized Prostitution: or Marriage As It Is, and Marriage As It Should Be, Philosophically Considered.* Boston: Bela March, 1862.

OTHER SOURCES

"An Address to the women of the State of New York From the Yearly Meeting of Congregational Friends, June 3–5, 1850: Proceedings of the Yearly Meeting of Congregational Friends held at Waterloo." Auburn, N.Y.: Henry Oliphant, 1850.
Bartlett, John, and Kaplan, eds. *Bartlett's Familiar Quotations,* 16th edition. Boston, New York, and London: Little, Brown and Company, 1992.
By Laws, National Spiritualist Association of Churches, Lily Dale, N.Y., October 10, 2003.
Clark, Franklin, W. *The Rochester Spirit Rappers,* unpublished master's thesis, University of Rochester, 1932.
Davis, H. W. C., and Weaver, J. R. H., eds. *The Dictionary of National Biography,* 1912–1921. London: Oxford University Press, 1927.
Elisha Kent Kane Papers, American Philosophical Society.
Hooker, Isabella Beecher. *Votes for Women: Selections from the National America Woman Suffrage Association Collection, 1840–1921,* "The Constitutional Rights of the Women of the United States: An Address Before the International Council of Women," Washington, D.C., March 30, 1888.
Horace Greeley Papers, New York Public Library, Manuscripts and Archives Division.
Lawton, George. "The Drama of Life After Death: A Study of the Spiritualist Religion," *Dictionary of American Biography.* New York: Henry Holt and Company, 1932.
Melton, Gordon J., ed. *Encyclopedia of Occultism and Parapsychology.* Detroit: Gale Research, 1996.
Post Family Papers, Friends Historical Library, Swarthmore College.
Proceedings of the Annual Meeting of the Friends of Human Progress, Held at Junius Meeting House, Waterloo, Seneca County, NY. Rochester Steam Press: Curtis, Butts & Co., Daily Union Advertiser, 1957.
Society for the Diffusion of Spiritual Knowledge, The Charter and By-Laws of the Society for the Diffusion of Spiritualist Knowledge, With a List of Officers for the year 1854, And an Address to the Citizens of the United States. New York: The Society, 1854.
The Isaac and Amy Post Family Papers, Rare Books and Special Collections, University of Rochester Library.